The Enduring Vision

The Enduring Vision

A History of the American People

Essentials Edition

VOLUME 1: TO 1877

Paul S. Boyer
University of Wisconsin, Madison

Clifford E. Clark, Jr.
Carleton College

Sandra McNair Hawley
San Jacinto College

Joseph F. Kett
University of Virginia

Neal Salisbury
Smith College

Harvard Sitkoff
University of New Hampshire

Nancy Woloch
Barnard College

Houghton Mifflin Company   Boston   New York

Editor-in-chief: Pat Coryell
Associate sponsoring editor: Jeffrey Greene
Senior project editor: Rosemary Winfield
Production/design coordinator: Jennifer Meyer Dare
Senior designer: Henry Rachlin
Senior manufacturing coordinator: Sally Culler
Senior marketing manager: Sandra McGuire

Cover: design by Diana Coe

Printed in the U.S.A.

Library of Congress Catalog Card Number: 98-71992

ISBN: 0-395-98233-2

123456789-HP-02 01   00   99   98

Preface

For some years now, rapid advances in computer-based technology have made possible the creation of a number of products, services, and tools that can be used to enrich students' learning experience. The World Wide Web, e-mail, and CD-ROMs have also changed the way we communicate, conduct research, and, in some cases, teach. As we end the twentieth century, almost every historian uses e-mail to communicate and the Internet to do research, but far fewer use any of these products or tools in their teaching. In most cases, this is the result not of inferior technology but of a failure to combine new and old technologies in a way that is effective and easy to use. Early attempts at this marriage, such as putting a textbook on CD-ROM, failed because, among other reasons, it wasn't clear what one was supposed to do with this new product and what the relationship of the printed textbook to the CD-ROM was. We have a better idea for how to use this new technology effectively and how to tie it to a traditional narrative U.S. history survey textbook. The result is *The Enduring Vision*, Essentials/Multimedia Edition.

In a sense we have created an interactive book, one that combines a number of media to offer the instructor and the student a rich resource that uses each medium for its best purpose. You can view history on the CD-ROM and the web site and you can read about it in the book.

This Essentials/Multimedia Edition of *The Enduring Vision* is the first United States history textbook to integrate a traditional print text with a CD-ROM and a web site to create a true multimedia teaching and learning package for the U.S. history survey course. To create this package, we have written a book to do what a text can do best—present history that is designed to be read as a narrative, focused on the essential aspects of United States history. The other components of this package—the CD-ROM and the web site—are used to present still and moving images, sound, and extensive additional documentary resources that are best experienced in the dynamic environment of multimedia. The contents of the CD-ROM and web site have been selected and the activities prepared by Paula Petrik of the University of Maine and Kelly Woestman of Pittsburg State University.

We have pared down *The Enduring Vision*, Third Edition, to create the Essentials/Multimedia Edition, leaving what we regard as the essential elements of U.S. history. The strengths of *The Enduring Vision* remain—a strong narrative that interweaves political, diplomatic, and economic history with social, cultural, and environmental analysis in a text that reflects both traditional concerns and the cutting edge of contemporary historical research. We have tried to retain the readable style while integrating social history, cultural history, the histories of the diverse peoples who make up our pluralistic society, and environmental history—a blend of the best of both traditional and the new emphases in historical scholarship that will serve the modern student well. We have retained all the major topics and issues from the original text to make this a book suitable for any introductory United States history, whether in four-year colleges and universities or two-year community and junior colleges.

The great advantage of this edition is that it allows instructors to use multimedia technology to enrich their survey courses in a way not possible until now. On one CD-ROM are approximately 1,000 primary sources that cover the span of U.S. history and include sources on political, social, economic, diplomatic, environmental, and cultural history. A gateway on the *@history* web site provides access to hundreds more sites, all of which have been categorized for easy searching.

A distiguishing feature of this edition is the placement of annotations in the margins of the text that direct the reader to a primary source in the CD-ROM that is relevant to a particular topic under discussion. This annotation contains the title of the source, making it easy to locate it on the CD-ROM. The sources are searchable by title and key words. These primary sources enrich the text discussion by providing a text document, a photograph, a map, a speech, or some other representative source from the period. About half of these sources include critical thinking activities for students. These activities are framed as questions to help the student think about the source and provide an opportunity for discussion or written responses. Together, the book and the CD-ROM provide everything one expects from a traditional textbook plus the additional benefit of hundreds of primary sources available immediately.

In addition to the text and the CD-ROM, the @history web site offers instructors and students a gateway to hundreds of other relevant web sites that have been selected and categorized by Professor Woestman. These sites are searchable by various common categories such as historical period and theme, so instructors and students can immediately go right to the site in which they are interested. These sites are reviewed periodically to ensure that the links are always live and new ones are added.

The CD-ROM comes in both a student version and an instructor's version. The instructor's version contains everything that is on the student version plus additional notes suggesting ways to use a particular source with students. The activities have also been classified by level of thinking skill required to complete them. This is also available exclusively on the instructor's version. For instructors who want to create multimedia lectures and use these sources as presentation material, sample e-lectures offer examples of how to create a multimedia lecture. Instructors can use the sample e-lectures as they are or edit them by importing sources on the CD-ROM or by importing their own material. Flexibility and customization are built in to this package.

Explicit instructions are packaged with the CD-ROM to provide information on navigation, and a special section in the *Instructor's Manual with Test Items* provides instructors with tips on how to use this package in both small and large classes. In addition to the *Instructor's Manual with Test Items*, there is a wide range of ancillaries available with *The Enduring Vision*, Essentials/Multimedia Edition, including a computerized test bank for Macintosh and IBM-compatible computers. The instructor may also opt to use some of the following additional supplements for the course and should contact a Houghton Mifflin sales representative for more information:

- *Getting the Most out of Your U.S. History Course: The History Student's Vade Mecum* by Neil R. Stout—a handy, concise student guide to getting the most out of the U.S. history survey course

- *Reading and Writing American History* by Peter Charles Hoffer and William W. Stueck, Volumes 1 and 2—a skills-based sourcebook for U.S. history students

- Map transparencies

- *Enduring Voices Document Sets* by James J. Lorence, Volumes 1 and 2

- *Surveying the Land: Skills and Exercises in U.S. Historical Geography* by Robert B. Grant, Volumes 1 and 2

- *Atlas of American History*

- *The Houghton Mifflin Guide to the Internet for History*

No book is ever the product of just one set of hands or just one mind. This is no exception. I want to express my thanks and gratitude to friends and colleagues who have been particularly helpful and supportive: James Hall, James Heil, Dean Minix, and Chuck Prosch. As usual, my daughter, Lee Anne Hawley, has been both a great help and a great pleasure. The production team at Houghton Mifflin—Rosemary Winfield, senior project editor, Jennifer Meyer Dare, production/design coordinator, and Sally Culler, senior manufacturing coordinator—are professional, helpful, and highly intelligent; much of what there is of style, syntax, and coherence in this book derives from their combined skills. They have been wonderful to work with.

S.M.H.

Contents

America Begins

1

Transatlantic Encounters and Colonial Beginnings, 1492–1630

10

Expansion and Diversity:
The Rise of Colonial America

25

Colonial Society Comes of Age, 1660–1750

43

The Road to Revolution, 1744–1776

57

The Forge of Nationhood,
1776–1788

74

Launching the New Republic, 1789–1800

92

Jeffersonianism and the Era of Good Feelings

107

The Transformation of American Society, 1815–1840

121

Politics, Religion, and Reform
in Antebellum America

131

Life, Leisure, and Culture 1840–1860

144

The Old South and Slavery, 1800–1860

155

Immigration, Expansion, and Sectional Conflict, 1840–1848

168

From Compromise to Secession, 1850–1861

179

Reforging the Union: Civil War, 1861–1865

191

The Crises of Reconstruction, 1865–1877

207

APPENDIX   A-1

INDEX   I-1

Maps

The Enduring Vision

Volume 1: To 1877

1

America Begins

〜〜

The First Americans

The origins of the human species extend far back in time. More than 5 million years ago, direct human ancestors evolved in the temperate grasslands of Africa. Between 300,000 and 100,000 years ago, humans began peopling the Old World. Between 40,000 and 15,000 years ago, northern Asian hunting bands pursued large game animals across a broad land bridge then connecting Siberia and Alaska. In doing so, they became the first Americans. Most Native Americans are descended from these earliest migrants, but a few trace their ancestry to later arrivals.

The Peopling of North America:
The Paleo-Indians

About 10,000 B.C., the Ice Age neared its end. Melting glaciers opened an ice-free corridor from Alaska to the northern Plains, and bands of hunters moved along this route. Others probably traveled south along the Pacific coast in boats. As they emerged from the glacier-covered north, they discovered a hunter's paradise. Giant mammoths, mastodons, bison, caribou, and moose roamed the continent. In this bountiful world, the Paleo-Indians, as archaeologists call these hunters, fanned out and multiplied with astonishing speed. Within 1,000 years, descendants of the first Americans had spread throughout the Western Hemisphere.

Most Paleo-Indians lived in small bands of fifteen to fifty people. The men hunted; the women prepared the food and cared for the children. The band lived together for the summer but split into smaller groups of one or two families for fall and winter.

Even before leaving Alaska, the Paleo-Indians developed distinctly "American" ways. Their most characteristic innovation was the fluted point, which the Indians fitted to spears. By 9000 B.C. many big-game species, including mammoths and mastodons, had vanished. Paleo-Indian hunters contributed to this extinction, as did a warming climate and ecological changes that altered or destroyed the large animals' food chains.

Archaic Societies

Climatic warming continued until about 4000 B.C. with dramatic effects for North America. Sea levels

1

rose, flooding the shallow continental shelf, and glacial runoff filled the Great Lakes, the Mississippi River basin, and other waters. Treeless plains and evergreen forests yielded to deciduous forests in the East, grassland prairies on the Plains, and desert in much of the West. An immense range of plants and animals covered the landscape.

Descendants of the Paleo-Indians prospered amid this abundance and diversity. These Archaic peoples, as archaeologists term native North Americans from 8000 B.C. to 1500 B.C., lived off wide varieties of smaller mammals, fish, and wild plants rather than big game. Greater efficiency in hunting and gathering permitted larger populations to inhabit smaller areas.

Archaic peoples' cultures were diverse in other ways. Besides using many varieties of stone, they utilized bone, shell, copper, ivory, clay, leather, asphalt, and horn to make tools, weapons, utensils, and ornaments. Often Native Americans obtained these materials through trade with neighbors and through long-distance networks. Obsidian from the Yellowstone region, copper from the Great Lakes, and marine shells from ocean coasts appear at sites thousands of miles from their points of origin.

Ideas as well as materials traveled along the trade networks. Techniques that developed in one place for making tools, procuring food, or using medicinal plants eventually spread over wide areas, far beyond the boundaries of community, language, and ethnicity. This diffusion created regional cultural patterns. Trade also served to spread religious beliefs, including ideas and practices relating to death. Archaic burials grew increasingly elaborate as Native Americans interred their dead with personal possessions and with objects fashioned from valued substances such as obsidian and copper.

Archaic Americans developed neither ranks nor classes, nor did they centralize political power. However, the growing complexity of their diets and technologies led them to sharpen many distinctions between women's and men's roles. Men took responsibility for fishing and hunting; women harvested and prepared wild plants, including grinding and milling seeds. Men and women each made the tools needed for their tasks. In general, men's activities entailed travel, and women's work kept them close to the village, where they bore and raised children. At Indian Knoll and elsewhere, men were buried with tools related to hunting and fishing, and women with implements related to nut cracking and seed grinding. Objects used by shamans, or religious healers, were distributed equally between male and female graves, a practice implying that these key roles were not divided by gender.

The Indians' Continent

By 1500 B.C. in much of North America, Indians were developing new cultures that transcended those of the Archaic peoples. In the Southwest, the Southeast, and the Eastern Woodlands, the advent of agriculture and of large centers of trade and population constituted a radical departure from Archaic patterns and hunting-gathering bands. Despite the differences emerging among native societies, ties among them remained strong. Expanded trade networks permitted goods and ideas to be carried over ever-widening areas.

The Northern and Western Perimeters

In western Alaska the post-Archaic period marked the beginning of a new arctic way of life. Eskimos and Aleuts had brought sophisticated tools and weapons from their Siberian homeland, including harpoons and spears for hunting sea mammals and caribou. By 1500 B.C., through their continued contacts with Siberia, the Eskimos were making and using the Americas' first bows and arrows, ceramic pottery, and pit houses, structures set partially below ground level. As they perfected ways of living in regions of vast tundras (treeless plains with a permanently frozen subsoil), Eskimos spread across upper Canada to the shores of Labrador, western Newfoundland, and Greenland.

Long before Columbus, the Eskimos made contact with Europeans and used certain of their material goods. From about A.D. 1 some iron tools reached

Alaska by way of Russia and Siberia, but not enough to affect Eskimo culture substantially. Direct contacts with Europeans began in Greenland, Newfoundland, and Labrador, where Norse people from Scandinavia planted colonies in the late tenth century. However, Norse colonies had no long-term impact on the indigenous peoples of North America. The colonies were short-lived, colonists were few, and, most important, the Norse did not carry the epidemic diseases that would be brought, with disastrous results for the Native Americans, by later colonists.

Along the Pacific coast, from Alaska to southern California, improvements in the production and storage of food enabled Indians to develop more settled ways of life. From the Alaskan panhandle to northern California, natives spent brief periods each year catching salmon and other fish. The Northwest Coast Indians dried and stored enough fish to last the year, and their seasonal movements gradually gave way to settled life in permanent villages of cedar-plank houses.

By A.D. 1 many Northwest Coast villages numbered several hundred people. Trade and warfare strengthened the power of chiefs and other leaders, whose families had greater wealth and prestige than commoners. Leading families proclaimed their status in elaborate totem poles depicting supernatural beings linked to their ancestors and in potlatches, ceremonies in which the Indians gave away or destroyed much of their material wealth.

At about the same time, Indians farther south, along the coast and in the interior valleys of what is now California, began to live in villages of one hundred or more people. Acorns dominated their diet. After the fall harvest, Indians ground the acorns into meal, leached them of bitter tannic acid, and then roasted, boiled, or baked the nuts before eating or storing them. Intense competition for acorns forced California bands to define territorial boundaries rigidly and to combine several villages under a single chief. Chiefs conducted trade, diplomacy, and religious ceremonies with neighboring groups and, when necessary, led their people in battle.

The end of the Archaic period saw little change in the hunting and gathering bands that braved the forbidding aridity of the Great Basin, which encompassed present-day Nevada, western Utah, southern Idaho, and eastern Oregon. Change came only in the fourteenth or fifteenth century A.D., when Paiute, Ute, and Shoshone Indians absorbed or displaced these earlier inhabitants. The newcomers' more efficient seed processing enabled them to support increased populations, which in turn occupied ever-larger territories.

The Southwest

Although peoples of the Pacific coast cultivated tobacco, they never farmed food-bearing plants. Abundant food resources left them little incentive to take the risks that agriculture entailed, especially in California, with its dry summers. In other areas of North America, however, agriculture became central to Indian life. In the arid Southwest, natives concentrated community energies on irrigation for agriculture, but the advent of agriculture was a long, slow process that never entirely replaced other food-procuring activities.

New World farming began about 5000 B.C.—the same era in which agriculture was being introduced in Europe from southwestern Asia—when Indians in central Mexico planted seeds of certain wild crops that they had customarily harvested, including squash, corn, and beans. Plant domestication slowly spread, first reaching western New Mexico about 3500 B.C. Agriculture remained relatively unimportant for several thousand years, until a more drought-resistant strain of corn from Mexico enabled the inhabitants to move to dry lowlands. Populations then rose rapidly, and two influential new cultures arose, the Hohokam and the Anasazi.

Hohokam culture emerged in the third century B.C. when ancestors of Pima and Papago Indians began farming in the Gila River and Salt River valleys of southern Arizona. The Hohokam people built elaborate canal systems for irrigation that enabled them to harvest two crops each year, an amazing feat in such an arid environment. The construction and maintenance of the canals demanded large, coordinated work forces. The Hohokams therefore built permanent villages of several hundred residents, and many such communities were joined in confederations linked by canals.

The Hohokam way of life drew on materials and ideas from outside the Southwest. From about the sixth century A.D., the larger Hohokam villages had ball courts and platform mounds such as those in Mexico, and ball games became major public events. Mexican art influenced Hohokam artists, who used clay, stone, turquoise, and shell.

Among the last southwesterners to make farming the focus of their subsistence were a people known as the Anasazis, a Navajo term meaning "ancient ones." Their culture originated in the Four Corners area where Arizona, New Mexico, Colorado, and Utah meet. Although they adopted village life and agriculture late, the Anasazis expanded rapidly in the sixth century A.D. and dominated a wide area.

The Anasazis had a distinctive architecture. They constructed their early dwellings, round pit houses, in the shape of *kivas*, the partly underground, circular structures where Anasazi men conducted religious ceremonies. As their population grew, the Anasazis built aboveground, rectangular apartment houses containing small *kivas*. Anasazi-style apartments and *kivas* are characteristic of the architecture of the modern-day Pueblo Indians, who are descendants of the Anasazis.

From the tenth through the mid-twelfth century, an unusually wet period, the Anasazis expanded over much of what today is New Mexico and Arizona. In Chaco Canyon in northwestern New Mexico, a cluster of twelve villages forged a powerful confederation numbering 15,000 people. Perfectly straight roads radiated from the canyon to satellite pueblos up to sixty-five miles away. The largest village, Pueblo Bonito, had 1,200 inhabitants and two Great Kivas, each fifty feet in diameter. People traveled from outlying areas to Chaco Canyon for religious ceremonies. Chaco Canyon was the center of the turquoise industry that manufactured beads for trade with Mexico, and its pueblos supplied the outlying people with food in times of drought. An elaborate system of controlling rainwater runoff through small dams, terraces, and other devices permitted this agricultural surplus.

Devastating droughts in the late twelfth and thirteenth centuries destroyed classic Anasazi culture. The Indians abandoned the great Anasazi centers and scattered. Some formed new pueblos along the upper Rio Grande, and others moved south and west to establish the Zuñi and Hopi pueblos, which descendants of the Anasazis still inhabit. With farming peoples consequently clustered in the few areas with sufficient water, the drier southwestern lands attracted the foraging Apaches and Navajos, whose arrival at the end of the thirteenth century ended their long migration from northwestern Canada.

**@ Hopi
Snake Dancer**

The Eastern Woodlands

Indians of the Eastern Woodlands, the vast forests from the Mississippi Valley to the Atlantic coast, also experimented with village life and political centralization, but without farming. After doing so, however, they developed an extraordinarily productive agriculture.

By 1200 B.C. about 5,000 people had concentrated in a single village at Poverty Point on the Mississippi River in Louisiana. Two large mounds flanked the village, and six concentric embankments—the largest over half a mile in diameter—surrounded it.

Poverty Point lay at the center of a large political and economic unit. It imported quartz, copper, obsidian, crystal, and other sacred materials from eastern North America and distributed them to nearby communities, which almost certainly supplied the labor for the earthworks. The settlement flourished for only three centuries and then declined, for reasons that are unclear.

A different mound-building culture, the Adena, emerged in the Ohio Valley in the fifth century B.C. Adena villages rarely exceeded 400 inhabitants, but the Adena people spread over a wide area and built hundreds of mounds, most of them containing graves. The largest, Grave Creek Mound in West Virginia, was 240 feet in diameter and 70 feet high.

The Adena mounds constituted the heart of a religious movement whose adherents scattered over much of the Northeast. Although Adena burial practices—the inclusion of grave goods, the painting of red

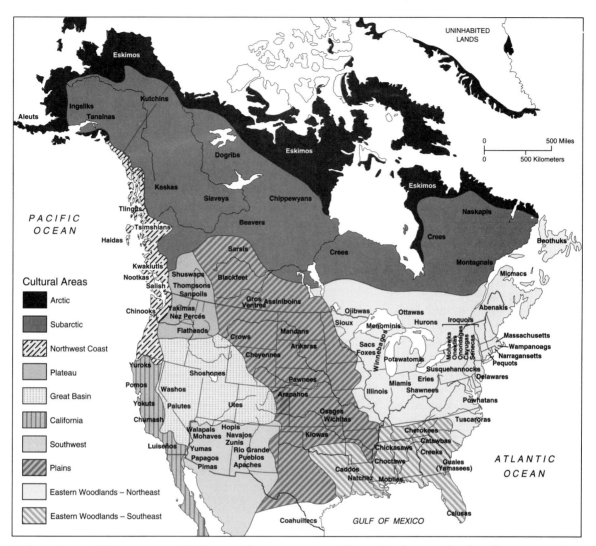

Culture Areas of Native Americans and Locations of Selected Tribes, A.D. 1500

"Culture area" is a convention enabling archaeologists and anthropologists to generalize about regional patterns among pre-Columbian Native American cultures.

hematite (an iron-bearing ore) on some corpses—were familiar in the Northeast, the burial rituals themselves and many of the manufactured objects were new.

During the first century B.C., Adena culture evolved into a more developed and widespread culture known as Hopewell. Hopewell ceremonial centers, larger and more elaborate than those of the Adena, mushroomed along the Ohio and Illinois

River valleys. Some centers contained two or three dozen mounds within enclosures of several square miles. Hopewell artisans used raw materials from throughout America east of the Rockies. Through trade networks Hopewell influence spread to communities as distant as places in modern-day Wisconsin, Florida, and New York. The great Hopewell centers of the Ohio and Illinois Valleys were abandoned in the fifth century A.D. for reasons that remain unknown, but they exerted enormous influence.

The first full-time farmers in the East were the Mississippians, who lived on the flood plains of the Mississippi River and its major tributaries. Their culture incorporated elements from the Hopewell culture and new ideas from Mexico. Mississippian towns, containing hundreds or even thousands of people, were built around open plazas like those of central Mexico. Religious temples and elite residences stood atop large mounds next to the plazas. Religious ceremonies focused on worship of the sun as the source of agricultural fertility. Chiefs claimed to be related to the sun, and when they died, wives and servants were killed to accompany them to the afterlife. Artisans produced sophisticated work in clay, stone, shell, copper, and wood, largely for religious and funeral rituals.

By the tenth century most Mississippian centers were part of larger confederacies based on trade and shared religious beliefs. Powerful "supercenters" and their chiefs dominated these confederacies. The most powerful confederacy revolved around the magnificent city of Cahokia, near modern St. Louis; its influence extended from the Appalachians to the edge of the Plains and from the Great Lakes to the Gulf of Mexico.

@ **Cahokia: The Great Mound and Its Surroundings**

A city of about 20,000 people, Cahokia covered more than 6 square miles and contained more than 120 earthworks. Surrounding the city, a 125-square-mile metropolitan area encompassed ten large towns and more than fifty farming villages. In addition, Cahokia dominated a giant network of commercial and political alliances extending over much of the American heartland. Like other Mississippian societies, Cahokia, influenced by ideas and crops from Mexico, erected ever-more-complex political, economic, and religious institutions. Many scholars believe that by the twelfth century, Cahokia was the capital of a potential nation-state.

Cahokia reigned supreme for two and a half centuries, but by the thirteenth century, it and allied centers were beginning to suffer food shortages. Neighboring peoples, moreover, challenged them militarily, and the inhabitants fled. By the fifteenth century, Indians in the central Mississippi Valley were living in small villages linked by mutual interdependence, not coercion.

The demise of the Mississippian culture, like that of the Hopewell, ended a trend toward political centralization among Indians in eastern North America. Nonetheless, the Mississippians profoundly affected native culture in the East. They spread not only new strains of corn and beans but also the techniques and tools to cultivate them. Only northern New England and the upper Great Lakes had growing seasons too short for corn to become a reliable crop.

New World Peoples on the Eve of European Contact

In 1492 the entire Western Hemisphere had about 75 million people, clustered thickly in Mexico and Central America, the Caribbean islands, and Peru. Between 7 and 10 million Native Americans lived north of Mexico. Sparse nomad populations inhabited the Great Basin, the high plains, and the northern forests. Denser concentrations, however, thrived along the Pacific coast, in the Southwest and Southeast, in the Mississippi Valley, and along the Atlantic coast. Speaking many diverse languages and dialects, these people constituted several hundred Indian nations and tribes.

Family and Community

Kinship cemented Indian societies together. Ties to cousins, aunts, and uncles created complex patterns of social obligation. So did membership in a clan—a large kin group whose members reckoned their descent from a common ancestor embodying the admired qualities of some animal. Several different clans usually dwelled together in a single village. Clans in turn linked widely scattered groups within a larger social unit known as a tribe.

Kinship bonds were more important in Indian society than the bonds within nuclear families, that is, among married couples and their children. Indians did not necessarily expect spouses to be bound together forever; but kinship lasted for life. Divorce thus did not threaten the social order. Customs regulating marriage varied, but strict rules prevailed. In most cultures young people married in their teens, generally after a period of sexual experimentation. Although male leaders sometimes took several wives, nuclear families never stood alone. Instead, strong ties of residence and deference bound each couple to one or both sets of parents, producing what social scientists call extended families.

In addition, kinship was the basis for armed conflict. Indian societies typically considered homicide a matter to be resolved by the extended families of the victim and the perpetrator. If the perpetrator's family offered a gift that the victim's family considered appropriate, the question was settled. If not, the victim's kin might avenge the killing by armed retaliation. Chiefs or other leaders intervened to resolve disputes within the same village or tribe, but disputes between members of different groups could escalate into war. Densely populated societies that competed for scarce resources, as on the California coast, and centralized societies that attempted to dominate trade networks through coercion, such as the Hopewell culture, experienced frequent and intense warfare. However, warfare remained a low-level affair in most of North America. An exasperated New England officer, writing of his effort to obtain Indian allies in the early seventeenth century, described a battle between two Indian groups as "more for pastime than to conquer and subdue enemies."

Among almost all agricultural Indians except those in the Southwest, women did the cultivating. Fieldwork easily meshed with child care, as did such other tasks as preparing animal hides and gathering wild plants. Men did jobs that took them away from women and children: hunting, fishing, trading, negotiating, and fighting. With women producing much of the food supply, these communities gave women more power than European societies did. Among the Iroquois of what today is upstate New York, for example, women collectively owned the fields, distributed food, and played a major role in tribal councils.

@ A Jesuit's Interpretation of Gender Roles Among Indians in Acadia

In the Southwest wresting a living from the severe environment demanded concentrated effort, but the native peoples succeeded. The population was comparatively dense: 100,000 people may have lived in the pueblos and in river-valley settlements by the early sixteenth century.

Patterns of property ownership and gender roles in the Southwest differed considerably from those of Native Americans elsewhere. In addition, differences prevailed among local cultures. Unlike Indians elsewhere, men and women in the Southwest shared agricultural labor. River-valley peoples of the Southwest, moreover, owned land privately and passed it through the male line, and men dominated decision making. In pueblo society, land was communally owned, and women played an influential role in community affairs. Clan membership passed through the mother's line. Yet pueblo communities depended on secret male societies to perform rituals that would secure the gods' blessings and bring life-giving rain. More than other Indians, pueblo society strictly subordinated the individual to the group and demanded rigorous cooperation.

Religion and Social Values

Native American religions revolved around the conviction that nature was alive, pulsating with spiritual power— *manitou* in the Algonquian language.

@ Indians of New Netherlands Account For Creation

A mysterious, awe-inspiring force that affected human life for both good and evil, such power united all nature in an unbroken web. Belief in supernatural power led most Indians to seek constantly to conciliate all the spiritual forces in nature: living things, rocks, water, the sun and moon, even ghosts and witches. For example, Indians prayed to the spirits of animals that they hunted and generally killed just enough game to sustain themselves. To the Indians, humanity was only one link in the great chain of living nature.

Indians had many ways of gaining access to spiritual power. One was dreaming; most Native Americans took seriously the visions that came to them in sleep. They also sought access to the supernatural by using physical ordeals to alter their consciousness. Young men, for instance, commonly endured a traumatic rite of passage. Such rites often involved "questing"—going alone into a forest or up a mountain, fasting, and awaiting a mystical experience in which an animal spirit would reveal itself as a guide and offer a vision of the future. Girls went through comparable rituals at the onset of menstruation to initiate them into the spiritual world from which female reproductive power flowed.

Indians normally relied on shamans to understand the unseen. Shamans were healers who used medicinal plants and magical chants, but their role went further. They interpreted dreams, guided "questing" and other rituals, invoked war or peace spirits, and figured prominently in community councils.

Indian societies maintained a strong sense of interdependence. Consequently, they demanded conformity and cooperation. From early childhood, Indians learned to be accommodating and reserved—careful not to reveal their feelings before they could sense others'. Indian parents generally punished by shaming. Fear of becoming an isolated social outcast forced individuals to maintain strict self-control. Communities made decisions by consensus, and leaders articulated slowly emerging agreements in passionate oratory.

Because Indians valued consensus so highly, their leaders' authority depended primarily on the respect that they invoked rather than on what they could demand by compulsion. Distributing gifts was central to establishing and maintaining leadership within a Native American community or to building alliances. Thus for Indians, trade was not only an economic activity but also a means of ensuring goodwill with other peoples and of building their own prestige. Trade in flint and other toolmaking materials, salt, dyes, furs, food, seeds, and tobacco (which Indians treated as a ceremonial drug) spanned the continent.

Prestige, not material possessions, counted in Native American societies. If Indians did accumulate worldly goods, they did so to give them away in order to win prestige. Potlatch ceremonies of the Pacific Northwest were the most dramatic examples. An aspiring leader invited neighbors to a potlatch, at which he gave away or destroyed most of his possessions while chanting about his own greatness and taunting his rivals. Those who received were expected later to give away even more. Whoever gave away the most won the highest prestige and gained the most people obligated to him.

Scholars have used the word *reciprocity* to characterize Indian religious and social values. Reciprocity involved mutual give-and-take but did not aim to confer equality. Instead, societies based on reciprocity tried to maintain equilibrium and interdependence between individuals of unequal power and prestige. Indians also applied reciprocity to their religious concepts, viewing nature as a web of interdependent spiritual powers into which humans had to fit. And in social organizations, reciprocity required that communities be places of face-to-face, lifelong interaction. Trade and gift giving solidified such reciprocal bonds. Further, faith in social reciprocity underlay Indians' ideas of property rights. They believed that the people of one area might agree to share with others the right to use land for different but complementary purposes: hunting, gathering, farming, trapping, or traveling.

But Native American society was hardly a simple, noncompetitive world. All Indian cultures possessed a strong sense of order. Custom, the demands of social conformity, and the rigors of nature strictly regulated life. Everyday affairs mingled with the spiritual world at every turn. Nature and the supernatural could be frightening. Indians feared ghosts and believed that nonconformists could invoke evil spirits by witchcraft, the most dreaded crime in Indian cultures. Much of Indian religion involved placating evil spirits that caused sickness and death. Even in the Southwest, where cooperation was stressed, life had an intensely competitive side. Individuals and communities eagerly strove to show physical prowess in such ritualized games as lacrosse, and some bet enthusiastically on the outcome.

A breakdown of order in Indian communities could bring fearful consequences: accusations of witchcraft, demands for revenge against wrongdoers, war against enemies. Going to war or exacting personal revenge was a ritualized way of restoring order. A captured male could expect to meet death after prolonged torture. Indian men learned from childhood to inflict, and to bear, physical pain out of loyalty to kin and neighbors. Endurance was central to Indian life.

CHRONOLOGY

c. 5,000,000 B.C.	Earliest human ancestors appear in Africa.
c. 2,000,000 B.C.	Ice Age begins.
c. 300,000–100,000 B.C.	Humans spread throughout Eastern Hemisphere.
c. 40,000–15,000 B.C.	Ancestors of Native Americans cross Alaska-Siberia land bridge.
c. 10,000 B.C.	Ice Age ends.
c. 10,000–9000 B.C.	Paleo-Indians spread throughout Western Hemisphere.
c. 9000 B.C.	Extinction of big-game mammals.
c. 8000 B.C.	Archaic era begins.
c. 7000 B.C.	Athapaskan-speaking peoples arrive in North America.
c. 5000 B.C.	First domesticated plants grown in Western Hemisphere.
c. 3500 B.C.	First domesticated plants grown in North America.
c. 3000–2000 B.C.	Eskimo and Aleut peoples arrive in North America.
c. 1500 B.C.	Archaic era ends. Bow and arrow and ceramic pottery introduced in North America.
c. 1200 B.C.	Poverty Point flourishes in Louisiana.
c. 400–100 B.C.	Adena culture flourishes in Ohio Valley.
c. 250 B.C.	Hohokam culture begins in Southwest.
c. 100 B.C.	Anasazi culture begins in Southwest.
c. 100 B.C.–A.D. 600	Hopewell culture thrives in Midwest.
c. A.D. 700	Mississippian culture begins.
c. A.D. 900	Stockade and first mounds built at Cahokia.
c. A.D. 1000–1100	Norse settlement of Vinland flourishes on Newfoundland.
c. A.D. 1150	Anasazi peoples disperse to form pueblos.
c. A.D. 1200–1300	Cahokia declines.
c. A.D. 1400	League of the Iroquois formed.

FOR FURTHER READING

John Bierhorst, *The Mythology of North America* (1985). An excellent introduction to Native American mythology, organized regionally.

Brian Fagen, *Ancient North America: The Archaeology of a Continent* (1991). An informative, comprehensive introduction to the continent's history before Europeans' arrival.

Åke Hultkrantz, *The Religions of the American Indians* (1979). A stimulating discussion by the leading scholar on the subject.

Gwyn Jones, *The Norse Atlantic Saga*, rev. ed. (1986). A single volume combining recent scholarship on Norse, Eskimos, and Indians with translations of the most important sagas.

Alvin M. Josephy, Jr., *America in 1492: The World of the Indian Peoples Before the Arrival of Columbus* (1992). Outstanding essays on life in the Western Hemisphere on the eve of European contact.

William C. Sturtevant, gen. ed., *Handbook of North American Indians* (20 vols. projected, 1978–). A partially completed reference work providing basic information on the history and culture of virtually every known native society.

2

Transatlantic Encounters and Colonial Beginnings, 1492–1630

Old World Peoples

The Eastern Hemisphere gave birth to the human race. Early humans evolved for several million years on Africa's warm savannas (grasslands) before spreading slowly across the rest of Africa, Asia, and Europe.

West Africa and Its Peoples

For almost 5,000 years the barren Sahara Desert across northern Africa cut most of the continent off from the rest of the Old World. But a broad, hospitable savanna covered much of Africa south of the desert. In the first millennium B.C., the region's peoples radiated outward, eventually leaving their imprint on virtually all of sub-Saharan Africa. By the sixteenth century, sub-Saharan

Africa, twice the landmass of the United States, had a population of perhaps 20 million.

Camel caravans crossing the Sahara ended West Africa's isolation and stimulated trade in gold and salt with Mediterranean North Africa. Powerful West African empires—Ghana, Mali, and Songhai—arose and flourished for a millennium, from A.D. 600 to 1600. Nominally Islamic, these wealthy empires were famed throughout North Africa. By 1492 the last of the great empires, Songhai, stood at the height of its power, its bureaucracy and army dominating much of the African interior.

Compared to the savanna empires, coastal West Africa was relatively insignificant. During the first millennium A.D., small Islamic states arose in Senegambia, at Africa's westernmost bulge, and in Guinea's coastal forests.

Then in the fifteenth century foreign demand for the gold that Africans panned from streams and dug from the earth triggered a population rise in Guinea. Savanna warriors and merchants poured into Guinea and Senegambia, seeking opportunity and occasionally founding or expanding Islamic states.

In sub-Saharan Africa, kinship groups knitted societies together. Parents, aunts, uncles, distant cousins, and those who shared clan ties formed networks of mutual obligation. In centuries to come, the tradition of strong extended families would help enslaved Africans to endure the breakup of nuclear families by sale. Wives generally maintained lifelong links with their own kin group, and children traced descent through the mother's bloodline.

Sub-Saharan Africans believed that kin groups enjoyed inalienable rights to land that their ancestors had cultivated and that they had a duty to honor ancestors and earth spirits by proper cultivation. Like North Americans, Africans did not treat land as a commodity to be bought and sold.

Cultivation was difficult in Africa and required the labor of both genders. As in all tropical regions, scorching sunlight and frequent downpours lowered soil fertility. Like Indians in eastern North America, many Africans practiced slash-and-burn agriculture to maintain soil fertility. In coastal rain forests, root crops, primarily yams, dominated. On the Senegambia savanna, rice was the staff of life. In the seventeenth and eighteenth centuries, both rice and its Senegambian cultivators would be transplanted (the latter, as slaves) to North America.

Religion permeated African life. West African, like Native American, religion recognized spiritual presences throughout nature. The power of earth spirits and of agricultural ancestors reinforced the esteem that Africans accorded to cultivators.

Magic and the placating of spiritual powers, moreover, were important in African life. In both African and Native American societies, shamans maintained contact with the spiritual world, and belief in witchcraft was widespread.

Religious motifs saturated African art. West Africans used their ivory, cast-iron, and wood sculptures in ceremonies reenacting creation myths and honoring spirits. A strong moralistic streak ran through African folktales. Oral reciters transmitted these stories in dramatic public presentations with ritual masks, dance, and music of a complex rhythmic structure.

Much in traditional African culture clashed with the great monotheistic religions, Islam and Christianity. Among Africans, Islam appealed primarily to merchants trading with Muslim North Africa and to grassland rulers eager to consolidate their power. By the sixteenth century, Islam had only just begun to affect the daily lives of grassland cultivators and artisans.

European Culture and Society

When Columbus reached the New World in 1492, Europe was approaching the height of the Renaissance, the rebirth of classical Greek and Roman culture. The era's artistic and intellectual creativity reflected intense social and spiritual stress as Europeans groped for stability by glorifying order, hierarchy, and beauty. A concern for power and rank, or "degree," dominated European life in the fifteenth and sixteenth centuries. Gender, wealth, inherited position, and political power affected every European's status, and few lived beyond the reach of some political authority's claim to tax and rule.

Democracy had no place in this world. To Europeans of the era, democracy meant mob rule and the destruction of social distinctions. Hierarchy and its strict rules seemed safer. Kings dominated the European hierarchy, but they were concerned less with their people's welfare than with consolidating and enlarging their own power.

But royal power depended on the cooperation of the upper classes. Titled noblemen served in Parliament, and in defending their own liberties, they preserved the principle of limited government against encroaching despotism. The gentry (well-to-do untitled landowners) also played prominent roles in local government and Parliament.

At the bottom of the social heap toiled the ordinary people. Europe remained rural in these times, and four-fifths of its population were peasants. Taxes, rents, and other dues to landlords and church officials were heavy. Poor harvests or war drove even well-to-do peasants to starvation.

Sharp population increases worsened conditions. The plague known as the Black Death had killed one-third of Europe's people in the late fourteenth century, but by 1660 dramatic growth was driving up the population to 100 million. Food supplies, however, did not rise as rapidly. Peasant families survived on pitifully low yields of wheat, barley, and oats. Plowing, sowing, and harvesting together, they also grazed livestock on jointly owned "commons" composed of pastureland and forest. But with new land at a premium, landlords, especially the English gentry, began to "enclose" the commons, thus making them private property.

Though numerous, European towns usually contained only a few thousand inhabitants. London, a great metropolis of 200,000 people by 1600, was an exception. Large or small, towns were dirty and disease-ridden, and townspeople lived close-packed with their neighbors.

People of the times saw towns as centers of opportunity for the ambitious. Immigration from the countryside therefore swelled urban populations. But peasants transplanted to towns remained at the bottom of the social order, unable to earn enough money to marry and to live independently.

The consequences of rapid population growth were acute in England, where the population doubled from 2.5 million in 1500 to 5 million by 1620. Some of the gentry grew rich selling wool, but because of technological stagnation, per capita output and household income among textile workers fell. In effect, more workers competed for fewer jobs as European markets for English cloth diminished and as food prices rose. Land enclosure aggravated unemployment and forced large numbers of people to wander the countryside in search of work.

Thus the hopes and ambitions that drew people to towns usually yielded to frustration. Some English people blamed the wealthy for raising prices, goading the poor to revolt, and giving too little to charity.

Conservative moralists stoutly upheld the value of social reciprocity. As in the New World and Africa, traditional society in Europe rested on long-term, reciprocal relationships. Because it sought smooth social relationships between individuals of unequal status, reciprocity required the upper classes to act with self-restraint and dignity and the lower classes to show deference to their "betters." It demanded strict economic regulation, too, to ensure that sellers charged a "just" price—one that covered costs and allowed the seller to profit but barred him from taking advantage of buyers' and borrowers' mis-

fortunes, or of shortages, to make "excessive" profits.

Yet the ideals of traditional economic behavior had been withering for centuries. By the sixteenth century, nothing could stop the practices of charging interest on borrowed money and of increasing prices in response to demand. New forms of business organization such as the joint-stock company, the ancestor of the modern corporation, steadily spread. Demand for capital investment grew, and so did the supply of accumulated wealth. Gradually, a new economic outlook arose that justified the unimpeded acquisition of wealth and unregulated economic competition. Its adherents insisted that individuals owed one another only the money necessary to settle each market transaction. This "market economy" capitalism stood counter to traditional demands for the strict regulation of economic activity to ensure social reciprocity.

Sixteenth- and seventeenth-century Europeans therefore were ambivalent about economic enterprise and social change. A restless desire for fresh opportunity kept life simmering with competitive tension. However, even those who prospered sought the security and prestige of traditional social distinctions, and the poor longed for the age-old values that they hoped would restrain irresponsible greed.

Change in European society could also be seen in the rising importance of the nuclear family. In such a family, the power of the senior male challenged traditional kinship networks. The nuclear family represented a "little commonwealth" within which the father's rule mirrored God's rule over Creation and kings' lordship over their subjects.

Europeans and Their God

Sixteenth-century Europeans believed in the biblical explanation of the origins of the world and its peoples. Christianity taught that Jesus Christ, God's Son, redeemed sinners through his crucifixion and resurrection. As real as God to European Christians was the devil, Satan, who lured people to damnation by tempting them to do evil. But many sixteenth-century Europeans also believed in witchcraft, magic, and astrology. They saw nature as a "chain of being" infused by God with life and tingling with spiritual forces.

The medieval Christian church taught that Christ had founded the church to save sinners from hell. Every time a priest said Mass, Christ's sacrifice was repeated, and divine grace flowed to sinners through sacraments that priests alone could administer—especially baptism, confession, and the Eucharist (communion). In most of Europe the "church" was a huge network of clergymen set apart from laypeople by ordination into the priesthood and by the fact that they did not marry. The pope, the "vicar (representative) of Christ," topped this hierarchy.

The papacy wielded awesome spiritual power. Fifteenth- and sixteenth-century popes claimed the authority to dispense extra blessings, or "indulgences," to repentant sinners in return for "good works," such as donating money to the church. Indulgences also promised time off from future punishment in purgatory.

But the sale of indulgences provoked charges of materialism and corruption. In 1517 Martin Luther, a German friar, attacked the practice. When the papacy tried to silence him, Luther broadened his criticism to include the Mass, priests, and the pope. His revolt sparked the Protestant Reformation, which changed Christianity forever.

To Luther, the selling of indulgences was evil not only because it bilked people but also because the church did harm by falsely assuring people that they could "earn" salvation by doing good works. Luther believed instead that God alone chose whom to save and that believers should trust only God's love, not the word of priests and the pope. Luther's own spiritual struggle and experience of being "born again" constituted a classic conversion experience—the heart of Protestant religion as it would be preached and practiced for centuries in England and North America.

Luther's assault on church abuses won a fervent following among the German public, but Protestant reformers themselves could not agree on what God's word really meant. Thus Luther and French reformer John Calvin (1509–1564) interpreted salvation dif-

ferently. Calvin, unlike Luther, insisted on the doctrine of predestination, in which an omnipotent God "predestined" most sinful humans to hell, saving only a few to exemplify his grace. Calvinists and Lutherans, as the followers of the two Reformation leaders came to be called, alike were horrified by radical Protestants such as the Anabaptists, who criticized the rich and powerful and restricted baptism to adults who had undergone a conversion.

The Catholic church's remarkable resilience also dismayed Protestants. Indeed, the papacy vigorously attacked church corruption and combated Protestant viewpoints. The popes also sponsored a new religious order, the Jesuits, whose members would distinguish themselves for centuries as teachers, missionaries, and royal advisers. This Catholic revival, known as the Counter-Reformation, created the modern Roman Catholic church.

Religious warfare consumed much of western and central Europe from the mid-sixteenth to the mid-seventeenth century. Well-established international rivalries, such as those between Protestant England and Catholic Spain, assumed religious dimensions. In England the crown itself was entangled in religious controversy. Henry VIII (ruled 1509–1547) wanted a male heir to ensure political stability. But when his queen, Catherine of Aragon, failed to bear a son, Henry in 1527 requested a papal annulment of their marriage. When the pope denied his request, in 1533–1534 Henry had Parliament dissolve his marriage and proclaim him "supreme head" of the Church of England (Anglican church).

The Rise of Puritanism in England

Religious strife troubled England for over a century after Henry's break with Rome. The reign of Elizabeth I, who became queen in 1558, marked a crucial watershed. Most English people were now Protestant; *how* Protestant was the question. A militant Calvinist minority, the Puritans, demanded wholesale "purification" of the Church of England from "popish abuses." As Calvinists, they affirmed salvation by predestination, denied Christ's presence in the Eucharist, and believed that a learned sermon was the heart of true worship. They wished to free each congregation from outside interference and encouraged lay members to participate in parish affairs.

Puritans argued that leading an outwardly moral life was not enough to earn salvation. They believed that Christians also must forge a commitment to serve God through an act of spiritual rebirth, the conversion experience. At this moment of being "reborn," a soul confronted its own unworthiness and felt the power of God's grace. Through "sanctification," the convert was cemented to God as a "saint"—a member of the "elect," or the chosen. Only saints could join Puritan congregations.

In preparing for spiritual rebirth, Puritans struggled to master their own wills, to internalize an idealistic code of ethics, and to forge the inner strength to survive in a world of economic and moral chaos. By the time of his or her redemption, the Puritan had undergone a radical transformation that replaced doubt with certainty, producing a strong sense of purpose, a willingness to sacrifice, and an ironclad discipline.

Puritanism appealed mainly to the growing middle sectors of English society—the gentry, university-educated clergymen and intellectuals, merchants, shopkeepers, artisans, and well-to-do peasants. Self-discipline had become central to both the worldly and the spiritual dimensions of these people's lives, and from their ranks would come the settlers of New England (see Chapter 3).

The Stuart monarchs, James I (ruled 1603–1625) and Charles I (ruled 1625–1649), bitterly opposed Puritan efforts to eliminate the office of bishop; not only did bishops, appointed by the king, compose one-quarter of Parliament's upper house, but they also could, and did, silence clerical critics of the monarchs.

Abandoning the earlier hope of transforming the Church of England into independent congregations of "saints," Puritan *Separatists* decided to leave the corrupt state church. Some Separatists went first to Calvinist Holland and from there to Plymouth Plantation in New England. *Nonseparatists* continued to strive to reform the Church of England from within. Some of their rank would later lead the colonization of Massachusetts Bay and Connecticut.

Under Charles I, Anglican authorities campaigned to eliminate Puritan influence within the church. Church courts harassed Puritans with fines and even excommunication.

Hard economic times compounded the Puritans' plight. Wages fell by 50 percent between 1550 and 1650, a growing population spawned massive unemployment, and war on the European continent threw the weaving industry of England's heavily Puritan southeastern counties into a recession. Puritans believed that these problems were contributing to a spiritual and moral crisis in England.

Seeking escape from religious, political, and economic misery, a group of Puritan merchants bought the charter of the failed Virginia Company of Plymouth in 1628 and obtained a royal charter for land north of the Plymouth colony between the Charles and Merrimack Rivers in 1629.

Legacies of the Reformation

The Reformation left four major legacies. First, it created almost all the major Christian traditions that took root on American soil: Protestantism, modern Roman Catholicism, and the radical Protestantism that would later flower into dozens of denominations. Second, Protestants valued literacy. Luther's conversion sprang from his long study of the Bible, and Protestants demanded that believers carefully read God's Word translated from Latin into contemporary spoken languages. Newly invented printing presses spread the new faith; wherever Protestantism flourished, so did general education and religious teaching. Third, Protestants denied that God endowed priests with special powers. Instead, Luther claimed, the church was a "priesthood of all believers." People were responsible for their own spiritual and moral condition. Finally, the Reformation and Counter-Reformation created a new crusading spirit in Europe that coincided with overseas expansion. From Christopher Columbus onward, this spirit justified Europeans' assumption of superiority over the non-Christian peoples of Africa and the Americas and the seizing of their land, resources, and labor.

The Reformation also created in many people a longing for the simplicity and purity of the ancient Christian church. Protestantism condemned the replacement of traditional reciprocity by marketplace values and questioned the pursuit of excessive wealth. In a world of troubling change, it forged individuals of strong moral determination and gave them the fortitude to survive and prosper.

European Expansion

Europe's outward thrust began centuries before Columbus's first voyage in 1492. Norse adventurers had reached North America in the tenth century, but their colonies had collapsed. European attention had turned eastward after 1096 as a series of crusading armies tried to wrest Palestine from Muslim control. A brisk trade with the Middle East begun in these years had brought silks and spices to Europe.

Seaborne Expansion

In the mid-fifteenth century Europe experienced renewed prosperity and population growth. Competing for commercial advantage, the newly centralized European states projected their power overseas.

The Portuguese first felt the itch to explore new worlds. Their zeal for continuing the struggle against the Muslims, recently driven from Portugal, combined with an anxious search for new markets. Prince Henry "the Navigator" of Portugal (1394–1460) embodied both impulses. He encouraged Portuguese seamen to pilot their caravels farther down the African coast searching for weak spots in Muslim defenses and for trade opportunities. By the time of Henry's death, the Portuguese had built a profitable slaving station at Arguin; shortly after, they had penetrated south of the equator. In 1488 Bartolomeu Días reached Africa's southern tip, the Cape of Good Hope, opening the possibility of direct trade with India, and in 1498 Vasco da Gama led a Portuguese fleet around the cape and on to India. These voyages brought Europeans face to face with black Africans.

@ **The Age of Exploration: Routes of the Explorers**

The "New Slavery" and Racism

Slavery was well established in fifteenth-century West Africa, as elsewhere. The grassland emperors as well as individual families depended on slave labor. But most slaves or their children were absorbed into African families over time. First Arabs, and then Europeans, however, turned African slavery into an intercontinental business.

The Portuguese kept most competitors from the lucrative African slave trade until about 1600. They exploited existing African commercial and social patterns, often trading slaves and local products to other Africans for gold. African kings and their communities used the slave trade to dispose of "undesirables," including troublesome slaves whom they already owned, lawbreakers, and persons accused of witchcraft. But most slaves were simply victims of raids or wars. Muslim and European slave trading greatly stimulated conflicts among communities in Africa.

Europeans had used slaves since ancient Greece and Rome, but ominous changes took place in European slavery once the Portuguese began making voyages to Africa. First, the new slave trade was a high-volume business that expanded at a steady rate as Europeans colonized the Western Hemisphere and established plantation societies there. Between 1500 and 1600, perhaps 250,000 African slaves would reach the New World. Before the Atlantic slave trade ended in the nineteenth century, nearly 12 million Africans would be shipped across the sea. Second, African slaves received exceptionally harsh treatment. In medieval Europe slaves had primarily performed domestic service, but by 1450 the Portuguese and Spanish had created large slave-labor plantations on their Atlantic and Mediterranean islands. Using African slaves who toiled until death, these plantations produced sugar for European markets. By 1600 the "new slavery" had become a brutal link in an expanding commerce that ultimately would encompass all major Western nations.

Finally, race became the explicit basis of the "new slavery." Africans' blackness and alien religion dehumanized them in European eyes. As racial prejudice hardened, Europeans found it easy to justify black slavery. European Christianity, moreover, made few attempts to soften slavery's rigors. Because the victims of the "new slavery" were physically distinctive and culturally alien, slavery became a lifelong, hereditary, and despised status.

Europeans Reach America

The fascinating, contradictory figure of Christopher Columbus (1451–1506) embodied Europeans' varied motives for expansion. The son of an Italian weaver, Columbus became obsessed by the idea that Europeans could reach Asia by sailing westward across the Atlantic. Combining an overestimation of Asia's eastward thrust with an underestimation of the earth's circumference, he concluded that the world was much smaller than it actually is and that the open-sea distance from Europe to Asia was roughly 3,000 miles, not the actual 12,000 miles.

Europeans had ventured far into the Atlantic before Columbus: what distinguished Columbus was his persistence in hawking his "enterprise of the Indies" around Europe's royal courts. In 1492 the rulers of newly united Spain, Isabella of Castile and Ferdinand of Aragon, accepted Columbus's offer, hoping to break a threatened Portuguese monopoly on Asian trade. Picking up the westerly trade winds, Columbus's three small ships made landfall within a month off the North American coast at a small island that he named San Salvador.

Word of Columbus's discovery fired Europeans' imaginations. It also induced the Spanish and Portuguese to sign the Treaty of Tordesillas in 1494, dividing all future discoveries between themselves. Columbus made three further voyages, in the course of which he established Spanish colonies, but never fulfilled his promise of reaching Asia. Meanwhile, England's Henry VII (ruled 1485–1509) ignored the Treaty of Tordesillas and sent an Italian navigator known as John Cabot westward across the northern Atlantic in 1497. Cabot claimed Nova Scotia, Newfoundland, and the rich Grand Banks fisheries for England.

The more Columbus and others explored, the more apparent it became that a vast landmass blocked the western route to Asia. In 1500 the Por-

tuguese claimed Brazil, and other voyages outlined a continuous coastline from the Caribbean to Brazil. In 1507 a publisher brought out a collection of voyagers' tales, including one from the Italian Amerigo Vespucci. A shrewd marketer, the publisher devised a catchy name for the new continent: America.

The Conquerors

Columbus was America's first slave trader and the first Spanish *conquistador*, or conqueror. On Hispaniola he exported Indian slaves and created *encomiendas*, grants for both land and the labor of the Indians who lived on it. From the beginning, *encomienderos*, those given the *encomiendas*, harshly exploited the native people. As disease, overwork, and malnutrition killed thousands of Indians, Portuguese slave traders supplied shiploads of Africans to replace them.

Spanish settlers were soon fanning out across the Caribbean in pursuit of slaves and gold. In 1519 the young nobleman Hernán Cortés (1485–1547) led a small band of Spaniards to the Mexican coast. Destroying his boats and enlisting Indian allies, he marched inland to conquer Mexico. Since reaching America, Spaniards had dreamed of a prize as rich as Mexico. The Aztec civilization, the product of 3,000 years of cultural evolution, was both powerful and wealthy, and the Aztecs offered golden gifts in vain hopes of buying off the invaders.

Cortés attacked and swiftly prevailed, owing partly to firearms and horses, which terrified the Aztecs, and partly to initial Aztec suppositions that the Spanish were the white, bearded gods foretold in legends. By 1521 Cortés had defeated the Aztecs and had begun to build Mexico City on the ruins of the Aztec capital, Tenochtitlán.

During the rest of the sixteenth century, other *conquistadores* consolidated a great Hispanic empire stretching from New Spain (Mexico) to Chile. Spaniards stilled any doubts about the legitimacy of conquest by demanding that the Indians convert to Christianity—and by attacking them if they refused.

The conquest came at enormous human cost. When Cortés landed in 1519, the Aztec empire contained 25 million people. By 1600 it had shrunk to

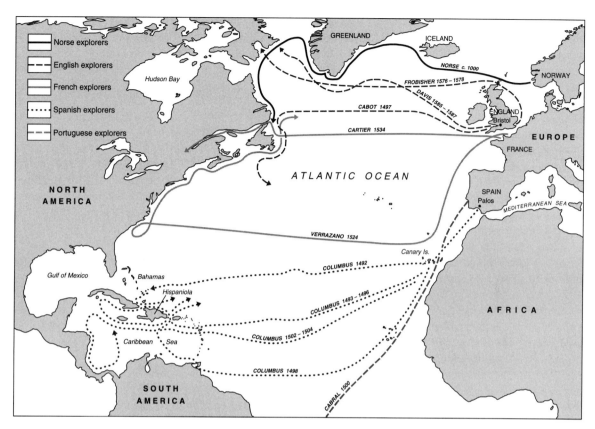

Major Transatlantic Explorations, 1000–1587

Following Columbus's 1492 voyage, Spain's rivals soon began laying claim to parts of the New World based on the voyages of Cabot for England, Cabral for Portugal, and Verrazano for France. Later English and French exploration focused on finding a passage to Asia around or through Canada.

between 1 and 2 million. Peru experienced similar devastation. Disease, not war or slavery, was the greatest killer. Native Americans lacked resistance to European and African infections, especially the deadly, highly communicable smallpox. From the first years of contact with Europeans, terrible epidemics decimated Indian communities. In the West Indies the native population vanished within a half century, and disease opened the mainland for conquest as well.

@ **How Savages Roast Their Enemies**

The "Columbian exchange"—the biological encounter of the Old and New Worlds—went beyond deadly germs. Europeans brought horses, cattle, sheep, swine, chickens, wheat, coffee, sugar cane, and numerous fruits and vegetables with them, as well as an astonishing variety of weeds. African slaves carried rice and yams across the Atlantic. The list of New World gifts to the Old was equally impressive: it included corn, white and sweet potatoes, many varieties of beans, tomatoes, squash, pumpkins, peanuts, vanilla, chocolate, avocados, pineapples, chilis, tobacco, turkeys, canoes, kayaks, hammocks, snowshoes, and moccasins. European weeds and domesticated animals often, especially in North America, overwhelmed indigenous plant life and drove away native animals dependent on those plants. Nonetheless, the worldwide exchange of food products

@ **The Plant Exchange: New and Old World Crops**

enriched human diets and made possible enormous population growth.

Another dimension of the meeting of the two worlds was the mixing of peoples. Within Spain's empire, a great human intermingling occurred. From 1500 to 1600 between 100,000 and 300,000 Spaniards immigrated to the New World, 90 percent of them male. A racially mixed population developed as Spaniards fathered numerous children with African or Indian mothers.

The New World supplied seemingly endless wealth for Spain. West Indian sugar plantations and Mexican sheep and cattle ranches enriched many. Much of Spain's wealth, however, was dug from the silver mines of Mexico and Peru. After 1540 enormous amounts of silver flowed across the Atlantic, far more than the small Spanish economy could absorb, setting off an inflation that eventually engulfed Europe.

The bloody history of Spain's American conquests and efforts to dominate Europe created the "Black Legend"—Protestant Europeans' vision of tyrannical, fanatically Catholic Spain intent on conquering everything in sight. Ironically, much of this grimly lurid picture came from the writings of a devout Spanish friar, Bartolomé de Las Casas (1474–1566), who had repented his own participation in the subjugation of Hispaniola and argued for a more humane Indian policy.

@ A Spanish Monk Pleads for Better Treatment of the Indians.

Footholds in North America

Spain's New World wealth attracted other Europeans to the North American coast. But except for a Spanish fort at St. Augustine, Florida, all sixteenth-century attempts at colonizing North America failed. Unrealistic dreams of easy wealth and pliant Indians brought French, English, and Spanish attempts to grief. Only the continued ravaging of the Indians by disease, declining Spanish power, and rising French, Dutch, and English power finally made colonization possible.

In 1607–1608 the English and French finally established permanent colonies. By 1614 the Dutch had followed. Within a generation North America's

modern history took shape as each colony developed an economic orientation, pattern of Indian relations, and direction of geographic expansion.

New Spain's Northern Frontier

The Spanish built their New World empire on the wealth of the Aztec and other Indian states. But in the frontier lands north of Mexico, the absence of visible wealth and organized states discouraged conquest. Nonetheless, a succession of hopeful *conquistadores* marched across much of what would become the United States. Earliest came Juan Ponce de León, the conqueror of Puerto Rico, who trudged through Florida in search of gold and slaves twice, in 1512–1513 and in 1521, and then died in an Indian skirmish. The most astonishing early expedition began when 300 explorers left Florida in 1527 to explore the Gulf of Mexico. Indian attacks whittled their numbers until only four survived. Stranded in Texas, the survivors, led by Cabeza de Vaca, were passed from Indian tribe to tribe, often as slaves. They finally escaped and made their way to New Mexico and then south to Mexico in 1536.

Cabeza de Vaca inspired two would-be conquerors, Hernando de Soto and Francisco Vásquez de Coronado. In 1539–1543 de Soto and his party blundered from Tampa Bay to the Appalachians and back to southern Texas, scouring the land for gold and harrying the Indians. Although de Soto died without finding gold or conquering any Indians, his and other expeditions touched off epidemics that destroyed most of the remaining Mississippian societies.

As de Soto roamed the Southeast, the Southwest drew others with dreams of conquest, lured by rumors that the fabled Seven Golden Cities of Cíbola lay north of Mexico. In 1538 an expedition sighted the Zuñi pueblos and assumed them to be the golden cities. In 1540–1542 Francisco Vásquez de Coronado led a massive expedition bent on conquest. Coronado plundered several pueblos and roamed from the Grand Canyon to Kansas before returning to Mexico, thinking himself a failure.

For decades after these failures, Spain's principal interest in the lands north of Mexico lay in establishing a few strategic bases in Florida to keep out intruders. In 1565 Spain planted the first successful European settlement on mainland North America, the fortress of St. Augustine. Then in the 1580s the Spanish returned to the southwestern pueblo country, preaching Christianity and scouting for wealth. In 1598 Juan de Oñate led 500 Spaniards into the upper Rio Grande valley, where he proclaimed the royal colony of New Mexico and demanded tribute from the Indians.

The new colony barely survived. In 1606 the Spanish replaced Oñate because of his excessive brutality. Finding no gold, many settlers left. In 1609 those who remained established Santa Fe; still others migrated to isolated ranches and fought off Navajo and Apache raiders. By 1630 Franciscan missionaries had established more than thirty missions stretching from the Rio Grande valley to Hopi villages in Arizona, 250 miles to the west.

@ **The Pacification of the Southwest**

France: Initial Failures

In 1534 Jacques Cartier of France, searching for the northwest passage, explored the St. Lawrence River, the center of French colonization after 1600. But a half century of failure preceded France's ultimate success.

France made its first attempt at colonizing North America in 1541, when ten ships sailed into the St. Lawrence Valley. Having alienated many of the Indians along the St. Lawrence in two previous expeditions, Cartier built a fortified settlement on Indian land and thus ended all possibility of peaceful Indian-French relations. Steady Indian attacks and scurvy (for which the Indians could have shown them a cure) drove the French off within two years.

In 1562 French Huguenots (Calvinists) made the next French attempt at colonization, establishing a base in modern South Carolina. Two years later they founded a settlement in Florida, which the Spanish quickly destroyed. These failures as well as a civil war between French Catholics and Huguenots ended France's first attempts at colonization.

@ **A Timucan Shows Frenchmen How His People Respect a Pillar Erected by an Earlier Party.**

The Enterprising Dutch

Having secured independence from Spain by 1588, the Dutch Republic became one of the seventeenth century's great powers. The Dutch empire, based on sea power, would stretch from Brazil to West Africa to the East Indies, modern Indonesia. North American colonies were a small part of this vast empire, but the Dutch nonetheless played a key role in European colonization of the continent.

In 1609 Henry Hudson sailed up the broad, deep river that today bears his name, and in the next year Dutch ships sailed up the Hudson to trade with Indians. In 1614 the Dutch established Fort Nassau at the site of modern Albany, New York, thus founding the colony of New Netherland. In 1625 they planted another fort on an island at the mouth of the Hudson. Within two years Peter Minuit, director-general of the colony, bought the island from local Indians, named it Manhattan, and began a settlement christened New Amsterdam. Furs, particularly beaver pelts, became the New Netherlanders' chief economic staple.

Elizabethan England and the Wider World

When Elizabeth I became queen in 1558, England, a minor power, stood on the sidelines as Spain and France grappled for European supremacy. England's claims to North America had receded, and religious division and domestic instability preoccupied the English.

This very instability, however, helped to propel Elizabethan expansion. Shipping the unemployed poor overseas would relieve England's economic woes, and these "surplus" people could provide markets for English cloth and produce raw materials.

But Spain blocked the way. Good relations between Elizabethan England and imperial Spain had broken down as England worried about Spanish attempts to crush rebellion in the Netherlands and about Spain's intervention in France's religious wars. By 1570 Elizabeth was secretly aiding the French Huguenots and Dutch rebels as well as encouraging English "sea dogs" such as Sir Francis Drake and Sir

John Hawkins, from whose voyages she took a share of the plunder.

Meanwhile, England's position in Ireland had deteriorated. By 1565 English troops were fighting to impose Elizabeth's rule throughout the island, where a Protestant English government was battling Irish Catholic rebels aided by Spain. In a war that ground on through the 1580s, English troops drove the Irish clans from their strongholds and established "plantations," or settlements, of Scottish and English Protestants. The English resorted to starvation and mass slaughter to break the Irish spirit. Elizabeth's generals justified these atrocities by calling the Irish savages. The Irish experience gave England strategies that it later used against North American Indians, whose customs, religion, and method of fighting seemed to absolve the English from guilt in waging exceptionally cruel warfare.

England had two objectives in the Western Hemisphere in the 1570s. The first was to find the northwest passage to Asia, preferably one lined with gold. The second, as Drake said, was to "singe the king of Spain's beard" by raiding Spanish fleets and cities. The search for a northwest passage proved fruitless, but the English did stage spectacularly profitable privateering raids against the Spanish.

In 1587 Sir Walter Raleigh, dreaming of founding an American colony where English, Indians, and even blacks liberated from Spanish slavery could live together productively, sponsored a colony on Roanoke Island, off the modern North Carolina coast. One hundred ten colonists, many of them members of families, reached Roanoke in late summer 1587. Almost immediately the colony's leader, John White, returned to England for more supplies, leaving behind the settlers.

Spain's attempt to crush England with the Great Armada in 1588 prevented White from returning to Roanoke until 1590. When he did, he found only rusty armor, moldy books, and the word CROATOAN carved into a post. To this day, no one knows what happened to the "Lost Colony."

Roanoke's fate illustrated several stubborn realities. First, even a large-scale, well-financed colony could fail, given settlers' unpreparedness for the American environment. Second, Europeans falsely assumed that the Indians would feed them and thus neglected to carry enough food supplies to carry them through the first winter. Third, colonizing attempts would have to be self-financing: a fiscally strapped monarch such as Elizabeth would not throw good money after bad. Finally, conflict with Spain hung menacingly over every other European attempt to gain a foothold in North America.

England's victory over the Spanish Armada in 1588 preserved English independence, kept the island Protestant, and demonstrated that England could repel invaders. But the war with Spain churned on.

Meanwhile, a new means of financing colonies appeared, the joint-stock company. A kind of business corporation, the joint-stock company raised capital through the sale of stock to the public. Each investor faced only a limited risk, but large sums could be amassed. The English government henceforth would leave colonization to the private initiative of individuals or groups.

The Beginnings of English Colonization: Virginia

The hopes of would-be English colonial investors rose after 1600. Peace between England and Spain, concluded in 1604 by Elizabeth's successor, James I (ruled 1603–1625), opened the way for new colonization attempts in the New World.

On April 10, 1606, James I granted charters to two separate joint-stock companies, one based in London and the other in Plymouth. The Virginia Company of Plymouth received a grant extending from modern Maine to the Potomac River; the Virginia Company of London, a grant from Cape Fear north to the Hudson River. Both companies dispatched colonists in 1607.

The Virginia Company of Plymouth sent 120 men to Sagadahoc at the mouth of the Kennebec River in Maine. The following year the colony disintegrated, the victim of Indian hostility (generally provoked) and hard Maine winters. The Virginia Company of London dispatched 105 settlers to a site on the James River near Chesapeake Bay that they named Jamestown. But the first colonists, who included many gentry, hunted for gold and failed to plant crops. When relief ships arrived in January 1608, they found only 38 survivors.

Near anarchy reigned at Jamestown until September 1608, when desperate councilors, representatives of the Virginia Company of London, turned to a brash soldier of fortune, Captain John Smith. Only twenty-eight, Smith found that his experiences fighting the Spanish and the Turks had prepared him well to assume control in Virginia. By instituting harsh discipline, organizing the settlers, and requiring them to build houses and plant food, he ensured Jamestown's survival.

Smith also became the colony's best diplomat. After local Indians captured him late in 1607, Smith displayed such impressive courage that Powhatan, the leader of the nearby Powhatan Confederacy, arranged an elaborate ceremony in which Pocahontas, his daughter, "saved" Smith's life during a mock execution.

When serious injuries forced Smith to return to England in 1609, discipline again crumbled. Expecting the Indians to furnish corn, the settlers had not laid away enough food for winter. Of the 500 residents at Jamestown in September 1609, only 100 lived to May 1610. An influx of new recruits and the imposition of military rule, however, enabled Virginia to win the First Anglo-Powhatan War (1610–1614) and, by 1611, to expand west to modern Richmond. The English population remained small—only 380 by 1616—and produced nothing of value for the stockholders.

Tobacco saved Virginia. John Rolfe, an Englishman who married Pocahontas, perfected a salable

European Settlements in Eastern North America, 1565–1625

Except for St. Augustine, Florida, and Santa Fe, New Mexico, all European settlements founded before 1607 were abandoned by 1625. Despite the migration of 10,000 Europeans to North America's Atlantic coast by 1625, the total number of Spanish, English, French, and Dutch on the continent was then about 1,800, of whom two-thirds lived in Virginia. For French and Spanish settlement in the late colonial period, see map on p. 52.

variety of tobacco for planting there, and by 1619 Virginia was exporting large, profitable amounts of the crop. Thereafter the Virginia Company poured supplies and settlers into the colony.

To attract labor and capital, the company awarded fifty-acre land grants ("headrights") to anyone paying his or her own passage or that of a laborer. By financing the passage of indentured servants, planters could accumulate large tracts of land. Thousands of single young men and a few hundred women became indentured servants, choosing the uncertainty of Virginia over poverty in England. In return for their passage, they worked a fixed term, usually four to seven years.

In 1619 the Virginia Company ended military rule and provided for an elected assembly, the House of Burgesses. Although the company could veto the assembly's actions, 1619 marked the beginning of representative government in North America. However, Virginia still faced three serious problems. First, local officials systematically defrauded shareholders, in the process sinking the company deeply into debt. Second, the colony's death rate soared. Malnutrition, typhus, dysentery, and salt poisoning (from drinking polluted river water) killed thousands of immigrants. Third, Indian relations worsened. After Powhatan's death in 1618, the new leader, Opechancanough, worried about the relentless expansion of the English colony. In 1622 the Indians killed 347 of the 1,200 settlers in a surprise attack.

The Virginia Company sent more men, and Governor Francis Wyatt took the offensive. Using tactics developed during the Irish war, Wyatt destroyed the Indians' food supplies and conducted winter campaigns to drive them from their homes when they would suffer most. By 1625 the English had won the war, and the Indians had lost their best chance of forcing out the intruders.

But the struggle bankrupted the Virginia Company. After receiving complaints about its management, James revoked its charter and made Virginia a royal colony in 1624. Only 500 Old World settlers lived there, including a handful of Africans of uncertain status.

The Origins of New England: Plymouth Plantation

Another rival entered the competition for the North American fur trade: the English who settled New England. In 1620 the Virginia Company of London granted a patent for a settlement to some English merchants headed by Thomas Weston. Weston dispatched eighteen families (102 people) in a small, leaky ship, the *Mayflower*. The colonists promised to send back lumber, furs, and fish for seven years, after which they would own the tract.

The expedition's leaders, and half its members, belonged to a small religious community from the northern English town of Scrooby. Separatist Puritans, they had earlier fled to the Netherlands to practice their religion freely. Fearing that their children were adopting Dutch ways, they decided to immigrate to America under Weston's sponsorship.

In November 1620 the *Mayflower* landed at Plymouth, outside the bounds of Virginia. Because they had no legal right to be there, the leaders forced the adult males in the group to sign the Mayflower Compact before they landed. By this document they constituted themselves a "civil body politic"—a civil government—under James I's sovereignty and established the colony of Plymouth Plantation.

Weakened by their journey and unprepared for winter, half the self-styled Pilgrims died within four months. To stop the Pilgrims from stealing their food, the Indians taught the newcomers how to grow corn.

Plymouth's relations with the Indians gradually worsened. Learning of the Virginia massacre of 1622, the Pilgrims militarized their colony and threatened their Indian "allies" with their monopoly of firepower.

Meanwhile, systematically cheated by English patrons, the Pilgrims had sunk deeply into debt after seven years and faced fifteen years' additional labor to free themselves. By the time Plymouth fulfilled its financial obligations, the settlement had grown to several hundred people on Cape Cod and in the southeastern corner of modern Massachusetts.

The Pilgrims' importance was twofold. First, they helped to inspire the ideal of Americans as sturdy, self-reliant, God-fearing folk who endured hardship to govern themselves freely. Second, they fore- 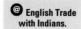 @ **English Trade with Indians.** shadowed the coercive methods that later generations of white Americans would use to gain mastery over the Indians.

CHRONOLOGY

c. 1400–1600	Renaissance era—first in Italy, then elsewhere in Europe.
1440	Portuguese slave trade in West Africa begins.
1488	Bartolomeu Días reaches the Cape of Good Hope.
1492	Christopher Columbus lands at San Salvador.
1497	John Cabot reaches Nova Scotia and Newfoundland.
1512–1521	Juan Ponce de León explores Florida.
1517	Protestant Reformation begins in Germany.
1519	Hernán Cortés begins conquest of Aztec empire.
1534	Church of England breaks from Roman Catholic church.
1534–1542	Jacques Cartier explores eastern Canada for France.
1539–1543	Hernando de Soto explores the southeastern United States.
1540–1542	Francisco Vásquez de Coronado explores the southwestern United States.
1558	Elizabeth I becomes queen of England.
1565	St. Augustine founded by Spanish.
1565–1580s	English attempt to subdue Ireland.
1584–1587	Roanoke colony explored and founded.
1588	English defeat the Spanish Armada.
1598	New Mexico colony founded.
1603	James I becomes king of England.
1607	English found colonies at Jamestown and Sagadahoc.
1609	Henry Hudson explores the Hudson River for the Dutch Republic.
1610–1614	First Anglo-Powhatan War.
1614	New Netherland colony founded.
1619	Large exports of tobacco from Virginia begin.
	House of Burgesses, first elected assembly, established in Virginia.
	First Africans arrive in Virginia.
1620	Mayflower Compact signed; Plymouth Plantation founded.
1622–1632	Second Anglo-Powhatan War.
1624	James I revokes Virginia Company's charter.

FOR FURTHER READING

J. F. A. Aiayi and Michael Crowder, eds., *History of West Africa,* vol. I (1972). A comprehensive collection of essays covering the period prior to 1800.

Robert J. Berkhofer, Jr., *The White Man's Burden: Images of the American Indian from Columbus to the Present* (1978). A penetrating analysis of the shaping of European and American attitudes, ideologies, and policies toward Native Americans.

Carl Bridenbaugh, *Vexed and Troubled Englishmen, 1590–1642* (1968). A highly readable account of England at the start of the colonial era.

Alfred W. Crosby, Jr., *Ecological Imperialism: The Biological Expansion of Europe, 900–1900* (1986). An outstanding discussion of the environmental and medical history of European overseas expansion.

D. W. Menig, *The Shaping of America, vol. I: Atlantic America, 1492–1800* (1986). A geographer's engrossing study of Europeans' encounter with North America and the rise of colonial society.

J. H. Parry, *The Age of Reconnaissance* (1963). A comprehensive analysis of European exploration and the rise of European overseas empires from the fifteenth to the seventeenth century.

David B. Quinn, *North America from Earliest Discoveries to First Settlements: The Norse Voyages to 1612* (1977). A thorough, learned account of European exploration, based on a wide range of scholarship.

Kirkpatrick Sale, *The Conquest of Paradise: Christopher Columbus and the Columbian Legacy* (1990). A polemical but informed critique of Columbus and his role in opening the Americas to European exploitation.

Eric Wolf, *Europe and the People Without History* (1982). An anthropologist's sweeping view of the causes and consequences of Europe's worldwide expansion.

3

Expansion and Diversity: The Rise of Colonial America

The New England Way

Chesapeake Society

Spread of Slavery: The Caribbean and Carolina

The Middle Colonies

Rivals for North America

Invading Englishmen and their African slaves settled not in wilderness but on lands that Indian peoples had long inhabited.

The New England Way

In 1628 several Puritan merchants obtained a charter to settle north of the Separatist colony at Plymouth. Organized as the Massachusetts Bay Company, they moved the seat of their colony's government to New England, paving the way for Massachusetts to be self-governing.

A City upon a Hill

In 1630 the Massachusetts Bay Company dispatched a "great fleet," eleven ships and 700 passengers, to New England. As the ships crossed the Atlantic, Governor John Winthrop delivered a lay sermon, "A Model of Christian Charity," in which he explained how and why the new colony would differ from England itself.

Winthrop boldly announced that "we shall be as a city upon a hill, the eyes of all people are upon us." The settlers would build a godly community whose compelling example would shame England. Denouncing economic jealousy, Winthrop explained that God intended "in all times some must be rich and some poor." The rich would practice charity and mercy, and the poor show their faith in God's will by practicing patience and fortitude. In a godly state, the government would prevent the greedy among the rich from exploiting the poor and the lazy among the poor from burdening their fellow citizens.

Winthrop's sermon expressed both traditional European ideas of social reciprocity (see Chapter 2) and the Puritans' dismay at the economic forces battering—and changing—English society.

For much of England's village population, life was brutal and desperate. Lacking land, England's people competed fiercely for jobs and became individualistic, acquisitive, and materialistic. Winthrop blamed this competitive spirit for fostering apathy toward human suffering. Charity should moderate the drive for profit, he believed, so that goods would be exchanged, wages set, and interest calculated in a way that would allow a decent life for all.

Winthrop and his fellow Puritans saw Massachusetts Bay not, like other colonies, as an extension of England and its harshly competitive ways, but as a reaction to it. Moral self-restraint would prevent merchants from squeezing out excessive profits; if necessary, the government could step in. Above all, the Puritans wanted to turn religious idealism into a renewed sense of community.

Development of a Puritan Orthodoxy

The great fleet of Puritans reached Boston Harbor in June 1630; by fall six towns had sprung up. During the unusually severe first winter, one-third of the Puritans died; however, spring brought 1,300 new settlers, and thousands more followed. The disciplined and highly motivated Puritans put Massachusetts Bay Colony on a firm footing in its first year. Though Nonseparatists, they created a system of self-governing congregations (congregationalism) unique to America. In New England the male saints chose their minister, elected "elders" to handle finances, and otherwise controlled their church.

Congregationalism fused elements of separating and nonseparating Puritanism. It followed the Separatist tradition by allowing only saints to take communion and to baptize their children, but adopted the Nonseparatist practice of requiring all adults (except for a few scandalously wicked individuals) to attend services and to pay for the support of the churches. New England thus had a state-sponsored, "established" church; the meetinghouse, used for both religious services and town business, symbolized the relationship of church to government.

This "New England Way" set high standards for identifying saints. Massachusetts Puritans insisted that candidates for church membership provide a soul-baring "relation," or account of their conver-sion, before the congregation. This public revelation of intimate spiritual matters could be embarrassing and painful for candidate and congregation, and it often intimidated those seeking church membership. The conversion relation ultimately became the New England Way's most vulnerable point and a major cause of its demise.

Literacy was essential to conversion. Children were drilled in catechism, young people read the Bible to feel the quickening of God's grace, and saints recorded their lapses and spiritual insights in diaries. In 1647 the Massachusetts Bay Colony passed the Old Deluder Act because "one chief project of that old deluder, Satan [is] to keep men from knowledge of the Scriptures." Every town of fifty or more households was to appoint one teacher from whom all children could receive instruction, and every town of one hundred households or more was to maintain a grammar school with a teacher capable of preparing students for university-level learning.

@ Cotton Mather on the Education of His Children.

Clergymen bore responsibility for leading people to repentance and for stimulating piety. The minister was to stir his congregation's faith with direct, logical, and moving sermons understandable to average listeners. An educated clergy was essential, and so in 1636 Massachusetts founded Harvard College to produce learned ministers. In its first thirty-five years, the college turned out 201 graduates, 111 of them ministers.

Dissenting Puritans

Some Puritans dissented from their leaders' vision of social order and religious conformity. The first to challenge the New England Way was Roger Williams, who arrived in America in 1631. Radiating the joy of serving God, he quickly became one of the most respected and popular figures in Massachusetts Bay. But when he questioned the legal basis of congregationalism, insisting that church and state be separate, the Massachusetts Bay government silenced him.

Although agreeing that the church must be free of state control, Puritans believed that a holy commonwealth required cooperation between church and state. Williams argued that civil government had to remain absolutely uninvolved with religous matters.

Believing that the purpose of the colony was to protect true religion and to prevent heresy, political authorities declared Williams's opinions subversive and banished him in 1635. Williams went south to the edge of Narragansett Bay to a place that he later named Providence, which he purchased from the Indians. A steady stream of dissenters drifted to the group of settlements near Providence, forming Rhode Island in 1647. The only New England colony to practice religious toleration, Rhode Island grew to 800 settlers by 1650.

Anne Hutchinson, "a woman of haughty and fierce carriage, of a nimble wit and active spirit" according to her enemy John Winthrop, presented a second challenge to the New England Way. Ironically, Hutchinson's ideas derived from the much-respected minister John Cotton. Cotton insisted that true congregationalism required the saints to be free of religious or political control by anyone who had not undergone a conversion experience.

Hutchinson extended Cotton's ideas to a broad attack on clerical authority. She began to imply that her own minister was not a saint and then asserted that saints in the congregation could ignore his views if they believed that he lacked saving grace.

Hutchinson's ideas directly attacked the clergy's authority to interpret and teach Scripture; critics charged that her beliefs would delude individuals into imagining that they were accountable only to themselves. Her followers were labeled Antinomians, meaning those opposed to the rule of law. Anne Hutchinson bore the additional liability of being a woman challenging traditional male roles in church and state. Her gender made her seem an especially dangerous foe.

Massachusetts Bay split into pro- and anti-Hutchinson forces. Her opponents prevailed, bringing Hutchinson to trial for sedition before the Massachusetts Bay legislature (the General Court) and then for heresy before a panel of ministers. Hutchinson's knowledge of Scripture was so superior to that of her inquisitors that she might well have

been acquitted had she not claimed to communicate directly with the Holy Spirit. Because Puritans believed that God had ceased to make known matters of faith by personal revelation since New Testament times, Hutchinson was condemned by her own words. Hutchinson and other Antinomians were banished from the colony, effectively ending the last challenge capable of splitting congregationalism and ensured the survival of the New England Way for two more generations.

New restrictions on women's independence and on equality within Puritan congregations followed antinomianism's defeat. Increasingly, women were prohibited from assuming the kind of public religious role claimed by Hutchinson and were even required to relate their conversion experiences in private to their ministers rather than publicly before their congregations.

Economics as well as ideas posed serious threats to Winthrop's "city upon a hill." While most Puritans shared Winthrop's view of community, self-discipline, and mutual obligation, a large minority had come to America for prosperity and social mobility. The most visibly ambitious colonists were merchants, whose activities fueled New England's economy but whose way of life challenged its ideals.

Merchants fit uneasily into a religious society that equated financial shrewdness with greed. They clashed repeatedly with government leaders, who were trying to regulate prices so that consumers would not suffer from the chronic shortage of manufactured goods that afflicted New England. At stake was the Puritans' ability to insulate their city upon a hill from a market economy that threatened to strangle the spirit of community within a harsh world of frantic competition.

Puritan Government and Community Life

To preserve the New England Way, the Puritans created political and religious institutions with far more popular participation than those in England. Its headquarters established in America, the Massachusetts Bay Company allowed all male saints to elect the governor and his council. By 1634 each town had gained the right to send two delegates to the General Court; ten years later court and council separated to create a bicameral (two-chamber) legislature. Although in England stringent property requirements allowed less than 30 percent of adult males to vote, 55 percent of Massachusetts's adult males could vote.

Towns were formed when a legislature granted land to several dozen heads of families. These individuals had almost unlimited freedom to lay out the settlement, design its church, distribute land among themselves, and make local laws. Generally, all adult male taxpayers, even nonsaints, participated in town meetings. In turn, the meetings ran the town and granted land rights to new settlers.

Most New England towns were uniform farm communities resembling traditional English villages; seaports, with their transient populations, were the chief exception. Each family generally received a one-acre house lot (just enough room for a vegetable garden) within a half mile of the meetinghouse. Each household also received strips of land or small fields farther away for crops and livestock. Individuals often owned several scattered parcels of land and had the right to graze a few extra animals on the town "commons."

Most towns attempted to maintain communities of tightly clustered settlers by distributing only as much land as was necessary for each family to support itself. The remaining land would be distributed to future generations as needed. Forcing residents to live close together was an attempt to foster social reciprocity. New England's generally compact system of settlement made people interact with each other and established an atmosphere of mutual watchfulness that promoted godly order.

> @ **Land Division for a Typical Puritan Town**

> @ **Land Division in New Orleans Clearly Shows Different Social Goals than the Puritans Held.**

Puritan Families

"The little commonwealth"—the nuclear family—was the foundation of Puritan society. "*Well-ordered families*," declared minister Cotton Mather in 1699,

"naturally produce a *Good Order* in other *Societies*." A well-ordered family was one in which wife, children, and servants dutifully obeyed the husband and in which the "true wife" thought of herself "in subjection to her husband's authority."

> @ **Excerpts from an Early Advice Book: How Puritans Can Maintain "a Well-ordered Family"**

New Englanders defined matrimony as a contract, not a sacrament. Puritans were thus married by justices of the peace rather than ministers. As a civil institution, marriage could be dissolved by the courts in cases of desertion, bigamy, adultery, or physical cruelty. However, New England courts saw divorce as a remedy only for extremely wronged spouses, such as the Plymouth woman who discovered that her husband also had wives in Boston, Barbados, and England.

Because Puritans believed that healthy families were crucial to the community's welfare, they intervened whenever they discovered serious problems in a household. Courts disciplined unruly youngsters, disobedient servants, disrespectful wives, and irresponsible husbands. Churches also censured, and even expelled, spouses who did not maintain domestic tranquillity.

New England wives enjoyed significant legal protections against spousal violence and nonsupport and had more freedom than their English counterparts to escape a failed marriage. But they suffered the legal disabilities borne by all women under English law. A wife had no property rights independent of her husband except by premarital agreement. Only if there were no other heirs or if a will so specified would a widow receive control of household property, although law entitled her to lifetime use of one-third of the estate.

> @ **A Puritan Prescription for Marital Concord**

New England's families enjoyed greater stability and lived longer lives than their English counterparts. The region's cold climate limited the impact of disease, especially in winter, when limited travel between towns slowed the spread of infection. Easy access to land contributed to a healthy diet, which strengthened resistance to disease and lowered death rates associated with

> @ **An Early Prenuptial Agreement to Protect the Economic Rights of the Wife**

childbirth. Life expectancy for Puritan men reached sixty-five, and women lived nearly that long. These life spans were ten years or more longer than those of England. Because so many of the 20,000 immigrants who arrived in New England between 1630 and 1642 came as members of families, an even sex ratio and a rapid natural increase of population followed.

> @ **Mortality at Plymouth Plantation**
>
> @ **Gender Differences in Life Expectancy at Plymouth**

Families were economically interdependent. Male heads of family managed the household's crops and livestock, conducted its business transactions, and represented it at town meetings. Wives bore and nurtured children; performed or oversaw work in the house, garden, and barn; and participated in community networks that assisted at childbirths and aided the poor and vulnerable. Sons depended on parents to provide them with acreage for a farm, and parents encouraged sons to stay at home and work in return for a bequest of land later on. Young males often tended their fathers' fields until their late twenties before receiving their own land. The average family, raising four sons to adulthood, could count on thirty to forty years of work if their sons delayed marriage until age twenty-six.

> @ **"Before the Birth of One of Her Children"—Poem by Anne Bradstreet**
>
> @ **Family Ties: a Puritan Woman's Advice on Dealing with an Elderly Family Member**

There were other benefits. Prolonged dependence for sons ensured that the family property would continue in the hands of capable, experienced men. Although daughters performed vital labor, they would marry into another family. Young women with many childbearing years ahead were the most valuable potential wives, and first-generation women tended to marry by the age of twenty-one.

Saddled with the triple burdens of a short growing season, rocky soil salted with gravel, and an inefficient system of land distribution that forced farmers to cultivate widely scattered strips, the colonists nevertheless managed to feed their families and to keep ahead of their debts. Few grew wealthy from farming. For wealth, New Englanders turned lumbering, shipbuilding, fishing, and rum distilling into major industries that employed perhaps one-fifth of all adults full-time. As its economy diversified, New England prospered. Increasingly concerned more with profit than prophecy, the Puritans discovered, to their dismay, that fewer of their children were emerging as saints.

The Demise of the Puritan Errand

As New England struggled for stability and conformity, old England fell into chaos and civil war. Alienated by years of religious harassment, Puritans gained control of the revolt, beheaded Charles I in 1649, and governed without a king for more than a decade. In 1660 a provisional English government recalled the Stuarts and restored Charles II to the throne.

The Stuart Restoration doomed Puritanism in England as High Church Anglicans took their revenge; "God has spit in our face," lamented one Puritan. The Restoration also left American Puritans without a mission. Having conquered a wilderness and built their city upon a hill, they found that the eyes of the world were no longer fixed on them.

An internal crisis also gripped New England. First-generation Puritans had believed that they held a covenant, a holy contract, with God to establish a scripturally ordained church and to charge their descendants with its preservation. However, reluctant to submit to a public review of their spirituality, relatively few second-generation Puritans were willing to join the elect by making the required conversion relation before the congregation.

Because Puritan churches baptized only babies born to saints, first-generation Puritans faced the prospect that their own grandchildren would remain unbaptized unless the standards for church membership were lowered. They solved their dilemma in 1662 through a compromise known as the Half-Way Covenant, which permitted the children of all baptized members, including nonsaints, to be baptized. Church membership would pass down from generation to generation, but nonsaints would be "halfway" members, unable to take communion or to vote in church affairs. When forced to choose between a church system founded on a pure membership of the elect and one that embraced the entire community,

New Englanders opted to sacrifice purity for community.

The Half-Way Covenant marked the end of the New England Way. The elect had been unable to raise a new generation of saints whose religious fervor equaled their own. Most adults chose to remain in "halfway" status for life, and the saints became a shrinking minority in the third and fourth generations.

Expansion and Native Americans

In contrast to the settlement of Virginia, the Puritan colonization of New England initially met little resistance from Native Americans, whose numbers had been drastically reduced by disease. Between 1616 and 1618 an epidemic killed 90 percent of New England's coastal Indians, and a second epidemic in 1643–1644 inflicted comparable casualties on Indians throughout the Northeast.

The expansion of English settlement farther inland, however, aroused Indian resistance. As settlers moved into the Connecticut River valley, beginning in 1633, friction developed with the Pequots, who controlled the trade in furs and wampum with New Netherland. After tensions escalated into violence, the English waged a ruthless campaign against the Pequots, using tactics similar to those devised to break Irish resistance (see Chapter 2). By late 1637 Pequot resistance was crushed, and English settlement of the new colonies of Connecticut and New Haven could proceed unimpeded.

Indians felt the English presence in many ways. The fur trade, initially beneficial to Native Americans of the interior, became a burden. Once Indians began hunting for trade instead of for their subsistence needs alone, they quickly depleted the supply of beavers and other fur-bearing animals. Because English traders advanced trade goods on credit before the hunting season began, many Indians fell into debt. Traders increasingly took Indian land as collateral and sold it to settlers.

English townspeople, eager to expand their agricultural output and provide for their sons, voted themselves much larger amounts of land after 1660.

> **@ A Narragansett Leader Complains of English Encroachment.**

For example, Dedham, Massachusetts, had distributed only 3,000 acres from 1636 to 1656; by 1668 it had allocated another 15,000 acres. Many farmers built their homes on their outlying tracts, crowding closer to the Indians' settlements and their hunting, fishing, and gathering areas.

Expansion put pressure on the natives and the land alike. By clearing trees for fields and for use as fuel and building material, the colonists were altering the entire ecosystem by the mid-1600s. Deer no longer grazed freely, and the wild plants on which the Indians depended for food and medicine could not grow. Deforestation not only dried the soil but also brought frequent flooding. Encroaching white settlers allowed their livestock to run wild, according to English custom. Pigs damaged Indian cornfields and shellfish-gathering sites. Cattle and horses devoured native grasses, which the settlers replaced with English varieties.

Powerless to reverse the alarming decline of population, land, and food supplies, many Indians became demoralized. Some turned to alcohol, increasingly available during the 1660s despite colonial attempts to suppress its sale to Native Americans. Interpreting the crisis as one of belief, other Indians converted to Christianity. By 1675 Puritan missionaries had established about thirty "praying towns." Supervised by missionaries, each praying town had its own Native American magistrate, and many congregations had Indian preachers.

Anglo-Indian conflict became acute in the 1670s because of pressure on the Indians to sell their land and to accept missionaries and the legal authority of white courts. Tension was especially high in the Plymouth colony, where Puritans had engulfed the Wampanoag tribe and forced a series of humiliating concessions from their leader Metacom, "King Philip," the son of the Pilgrims' onetime ally Massasoit.

In 1675 Plymouth hanged three Wampanoags for killing a Christian Indian; several other Wampanoags were shot while burglarizing a farmhouse. In response to the escalation of violence, Metacom organized two-thirds of the Native Americans, including many praying Indians, into a military alliance. "But little remains of my ancestors' domain.

I am resolved not to see the day when I have no country," Metacom declared as he and his men touched off the conflict known as King Philip's War.

The war raged across New England. Metacom's forces, as well armed as the Puritans, devastated the countryside, wiping out twelve of New England's ninety towns and killing 600 colonists. The following year, 1676, saw the tide turn as Puritan militia destroyed their enemies' food supplies and sold hundreds of captives into slavery, including Metacom's wife and child. Perhaps 3,000 Indians died in battle or starved, including Metacom himself.

King Philip's War reduced southern New England's Indian population by almost 40 percent and eliminated open Indian resistance to white expansion. It also deepened whites' hostility toward all Native Americans, even the Christian Indians who had fought against King Philip. In 1677 ten praying towns were disbanded and all Indians were restricted to the remaining four. Missionary work ceased.

Economics, Gender, and Satan in Salem

In the three decades after adoption of the Half-Way Covenant, the Puritan clergy unleashed a stream of jeremiads (angry lamentations, named after the Old Testament prophet Jeremiah) at their congregations, berating them for failing to preserve the idealism of the first generation. Indeed, by 1690 the Puritans, having built a society from the ground up, no longer felt an overriding need to place collective, community interests first. As New Englanders pursued economic gain more openly and as populations dispersed away from town centers, the fabric of community frayed. Friction easily arose between the townspeople still dwelling near the meetinghouse (who usually dominated politics) and the "outlivers," those living on outlying tracts of land, who were less influential because of their distance from town.

Nowhere in New England did these trends have more disturbing effects than in Salem, Massachusetts, made up of the port of Salem Town and the farm community of Salem Village. Trade and rapid growth

had made Salem Town the region's second-largest port. By 1690 prosperous merchants controlled much of the wealth and political power of Salem as a whole, and the community was vulnerable to conflict between its prosperous merchants and its struggling farmers.

@ Factionalism and Wealth in Salem Village

Salem Village (now Danvers) lay six miles west of Salem Town's meetinghouse, and its citizens resented Salem Town's political dominance. Salem Village was divided between the supporters of two families, the Porters and the Putnams. Well connected with the merchant elite, the Porters enjoyed political prestige in Salem Town and lived in the village's eastern section, whose residents farmed richer soils and benefited more from Salem Town's prosperity. In contrast, most Putnams lived in Salem Village's less fertile western half, shared little in Salem Town's commercial expansion, and had lost their political influence. Rivalry between Porters and Putnams mirrored the tensions between Salem's urban and rural dwellers.

In late 1691 several Salem Village girls encouraged an African slave woman, Tituba, to tell fortunes and talk about sorcery. When the girls began behaving strangely, villagers assumed that they were victims of witchcraft. Pressed to identify their tormenters, they named two local white women and Tituba.

So far the incident was not unusual. Belief in witchcraft existed at all levels of American and European society. But by April 1692 the girls had denounced two prosperous farm wives long considered saints in the local church and had identified the village's former minister as a wizard (male witch). Fear of witchcraft soon overrode considerable doubts about the girls' credibility and led local judges to sweep aside normal procedural safeguards. Specifically, the judges ignored legal bans on "spectral evidence," testimony that a spirit resembling the accused had been seen tormenting a victim. Thereafter charges multiplied until the jails overflowed with accused witches.

@ Samuel Parris Sets a Tone.

@ Wonders of the Invisible World, by Cotton Mather

The pattern of hysteria and accusations reflected Salem Village's internal divisions. Most charges came from the western side of the village—one-third from the Putnams alone—and were lodged against people who lived outside the western half and who were connected by economics or marriage to the Porters. Two-thirds of all accusers were girls aged eleven to twenty, and more than one-half had lost one or more parents in conflicts between Indians and settlers in Maine. They most frequently named as witches middle-aged wives and widows—women who had escaped the poverty and uncertainty that they themselves faced.

@ **Witchcraft in Salem**

Those found guilty of witchcraft tried to stave off death by implicating others. As the pandemonium spread, fear dissolved ties of friendship and family. A minister was condemned by his granddaughter, a mother by her seven-year-old daughter, and a husband and father by his wife and daughter. Fifty saved themselves by confessing, but twenty were condemned and executed.

@ **Petition for Bail from Accused Witches**

@ **Ann Putnam's Deposition**

By late 1692 doubts about the charges were surfacing. Clergymen objected to the emphasis on spectral evidence, crucial to most convictions. In October Governor William Phips forbade any further imprisonments for witchcraft. One hundred were still in jail, and 200 more stood accused. In early 1693 Phips ended the terror by pardoning all those who were convicted or suspected of practicing witchcraft.

@ **Ann Putnam's Confession**

@ **The Conclusions of the Massachusetts Bay Elders**

The witchcraft hysteria reflected profound anxieties over social change. The underlying causes of this tension became clear as Salem Village's communally oriented farmers directed their wrath toward Salem Town's competitive and individualistic merchants. This clash of values revealed the extent to which John Winthrop's city upon a hill had lost its relevance to new generations forced into economic enterprise by New England's stingy soil, harsh climate, and meager natural resources.

By 1700 New Englanders had begun a transition from Puritans to "Yankees." True to their Puritan roots, they retained strong religious convictions and an extraordinary capacity for perseverance. Increasingly grafted to these roots were ingenuity, sharpness, and an eye for opportunity, traits that would enable New Englanders to build a thriving international commerce and later an industrial revolution.

@ **Portraits of a Boston Merchant and His Wife**

As New England moved away from its roots, the Chesapeake region to the south also underwent radical transformation.

Chesapeake Society

Virtually ignored by King James I (who took over the colony in 1624 from the bankrupt Virginia Company) and his successors, Virginia developed on its own. The English monarch's indifference worked to the colonial elite's advantage, leaving them room to experiment with local administration. Tobacco and the environment shaped the colonists' destiny not only in Virginia but also in Maryland and in what became North Carolina.

State and Church in Virginia

James I planned to rule Virginia through appointed officials, but Virginians petitioned repeatedly for the restoration of their elected assembly, the first in the New World. James I's successor, Charles I, grudgingly relented in 1628. After 1630, seeking more taxes, Virginia's royal governors called regular assemblies. During the 1650s the assembly split into two chambers, the elected House of Burgesses and the appointed Governor's Council. Later royal colonies also adopted this bicameral pattern.

Local government officials were appointed, rather than elected, during Virginia's first quarter-century. In 1634 Virginia adopted England's county-court system. Royal governors appointed justices of the peace to preside over the county courts. They acted as judges, set local tax rates, paid county officials, and oversaw the construction and maintenance of roads, bridges, and public buildings.

In contrast to Puritan New England, Virginia had the Church of England as its established church. Anglican vestries governed each parish; elected vestrymen handled church finances, determined poor relief, and investigated complaints against the minister. Taxpayers were legally obliged to pay fixed rates to the Anglican church. Because of the large distances between settlements and churches as well as a chronic shortage of clergymen, few Virginians regularly attended services.

Maryland

Beginning in the 1630s, grants by the crown to reward English politicians replaced joint-stock companies as the primary mechanism of colonization. The first such grant, or proprietorship, went in 1632 to Lord Baltimore (Cecilius Calvert); he named the large tract east of Chesapeake Bay Maryland in honor of England's Queen Henrietta Maria.

With Charles I's consent, Baltimore intended to make Maryland a refuge for England's Catholics, who could neither worship in public nor hold political office and who had to pay tithes to the Anglican church. Baltimore tried to install the old English manor system, with a manor lord taking on tenants and employing a Catholic priest as chaplain. However, relatively few Catholics settled in Maryland, which was overwhelmingly Protestant from the beginning. Cheap land lured settlers who did not need to become tenants on the manors, and Baltimore's scheme fell apart. By 1675 all sixty of Maryland's nonproprietary manors had become plantations.

Religious tension gradually developed in Maryland society. The Protestant majority dominated the elected lower house of government, but many Catholics had become large landowners, held high public office, and dominated the appointive upper house. Until 1642 Catholics and Protestants shared the chapel at St. Mary's, the capital, but they began to argue over its use. As antagonisms intensified, Baltimore drafted, and the assembly passed, the Act for Religious Toleration (1649), America's first law affirming liberty of worship.

Unfortunately, the toleration act did not secure religious peace. In 1654 the Protestant majority barred Catholics from voting; ousted Governor William Stone, a Protestant; and repealed the toleration act. Stone raised an army, both Protestant and Catholic, to regain the government but met defeat at the Battle of the Severn River in 1655. The victors imprisoned Stone and hanged three Catholic leaders. Maryland remained in Protestant hands until 1658.

Tobacco Shapes a Way of Life

Chesapeake settlers were scattered across the landscape. A typical community included only 24 families in a twenty-five-square-mile area, a mere six people per square mile. (In contrast, New England often had 500 people squeezed onto one square mile.) Most Chesapeake inhabitants lived in a world of few friendships and considerable isolation.

Isolated Chesapeake settlers shared a life governed by one overriding factor: the price of tobacco. After an initial boom, tobacco prices plunged 97 percent in 1629 before stabilizing at 10 percent of their original high. Tobacco was still profitable as long as it was grown on fertile soil near navigable water. As a result, 80 percent of Chesapeake homes were located along a riverbank, both for the fertile soil and for the cheap transportation thus afforded; ships literally could come to the plantation's front door. Wealthy planters shipped their tobacco and small farmers' crops from their own wharves and distributed imported goods. Neither towns nor a merchant class was needed, and urbanization was slow.

Wealth lay in the cultivation of large amounts of tobacco, and that in turn required a large work force. From 1630 to 1700, 110,000 English, most of them indentured servants, migrated to the Chesapeake. Because most of these immigrants were destined for field work, men dominated; four out of every five servants were males aged about twenty.

Mortality, Gender, and Kinship

So few women immigrated to the Chesapeake that before 1650, only one-third of male servants could find brides and then only after completing their indentures. Female scarcity gave women an advantage in negotiating favorable marriages.

> @ **Divorce in Maryland**

Death ravaged Chesapeake society and left domestic life exceptionally fragile. In 1650 malaria joined the killer diseases typhoid, dysentery, and salt poisoning as the marshy lowlands of the tidewater Chesapeake became fertile breeding grounds for the mosquitoes that spread malaria. Life expectancy in the 1600s was twenty years lower in the Chesapeake than in New England. Servants died at appalling rates; 40 percent were dead within a decade of arrival and 70 percent before reaching age fifty.

Chesapeake widows often enjoyed substantial property rights. The region's men wrote wills giving their wives perpetual and complete control of their estates so that their own children could inherit them. A widow in such circumstances had a degree of economic independence but faced enormous pressure to remarry, particularly a man who could produce income by farming her fields.

> @ **A Puritan Prescription for Marital Concord**

> @ **Pattern of Bequests to Wives in Colonial Maryland**

The lopsided sex ratio and high death rates contributed to slow population growth in the Chesapeake. Although perhaps 110,000 English immigrated to the Chesapeake between 1630 and 1700, the white population was just 69,000 in 1700. Change came gradually as children acquired childhood immunities, life spans lengthened, and the sex ratio evened out. By 1720 most Chesapeake residents were native born.

Tobacco's Troubles

Chesapeake society became increasingly unequal. A few planters used the headright system to build up large landholdings and to profit from their servants' labor. Wretchedly exploited, and poorly fed, clothed, and housed, servants faced a bleak future even when their indentures ended.

> @ **A Virginia Case Involving Runaway Indentured Servants**

In 1660 Chesapeake tobacco prices plunged by 50 percent, setting off a depression that lasted fifty years. Despite losses, large planters earned some income from rents, interest on loans, and shopkeeping, while small landowners scrambled to sell corn and cattle in the West Indies. A typical family in this depression era lived in a small wooden shack, slept on rags, and ate mush or stew cooked in the single pot. Having fled poverty in England or the West Indies, people often found utter destitution in the Chesapeake.

Bacon's Rebellion

By the 1670s these bleak conditions had locked most Virginia landowners into a losing battle against poverty and had left the colony's freedmen in despair. Both groups were capable of striking out in blind rage if an opportunity to stave off economic disaster presented itself. In 1676 this human powder keg exploded in violence.

Virginians had been free of serious conflict with the Indians since the end of the Third Anglo-Powhatan War in 1646. By 1653 tribes encircled by English settlements had begun agreeing to remain within boundaries set by the government—in effect, on reservations.

In June 1675 a dispute between some Doeg Indians and a Virginia farmer escalated. A force of Virginia and Maryland militia pursuing the Doegs murdered fourteen friendly Susquehannocks and later executed five of their chiefs. The violence was now unstoppable. While Governor William Berkeley proposed defending the frontier by a costly system of forts, small farmers preferred the cheaper solution: a war of extermination against the Indians. Some 300 settlers elected Nathaniel Bacon, a distant relative of Berkeley and member of the Royal Council, to lead them against nearby Indians in April 1676. The expedition found only peaceful Indians but slaughtered them anyhow.

Returning to Jamestown, Virginia's capital, in June 1676, Bacon asked for authority to wage war "against all Indians in general." The legislature voted for a program designed to appeal to both hard-pressed taxpayers and landless ex-servants. All Indians who had left their villages without permission (even if fleeing Bacon) were declared enemies, and their lands were forfeited. Bacon's troops could seize any "enemy" property and enslave Indian prisoners.

But Governor Berkeley soon had second thoughts about the slaughter and recalled Bacon and his 1,300 men. Forbidden to attack Indians, Bacon's forces turned against the government and burned Jamestown. The rebels offered freedom to any servants or slaves owned by Berkeley's allies who would join them and then looted enemy plantations. What had begun as Indian warfare was now a social rebellion. Before the uprising could proceed further, however, Bacon died of dysentery in late 1676, and his followers dispersed.

Bacon's Rebellion revealed a society under deep internal stress. Begun as an effort to displace escalating tensions among whites onto the Indians, it became an excuse to plunder other whites.

Slavery

Racial slavery developed in three stages in the Chesapeake. Africans first appeared in 1619, but their early status was generally indistinguishable from the standing of white servants. By 1640 blacks and some Indians were being treated as slaves, and their children inherited their status. Thus their situation had become inferior to that of indentured white servants. In the final phase, after 1660, laws defined slavery as a lifelong, inheritable status based on color. By 1705 strict legal codes defined the place of slaves in society and set standards of racial etiquette. Slavery was a system for blacks and Indians only. The English embarked on slavery as a response to nonwhite peoples, whom they considered inferior to whites.

@ **Main Sources of African Slaves**

Not until the 1680s were there significant numbers of black slaves in the Chesapeake, but by 1700 nearly 20,000 slaves resided in the region. Economics as well as race underlay the replacement of indentured servitude by slavery. In England a pop-

@ **Excerpts of Virginia Law on Indentured Servitude**

ulation decline between 1650 and 1700 reduced the potential pool for overseas labor and drove up wages. In addition, with the end of the Royal African Company's monopoly on the shipping and sale of slaves in the 1690s, an expanded supply of slaves arrived in the Chesapeake.

@ **Early Evidence of Sexual Tensions Within Slavery**

The emergence of slavery served to relax the economic tensions that had triggered Bacon's Rebellion. After 1690 even poor whites who owned no slaves believed that they shared a common interest with upper-class planters in maintaining social control over an alien and dangerous race.

Slavery's establishment as the principal form of labor in the Chesapeake was part of a larger trend among England's plantation colonies, one that had begun in the Caribbean and would spread to the new mainland colony of Carolina.

Spread of Slavery: The Caribbean and Carolina

As Puritans settled New England, a second immigrant wave carried twice their number, some 40,000 English people, to the West Indian islands in the Caribbean. The English West Indies strongly influenced English North America. The islands were a major market for New England's surplus foodstuffs, dried fish, and lumber. The West Indies pioneered techniques of racial control that were later adopted in the mainland colonies' plantation societies.

After 1660 large numbers of English islanders migrated to the Chesapeake and to Carolina, carrying with them the habits and prejudices of plantation slaveholding.

The Chaotic Caribbean

In the sixteenth century Spain claimed the entire Caribbean but concentrated on holding the four largest islands: Santo Domingo (Hispaniola), Puerto Rico, Cuba, and Jamaica. The English, French, and

Dutch all scrambled to settle the uninhabited Caribbean islands. By 1640 England had established twenty communities from the Bahamas to the Nicaraguan coast. St. Kitts, Barbados, Montserrat, Nevis, and Antigua survived a Spanish counterattack, and Jamaica fell to England in 1655.

Born of war, England's West Indian colonies matured in turmoil. Between 1640 and 1713 they suffered the constant threat and frequent reality of both invasion and piracy. Seven slave revolts rocked the English islands before 1713 and left a bitter legacy of racial hatred.

Caribbean life went on amid constant violence inflicted on slaves by masters, on Catholics by Protestants, and on humans by nature. Bubonic plague killed one-third of the islanders from 1647 to 1649. Five thousand militiamen (every sixth Englishman in the Caribbean) died in the battle to capture Jamaica from Spain in the 1650s. Hurricanes regularly killed hundreds, and malaria and yellow fever felled thousands. Few lived more than twenty years from their arrival in the islands.

Sugar and Slaves

Initially, the English West Indies developed along lines similar to Virginia, with tobacco the dominant crop. Because a single worker could tend only three acres of tobacco, tobacco farming demanded a large population. By 1640 more colonists lived on England's five West Indian islands than in all of Virginia.

Tobacco, requiring little equipment beyond a curing shed, was cheap to raise, and tobacco cultivation gave individuals with little money a chance at upward mobility. Sugar cane soon changed that, revolutionizing the islands' economy and society. Encouraged by Dutch merchants, wealthy English planters began to raise this enormously lucrative crop. Sugar sold at high prices, which escalated steadily over the next century, and could make a planter fabulously wealthy, but it required large amounts of capital and labor and elaborate machinery. With tobacco prices remaining low, most farmers could not afford to raise sugar. On Barbados a few sugar planters closed off all opportunity to small farmers by aggressively bidding up the price of land by more than 1,000 percent; by 1680 a mere 7 percent of landowners held over half the acreage. A typical sugar planter's estate was 200 acres, whereas most Barbadians scratched a meager living from 10 acres or less.

Because the profit from sugar vastly exceeded that from any other crop, West Indian planters turned every available acre into cane fields. Deforesting the islands (except Jamaica's mountains), they also virtually eliminated land for growing grain or raising livestock. Suddenly dependent on outside sources even for food, the Indies became a flourishing market for New England farmers, fishers, and loggers.

Moreover, the demand for labor soared because sugar required triple the labor force of tobacco. African slaves soon replaced indentured white servants in the fields. Most planters preferred black slaves to white servants because they could be driven harder and maintained more cheaply. Also, African slaves could better withstand the tropical diseases of the Caribbean, they had no rights under contract, and they toiled until they died.

By 1670 the sugar revolution had transformed the British West Indies into a predominantly black and slave society. In 1713 slaves outnumbered whites by four to one; the slave population had leaped from 40,000 in 1670 to 130,000 in 1713, with the white population remaining stable at 33,000. Meanwhile, driven from the Indies by high land prices, thousands of English settlers went north to the mainland. Settling in Carolina, they resumed tobacco cultivation.

West Indian Society

Caribbean slaves lived under a ruthless system of racial control expressed in laws known as slave codes. The Barbados slave code of 1661 served as a model for both the Caribbean and the mainland colonies. The code required but never defined adequate shelter and diet for slaves, in effect allowing masters to let their slaves run almost naked, to house them in rickety shacks, and to work them to exhaustion. Slaves were stripped of all legal rights and protections: they could not be tried by juries and had no guarantee of a fair legal hearing.

In this way West Indian governments granted masters almost total control over their human property. As there were no limits on punishment, slaves suffered vicious beatings and whippings. A master who killed a slave could be punished only if a jury determined that the act was intentional—and then the punishment was limited to fines. Slave codes effectively legalized assault, battery, and manslaughter. Cruel and extreme punishments were prescribed to guarantee obedience. Judges could order ears sliced off, slaves torn limb from limb, and accused rebels burned alive.

Mortality among slaves was frightfully high. Sugar production required arduous labor, but it was so profitable that planters had little incentive to keep slaves healthy; they could easily replace those killed by overwork. Exhaustion and abuse killed most slaves within a decade of their arrival. Although planters imported 264,000 slaves between 1640 and 1699, the slave population stood at just 100,000 in 1700.

Despite these appalling conditions, slaves tried to maintain a semblance of normal existence. Many married and formed families. But the staggering rate of mortality cut most slave marriages short, and more than one-half of slave children died before reaching age five. Slaves preserved much of their African heritage in work songs, ceremonial dances and chants, and lamentations. The islands' black culture retained far more of an African imprint than the African-American life that would emerge on the mainland.

Among island whites, family cohesion was weak. Men outnumbered women four to one, and most white islanders lived wild bachelor lives. Organized religion withered in the absence of family and community support. A Caribbean joke maintained that on founding a settlement, the Spanish built a church, the Dutch built a fort, and the English built a barroom. "Old Kill-Devil," the local rum, was consumed in great quantities.

The West Indies were the first English colonies to become plantation societies. They contained the most extreme examples of labor exploitation, racial subordination, and social inequality, but similar patterns would also characterize the Chesapeake Bay settlements and the coastal region known as Carolina.

Carolina: The First Restoration Colony

In 1663 Charles II bestowed the swampy coast between Virginia and Spanish Florida on several English supporters, making it the first of several Restoration colonies. The proprietors named their colony Carolina in honor of Charles (*Carolus* in Latin).

Settlers from New England and the West Indies had established outposts along the northern Carolina coast in the 1650s; the proprietors organized them into a separate district with a bicameral legislature. In 1669 one of the proprietors, Anthony Ashley Cooper, offered immigrants fifty-acre headright grants for every family member, indentured servant, or slave they brought in. The next year 200 Barbadian and English people began the settlement of southern Carolina near modern Charleston, "in the very chops of the Spanish." In the settlement they called Charles Town, they formed the colony's nucleus, with a bicameral legislature distinct from that of the northern district.

In the early years Carolina's population mainly consisted of small landowners. Southern Carolinians raised livestock, and colonists in northern Carolina exported tobacco, lumber, and pitch. In neither north nor south did the people realize enough profit to maintain slaves, and so self-sufficient white families predominated. But southern Carolinians eagerly sought a cash crop. In the early 1690s they found it—rice. Probably introduced to America by enslaved West Africans, rice cultivation enriched the few settlers with capital enough to acquire the dikes, dams, and slaves necessary to grow it. By earning annual profits of 25 percent, successful rice planters within a generation became the only colonial mainland elite whose wealth rivaled that of the Caribbean sugar planters.

Rice planters reaped their riches at the expense of African slaves. Knowledgeable about rice cultivation, slaves became tutors to their owners. The typical rice planter, with 130 acres in cultivation, needed sixty-five slaves. Demand drove the proportion of slaves in southern Carolina's population from 17 percent in 1680 to 67 percent in 1720, when the region officially became South Carolina. By 1776 the colony, with at least 100,000 slaves, would have more bondsmen than any other mainland colony in the eighteenth century.

As the black majority increased, whites relied on force and fear to control their slaves. In 1696 Carolina adopted the galling restrictions and gruesome punishments of the Barbados slave code. Bondage in the mainland colony grew as cruel and harsh as in the West Indies.

White Carolinians' attitudes toward Native Americans likewise hardened. The most vicious result was the trade in Indian slaves. White Carolinians armed allied Indians, encouraged them to raid and capture unarmed Indians to the south and west, and sold the captives to the West Indies during the 1670s and 1680s. A recent study estimates that the Carolina traders enslaved tens of thousands of Indians.

Not surprisingly, Indian wars racked Carolina in the early eighteenth century. In 1711 some Tuscaroras, provoked by whites' encroachments and enslavement of Indians, destroyed the frontier settlement of New Bern. North Carolinians enlisted the aid of southern Carolina and its Indian allies. By 1713, after 1,000 Tuscaroras (about one-fifth of their population) had been killed or enslaved, the Native Americans surrendered.

In two generations Carolinians, with little help from distant proprietors, had developed a thriving economy and had ended resistance from hostile Native Americans. Hoping for a more capable government, South Carolinians asked the British monarchy to take control, and in 1720 a temporary royal governor was appointed. Proprietary rule came to an end in 1729 when both North Carolina and South Carolina became royal colonies.

The Middle Colonies

Between the Chesapeake and New England, the third mainland colonial region, the middle colonies,

gradually emerged. By the end of the seventeenth century, the colonies of New York, New Jersey, and Pennsylvania composed North America's fastest-growing region.

Precursors: New Netherland and New Sweden

New Netherland became North America's first multiethnic society. Barely half the settlers were Dutch; most of the rest comprised Germans, French, Scandinavians, and Africans, both free and slave. In 1643 the population included Protestants, Catholics, Jews, and Muslims, speaking eighteen European and African languages. The trading company that had established the settlement struggled to control the settlers, whose get-rich-quick attitude sapped company profits as private individuals traded illegally in furs. Eventually, the company legalized the private trade.

Privatization rapidly increased the number of guns in the hands of New Netherland's Iroquois allies, giving them a distinct advantage over other tribes. As overhunting depleted local fur supplies and smallpox epidemics raged, the Iroquois encroached on Huron territory for pelts and captives (who were adopted into Iroquois families to replace the dead). After 1648 the Dutch-armed Iroquois destroyed the Hurons and attacked French settlements along the St. Lawrence.

Although the Dutch had allied with the Iroquois, relations with the nearer Indian neighbors were terrible. In 1643 an all-out war erupted when Governor Willem Kiefft massacred previously friendly Algonquian-speaking Indians. By 1645 the Dutch had temporarily prevailed, but only by enlisting English help and by inflicting atrocities.

Another European challenger, Sweden, distracted the Dutch in their war with the Algonquians. In 1638 Sweden had planted a small fur-trading colony in the lower Delaware Valley that was diverting furs from New Netherland. In 1655 the Dutch colony's stern soldier-governor Peter Stuyvesant marched against New Sweden, whose 400 residents peacefully accepted Dutch annexation.

New Netherland fell to the English in 1664, but the Dutch presence in what became New York has lent a distinctive flavor to American life. Even short-lived New Sweden left a mark, the log cabin, introduced to the continent by Finnish settlers in the Swedish colony. Above all, the Dutch and Swedish colonies bequeathed a religious and ethnic diversity that would continue in England's "middle colonies."

English Conquests: New York and the Jerseys

Like the Carolinas, New York and the Jerseys originated with Restoration-era proprietors hoping to grow rich from rents collected from settlers within a hierarchical society.

In 1664, at war with the Dutch Republic, Charles II attacked the Dutch colony of New Netherland. Four hundred poorly armed Dutch civilians under Governor Peter Stuyvesant surrendered peacefully. Charles II made his brother James, duke of York, proprietor of the new English colony and renamed it New York. With James's ascension to the throne in 1685, he converted New York into a royal colony. By 1700 immigration had swelled the population to 20,000, of whom just 44 percent were descended from the original Dutch settlers.

New York's governors rewarded their influential political supporters with large land grants. By 1703 five families held 1.75 million acres, which they carved into manors and rented to tenants. By 1750 the enormous income they earned from rents had made the New York *patroons* a landed elite second in wealth only to the Carolina rice planters.

Ambitious plans collided with American realities in the Jerseys, also carved out of New Netherland. In 1664 the duke of York awarded a group of supporters the Jerseys, at the time inhabited by a few hundred Dutch and Swedes and several thousand Delaware Indians. Within a decade thousands of troublesome New England Puritans settled in the Jerseys, and the proprietors sold the region to Quakers, who split the territory into East and West Jersey.

East Jersey's new Scottish Quaker proprietors worked no more successfully with the local Puritans than had their predecessors, and in West Jersey the English Quakers squabbled constantly among them-

selves. The Jerseys' Quakers, Anglicans, Puritans, Scottish Presbyterians, and Dutch Calvinists quarreled with each other and got along even worse with the proprietors. The governments collapsed between 1698 and 1701, and in 1702 the disillusioned proprietors surrendered their political powers to the Crown, which made New Jersey a royal colony.

Quaker Pennsylvania

In 1681 Charles II paid off a huge debt by appointing a supporter's son, William Penn, as proprietor of the last unallocated tract of American territory at the king's disposal. Penn, a Quaker, thus founded the colony as a "holy experiment" based on the teachings of the English preacher George Fox. Penn also hoped for financial gain.

Quakers in late-seventeenth-century England stood well beyond the fringe of respectability. Challenging conventional foundations of social order, they appealed to those at the bottom of the economic ladder. But they also attracted some well-educated, well-to-do individuals disillusioned by the quarreling of rival religious faiths, including significant numbers of merchants. Constant persecution seemed only to add to the resolve of the Quakers and strengthen their egalitarian and pacifist principles.

At the heart of their founder George Fox's theology was the belief that the Holy Spirit, or "Inner Light," could inspire every soul. Although trusting such direct inspiration, Quakers took pains to ensure that individual opinions would not be mistaken for God's will. Indeed, they felt confident that they understood the Inner Light only after having reached near-unanimous agreement through intensive discussion. In their religious services ("meetings"), Quakers sat silently until the Inner Light prompted one of them to speak.

Care and planning made the Quaker migration to Pennsylvania one of the most successful initial transplantations of Europeans in any North American colony. After sending an advance party, Penn arrived in 1682. He named his new capital Philadelphia, the "City of Brotherly Love." Within five years, 8,000 English Quakers had joined him. Quakers migrated in family groups, and the resulting high birthrate generated rapid population growth. (Pennsylvania's religious toleration attracted not only Quakers but also many other religious groups: Presbyterians, Baptists, Anglicans, and Catholics from England and Lutherans and radical sectarians from Germany.)

A victim of persecution, Penn hated intolerance and arbitrary governance. He offered Quakers the opportunity to make laws according to their ideals. His Frame of Government (constitution) featured a strong executive branch (a governor and governor's council) and a lower chamber (the assembly) with limited power. Quakers, a majority in the colony, dominated the assembly and held most governmental offices. To prevent wrangling and to achieve an orderly disposition of property, Penn personally oversaw land sales. He also designed a grid plan for Philadelphia, reserving park areas to keep it a "greene country towne." Penn sought peace with Native Americans by reassuring the Indians that the Quakers wished "to live together as Neighbours and Friends" and by buying land from them fairly.

Pennsylvania seemed an ideal colony—intelligently organized, well financed, tolerant, open to all industrious settlers, and at peace with the Indians. Rich lands and a lengthy growing season produced bumper crops. West Indian demand for grain generated widespread prosperity. By 1700 Philadelphia had become a major port. In 1704 counties along the lower Delaware River, where Swedes and Dutch had settled long before Penn, gained the right to elect their own legislature and became the colony of Delaware.

However, by this time Penn's "peaceable kingdom" had bogged down in human bickering. In 1684 Penn had returned to England, and during his fifteen-year absence the settlers had quarreled incessantly. An opposition party had attacked his efforts to monopolize foreign trade and to collect a small annual fee from each landowner. Struggles between pro- and anti-Penn forces had deadlocked the government. Penn's return from 1699 to 1701 had restored some order, but before leaving again, he made the legislature unicameral (one chamber) and allowed it to initiate measures.

Sadness darkened Penn's last years. His fortune spent in Pennsylvania, he served time in a debtor's prison and died in debt in 1718. He had long despaired at battling the legislature's politicians, bent as they were on economic and political advantage. As early as 1685 he had begged them, "For the love of God, me, and the poor country, be not so governmentish; so noisy and open in your disaffection."

Penn's anguish summed up the dilemmas of the English who had established the Restoration colonies. Little had gone as planned. Yet the Restoration colonies had succeeded. Before they were a quarter century old, the middle colonies had demonstrated that English America could benefit by encouraging pluralism. But the virtual completion of English claim staking along the Atlantic coast had set England on a collision course with France and Spain.

Rivals for North America

Unlike England, with its compact seacoast colonial settlements in North America, France and Spain had cast enormous nets of widely separated trading posts and missions across the interior. The two Catholic nations had converted many Indians to Christianity and made them trading partners and allies. By 1720 scattered missionaries, fur traders, and merchants had spread French and Spanish influence across two-thirds of today's United States.

France Claims a Continent

Under King Louis XIV (reigned 1661–1715), France sought to subordinate its American colony to French interests, following the doctrine of *mercantilism*. According to this doctrine, colonies should serve as sources of raw materials and as markets for manufactured goods so that the colonial power did not have to depend on rival nations for trade. The French wanted New France in order to increase fur trade, provide agricultural surplus to ship to France's West Indies colonies, and export timber for those colonies, and for the French Navy.

The Iroquois had long limited French colonial profits by intercepting convoys of fur pelts. In the 1660s Louis XIV had dispatched French troops to New France. The French Army had burned Mohawk villages. Sobered by the destruction, the Iroquois Confederacy had made a peace that had permitted New France's rapid expansion of fur exports.

In the 1660s France dispatched about 600 settlers a year to Canada, half of them indentured servants. But many immigrants gave up farming for the fur trade. By 1670 one-fifth had become *coureurs de bois*, independent traders free of government authority. Living and intermarrying with the Indians, the *coureurs* built a French empire resting on trade and goodwill among native peoples throughout central North America.

The Spanish Borderlands

English and French expansion, particularly René-Robert La Salle's building a fort in Spanish Texas in the 1680s, alarmed the Spanish. Yet the first permanent Spanish settlements in Texas did not appear until 1716. Instead, Spain concentrated on New Mexico. By 1680, 2,300 Europeans and 17,000 Pueblo Indians lived in New Mexico's Rio Grande valley.

However, many of the Indians chafed under Spanish control. Taos, a large pueblo in northern New Mexico, had long been a magnet for Native Americans resentful of Spanish rule, and in 1680 it would become the center of a major rebellion against the Spanish. The leader of the Taos revolt was Popé, a religious leader from a nearby pueblo who had fled to Taos to avoid persecution. In August 1680 Popé and others—many disillusioned Christian converts—led a massive uprising against the Spanish. The rebels slew more than 400 colonists and missionaries; hundreds more fled south into Mexico, leaving behind their horse herds and other livestock. Twelve years would pass before the Spanish recaptured Taos and the rebel Indians submitted to Spanish rule once again. Perhaps the most important legacy of the Pueblo Revolt was the acquisition of the horse by Plains Indians quick to recognize the enormous advantages of mobility and speed; within a generation mounted warriors peopled the Great Plains from Canada to Texas, a formidable force arrayed first against Spanish and then against Anglo-American settlers.

In Florida the Spanish fared little better. Forced labor and missionization led to periodic Indian rebellions before 1680, and after that slave raiders from Carolina wreaked havoc among Indians under Spanish rule, as did disease. When a new round of warfare erupted in Europe early in the eighteenth century, Spain was ill prepared to defend its beleaguered North American colonies.

CHRONOLOGY

1627 English establish Barbados.

1630 John Winthrop, "A Model of Christian Charity." Massachusetts Bay colony founded.

1630–1660 The great English migration to North America.

1633 First English settlements in Connecticut.

1634 Cecilius Calvert (Lord Baltimore) founds proprietary colony of Maryland.

1635 Roger Williams banished from Massachusetts Bay; founds Providence, Rhode Island, in 1636.

1636 Harvard College established.

1637 Anne Hutchinson tried by Massachusetts Bay Colony and banished to Rhode Island. Pequot War.

1638 New Sweden established.

1640s Large-scale slave-labor system takes hold in the West Indies.

1642 English Civil War begins.

1644 Williams obtains permission to establish a legal government in Rhode Island.

1644–1646 Third Anglo-Powhatan War in Virginia.

1649	Maryland's Act for Religious Toleration. King Charles I beheaded.
1653	First Indian reservation established in Virginia.
1655	New Netherland annexes New Sweden.
1660	Charles II becomes king of England.
1661	Barbados government creates first comprehensive slave code. Maryland defines slavery as a lifelong, inheritable racial status.
1662	Half-Way Covenant drafted.
1663	Carolina founded as English colony. New France made a royal colony.
1664	English conquer the Dutch colony of New Netherland, which becomes the English colony of New York. New Jersey established.
1670	Settlement of southern Carolina begins. Virginia defines slavery as a lifelong, inheritable racial status.
1675– 1676	King Philip's War in New England.

1676	Bacon's Rebellion in Virginia. Quakers organize the colony of West Jersey.
1680– 1692	Pueblo Revolt in New Mexico.
1681	William Penn founds the Pennsylvania colony.
1682	Quakers organize the colony of East Jersey. The Sieur de La Salle descends the Mississippi River to the Gulf of Mexico and claims the Mississippi basin for France.
1690s	Collapse of the Royal African Company's monopoly on selling slaves to the English colonies; large shipments of Africans begin reaching the Chesapeake.
1692– 1693	Salem witchcraft trials.
1698	French begin settlements near the mouth of the Mississippi River.
1711– 1713	Tuscarora War in Carolina.

FOR FURTHER READING

Paul Boyer and Stephen Nissenbaum, *Salem Possessed: The Social Origins of Witchcraft* (1974). A study of the witchcraft episode as the expression of social conflict in one New England community.

William Cronon, *Changes in the Land: Indians, Colonists, and the Ecology of New England* (1983). A pioneering study of the interactions of Native Americans and European settlers with the New England environment.

W. J. Eccles, *France in America*, rev. ed. (1991). An interpretive overview of French colonization in North America and the Caribbean by a distinguished scholar.

Jack P. Greene, *Pursuits of Happiness: The Social Development of Early Modern British Colonies and the Formation of American Culture* (1988). A brilliant synthesis of the colonial history of English America.

Winthrop D. Jordan, *The White Man's Burden: Historical Origins of Racism in the United States* (1974). A brief, yet definitive analysis of racism's origins.

Carol F. Karlsen, *The Devil in the Shape of a Woman: Witchcraft in Colonial New England* (1987). An examination of the relationship between witchcraft episodes and gender in New England society.

Edmund S. Morgan, *American Slavery, American Freedom: The Ordeal of Colonial Virginia* (1975). The most penetrating analysis yet written on the origins of southern slavery.

Alan Simpson, *Puritanism in Old and New England* (1955). A good brief introduction to Puritanism.

David J. Weber, *The Spanish Frontier in North America* (1992). A masterful synthesis of Spanish colonial history north of the Caribbean and Mexico.

4

Colonial Society Comes of Age,
1660–1750

Restoration and Rebellion

Although English colonies dated to Virginia in 1607, there was no serious attempt to weld the diverse colonies into an empire until Charles II (ruled 1660–1685) ascended the throne. With the "restoration" of the Stuart dynasty, England began to place its own interests ahead of the commercial and political interests of the colonies.

Stuart Policies

To benefit England's commercial interests, Parliament began "tidying up" the North American colonies by passing a series of laws collectively known as the Navigation Acts beginning in 1651. The 1660 and 1663 acts, expanding on the 1651 act, forced colonial merchants to export valuable commodities such as sugar and tobacco only to England and banned the importation of goods in non-English

ships. Meanwhile, a new wave of colony building gave England control of the North American coast from Maine to South Carolina.

Charles II intended the Navigation Acts and the new colonies to reward his supporters in England. The proprietors who oversaw the colonies' government expected to create prosperous settlements and a stable social hierarchy. But by 1689 English attempts to impose a uniform system of rule had provoked a series of colonial rebellions.

Royal Centralization

The sons of a king executed by Parliament, the last Stuart monarchs, Charles II and James II, disliked representative government. They tried to rule England as much as possible without Parliament and eyed American colonial assemblies suspiciously.

As Duke of York during his brother Charles's rule, James showed his disdain for colonial assemblies almost as soon as he became the proprietor of New York. Calling elected assemblies "of dangerous consequence," he forbade legislatures to meet from 1664 to 1682.

Ever resentful of outside meddling, New Englanders resisted royal interference. In 1661 the Massachusetts assembly declared its citizens exempt from all English laws and royal decrees except declarations of war. Ignoring the Navigation Acts, New Englanders welcomed Dutch traders.

The Restoration Colonies

England's Restoration colonies were carved out of the claims or earlier colonial territory of rival European powers. Spain claimed the territory chartered as Carolina in 1663. Out of England's takeover of Dutch New Netherland in 1664 came the colonies of New York, East Jersey, West Jersey, Pennsylvania, and Delaware.

Provoked, Charles targeted Massachusetts for punishment. In 1679 he carved a new royal territory, New Hampshire, from Massachusetts. In 1684 he declared Massachusetts a royal colony and revoked its charter, the very foundation of the Puritan city upon a hill.

James II's accession to the throne intensified royal centralization in America. In 1686 the new king merged five separate colonies—Massachusetts, New Hampshire, Connecticut, Rhode Island, and Plymouth—into the Dominion of New England, later adding New York and the Jerseys. Under the new system, these colonies' legislatures ceased to exist. Sir Edmund Andros, a former army officer, became the Dominion's governor.

Andros's arbitrary actions ignited burning hatred. "You have no more privileges left you," Andros reportedly told a group of colonists, "than not to be sold for slaves."

The Glorious Revolution in England and America

Puritans in England also worriedly monitored Stuart displays of pro-Catholic sympathies. The Duke of York himself became a Catholic in 1676, and Charles II converted on his deathbed.

The English tolerated James II's Catholicism only because his heirs, daughters Mary and Anne, remained Anglican. But in 1688 his second wife bore a son, who would be raised—and perhaps would rule—as a Catholic. Aghast at the idea, English political leaders asked Mary and her husband, William of Orange (the Dutch Republic's leader), to intervene. When William and Mary led a small army to England in November 1688, royal troops defected to them, and James II fled to France.

This bloodless coup, the "Glorious Revolution," created a "limited monarchy" as defined by England's Bill of Rights of 1689. The monarchs promised to summon Parliament annually, to sign its bills, and to respect civil liberties.

News of the Glorious Revolution electrified Massachusetts Puritans, who arrested Andros and his councilors. The new monarchs allowed Connecticut and Rhode Island to resume election of their own governors and permitted Massachusetts to absorb the Plymouth colony. But Massachusetts enjoyed only a partial victory. The colony's new royal charter of 1691 reserved to the crown the appointment of the governor.

New York's counterpart of the anti-Stuart uprising was Leisler's Rebellion. In May 1689 the city militia, under Captain Jacob Leisler, had seized the harbor's main fort and called elections for an assembly. In 1691 Leisler denied newly arrived English troops entry for fear that they were loyal to James II. Leisler was arrested and charged with treason; he and his son-in-law were convicted and hanged.

Arbitrary government and fears of Catholic plots had also brought turmoil to Maryland by 1689, where Protestants widely suspected that their proprietor was a traitor who supported James II. Protestant rebel John Coode organized the Protestant Association to secure Maryland for William and Mary. In July 1689 Coode and his coconspirators seized the capital, removed Catholics from office, and requested that the crown take over the colony. Maryland became a royal province in 1691 and made the Church of England an established religion in 1692. Catholics, composing less than one-fourth of the population, lost the right to vote and to worship in public.

The revolutionary events of 1688–1689 reestablished the colonies' legislative government and ensured Protestant religious freedom. William and Mary allowed colonial elites to reassert local control and encouraged Americans to identify their interests with England, laying the foundation for an empire based on voluntary allegiance, not raw force.

A Generation of War

The Glorious Revolution ushered in a quarter century of war that convulsed both England and the colonies. In 1689 England joined a European coalition against France's Louis XIV and plunged into the War of the League of Augsburg (which Anglo-Americans called King William's War).

In 1690, at the outbreak of King William's War, New Yorkers and New Englanders launched an invasion of England's enemy, New France. The invasion deteriorated into cruel but inconclusive border raids by both sides. The Iroquois, allied to the English and Dutch, bore the brunt of the war. In twelve years their population fell from 8,600 to 7,000. In 1701 the Iroquois agreed to let Canada's governor settle their disputes with other Indians and to remain neutral in future wars. Thereafter, the Iroquois maintained control of their lands, rebuilt their population, and held the balance of power along the Great Lakes.

In 1702 a new European war, known as Queen Anne's War, pitted England against France and Spain. French and Indian raiders from Canada destroyed New England towns, while the Spanish invaded southern Carolina and nearly took Charles Town in 1706. English forces, however, gained control of the Hudson Bay region, Newfoundland, and Acadia (henceforth called Nova Scotia). The peace signed in 1713 allowed Britain to keep these lands but left the French and Indians in control of their interior.

These wars had a profound political consequence. Anglo-Americans, newly aware of their military weakness, realized how much they needed the protection of the Royal Navy, and they became more loyal than ever to the English crown.

A Maturing Colonial Economy and Society

By 1750 the colonies' brisk economic growth had been under way for fifty to seventy-five years. Colonial exports had grown steadily, allowing Anglo-Americans to enjoy a relatively high living standard despite parliamentary controls.

British Economic Policy Toward America

Between 1651 and 1733 Parliament enacted laws to govern commerce between Britain and its overseas colonies. Historians label the rules of trade set forth in these laws the navigation system, and they use the word *mercantilism* to describe the underlying legal assumptions.

The word refers in general to European policies aimed at guaranteeing prosperity by making their own country as self-sufficient as possible—by eliminating its dependence on foreign suppliers, damaging its foreign competitors' commerce, and increasing the national stock of gold and silver by selling more goods abroad than it bought. Mercantilism was the direct opposite of a competitive free-market system.

In 1651 the English Parliament passed the first Navigation Act to exclude the Dutch from English trade. The Stuart restoration in 1660 brought more laws to protect English manufacturers from foreign competition. By 1750 a long series of Navigation Acts was affecting the colonial economy in four major ways.

First, the laws limited imperial trade to British-owned ships whose crews were three-quarters British (which was broadly defined to include all colonists, even slaves). This new shipping restriction helped Britain to become Europe's foremost shipping nation and laid the foundations for an American merchant marine.

Second, the Navigation Acts barred the colonies' export of "enumerated goods" unless they first passed through England or Scotland. Among these were tobacco, rice, furs, indigo, and naval stores (masts, hemp, tar, and turpentine). In return, American tobacco exporters received a monopoly on the British tobacco market.

Third, the navigation system encouraged economic diversification. Parliament paid modest bounties to Americans producing silk, iron, dyes, hemp, lumber, and other products that Britain would otherwise have had to import from foreign countries. Parliament also erected protective tariffs against foreign goods.

Fourth, the trade laws forbade Americans from competing with British manufacturers of clothing and steel. In practice this regulation meant little because it referred to *large-scale* manufacturing and thus did not interfere with the tailors, hatters, and housewives who produced most American clothing in their households or in small shops.

Before the mid-eighteenth century, the Navigation Acts did not over-burden the colonists. The great volume of colonial trade proceeded lawfully, and British North America's economy grew at a per capita rate of 0.6 percent annually from 1650 to 1770—twice as fast as Britain's.

A Burgeoning, Diversifying Population

European cities were too poor and crowded for marriage and families, Benjamin Franklin noted in 1751, but British America, with its open spaces and small cities, seemed destined to grow and flourish. Estimating the colonies' population at 1 million, Franklin predicted that it would double every 25 years. He was right.

After 1700, when life expectancy and family size in the South rose to levels typical of those of the North, Anglo-America's growth far outpaced Britain's. Colonial women had an average of eight children and forty-two grandchildren, compared to five children and fifteen grandchildren for their British counterparts. In 1700 England's population outnumbered the colonies' by twenty to one; by 1775 the ratio would be only three to one.

In the eighteenth century continuing immigration contributed significantly to colonial population growth. In the forty years after Queen Anne's War, 350,000 newcomers had reached the colonies.

Ironically, some 140,000 enslaved Africans made up the largest group of newcomers. Most were from Africa's west coast, and all had survived a sea crossing of sickening brutality. Ship captains closely calculated how many slaves they could jam into their vessels. Kept below deck in near-darkness, surrounded by filth and stench, numbed by depression, the Africans often fell victim to disease.

More than 100,000 newcomers in this era were from Ireland. Two-thirds of these were "Scots-Irish," the descendants of sixteenth-century Scottish Presbyterian settlers of northern Ireland. Germany contributed some 65,000 settlers, the majority seeking escape from desperate poverty; a significant minority belonged to small, pacifist sects that desired above all to be left alone.

The piedmont, a broad, rolling upland stretching along the eastern slope of the Appalachians, drew many immigrants. Upper New York, Pennsylvania, and Maryland attracted large numbers of Germans and Scots-Irish. Charles Town became a popular gateway for immigrants who later moved westward to the Carolina piedmont to become small farmers. In 1713 few Anglo-Americans lived more than fifty miles from the Atlantic, but by 1750 one-third of the colonists resided in the piedmont.

Eighteenth-Century Living Standards

A tenfold increase in exports drove colonial living standards up dramatically after 1700, especially in the Chesapeake. A landholding small-planter class arose, and a wealthy elite of large landowners and slavemasters flourished atop Chesapeake society after 1700.

@ Portraits of Well-to-Do Colonists

The mid-Atlantic, stretching from New York to Delaware, had the highest living standards. In 1770 per capita wealth here stood 40 percent above the colonial average. Prosperity rested on the region's rich soil, on a long-term climatic warming that lengthened the growing season, and on a brisk demand for livestock, wheat, and corn in the West Indies and southern Europe.

New Englanders prospered least. Their wealth, on average, was only half that of other colonists. Mediocre soil and a short growing season forced New Englanders to import grain. By 1750 New England towns teemed with more young men than the land could support. The sea also provided a means of survival for many New Englanders. By 1700 the Yankee merchant marine and fishing industry were the largest in the colonies.

By 1750 the American colonies enjoyed a standard of living roughly equal to that of England and far higher than those of Scotland and Ireland.

Rural Men and Women

Because the vast majority of colonial landowners had just enough acreage for a working farm, most could not provide land for their children when they married. Moreover, with longevity increasing, children often did not receive their inheritances until middle age or later; and, because families were large, a farmer's wealth was typically divided into small portions. Under these circumstances, a young man typically worked from about age sixteen to twenty-three as a field hand to save money just to buy farm equipment, and a young husband generally had to rent land until he reached his mid-thirties.

The payment of mortgages was slow. A farmer could expect to earn 6 percent cash income per year, which barely equaled mortgage interest. After making a down payment of one-third, a husband and wife generally paid the next third through their inheritances. The final third would be paid when the children reached their teens and helped to double the regular farm income.

Rural families depended somewhat on barter and much more on the economic contributions of wives and daughters: soap, preserved food, knitted goods, yarn, and the products of dairy, orchard, and

Immigration and Frontier Expansion, to 1755
A sharp rise in the importance of African slaves made much of the southern tidewater a predominantly African-American region. Immigrants from Germany, Ireland, and Scotland tended to settle in the piedmont. A significant Jewish population emerged in the seaports.

garden. Legal constraints, however, bound colonial women. A woman's most independent decision was her choice of a husband. Once married, she lost control of her dowry. Nevertheless, widows controlled substantial property—an estimated 8 to 10 percent of all property in eighteenth-century Anglo-America—and some ran large estates or plantations.

Colonial Farmers and the Environment

As English settlement expanded, the environment east of the Appalachians changed rapidly. Eighteenth-century settlers cleared forest land in order to plant crops in its fertile soil.

Removal of trees (deforestation) deprived large forest creatures such as bears, panthers, and wild turkeys of their habitat, while the planted land provided free lunch for rabbits, mice, and possums. Deforestation removed protection from winds and sun, producing warmer summers and harsher winters and, ironically, reinforcing the demand for firewood. By hastening the runoff of spring waters, deforestation led to heavier flooding. Volatile temperatures and water levels rapidly reduced the number of fish in colonial streams and lakes.

Deforestation also dried and hardened the soil; colonial crops had even more drastic effects. Native Americans had rotated their crops to protect against soil depletion, but many colonial farmers lacked enough land to do so—and many more were unwilling to sacrifice short-term profits for long-term benefits. As early as 1637 a dismayed New England farmer found that his soil "after five or six years [of planting corn] grows barren beyond belief and puts on the face of winter in the time of summer." Tobacco yields in the Chesapeake region declined in fields planted only three or four consecutive years. By 1750, in order to remain productive, many planters had shifted from tobacco to wheat.

Well-to-do Europeans had already turned to conservation and "scientific farming." North American colonists ignored such techniques, believing that America's vast lands would sustain them and future generations indefinitely.

The Urban Paradox

Cities were colonial America's economic paradox. Although they shipped the livestock, grain, and lumber that enriched the countryside, at the same time they were caught in a downward spiral of declining opportunity.

After 1740 the 4 percent of colonists in cities found economic success elusive. Philadelphia, New York, and Boston faced escalating poverty. Debilitating ocean voyages left many immigrants too weak to work, and every ship from Europe carried widows and orphans. The cities' poor rolls, moreover, always bulged with the survivors of mariners lost at sea; unskilled, landless men; and women (often widows) and children from the countryside. High population density and poor sanitation left colonial cities vulnerable to the spread of contagious diseases.

Even the able-bodied found cities economically treacherous. Traditionally, artisans trained apprentices and employed them as journeymen until they could open their own shops. After 1750, however, more employers released their workers when business slowed. As urban populations ballooned, wages shrank, while the cost of rent, food, and firewood shot up.

In the South most cities were little more than large towns, although Charles Town was North America's fourth-largest city. South Carolina's capital offered gracious living to wealthy planters during the months of heat and insect infestations on their plantations. Like their counterparts in northern port cities, Charles Town's poor whites competed for work with urban slaves whose masters rented out their labor. Racial tensions simmered.

Middle-class urban women faced less manual drudgery than their rural counterparts. Nonetheless, they managed complex households, often including servants and other nonfamily members. Widows and less affluent wives took in boarders and often spun and wove cloth for local merchants. Grim conditions in Boston forced many widows with children to look to the community for relief.

Origin and proportion of slaves from each region

Angola 25%

North African coast

Desert

Grassland

Rain forest

Senegambia 19%

Windward Coast 11%

Gold Coast 16%

Niger Valley/Benin 27%

Congo Valley/Angola 25%

Madagascar and Mozambique 2%

WOLOFS
MALINKES
MANDINGOES
ASHANTIS
YORUBAS
HAUSAS
IBOS
BANTUS
UBANGIS
ZULUS
MALAGASIES
HOVAS

0   1000 Miles
0   1000 Kilometers

African Origins of North American Slaves, 1690–1807
Virtually all slaves brought to English North America came from West Africa, between Senegambia and Angola. Most were captured or bought inland and marched to the coast, where they were sold to African merchants who in turn sold them to European slave traders.

Slavery's Wages

From 1713 to 1754 five times as many slaves poured into mainland Anglo-America as in all the preceding years. The proportion of African-Americans in the colonies doubled, reaching 20 percent by midcentury.

Because West Indian and Brazilian slave buyers outbid North Americans, only 5 percent of transported Africans reached the mainland Anglo-American colonies. Mainland slave owners, unable to buy enough male field hands, bought female workers and protected their investment by maintaining their slaves' health. These factors promoted family formation and increased life expectancy far beyond the levels in the Caribbean.

Masters could usually afford to keep slaves healthy, but they rarely made their human chattels comfortable. Slave upkeep generally cost 60 percent less than the maintenance of indentured servants. Adult slaves received eight quarts of corn and one pound of pork weekly and were expected to grow vegetables and to raise poultry.

Slaves worked for a longer portion of their lives than whites. Slave children worked part-time from the age of seven and full-time as early as eleven. African-American women performed hard work alongside men and tended tobacco and rice crops even when pregnant. Most slaves toiled until they died, although those in their sixties rarely did hard labor. The rigors of bondage, however, did not crush the slaves' spirits.

By midcentury slaves constituted 20 percent of New York City's population and formed a majority in Charles Town and Savannah. Skilled urban slaves hired themselves out and kept part of their wages. By 1770 one-tenth of Savannah's slaves were living in rented rooms away from their owners.

The independence of South Carolina's slaves, and the fact that they constituted a majority in the colony, aroused planters' fears. To retain control, the white minority passed a number of laws restricting slaves' behavior. Concern about the dangers of gatherings of large numbers of blacks uncontrolled by whites led in 1721 to a 9:00 P.M. curfew on blacks in Charles Town; the colony of South Carolina placed local slave patrols under the colonial militia.

Tensions erupted in 1739 when a slave uprising known as the Stono Rebellion jolted South Carolina. Stealing guns and ammunition from a store at the Stono River Bridge, one hundred slaves headed for Floridia crying "Liberty!" Along the way they burned seven plantations and killed twenty whites. Within a day, however, mounted militiamen surrounded the runaways, cut them down, and spiked a rebel head on every milepost back to Charles Town. Whites expressed their fears in a new slave code stipulating constant surveillance for slaves. The code threatened masters with fines for not disciplining slaves and required legislative approval for manumission (the freeing of individual slaves). The Stono Rebellion thus accelerated South Carolina's emergence as a racist and fear-ridden society. The rebels' failure showed slaves that armed uprisings were suicidal. Not until 1831 would significant slave violence of a comparable scale erupt on the mainland.

The Rise of the Colonial Elites

For white colonial Americans, wealth defined status. Once wealthy, a man was expected to be responsible, dignified, and generous and to act as a community leader—to act like a gentleman. His wife was expected to be a skillful household manager and a refined, yet deferential hostess—a lady.

> @ A Virginia Gentleman Weighs "a Frail Woman's" Class Transgressions.

Before 1700 class structure in the colonies was relatively invisible; after 1720, however, the display of wealth became more ostentatious. The greater gentry—the richest 2 percent of the population—built splendid estate homes such as New Jersey's Low House and Virginia's Shirley Mansion. The gentry also exhibited their wealth by living in the European "grand style." They wore costly English fashions, drove carriages, and bought expensive china, books, and furniture. They pursued a gracious life by studying foreign languages and learning formal dances. Horse racing replaced cockfighting as a preferred spectator sport.

> @ An Eighteenth-Century Home: Exterior and Interior Views

> @ Typical Pieces of Eighteenth-Century furniture

Chesapeake planters, even the frugal, accumulated debt. Tobacco planters, perpetually short of cash, were in hock to British merchants who bought their crops and sold them expensive goods on credit. Planters had two options. They could strive for self-sufficiency, or they could diversify by growing wheat or cutting timber. Both self-sufficiency and economic diversification became more widespread as the eighteenth century progressed.

In eighteenth-century colonial cities wealth remained concentrated. New York's wealthiest 10 percent owned 45 percent of the property. Similar patterns characterized Philadelphia and Boston. Juxtaposed against the growth of a poor urban underclass, these statistics underscored the polarization of status and wealth in urban America on the eve of the Revolution.

Elites and Colonial Politics

The colonial elite dominated politics as well as society. Governors appointed members of the greater gentry to serve on councils and as judges in the highest courts. The upper gentry, along with militia majors and colonels, also dominated among the representatives elected to the legislatures' lower houses (the assemblies).

Outside New England property restrictions barred 80 percent of white men from running for the assembly. In any case few ordinary citizens could have afforded the high costs of elective office. Consequently, political leadership fell to a small number of wealthy families with a tradition of public service.

The colonies generally set liberal qualifications for property-owning male voters, but all excluded women, blacks, and Indians from voting. Most white males in Anglo-America could vote by age forty, whereas across the Atlantic, two-thirds of all Englishmen and 90 percent of Irishmen could never vote.

Political indifference was widespread. For example, to avoid paying legislators' expenses, many Massachusetts towns refused to elect assemblymen. From 1731 to 1760 one-third of South Carolina's elected assemblymen neglected to take their seats. Only in the major seaports did political life flourish. Here greater population density, better communications, and the use of secret ballots accounted for a relatively high voter turnout.

The most important political development after 1700 was the rise of the assembly as the dominant force in colonial government. Except in Connecticut and Rhode Island, the crown or proprietors chose colonial governors, who in turn named a council, or upper legislative house. Only in the lower house, or assembly, could members of the gentry defend their interests. Until 1689 governors and councils drafted laws, and the assemblies generally followed passively. Thereafter assemblies assumed a more central role in politics as colonial leaders argued that their legislatures should exercise the same rights as Parliament. Indeed, they viewed their assemblies as miniature Houses of Commons and believed that colonial governors should be as restricted as monarchs.

The lower houses refused to permit meddling in their procedures, took control over taxes and budgets, and kept a tight rein on executive salaries. Governors remained vulnerable to such financial pressure: they received no salary from Britain and relied on the assemblies for income. This "power of the purse" often forced governors to sign laws opposed by the crown. Moreover, Britain's lack of interest in colonial politics allowed the assemblies to seize considerable power. The autonomy that colonies gained during this period would backfire when the British attempted to rule more directly after 1763.

Competing for a Continent

Europeans transformed North America in the first half of the eighteenth century as they expanded their territorial claims, opened new areas for settlement, and engaged in more intensive trade and warfare with Native Americans.

France and Native Americans

With the end of the War of the Spanish Succession in 1713, France aggressively expanded and strengthened its North American empire, especially Louisiana. The French began to settle the mouth of the Mississippi and its environs, founding New Orleans in 1718. French traders moved onto the southern plains, exchanging goods, including guns, with Comanches and other Plains tribes that raided Spanish Texas.

Louisiana quickly acquired a foul reputation, and few French immigrated there willingly. To boost its population, the government sent paupers and criminals and encouraged slave importation. By 1732 two-thirds of lower Louisiana's 5,800 people were slaves.

French attention also turned to the Ohio Valley, which, thanks to Iroquois neutrality, had become a refuge for dislocated Native American tribes such as the Kickapoos, Shawnees, and Delawares. In order to counter English influence and to secure commercial and diplomatic ties with the Indians, the French expanded their trade. Several French posts, including Detroit, ballooned into sizable villages of Indian, French, and mixed-ancestry residents. Nonetheless, increased English trade in the area led most Indians to prefer an independent course.

By 1744 French traders had explored as far west as North Dakota and Colorado, buying beaver pelts and Indian slaves on the Great Plains. Meanwhile, Indians in the southern Plains and Great Basin had

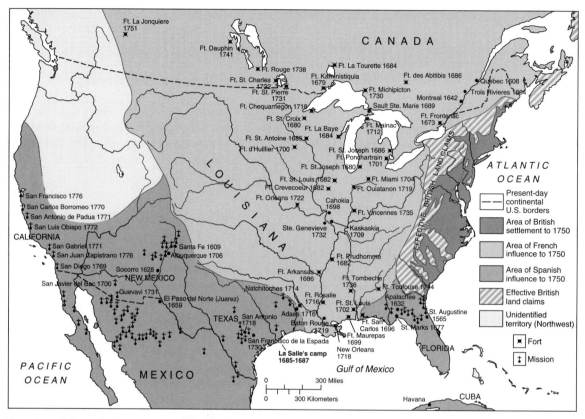

French and Spanish Occupation of North America, to 1776
French fur traders became entrenched along the Great Lakes and upper Mississippi River between 1666 and 1700, after which they built many settlements in territory claimed by Spain along the Gulf of Mexico. Spanish colonization was concentrated in Florida, central Texas, the Rio Grande valley, and (after 1769) southern California.

acquired horses from the thousands left behind by fleeing Spaniards after the Pueblo Revolt of 1680. Horses and guns enabled tribes such as the Lakota Sioux and Comanches to move onto the Plains and build a new, highly mobile way of life based on the pursuit of the buffalo. Widely scattered settlements along the Mississippi in modern-day Illinois and Missouri completed France's domain, an immense territory precariously dependent on often shaky relations with Native Americans.

Native Americans and British Expansion

The depopulation and dislocation of Native Americans made possible the colonies' rapid expansion. Pennsylvania coerced the Delawares into selling more than 818,000 acres between 1729 and 1734. In 1735 the colony's leaders produced a fraudulent treaty, in which the Delawares promised to sell

@ **Manifest Destiny: And Westward Expansion.**

their land as far west as a man could walk in a day and a half. They forced the Delawares to cede 1,200 square miles of land in what became known as the Walking Purchase.

By helping remove the Delawares from Pennsylvania, the Iroquois tried to accommodate the English and consolidate their own power. Late in the seventeenth century the Iroquois had entered into a series of agreements, known as the Covenant Chain, to relocate Indians whose lands the colonists desired. These tribes were moved to areas of New York and Pennsylvania, on the periphery of the Iroquois' homeland, to serve as buffers against English expansion.

British Settlement in the South: Georgia

In 1732 Parliament chartered a new colony, Georgia. It was to be a refuge for debtors, whose settlement would buffer South Carolina against attacks from Spanish Florida. Further, the new English colony would export expensive commodities such as wine and silk. To fulfill these plans, Parliament even spent money on the colony, the only North American colony except Nova Scotia in which the British government invested.

James Oglethorpe, who dominated the provincial board of trustees, shaped Georgia's early years. He established the port of entry, Savannah, in 1733. By 1740 nearly 3,000 colonists resided in Georgia. Almost half were non-English, immigrants from Germany, Switzerland, and Scotland, and most had their overseas passage paid by the government. A small number of Jews were among the early settlers. Thus Georgia began as the least English colony.

Idealism and concerns about security led Oglethorpe to ban slavery from Georgia. Oglethorpe thought that slavery degraded blacks and made whites lazy. Aware of the Stono Rebellion, he worried that reliance on slave labor courted a slave revolt. Parliament thus made Georgia the only colony where slavery was forbidden.

Oglethorpe's well-intentioned plans failed completely. Few debtors arrived because of Parliament's restrictions on their release from prison. Limitations

that Oglethorpe had secured on settlers' rights to enlarge or sell their holdings discouraged immigrants, as did the ban on slavery. Georgia exported neither wine nor silk; only rice proved profitable. After a decade of struggle against economic reality, Oglethorpe yielded. In 1750 slavery became legal, and restrictions on landholdings vanished. As a result, Georgia boomed. Its 4,000 residents of 1750 mushroomed to 23,000 by 1770, almost half of them African-American. Georgia's founding completed British settlement of the Atlantic seaboard.

Spain's Struggles

While trying to maintain an empire in the face of Native American, French, and British adversaries, Spain spread its language and culture over much of North America, especially the Southwest. To repopulate New Mexico with settlers after the Pueblo Revolt (see Chapter 3), Spain handed out huge land grants and constructed fortifications, primarily for defense against the Apaches. Livestock-raising *ranchos* (ranches) monopolized vast amounts of land along the Rio Grande and blocked the establishment of further towns. On these *ranchos* mounted herders of cattle and sheep (*vaqueros*) created the way of life later adopted by the American cowboy.

By 1750 New Mexico contained just 5,200 Spanish and 13,500 Pueblos. Integrated into New Mexico society, most Pueblos practiced both Catholicism and their traditional religion.

To counter growing French influence among the Comanches and other Native Americans on the southern plains, Spain colonized Texas. The Spanish presence in Texas remained light, however; by midcentury only 1,200 Spaniards and 1,300 mission Indians lived there under constant threat of Indian raids.

By 1750 the French and Spanish empires had reached their limits in North America. Spain controlled much of the Southeast and Southwest, and France claimed the Mississippi, Ohio, and Missouri River valleys. Both empires, spread thin, depended heavily on Indian goodwill. In contrast, British North

America, compact and aggressively expansionist, was generally antagonistic toward Native Americans.

Enlightenment and Awakening

Eighteenth-century Anglo-America was probably the world's most literate society. Ninety percent of New England's adult white males and 40 percent of its women could write well enough to sign documents. In other colonies the literacy rate varied from 35 to 50 percent. In contrast, in England it stood at just over 30 percent. Nevertheless, ordinary Americans' reading encompassed only a few books: an almanac, a psalter, and the Bible. They inhabited a world of oral culture, in which ideas were passed through conversations, debates, and sermons. The print culture and newly written works of the Enlightenment were accessible only to an intellectual elite.

The Enlightenment in America

American intellectuals drew inspiration from Enlightenment ideals, which combined confidence in reason with skepticism toward beliefs not based on science or logic. Enlightenment thought drew on the work of the English physicist Sir Isaac Newton (1642–1727), who explained how gravitation ruled the universe. Newton's work demonstrated the harmony of natural laws and stimulated others to search for rational principles in medicine, law, psychology, and government.

No American more embodied the Enlightenment spirit than Benjamin Franklin (1706–1790). To Franklin, science and community service were intertwined; true science would make everyone's life more comfortable. For example, his experiments in flying a kite during a thunderstorm proved that lightning was electricity and led to the invention of the lightning rod. In 1743 Franklin organized the American Philosophical Society to encourage "all philosophical experiments that let light into the nature of things, tend to increase the power of man over matter, and multiply the conveniences and pleasures of life."

Although some plantation owners, among them Thomas Jefferson, championed the Enlightenment, it flourished in the seaboard cities, where the latest ideas from Europe circulated and gentlemen and artisans met in small societies to investigate nature. Its adherents envisioned progress as gradual and proceeding from the top down. They trusted reason far more than they trusted the common people, whose judgment seemed too easily deranged.

Just as Newton inspired the scientific bent of Enlightenment intellectuals, the English philosopher John Locke's *Essay Concerning Human Understanding* (1690) led many to embrace "reasonable" or "rational" religion. Locke contended that ideas are not inborn but are acquired by investigation of, and reflection on, experience. Enlightenment intellectuals believed that the study of the harmony and order of nature provided the best argument for God, a rational Creator. A handful insisted that where the Bible conflicted with reason, one should follow reason. Those—including Franklin and Jefferson—who took the argument furthest were called Deists. They concluded that God, having created a perfect universe, did not miraculously intervene in its workings but instead left it alone to operate according to natural law.

Most Americans influenced by the Enlightenment described themselves as Christians and attended church. But they feared Christianity's excesses, especially the influence of fanatics who persecuted others in religion's name and of "enthusiasts" who claimed direct mandates from God.

The Great Awakening

Rationalists viewed the world as orderly and predictable. Many Americans, however, had neither worldly goods nor orderly and predictable lives. A diphtheria epidemic in 1737–1738 that killed every tenth child under sixteen from New Hampshire to Pennsylvania reminded the colonists how fragile life was and turned their thoughts to religion.

A quickening of religious fervor in scattered places in the 1730s became passionate revivalism throughout Anglo-America in the 1740s. This

"Great Awakening" cut across lines of class, status, and education as even elites realized the inadequacy of reason alone to move their hearts. Above all, the Great Awakening represented an unleashing of anxiety and longing among ordinary people—anxiety about sin, longing for salvation.

In contrast to rationalists, who stressed the human potential for betterment, the ministers of the Great Awakening emphasized the corruption of human nature, the fury of divine wrath, and the need for immediate repentance. Although well aware of contemporary philosophy and science, Congregationalist minister Jonathan Edwards drove home this message with breathtaking clarity. In 1735 during a revival in Northampton, Massachusetts, Edwards preached his great sermon "Sinners in the Hands of an Angry God." "The God that holds you over the pit of Hell, much as one holds a spider or other loathsome insect over the fire, abhors you," Edwards intoned. "He looks upon you as worthy of nothing else but to be cast into the fire."

In 1739 the charismatic English cleric George Whitefield arrived to stir the roiling emotions of the revival. A man of overpowering presence and a booming voice, Whitefield attracted some crowds exceeding 20,000. On a tour through the colonies Whitefield inspired thousands, mainly young adults, to seek salvation.

Colonial minister Gilbert Tennent and other radicals corroded support for revivals by lashing out at the established clergy. Increasingly, lines hardened between the revivalists, the "New Lights," and the rationalist clergymen, or "Old Lights," who dominated the Anglican, Presbyterian, and Congregational churches. In 1740 Tennent hinted that most Presbyterian ministers lacked saving grace and were bound for hell, and he urged parishioners to abandon them for the New Lights. By sowing doubts about ministers, Tennent undermined one of the foundations of the social order. Old Light rationalists fired back, condemning revivals as an epidemic of the "enthusiasm" that Enlightened intellectuals so hated.

The Great Awakening thus split American Protestantism. In 1741 Old and New Light Presbyterians formed rival branches that reunited in 1758 when the revivalists triumphed. The Anglican church lost many members to New Light Presbyterians and Baptists. Congregationalists also splintered badly; by 1760 New Lights had seceded from one-third of all churches and formed separate parishes.

The Great Awakening peaked in 1742 but made steady gains into the 1770s, and its long-term effects far exceeded its immediate impact. First, the revival started a decline in the influence of older sects such as the Quakers, Anglicans, and Congregationalists. In turn, the number of Presbyterians and Baptists increased after 1740, and that of Methodists rose steadily after 1770. Second, the Great Awakening stimulated the founding of new colleges unscarred by religious wars. The College of New Jersey (Princeton, 1746), King's College (Columbia, 1754), the College of Rhode Island (Brown, 1764), Queen's College (Rutgers, 1766), and Dartmouth (1769) trace their roots to this era. Third, the revival drew many African-Americans and Native Americans to Protestantism for the first time. Its oral and communal nature and emphasis on piety, rather than learning, blended aspects of both groups' traditional cultures.

The Great Awakening, moreover, gave women added prominence in colonial religion. For several decades ministers had praised women—the majority of church members—as the embodiment of Christian piety. Now some New Light sects, mainly Baptist and Congregationalist, granted women the right to speak and vote in church meetings. The Great Awakening also fostered religious tolerance by blurring theological differences among New Lights. Indeed, revivalism's emphasis on inner experience, rather than doctrinal fine points, helped to prepare Americans to accept the denominational pluralism that emerged after the Revolution.

And by empowering ordinary people to criticize those in authority, the revivals laid the groundwork for political revolutionaries a generation later who would preach that royal government had grown corrupt and unworthy of obedience.

CHRONOLOGY

1651– **1733**	Parliament creates the navigation system to regulate British imperial commerce.
1660	Restoration of the Stuart dynasty to the English throne.
1685	Duke of York becomes King James II of England.
1686– **1689**	Dominion of New England.
1688	Glorious Revolution in England; James II deposed.
1689	William and Mary ascend to English throne. Protestant Association seizes power in Maryland. Leisler's Rebellion in New York.
1689– **1697**	King William's War (in Europe, War of the League of Augsburg).
1690	John Locke, *Essay Concerning Human Understanding*.
1698	French begin settlements near the mouth of the Mississippi River.

1701	Iroquois adopt neutrality policy toward European powers.
1702– **1713**	Queen Anne's War (in Europe, War of the Spanish Succession).
1718	New Orleans founded.
1732	Georgia colony chartered.
1734	"Walking Purchase" of Delaware Indians in Pennsylvania.
1735	Jonathan Edwards leads revival in Northhampton, Massachusetts.
1739	Great Awakening begins. Stono Rebellion in South Carolina.
1750	Slavery legalized in Georgia.

FOR FURTHER READING

Bernard Bailyn, *The Peopling of British North America: An Introduction* (1986). A brief interpretive overview of the causes and effects of European immigration to British North America.

Bernard Bailyn and Philip D. Morgan, eds., *Strangers Within the Realm: Cultural Margins of the First British Empire* (1991). Essays by leading historians examine the interplay of ethnicity and empire occurring in North America, the Caribbean, Scotland, and Ireland.

Richard L. Bushman, *From Puritan to Yankee: Character and the Social Order in Connecticut, 1690–1765* (1967). The best examination of social and cultural transformation in any eighteenth-century colony.

Rhys Isaac, *The Transformation of Virginia, 1740–1790* (1982). Pulitzer Prize–winning study of class relationships, race relations, and folkways during the Great Awakening and American Revolution.

John J. McCusker and Russell R. Menard, *The Economy of British America, 1607–1789*, rev. ed. (1991). A comprehensive discussion of the colonial economy in light of current scholarship.

James H. Merrell, *The Indians' New World: Catawbas and Their Neighbors from European Contact Through the Era of Removal* (1989). A pathbreaking examination, with broad implications for understanding the Native American past, of the interaction between South Carolina colonists and Catawba Indians.

Gary B. Nash, *The Urban Crucible: The Northern Seaports and the Origins of the American Revolution*, abridged ed. (1986). A study of social, economic, and political change in Boston, New York, and Philadelphia during the eighteenth century.

Timothy Silver, *A New Face on the Countryside: Indians, Colonists, and Slaves in South Atlantic Forests, 1500–1800* (1990). A highly readable discussion of the interactions of humans and their environment in one region.

Peter H. Wood, *Black Majority: Negroes in Colonial South Carolina from 1670 Through the Stono Rebellion* (1974). An engrossing study of slavery, racism, and African-American life in the lower South.

5

The Road to Revolution,
1744–1776

Imperial Warfare

Imperial Reorganization

Era of Anglo-American Crisis

Toward Independence

Imperial Warfare

Imperial rivalries between England, on the one hand, and France and Spain, on the other, triggered two major wars that spilled into North America in the mid-eighteenth century. The War of the Austrian Succession (1740–1748), known as King George's War to the colonists, saw England and its allies emerge victorious. Within a few years the conflict resumed as the Seven Years' War (1756–1763). England and France fought these wars not on the continent of Europe but on the high seas; in India, where they were competing for influence among local rulers; and in North America. The conclusion of each war planted the seeds first of misunderstanding, then of suspicion, and finally of hostility between the colonists and the British.

King George's War

King George's War followed the pattern of earlier conflicts in the colonies. Battles generally involved

fewer than 600 men, and skirmishes consisted of raids along the New French–British frontier. In attacks on New England frontier towns, the French and Indians killed or captured many civilians.

King George's War produced a single major engagement. In 1745 almost 4,000 New Englanders captured the French bastion of Louisbourg in northern Nova Scotia, which guarded the entrance to the St. Lawrence River. But the triumph proved short-lived as Britain traded Louisbourg back to France in exchange for a British outpost in India. The memory of how the stunning achievement at Louisbourg went for naught would embitter the colonists for a decade.

A Fragile Peace

Neither Britain nor France emerged from King George's War as the dominant power in North America, and each prepared for another war. The Ohio Valley became the tinderbox for conflict.

By 1752 Virginia, Pennsylvania, France, the Iroquois, and several other tribes that had sought refuge there had all claimed the Ohio Valley. In 1753 France started building a chain of forts in order to regain control of the Virginia and Pennsylvania Indian trade. Virginia retaliated by sending a twenty-one-year-old surveyor, George Washington, to demand that the French abandon their forts. When the French refused, Washington recommended that Virginia occupy the point where the Monongahela and Allegheny Rivers joined. In 1754 he led 300 colonial volunteers and 100 British regulars west, only to find the French already constructing Fort Duquesne at the juncture of the rivers. Washington withdrew sixty miles southeast to build a crude defensive post christened Fort Necessity, near which his men killed several French soldiers in an ambush that brought swift retaliation. On July 4, 1754, with one-fourth of his men dead, Washington surrendered Fort Necessity.

In mid-1754 seven northern colonies sent delegates to Albany, New York, to plan their mutual defense in the face of certain French retaliation. By showering the wavering Iroquois with wagonloads of presents, the colonists bought Iroquois neutrality. The delegates endorsed a plan for a colonial confederation, the Albany Plan of Union, drawn up by Pennsylvania's Benjamin Franklin and Massachusetts's Thomas Hutchinson. However, the Albany Plan collapsed because no colonial legislature would

European Powers in the New World Before 1754 and in 1763
The Treaty of Paris (1763) divided France's North American empire between Britain and Spain. Hoping to prevent unnecessary violence between whites and Indians, Britain forbade any new white settlements west of the Appalachians' crest in the Proclamation of 1763.

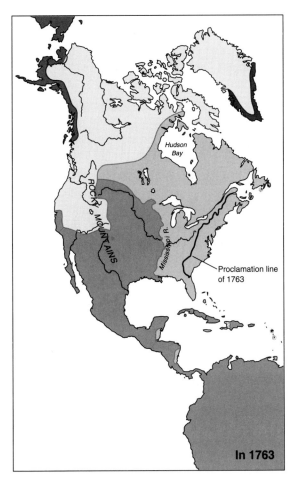

surrender control over its powers of taxation, not even to fellow Americans and in the face of grave danger. But the Albany Plan would provide a precedent for future American unity.

The Seven Years' War in America

Although France and Britain remained at peace in Europe until 1756, Washington's action at Fort Necessity had created a virtual state of war in North America. In response, nearly 8,000 colonists enlisted in 1755 to attack the French strongholds in New York and Nova Scotia. The British government sent General Edward Braddock and 1,000 regulars to take Fort Duquesne that same year.

Scornful of colonial soldiers, Braddock expected his disciplined regulars to make short work of the French. He only dimly perceived the strength and resourcefulness of the forces gathering against him. On July 9, 1755, about 850 French and Indians ambushed Braddock's 2,200 Britons and Virginians near Fort Duquesne. Nine hundred regular soldiers and colonists died, including Braddock.

After Braddock's defeat Indian raids convulsed Pennsylvania, Maryland, Virginia, and New Jersey. Two thousand New Englanders managed to seize two French forts that were threatening Nova Scotia. In the aftermath thousands of French-Canadians, or Acadians, were driven from Nova Scotia, and their villages were burned. French Louisiana became the new home for many of these people, who became known there as Cajuns.

In 1756–1757 New France's daring commanding general Louis Joseph Montcalm maintained the offensive. Anglo-Americans outnumbered Canadians twenty to one, but Montcalm benefited from large numbers of French regulars, Indian support (including that of the neutral but usually British-leaning Iroquois), and full-scale mobilization of the Canadian population. However, 1758 proved a turning point for the British. First, Indian support for the French evaporated, largely because France appeared to hold a decisive margin. Their withdrawal enabled Britain to easily capture Fort Duquesne and win control of the Ohio Valley. Second, British minister William Pitt took over Britain's military affairs. The imaginative and single-minded Pitt reinvigorated the military campaign. Hard-pressed in Europe by France and its allies (which after 1761 included Spain), Pitt believed that the mobilization of colonial forces would provide the key to crushing New France. He therefore kept fewer than 4,000 British regulars in North America, promising that Parliament would bear the cost of maintaining colonial troops.

Pitt's offer to free Americans from the war's financial burden generated unprecedented support. In 1758 and again in 1759 the colonies organized 21,000 troops. As a result, Britain took the offensive and captured Louisbourg and Fort Duquesne in 1758 and Quebec in 1759. In 1760, with Montreal's surrender, French resistance ended.

The Death of General Wolfe

In the Treaty of Paris of 1763 France ceded all its territories on the North American mainland. Britain received all French lands east of the Mississippi; Spain acquired the port of New Orleans and all French lands west of the Mississippi. Spain's New World empire thus remained intact, while France's shrank to a handful of islands off Newfoundland and the West Indies. Supreme in eastern North America and victorious in a first global war, Britain appeared unchallengeable.

Imperial Reorganization

After the Seven Years' War Britain tried to finance its greatly expanded empire through new revenue measures on both sides of the Atlantic and to exercise more direct control over its colonies. This effort coincided with the ascent of George III (ruled 1760–1820) to the throne. His attempts to play a strong role in government led to a dizzying succession of prime ministers and little chance of implementing a thoughtful policy.

Friction Among Allies

An extraordinary coalition of Britons, colonists, and Native Americans had defeated France, but when peace returned, so, too, did deep-seated tensions among these allies. In particular, Anglo-Americans chafed that they received little credit for their role in defeating New France.

Pitt's strategy caused much of the misunderstanding. Recognizing that Americans could not perform as well as veteran regulars, Pitt had used Americans in vital support roles: forming the reserve for battle, handling supplies, and garrisoning frontier forts.

These American contributions had freed large numbers of British regulars to fight, but British officers complained that colonial troops not only fought poorly but also tended to return home, even in the midst of campaigns, when their terms were up or when their pay lagged.

Tensions flared as well between British officers and colonial civilians. Officers groused about colonial unwillingness to provide food or shelter; colonists resented the officers' arrogance. Pitt's promise to reimburse the colonies for their military expenses enraged Britons. Staggering under debt and taxes, the British thought it outrageous to repay the Americans for defending themselves.

Many colonists felt equally burdened. Wartime profits had gone to pay for British goods as thousands of people purchased what they had previously produced. Now accustomed to new middle-class lifestyles, colonists went into debt, and British creditors obliged by extending repayment terms from six months to a full year. Mired in debt and even bankruptcy, many colonists began to suspect Britain of plotting to "enslave" the colonies in order to protect its own merchants and manufacturers.

Worse, Britain's victory over the French generated new Indian-white conflicts. No longer able to play the two imperial powers off against each other, Indians feared the consequences. They were right. To cut costs after the war, the British had stopped distributing food and ammunition to their Indian allies. Meanwhile, colonial squatters were moving onto Indian lands, raising both fears and tensions.

In early 1763 Pontiac, an Ottawa Indian, and other leaders forged an anti-British coalition of Indians that sacked eight British forts along the Great Lakes and besieged British positions at Detroit and

Pittsburgh. Short on food and ammunition, suffering a smallpox epidemic (deliberately spread by the British), and recognizing that the French would not return, the Indians surrendered in early fall.

But the British victory over the Indians was indecisive. Hoping to end the frontier fighting, the British government issued the Proclamation of 1763, which asserted royal control of land transactions, settlements, and trade of non-Indians west of the Appalachians and recognized existing Indian land titles everywhere west of the "proclamation line," which ran down the crest of the Appalachian Mountains. The policy angered the colonies by subordinating their western land claims to imperial authority and slowing colonial expansion.

Pontiac's rebellion also led the British government to station 10,000 regular troops in North America to occupy the western lands that France had ceded and to intimidate the Indians. The cost of administering British North America reached almost £440,000 yearly. Britons believed it perfectly reasonable for the colonists to help offset this expense. The colonists, however, struggling with their own postwar economic recession, saw it as none of their responsibility. Further, these troops raised fears of a peacetime "standing army" that could threaten American liberty.

The Writs of Assistance

To halt American trade with the enemy in the French West Indies during the Seven Years' War, Britain had cracked down on colonial smuggling. In 1760 the royal governor of Massachusetts authorized the use of the writ of assistance to seize illegally imported goods. A general search warrant, the writ permitted customs officials to enter any ship or building where smuggled goods might be hidden. Because it required no evidence of probable cause for suspicion, the writ was considered unconstitutional by most English legal authorities. It also allowed customs agents to ransack a house in search of illegal goods without any evidence of lawbreaking.

The writ of assistance proved a powerful weapon against smuggling. Merchants in Boston, the colonies' smuggling capital, hired James Otis to challenge the device's constitutionality. Before the Massachusetts supreme court in 1761, he argued that "an act against the Constitution is void"—even an act of Parliament. But the court, noting the use of an identical writ of assistance in England, ruled against the merchants.

Despite having lost his case, Otis had stated with clarity the colonial conception of Parliament's role under the British constitution. Like most colonists, Otis believed that Parliament had no authority to violate the traditional "rights of Englishmen" and that there were limits "beyond which if Parliaments go, their Acts bind not."

The Sugar Act

In 1764, at the urging of Prime Minister George Grenville, Parliament passed the Sugar Act to offset part of Britain's North American military expenses. In ending the long-standing exemption of colonial trade from revenue-raising measures, the Sugar Act triggered new tension between Britain and the colonies.

The Sugar Act amended the Molasses Act of 1733, a protective tariff against French molasses. The Molasses Act's 6-pence-per-gallon duty, however, was too high for American importers to pay, and they commonly bribed customs inspectors 1½ pence per gallon to look the other way when they unloaded smuggled molasses. In designing the Sugar Act, British officials, well aware of the widespread bribery, wrongly assumed that the colonists would willingly pay a lower, 3-pence-per-gallon tax.

The act brought a wide range of colonial commerce under imperial control. It stipulated that the colonists had to export valuable raw commodities *through* Britain instead of going directly to foreign ports, as they had been doing. It also slapped a heavy tax on the thriving American business of carrying duty-free Portuguese wine to the colonies.

The Sugar Act complicated the requirements for shipping colonial goods. A captain had to fill out a confusing series of documents certifying the legality of his trade. The absence of any document left his

cargo liable to seizure. The law's petty regulations made it virtually impossible for many colonial shippers to avoid committing technical violations of the act.

Finally, the Sugar Act discarded many traditional English protections for a fair trial. The law allowed customs officials to transfer smuggling cases from the colonial courts, in which juries decided the outcome, to vice-admiralty courts, in which a judge delivered the verdict. Until 1767 the law reversed normal procedure by presuming the guilt of the accused and requiring the defendant to prove innocence.

The Sugar Act alarmed the colonists because it sacrificed their economic interests and legal rights to benefit British merchants, but opposition to the law remained fragmented and ineffective. A far more controversial measure would soon overshadow the Sugar Act.

The Stamp Act

Revenues raised by the Sugar Act did little to ease Britain's financial crisis. Britons groaned under the second-highest tax rates in Europe and agreed with Prime Minister George Grenville that fairness demanded a larger colonial contribution.

In March 1765, to force colonists to pay their share of imperial expenses, Parliament passed the Stamp Act. The law obliged Americans to purchase and use specially marked or stamped paper for newspapers, customs documents, wills, contracts, and other public legal documents. Violators faced prosecution in vice-admiralty courts, without juries. Unlike the Sugar Act, an *external* tax levied on imports, the Stamp Act was an *internal* tax levied directly on property, goods, and services in the colonies.

Grenville agreed with Stamp Act opponents that Parliament could not tax British subjects unless they enjoyed representation in that body. He contended, however, that the colonists were *virtually* represented. Theoretically, with virtual representation, every member of Parliament considered the welfare of *all* subjects, not just his constituents, in deciding issues. Grenville and his supporters also held that the colonial assemblies had no powers other than those Parliament allowed them.

The Colonial Perspective

The Stamp Act made many colonists believe that they had to confront parliamentary taxation head-on or surrender any claim to meaningful self-government. In the American view, unless a lawmaker shared his constituents' interests, he would have no personal stake in opposing bills contrary to their welfare. Thus the colonists favored *actual,* rather than virtual, representation.

To the colonists, the Stamp Act demonstrated both Parliament's in- difference to their interests and the shallowness of virtual representation. The colonists did still concede, however, that Parliament possessed *limited* powers of legislation, and they accepted the parliamentary regulation of imperial trade.

Anglo-Americans considered the essential obligation of British allegiance to be loyalty to the Crown and their one unequivocal duty to be defending the empire in wartime. Otherwise, the colonists insisted, they enjoyed a substantial measure of self-government.

Resisting the Stamp Act

In 1765 a political storm generated by the Stamp Act rumbled through all the colonies. The tempest caught up nearly every member of colonial society, but before it ended, elite leaders had assumed direction of the resistance movement.

In late May Patrick Henry, a twenty-nine-year-old Virginia lawyer with a gift for fiery oratory, expressed the rising spirit of resistance. He persuaded Virginia's House of Burgesses to adopt strong resolutions denying Parliament's power to tax the colonies. By year's end, eight other colonial legislatures had rejected parliamentary taxation.

Meanwhile, active resistance took shape. In Boston by late summer, middle-class artisans and businessmen had created the Loyal Nine to fight the Stamp Act. They recognized that the stamp distributors, who alone could sell the specially watermarked paper, represented the law's weak link. If public pressure could force them to resign before the tax went into effect on November 1, the Stamp Act would not work.

Boston's preeminence in opposing Parliament was no accident. Bostonians lived primarily by trade and distilling, and in 1765 they were not living well, thanks to the Sugar Act.

This widespread economic distress produced an explosive situation. Furthermore, Bostonians seemed to enjoy mayhem for its own sake. The high point of each year was Guy Fawkes Day, November 5, when thousands commemorated the failure of a supposed Catholic plot in 1605 to blow up Parliament and to kill King James I. Crowds from the North End and the South End of Boston burned gigantic effigies of the pope as well as of local political leaders. High spirits overflowed into violent confrontations as crowds battled each other with fists, stones, and barrel staves. In 1764 after Guy Fawkes Day brawlers accidentally killed a small child, a truce united the rival mobs under a South End shoemaker named Ebenezer MacIntosh. The Loyal Nine enlisted MacIntosh's frustrated street fighters against Boston's stamp distributor, Andrew Oliver.

The morning of August 14, 1765, found a likeness of Oliver swinging from a tree. Oliver did not take the hint to resign, so at dusk MacIntosh and several hundred followers demolished a new building of his at the dock. The mob then surged toward Oliver's house and vandalized it. Oliver announced his resignation the following morning.

Groups similar to the Loyal Nine, calling themselves the Sons of Liberty, formed throughout the colonies. Several more houses were wrecked, and by November 1 the colonies had only two stamp distributors, who soon resigned.

In October 1765 representatives from nine colonies met in New York City in the Stamp Act Congress. There the colonies agreed on, and boldly articulated, the principle that Parliament had no authority to levy taxes outside Britain or to deny any person a jury trial. While emboldening and unifying the colonies, declarations of principle such as the Stamp Act Congress resolutions seemed futile to many colonists, in view of Parliament's earlier

@ **Stamp Act Protest**

@ **Hutchinson Recounts the Mob Reaction to the Stamp Act**

@ **John Holt's Account of the Stamp Act Riots in New York** refusal to consider their objections to the stamp duties.

Without the watermarked paper required by law, most customs officials and court officers refused to perform their duties. In response, legislators compelled them to resume operations by threatening to withhold their pay. By late December the colonial courts and harbors were again functioning.

The colonial upper class assumed control of the public outcry against the Stamp Act. Respectable gentlemen kept an explosive situation under 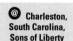 control by taking over leadership of local Sons of Liberty, by coordinating protest through the Stamp Act Congress, and by having colonial legislatures resume normal business. But the Stamp Act remained in effect. To force its repeal, New York's merchants agreed on October 31, 1765, to boycott all British goods. Others followed. Because the colonies purchased 40 percent of England's manufactures, this nonimportation strategy triggered panic within England's business community.

Meanwhile, the Marquis of Rockingham had succeeded George Grenville as prime minister. In March 1766 Parliament revoked the Stamp Act, but simultaneously passed the Declaratory Act, affirming parliamentary power to legislate for the colonies "in all cases whatsoever."

Because Americans interpreted the Declaratory Act as merely a face-saving measure on Parliament's part, they ignored it. In truth, however, the House of Commons intended that the colonists take the Declaratory Act literally to mean that they were not exempt from *any* parliamentary statute, including a tax law. The Stamp Act crisis thus ended in a fundamental disagreement between Britain and America over the colonists' political rights.

Ideology, Religion, and Resistance

The Stamp Act crisis had caused some Anglo-Americans to see for the first time a sinister quality in the imperial relationship with Britain. To understand these perceptions, some educated colonists turned to philosophers, historians, and political writers. Many more looked to religion.

The colonists were familiar with John Locke and other Enlightenment political thinkers. Locke argued that in a state of nature, people enjoyed the "natural rights" of life, liberty, and property. To form governments to protect these rights, people entered into a "social contract." A government that encroached on natural rights broke its contract with the people. In such cases the people could resist their government. To many colonial leaders, Locke's concept of natural rights justified opposition to Parliament's arbitrary legislation.

The political writers read most widely in the colonies included a group known as oppositionists. According to John Trenchard and Thomas Gordon, among others, Parliament—the freely elected representatives of the people—formed the foundation of England's unique political liberties and protected them against the tyranny of executive power. But since 1720, the oppositionists argued, most members of Parliament had sold their souls for financial gain and joined a "conspiracy against liberty."

During the 1760s and 1770s English radicals, notably Joseph Priestley and James Burgh, drew from both Enlightenment and oppositionist authors to fashion a critique of English government and a new way of thinking about politics. At the heart of all political relationships, they argued, raged a struggle between the aggressive extension of artificial *power*, represented by corrupt governments, and the natural *liberty* of the people. To protect their liberty, free people had to resist the encroachment of tyranny. Above all, they had to remain alert for "conspiracies" against liberty.

Influenced by such ideas, a number of colonists detected a conspiracy behind British policy during the Stamp Act crisis. Over the next decade a thundershower of pamphlets denounced British efforts to "enslave" the colonies through taxation and the imposition of officials, judges, and a standing army directed from London.

Educated colonists often looked to classical Greeks and Romans for models of virtuous devotion to liberty. The pamphlets and speeches of gentlemen such as Thomas Jefferson, John Dickinson, and Patrick Henry resounded with quotations from the ancients that served as constant reminders of the righteous dignity of their cause. But appeals to ordinary Americans drew on deeper wellsprings of belief, notably the religious fervor that the Great Awakening had stirred.

Beginning with the Stamp Act crisis, New England's clergymen summoned their flocks to stand up for God and liberty. A popular theme was how God sent the people woes only to strengthen and sustain them until victory. Even Virginia gentlemen not known for their piety felt moved by such messages and ordered their families to comply with the days of "fasting and public humiliation" proclaimed by the clerical leaders.

Era of Anglo-American Crisis

From 1767 to 1773 Parliament pursued a confrontational policy that eroded Americans' trust of Britain. The resulting climate of fear and alienation left most colonists convinced that the Stamp Act had been not an isolated mistake but part of a deliberate design to undermine colonial self-government.

The Quartering Act

In August 1766 George III dismissed the Rockingham government and summoned William Pitt to form a cabinet. An opponent of taxing the colonies, Pitt had the potential to repair the Stamp Act's damage; the colonists respected him highly. However, Pitt's health collapsed in March 1767, and Charles Townshend, the chancellor of the exchequer (treasurer), became the effective leader.

Just as Townshend took office, a conflict arose with the New York legislature over the Quartering Act of 1765, which ordered colonial legislatures to pay for certain goods used by British soldiers stationed within their borders. The law aroused resentment because it constituted an *indirect* tax. That is, although it did not empower royal officials to collect money directly from the colonists, it obligated assemblies to raise revenue by whatever means they considered appropriate. New York refused to grant the supplies.

New York's resistance unleashed a torrent of anti-American feeling in Parliament, still bitter after

revoking the Stamp Act. Townshend responded by drafting the New York Suspending Act, which threatened to nullify all laws passed by the colony after October 1, 1767, if it refused to vote the supplies. By the time George III signed the measure, New York had already appropriated the funds. Nonetheless, the conflict over the Quartering Act demonstrated that British leaders would not hesitate to defend Parliament's sovereignty through the most drastic of all steps: interfering with colonial self-government.

The Townshend Duties

This new wave of British resentment toward the colonies coincided with an outpouring of frustration over the government's failure to cut taxes from wartime levels. Discontent seethed among the landed gentry, whose members took advantage of their domination of the House of Commons to slash their own taxes in 1767. This move cost the government £500,000 and prompted Townshend to tax imports entering America and to propose laws to increase colonial customs revenues.

Townshend sought to tax the colonists by exploiting a loophole in their arguments against the Stamp Tax. Americans had emphasized their opposition to *internal* taxes but had said nothing about *external* taxes—Parliament's right to tax imports as they entered the colonies. Townshend interpreted this silence as evidence that the colonists accepted Britain's right to impose external taxes. Parliament passed Townshend's Revenue Act of 1767 (popularly called the Townshend duties), which taxed glass, paint, lead, paper, and tea imported into the colonies.

On the surface Townshend's case for external taxation was convincing, as the colonists had long accepted parliamentary regulation of trade and had in principle acknowledged taxation as a form of regulation. But the Townshend duties differed significantly from what Americans considered a legitimate way of regulating trade through taxation. To the colonists, charging a duty was a lawful way for British authorities to control trade only if it excluded foreign goods by making them prohibitively expensive. The Revenue Act of 1767, however, set moderate rates that did not price goods out of the colonial market; clearly, its purpose was to collect money for the treasury. Thus from the colonial standpoint, Townshend's duties were taxes just like the Stamp Act duties.

The Revenue Act never yielded the income that Townshend had anticipated. Of all the items taxed, only tea produced any significant revenue— £20,000 of the £37,000 expected. And because the measure would serve its purpose only if the colonists could afford British tea, Townshend eliminated £60,000 in import fees paid on East Indian tea entering Britain before transshipment to America. On balance, the Revenue Act *worsened* the British treasury's deficit by £23,000. By 1767 Britain's financial difficulties were no longer the driving force behind proposals to tax the colonies. From Parliament's standpoint, the conflict with America was becoming a test of national will over the *principle* of taxation.

The Colonists' Reaction

Americans learned of the Revenue Act shortly before it went into operation, and they hesitated over their response. Resistance to the act remained weak until December 1767, when John Dickinson, a Delaware planter and Philadelphia lawyer, published *Letters from a Farmer in Pennsylvania.* These twelve essays, which appeared in nearly every colonial newspaper, emphasized that Parliament had no right to tax trade for the simple purpose of raising revenue. No tax designed to produce revenue could be considered constitutional unless a people's elected representatives voted for it.

In early 1768 the Massachusetts assembly asked Samuel Adams to draft a "circular letter" to other legislatures. Possessing a flair for the push and shove of local politics, the Harvard-educated Adams had helped organize the Sons of Liberty in Boston. Adams's circular letter denounced taxation without representation and the threat to self-governance posed by Parliament's making governors and royal officials independent of the legislatures.

Virginia's assembly warmly approved Adams's eloquent measure and sent out a more strongly worded letter of its own, urging all the colonies to oppose imperial policies that would "have an immediate tendency to enslave them." Most colonial legislatures reacted indifferently to these letters. But the situation changed when British parliamentary leaders overreacted, denouncing even the mild Massachusetts letter as "little better than an incentive to Rebellion." The British government ordered the Massachusetts assembly to disown its letter, forbade all overseas assemblies to endorse it, and commanded royal governors to dissolve any legislature that violated these instructions.

The tactic backfired. Protesting such bullying, many legislatures previously indifferent to the Massachusetts letter adopted it enthusiastically. Royal governors responded by dismissing legislatures in Massachusetts and elsewhere, playing into the hands of Samuel Adams and others who wished to ignite widespread opposition to the Townshend duties.

Increasingly outraged, the colonists still needed an effective means of pressuring Parliament for repeal. Nonimportation seemed especially promising because it offered an alternative to violence and would distress Britain's economy. Thus in August 1768 Boston's merchants adopted a nonimportation agreement, and the tactic spread southward. Far from complete, the boycott probably kept out no more than 40 percent of British imports.

Wilkes and Liberty

British merchants and artisans, hit hard by the boycott, demanded repeal of the Townshend duties. Their protests became part of a larger movement in the 1760s against the policies of George III and a Parliament dominated by wealthy landowners. John Wilkes, a fiery London editor whose newspaper regularly and irreverently denounced the king, became both leader and focal point of the protest. A member of Parliament, Wilkes was tried for seditious libel and acquitted, to great popular acclaim. George III's government then shut down his newspaper and persuaded members of the House of Commons to deny Wilkes his seat.

In 1768 Wilkes returned to England, defying an arrest warrant, and again ran for Parliament. By then government policies, including the Townshend Acts, had unleashed a flood of protests against the "obnoxious" government ministers, a flood that swept along manufacturers and merchants as well as weavers and other workers. They all rallied around the cry "Wilkes and Liberty."

When the newly elected Wilkes was once again arrested 20,000 to 40,000 angry "Wilkesites" massed on St. George's Fields, outside the prison where he was being held. Soldiers and police responded to rock-throwing demonstrators by opening fire on them, killing eleven protesters. The "massacre of St. George's Fields" furnished martyrs to the protesters, and Wilkes received enormous public support from the North American colonies as well as from Britain.

Emboldened by the Wilkes and Liberty movement, William Pitt, Edmund Burke, and others forcefully denounced the government's colonial policies. The colonists themselves concluded that Parliament and the government represented a small but powerful minority whose authority they could legitimately question.

Women and Colonial Resistance

Nonimportation convinced the British—and the colonists—that all Americans were determined to sustain resistance, and it demonstrated that the American cause rested on foundations of impeccable morality and sensible moderation. It also provided a unique opportunity for women to join the protest.

Calling themselves Daughters of Liberty, upper-class female patriots assumed a highly visible role during the Townshend crisis. Convinced **@ A Society of Patriotic Ladies at Edenton in North Carolina** that colonial women could exert a persuasive moral influence on public opinion, American leaders encouraged them to protest the Revenue Act's tax on tea. Accordingly, in early 1770 more than 300 "mistresses of families" in Boston denounced the consumption of the beverage. In some ways nonconsumption was more effective than nonimportation, for the colonists' refusal to consume imports would chill merchants' economic incentive to import British goods.

Nonconsumption agreements therefore became popular and were extended to include other goods, mainly clothes. Again, women played a vital role because the boycott would fail unless the colonists replaced British imports with apparel of their own making. Responding to leaders' pleas for an expansion of domestic cloth production, women of all social ranks organized spinning bees.

Colonial leaders were waging a battle to convince British public opinion that their society would stand firm in opposing unconstitutional taxes. Female participation in symbolic protests forced the British public to appreciate the depth of colonial commitment.

Customs Racketeering

Townshend also sought to increase revenues by extending British surveillance of colonial trade. In 1767 he induced Parliament to create the American Board of Customs Commissioners to strictly enforce the Navigation Acts. **@ William Shepherd Attempts to Collect Customs Duties in Philadelphia** At the same time, Parliament increased the number of port officials, funded a colonial coast guard to catch smugglers, and provided money for secret informers. The law quickly drew protests because of the ways it was enforced and because it reversed traditional legal process by assuming the accused to be guilty until proved otherwise.

The rapid expansion of the customs service in 1767 coincided with new provisions that awarded an informer one-third of the value of all goods and ships appropriated through a conviction of smuggling. The fact that fines could be tripled under certain circumstances provided an even greater incentive to seize illegal cargoes. Smuggling cases were heard in vice-admiralty courts, where the probability of conviction was extremely high. The prospect of accumulating a small fortune proved too tempting to most commissioners.

Revenue agents commonly perverted the law by filing charges for technical violations of the Sugar Act even when no evidence existed of intent to conduct illegal trade. They most often exploited the provision that declared any cargo illegal unless it had been loaded or unloaded with a customs officer's written authorization.

Nowhere were customs agents and informers more detested than in Boston, where citizens retaliated in June 1768. When customs agents seized colonial merchant John Hancock's sloop *Liberty* on a technicality, a crowd tried to prevent the towing of Hancock's ship and then began assaulting customs officials.

The wealthy Hancock, a leading opponent of British taxation, had become a chief target of the customs commissioners. Despite a lack of evidence that he was a smuggler, customs commissioners in 1768 used a perjured statement from a customs inspector to seize the *Liberty* for allegedly avoiding £700 in duties on wine worth £3,000. During the prosecution that followed, British agents perjured themselves and the judge denied Hancock his right to a fair trial.

Hancock's case made Americans rethink their acceptance of the principle that Parliament had limited authority to pass laws for them. By 1770 it was clear that measures such as the Sugar Act and the act creating the American Board of Customs Commissioners endangered property rights and civil liberties as much as taxes. By 1774 a consensus had emerged that Parliament had no lawmaking authority over the colonies except the right to regulate imperial commerce.

Repeal of the Townshend Duties

Meanwhile, in January 1770 Lord North had become prime minister. An able administrator, North favored eliminating most of the Townshend duties to end the commercial boycott, but he insisted on retaining the tax on tea to underscore British authority. In April 1770 Parliament repealed most of the Townshend duties.

This partial repeal presented a dilemma to American politicians. They considered it intolerable that taxes remained on tea, the most profitable item for the royal treasury. The tea duty was a galling reminder that Parliament still claimed broad authority,

and it led to mounting colonial resentment of British rule.

The Boston Massacre

Nowhere was the fraying of loyalties more obvious than in Boston. In response to Bostonians' violence, 1,700 British troops landed in Boston in October 1768. In 1770 this military occupation provoked a fresh round of violence as armed sentries and resentful civilians traded insults. The mainly Protestant townspeople resented the authority of the soldiers, especially blacks and Irish Catholics, and bristled at job competition from enlisted men, most of whom could seek work after morning muster.

It was a situation tailor-made for Samuel Adams, a genius in shaping public opinion. By imposing nearly 2,000 redcoats on a crowded, economically distressed, and violence-prone city of 20,000 bullheaded Yankees, the British government had given Adams grist for his propaganda mill. In October 1768 he began publishing the *Journal of the Times*, a magazine claiming to offer factual accounts of abuses committed by the army and customs services. The *Journal* seldom lacked stories of citizens assaulted, insulted, or simply annoyed, and Adams exaggerated every incident.

Bostonians endured their first winter as a garrison town without undue trouble and saw half the British troops sail home in mid-1769. But relations between civilians and the remaining soldiers deteriorated. Resentment of British authority boiled over on February 22, 1770, when a customs informer fired birdshot at several children throwing rocks at his house and killed an eleven-year-old boy. Adams organized a burial procession to maximize the horror at a child's death, relying on grief to unite the community in opposition to British policies.

Although the army had played no part in the shooting, it became a target for Bostonians' rage. A week after the funeral, tension erupted at the guardpost protecting the customs office. When an officer tried to disperse a crowd led by Crispus Attucks, a seaman of African and Native American ancestry, the mob responded with a barrage of flying objects.

One soldier, knocked down by a block of ice, fired, and the others opened fire. Their volley killed five people, including Attucks.

Samuel Adams orchestrated a martyrs' funeral for the victims of this so-called Boston Massacre, named to recall the "St. George's Field Massacre" of Wilkes's supporters in London, and used the occasion to solidify American opposition to British authority. To defuse the explosive situation, royal authorities isolated the British troops on a fortified harbor island and promised a trial for the soldiers who had fired. Patriot leader John Adams defended the men to demonstrate American commitment to impartial justice. But the light punishments given these soldiers, who had shot unarmed civilians, forced the colonists to confront the stark possibility that Britain intended to coerce and suppress them through naked force.

> @ **The *Boston Gazette* Describes the Boston Massacre**
>
> @ **The Bloody Massacre Perpetrated in King Street, Boston, on March 5, 1770**
>
> @ **Captain Preston's Defense of Military Action in Boston**

The Committees of Correspondence

The colonies enjoyed a brief truce in their relations with Britain, but it ended in June 1772 when the customs schooner *Gaspee* ran aground near Providence, Rhode Island. A revenue cutter that engaged in customs racketeering by plundering cargoes for technical violations of the Sugar Act, the *Gaspee* also had an odious reputation among Rhode Islanders for its high-handed captain and crew of petty thieves. Stuck in the mud, the *Gaspee* presented an irresistible target for local inhabitants. That night more than 100 men took revenge by burning it to the water line.

The British government dispatched a commission with instructions to send all suspects to England for trial. Although the investigators failed to identify any raiders, colonists took alarm at the government's willingness to dispense with another essential civil liberty, an accused citizen's right to be tried by a local jury.

Meanwhile, in fall 1772 Lord North prepared to implement Townshend's goal of paying royal governors from customs revenue, freeing them from the control of the colonial assemblies. With representative government deeply threatened, Samuel Adams persuaded Boston's town meeting to request that every Massachusetts community appoint people to exchange information and to coordinate measures to defend colonial rights. Within a year most Massachusetts communities had established "committees of correspondence," and the idea spread throughout New England.

The committees of correspondence, the colonists' first attempt to maintain close political cooperation over a wide area, allowed Samuel Adams to conduct a campaign of political education for all New England. Tens of thousands of citizens faced evidence that their rights were endangered.

Patrick Henry, Thomas Jefferson, and Richard Henry Lee had proposed in March 1773 that Virginia establish committees of correspondence, and within a year every province but Pennsylvania had such committees. By early 1774 a communications web linked colonial leaders.

In contrast to the brief, intense Stamp Act crisis, the dissatisfaction spawned by the Townshend duties persisted and gradually poisoned relations between Britain and America.

Toward Independence

In early 1773 leading Americans still expected to see the tax on tea repealed. But Parliament's passage of the Tea Act soon shattered this hope and set off a chain reaction of events from the Boston Tea Party in late 1773 to the Declaration of Independence in 1776.

The Tea Act

Smuggling and nonconsumption had taken a heavy toll on Britain's East India Company, the holder of the legal monopoly on importing tea into the British Empire. By 1773, as tons of tea rotted in warehouses, the

East India Company was teetering on the brink of bankruptcy. But Lord North could not let the company fail because by maintaining British authority in India at its own expense, the East India Company had become a vital component in the British imperial structure.

If the company could control the colonial market, North reasoned, it could increase its profits and its survival would be guaranteed. In May 1773, to save the beleaguered East India Company, Parliament passed the Tea Act, which eliminated all import duties on tea entering England and thus lowered the selling price to consumers. To reduce the price further, the Tea Act also permitted the company to sell tea directly to consumers rather than through wholesalers. These provisions reduced the cost of East India Company tea in the colonies to well below the price of smuggled tea. Parliament expected economic self-interest to overcome American scruples about buying taxed tea.

But the Tea Act alarmed many Americans, who recognized that the revenues raised by the law would place royal governors' purses beyond the reach of the colonial assemblies. The law also threatened to seduce Americans into accepting parliamentary taxation in return for a frivolous luxury. The committees of correspondence decided to resist the importation of tea by pressuring the East India Company's agents to refuse acceptance or by preventing the landing of East India Company cargoes.

In Boston on November 28, 1773, the first ship came under jurisdiction of the customhouse, to which duties would have to be paid within twenty days or the cargo would be seized from the captain and the tea claimed by the company's agents and placed on sale. When Samuel Adams, John Hancock, and others asked customs officers to issue a special clearance for the ship's departure (to avoid the seizure and sale), Governor Hutchinson refused.

On the evening of December 16, 1773, Samuel Adams convened a meeting in Old South Church, at which he told 5,000 citizens about Hutchinson's insistence on landing the tea, warned them that the grace period would expire in a few hours, and proclaimed that "this meeting can do no more to save

the country." About fifty young men disguised as Indians then loosed a few war whoops and headed for the wharf, followed by the crowd. Thousands lined the waterfront to watch them heave forty-five tons of tea overboard; for an hour the only sounds echoing through the crisp, moonlit night were the steady chop of hatchets breaking open wooden chests and the soft splash of tea on the water. Their work finished, the participants left quietly.

The Coercive Acts

Boston's "Tea Party" enraged the British. Only "New England fanatics" could imagine that cheap tea oppressed them, fumed Lord North. The great orator Edmund Burke pled in vain for the one action that could end the crisis: "Leave America . . . to tax herself." But the British government swiftly asserted its authority through the passage of four Coercive Acts, which, along with the Quebec Act, became known to many colonists as the Intolerable Acts.

The first Coercive Act, the Boston Port Bill, was passed on April 1, 1774. It ordered the navy to close Boston Harbor unless the town arranged to pay for the ruined tea by June 1. The impossibly short deadline was meant to ensure the harbor's closing, which would plunge Boston into economic distress. The second Coercive Act, the Massachusetts Government Act, revoked the Massachusetts charter and made the colony's government less democratic.

The final two Coercive Acts—the Administration of Justice Act and a new Quartering Act—rubbed salt into the wounds. The first of these permitted any person charged with murder while enforcing royal authority in Massachusetts to be tried in England or in another colony. The second went beyond the Quartering Act of 1765 by allowing the governor to requisition *empty* private buildings for quartering, or housing, troops. These measures, coupled with the appointment of General Thomas Gage, Britain's military commander in North America, as governor of Massachusetts, struck New Englanders as proof of a plan to place them under a military despotism.

Americans learned of the unrelated Quebec Act at the same time as the Coercive Acts. Intended to cement loyalty to Britain among conquered French-Canadian Catholics, the law established Roman Catholicism as Quebec's official religion. Furthermore, the Quebec Act gave Canada's governor sweeping powers but established no legislature. The law extended Quebec's territorial claims south to the Ohio River and west to the Mississippi, a vast area populated by Indians and some French and claimed by several colonies.

The Intolerable Acts convinced New Englanders that the crown planned to corrode traditional English liberties throughout North America. Once the Coercive Acts destroyed these liberties in Massachusetts, many believed, the Quebec Act would serve as a blueprint for extinguishing representative government in other colonies.

Intended only to punish Massachusetts, the Coercive Acts thus pushed most colonies to the brink of revolution. Repeal of these laws became the colonists' nonnegotiable demand.

The First Continental Congress

In response to the Intolerable Acts, the committees of correspondence of every colony but Georgia sent delegates to a Continental Congress in Philadelphia. The fifty-six delegates who assembled on September 5, 1774, included the colonies' most prominent politicians: Samuel and John Adams of Massachusetts; John Jay of New York; Joseph Galloway and John Dickinson of Pennsylvania; and Patrick Henry, Richard Henry Lee, and George Washington of Virginia. They were determined to find a way to defend American rights without war.

The Continental Congress endorsed the Suffolk Resolves, extreme statements of principle that proclaimed that the colonies owed no obedience to the Coercive Acts, advocated a provisional government until restoration of the Massachusetts charter, and vowed that defensive measures should follow any attack by royal troops. The Continental Congress also voted to boycott British goods after December 1, 1774, and to stop exporting goods to Britain and its

West Indies possessions after September 1775. This agreement, called the Continental Association, would be enforced by locally elected committees of "observation" or "safety." But not all the delegates embraced such bold defiance. Jay, Dickinson, Galloway, and other moderates who dominated the middle-colony contingent vainly opposed nonimportation and unsuccessfully sought support of a plan for an American legislature that would share with Parliament the authority to tax and to govern the colonies.

@ **Gouverneur Morris Warns Against Democratic Revolution**

Finally, the delegates summarized their principles and demands in a petition to George III. They conceded to Parliament the power to regulate colonial commerce but argued that parliamentary efforts to impose taxes, enforce laws through admiralty courts, suspend assemblies, and revoke charters were unconstitutional.

The Fighting Begins

Most Americans hoped that resistance would jolt Parliament into renouncing its claims of authority over the colonies. But George III saw rebellion in Congress's actions. His instincts were correct: a revolution was indeed brewing.

In colony after colony, the committees elected to enforce the Continental Association assumed governmental functions by organizing volunteer military companies and extralegal legislatures. By spring 1775 colonial patriots had established provincial "congresses" that rivaled existing royal governments. Such organizations were greeted with indignation by loyalists—Americans loyal to England.

In April 1775 events in Massachusetts shattered the uneasy calm. Citizens had collected arms and organized militia units ("minutemen") to respond instantly in an emergency. The British government ordered Massachusetts governor Gage to quell the "rude rabble" and to arrest the patriot leaders. Aware that most of these had fled Boston, Gage, on April 19, 1775, sent 700 British soldiers to seize colonial military supplies stored at Concord. Two couriers, William Dawes and Paul Revere, alerted nearby towns of the British troop movements. At Lexington on the road to

Concord, about 70 minutemen faced the British on the town green. After a confused skirmish in which eight minutemen died and a single redcoat was wounded, the British marched to Concord. They found few munitions but encountered a swarm of armed Yankees. When some minutemen mistakenly concluded that the town was being burned, they exchanged fire with British regulars and touched off a running battle that continued most of the sixteen miles back to Boston. By day's end the redcoats had lost 273 men.

These engagements awakened the countryside. Within a day some 20,000 New Englanders were besieging the British garrison in Boston. In the New England interior the Green Mountain Boys under Ethan Allen overran Fort Ticonderoga on Lake Champlain on May 10, with the intent of using its captured cannon in the siege of Boston. That same day the Continental Congress reconvened in Philadelphia. Most delegates still opposed independence and agreed to send a "loyal message" to George III. The resulting Olive Branch Petition presented three demands: a cease-fire in Boston, repeal of the Coercive Acts, and negotiations to establish guarantees of American rights. But the Olive Branch Petition reached London along with news of the battles of Breed's Hill and Bunker Hill outside Boston. Although the British dislodged the Americans in the clashes, they suffered 2,200 casualties, compared to colonial losses of only 311. After Bunker Hill the British public wanted retaliation, not reconciliation. On August 23 the king proclaimed New England in a state of rebellion, and in December Parliament declared all the colonies rebellious.

The Failure of Reconciliation

Most Americans still clung to hopes of reconciliation. Yet the same Americans who pleaded for peace passed measures that the British could only see as rebellious. Delegates to the Continental Congress voted to establish an "American continental army" and appointed George Washington as commander.

Americans' sentimental attachment to the king, the last emotional barrier to independence, crumbled in January 1776 with the publication of Thomas Paine's *Common Sense*. Paine had immigrated to the colonies from England in 1774 with a penchant for radical politics and a gift for plain and pungent prose. Paine told Americans what they had been unable to bring themselves to say: that at the root of the conspiracy against American liberty lay not corrupt politicians but the very institutions of monarchy and empire. Further, America did not need its British connection. "The commerce by which she [America] hath enriched herself are the necessaries of life, and will always have a market while eating is the custom in Europe," Paine argued. And, he pointed out, the events of the preceding six months had made independence a reality. Finally, Paine linked America's awakening nationalism with a sense of religious mission: "We have it in our power to begin the world over again. A situation, similar to the present, hath not happened since the days of Noah until now." America, Paine wrote, would be a new *kind* of nation, a model society free of oppressive English beliefs and institutions.

Common Sense, "a landflood that sweeps all before it," sold more than 100,000 copies in three months, one copy for every fourth or fifth adult male in the colonies. By spring 1776 Paine's pamphlet had dissolved lingering allegiance to George III and removed the last psychological barrier to independence.

Independence at Last

John Adams described the movement toward independence as a coach drawn by thirteen horses, which could not reach its destination any faster than the slowest were willing to run. New England was already in rebellion, and Rhode Island declared itself independent in May 1776. The middle colonies hesitated to support revolution because they feared, correctly, that the war would largely be fought over control of Philadelphia and New York. The South began to press for separation. In April North Carolina authorized its congressional delegates to vote for independence, and in June Virginia followed suit. On July 2 the Continental Congress formally adopted the Virginia resolution and created the United States of America.

@ **A Maryland Preacher Resists the Patriots**

The drafting of a statement to justify the colonies' separation from England fell to Virginia's Thomas Jefferson. Congress approved his manuscript on July 4, 1776. Even though parliamentary authority had been the focal point of dispute since 1765, the Declaration of Independence never mentioned Parliament by name because Congress was unwilling to imply that Parliament held any authority over America. Jefferson instead focused on George III, citing "repeated injuries and usurpations" against the colonies.

Like Paine, Jefferson elevated colonial grievances to a struggle of universal dimensions. In the tradition of Enlightenment thought, Jefferson argued that Britain had violated its contract with the colonists, giving them the right to replace it with a government of their own. His emphasis on the equality of all individuals and their natural entitlement to justice, liberty, and self-fulfillment expressed the Enlightenment's deep longing for government that rested on neither legal privilege nor the exploitation of the majority by the few—and deliberately ignored the existence of slavery.

Jefferson addressed the Declaration of Independence as much to Americans uncertain about the wisdom of independence as to world opinion. He wanted to convince his fellow citizens that social and political progress could no longer be accomplished within the British Empire. The declaration challenged the Revolutionary generation and all who followed to bring its ideals closer to reality.

CHRONOLOGY

1733   Molasses Act.

1754– French and Indian War (in Europe, the Seven
1760   Years' War, 1756–1763).

1760   George III becomes king of Great Britain.
       Massachusetts controversy over writs of assistance.

1763   Indian uprising in Ohio Valley and Great Lakes.
       Proclamation of 1763.

1764   Sugar Act.

1765   Stamp Act.
       Quartering Act.
       Loyal Nine formed in Boston to oppose the Stamp Act.
       Sons of Liberty band together throughout the colonies.
       Stamp Act Congress.
       Colonists begin boycott of British goods.

1766   Stamp Act repealed.
       Declaratory Act.

1767   New York Suspending Act.
       Revenue Act (Townshend duties).
       John Dickinson, *Letters from a Farmer in Pennsylvania*.
       American Board of Customs Commissioners created.

1768   Massachusetts "circular letter."
       Boston merchants adopt the colonies' first nonimportation agreement.
       John Hancock's ship *Liberty* seized.
       British troops arrive in Boston.
       John Wilkes elected to Parliament; arrested.
       St. George's Fields Massacre in London.

1770   Townshend duties, except tea tax, repealed.
       Boston Massacre.

1772   *Gaspee* incident in Rhode Island.
       Committees of correspondence begin in Massachusetts and rapidly spread.

1773   Tea Act.
       Boston Tea Party.

1774   Coercive Acts.
       Quebec Act.
       First Continental Congress meets in Philadelphia and adopts Suffolk Resolves.
       Continental Association.

1775   Battles of Lexington and Concord.
       Second Continental Congress meets.
       Olive Branch Petition.
       Battles at Breed's Hill and Bunker Hill.

1776   Thomas Paine, *Common Sense*.
       Declaration of Independence.

FOR FURTHER READING

Bernard Bailyn, *The Ideological Origins of the American Revolution* (1967). Pulitzer Prize–winning examination of the political heritage that shaped colonial resistance to British authority.

Edward Countryman, *The American Revolution* (1985). An outstanding introduction to the Revolution.

Robert A. Gross, *The Minutemen and Their World* (1976). An eloquent and evocative examination of Concord, Massachusetts, in the revolutionary era.

Pauline Maier, *From Resistance to Revolution: Colonial Radicals and the Development of American Opposition to Britain, 1765–1776* (1972). An insightful, definitive examination of how colonial leaders strove to force the repeal of unconstitutional laws with a minimum use of violence.

Robert Middlekauff, *The Glorious Cause: The American Revolution, 1763–1789* (1982). A learned and highly readable narrative of the events leading to independence.

Edmund S. Morgan and Helen M. Morgan, *The Stamp Act Crisis: Prologue to Revolution*, rev. ed. (1963). A classic analysis of colonial constitutional principles regarding limits on Parliament's taxing power.

Robert R. Palmer, *The Age of the Democratic Revolution:* Vol. I, *The Challenge* (1959). Bancroft Prize–winning examination of the American Revolution in comparison to events in England, Ireland, and France.

Gordon S. Wood, *The Radicalism of the American Revolution* (1992). A sweeping account of the Revolution's long-range impact on American society.

6

The Forge of Nationhood,
1776–1788

America's First Civil War

Revolutionary Society

Forging New Governments

America's First Civil War

The Revolution was not just a collective struggle of the American people against Britain. It was also a civil war among North Americans, conducted without restraint, mutual respect, or compassion. Yet its supporters emerged from the war with a commitment to nationhood strong enough to unite the new country.

@ **Washington Crossing the Delaware (1851)**

Loyalists and Other British Sympathizers

When independence came in July 1776, many colonists remained unconvinced of its necessity. They refused to join the supporters of the Revolution, who were called Whigs. About 20 percent of all whites actively opposed the rebellion or supported it only when threatened with fines and imprisonment. These opponents of the Revolution

@ **A Socioeconomic Profile of Loyalist Claimants**

called themselves loyalists, but Whigs labeled them Tories.

Loyalists, like Whigs, typically opposed parliamentary taxation of the colonies. But loyalists believed that separation was illegal and was not necessary to preserve the colonists' rights. Above all, they revered the crown and equated any failure to defend their king with a sacrifice of personal honor.

Loyalist strength in an area depended on how well prominent local Whigs had convinced voters that the king and Parliament were endangering representative government. Whig leaders in New England and Virginia, for example, were active in winning public support, but such leadership was lacking in New York and New Jersey, which would become strongholds of loyalism.

A second major factor in loyalist strength was the geographic distribution of recent British immigrants, who identified closely with their homeland. These newcomers included thousands of British veterans of the French and Indian War who had remained in the colonies, usually in New York.

Third, loyalism thrived on the presence of ethnic and religious minorities outside the main currents of colonial society. For example, a few German, Dutch, and French religious congregations that had resisted use of the English language felt indebted to Britain for their religious freedom.

Canada's French Catholics became the most significant white loyalist minority. The Quebec Act of 1774 had guaranteed their religious freedom and their continued use of French civil law. The bitter denunciations of this measure by their southern neighbors convinced French Catholics that Protestant Anglo-Americans would be far less tolerant.

Black slaves and Native Americans also widely supported the British. Before 1776 the British, not the Americans, had most often offered liberty to American slaves. During the war itself at least 20,000 slaves would run away to sign on as laborers or soldiers in the Royal Army. Deeply alienated from white society, slaves realized that the Revolution would not benefit them. Finally, most Indians, recognizing the threat that expansion-minded colonists posed, likewise supported the British. Of the handful of tribes that sided with the colonists, the most prominent were two Iroquois tribes, the Oneidas and the Tuscaroras.

Whigs hated loyalists, and loyalists responded to Whigs with equal venom. Each side saw its cause as sacred and viewed opposition to it by a fellow American as a betrayal. The worst atrocities of the war were inflicted by Americans on each other.

> @ **A New Jersey Artisan Is Tarred and Feathered**
>
> @ **Grace Growdon Galloway Defies the Radicals in Philadelphia**

The Opposing Sides

Britain entered the war with what should have been two major advantages. First, Britain's 11 million people greatly outnumbered the 2.5 million colonists, one-third of whom were either slaves or loyalists. Second, Britain possessed the world's largest navy and one of its best armies. During the war the army's size more than doubled, from 48,000 to 111,000 men, and Britain hired 30,000 Hessian mercenaries and enlisted 21,000 loyalists to supplement its own fighting force.

Despite a smaller population, the new nation mobilized its people more effectively than Britain. By the war's end the rebels had enlisted or drafted half of all free males aged sixteen to forty-five—about 220,000 troops—compared to the 162,000 Britons, loyalists, and Hessians who served in the British army. Further, peacetime budget cuts after 1763 had weakened British sea power and thus Britain's ability to crush the rebellion. Midway

through the war, half of Britain's ships languished in dry dock, awaiting repairs. In addition, American privateers cost Britain's merchant marine dearly.

Britain could ill afford such losses, for supplying its troops in North America was a Herculean task. Although at various times the British army controlled all the major American cities, British soldiers seldom ventured into the agricultural hinterland and thus could not easily round up supplies. Virtually all the food consumed by the army, one-third of a ton per soldier per year, had to be imported from Britain.

Maintaining public support presented another serious problem for Britain. The war more than doubled the British national debt, adding to the problems of a people already paying record taxes.

The new United States faced different but equally severe problems. First, one-fifth of its population was openly pro-British. Second, state militias lacked the training to fight pitched battles. Their hit-and-run guerrilla tactics could not bring victory, nor could avoiding major battles and allowing the British to occupy population centers. The Continental Army would thus have to fight in European fashion, relying on precision movements of mass formations of troops.

In contrast to Britain, which had a well-trained army with a tradition of bravery under fire, the Continental Army had neither an inspirational heritage nor experienced officers in 1775. In the war's early years, it suffered heartbreaking defeats. However, to win, the Continentals did not have to destroy the British army but only to prolong the rebellion until Britain's taxpayers lost patience. Until then, American victory depended on the ability of one man to keep his army fighting despite defeat—George Washington.

George Washington

Few generals looked and acted the role as much as Washington. He spoke with authority and comported himself with dignity. At six feet two inches, he stood a half foot taller than an average contemporary. Powerfully built, athletic, and hardened by a rugged outdoor life, he could inspire troops to heroism.

Washington's military experience had begun at age twenty-two, when he had commanded a Virginia regiment raised to resist French claims in the Ohio Valley (see Chapter 5). Vastly outnumbered, he had lost his first battle. A year later at Braddock's defeat, Washington had assumed the point of greatest danger, had had two horses shot out from under him, and had had his hat shot off and his coat ripped by bullets. But Washington's mistakes and lost battles had taught him lessons that easy victories might not have. He had discovered the dangers of overconfidence and the need for determination. He had also learned that Americans fought best when led by example and treated with respect.

In 1758, with Virginia's borders secured, Washington had resigned his commission and become a tobacco planter. He had sat in the House of Burgesses, where he was greatly respected. An early opponent of parliamentary taxation, he had also served in the Continental Congress.

War in Earnest

In March 1776 the British evacuated Boston and moved south to New York, which they wished to use as a base for conquering New England. Under two brothers, General William Howe and Admiral Richard, Lord Howe, 130 warships carried 32,000 troops to New York City in summer 1776. Defending the city were 18,000 poorly trained soldiers under Washington. On August 27, 15,000 British troops nearly annihilated 10,500 American troops on Long Island, forcing Washington to execute a night evacuation.

In mid-September 1776 the Continental Army counted 16,000 men. Over the next three months the British killed or took prisoner one-quarter of these troops and drove the survivors across New Jersey. By early December, when Washington retreated from New Jersey into Pennsylvania, he commanded fewer than 7,000 men fit for duty. Thomas Paine called these demoralizing days "the times that try men's souls."

Washington took the offensive before military and national morale collapsed. On Christmas night 1776 he attacked a Hessian garrison at Trenton, New

Jersey, and captured nearly 1,000 Germans with the loss of only 4 men. On January 3, 1777, Washington attacked Princeton, New Jersey, killing or capturing one-third of his 1,200 British opponents and losing only 40. The American victories at Trenton and Princeton had important consequences. First, they boosted civilian and military morale. Second, they undermined the Howes' plans to rally skeptics to Britain's cause and forced the British evacuation of New Jersey in early 1777.

@ Washington Crossing the Delaware

The Turning Point

Shortly after the battles of Trenton and Princeton, the Marquis de Lafayette, a young French aristocrat, joined Washington's staff. Lafayette was twenty years old, idealistic, brave, infectiously optimistic—and closely connected to the French court. His arrival indicated that France might recognize American independence and declare war on Britain. However, the French first wanted proof that the Americans could win a major battle.

That victory came quickly. In summer 1777 the British planned a two-pronged attack to crush New York State and to isolate New England. Two British columns, one from Montreal and the other from Quebec, were to link up near Albany.

The first British column, moving south from Montreal, retreated north after failing to dislodge the Continentals from a choice point at Fort Stanwix. Meanwhile, the second British column, led by General John Burgoyne, outnumbered, surrendered to a force of 17,000 Continentals at Saratoga on October 17, 1777.

Saratoga was as important diplomatically as militarily. Already pro-American, the French court received news of the victory at Saratoga as proof that the Americans could win the war and thus deserved diplomatic recognition. In February 1778 France formally recognized the United States. Four months later France went to war with Britain. Spain and Holland ultimately joined the war as French allies.

The colonies' allies made their presence felt. Between 1779 and 1781 Spanish troops prevented the British from taking the Mississippi Valley, and begin-

The War in the North, 1776–1779

*Following the British evacuation of Boston, the war shifted to New York City, which the
British held from 1776 to 1783. In 1777 Britain's success in taking the U.S. capital,
Philadelphia, was offset by defeat in upstate New York. The hard-fought battle of Monmouth
Court House, New Jersey, ended the northern campaigns in 1778.*

ning in 1781 French troops contributed to rebel victories. The French and Spanish navies, which together approximately equaled the British fleet, won several large battles and punctured the Royal Navy's blockade.

The Continentals Mature

The British and American armies collided on September 11, 1777, at Brandywine Creek, Pennsylvania. After the Continentals crumbled in the face of superior British discipline, Congress fled Philadelphia, allowing General Howe to occupy it. In four bloody weeks 20 percent of the Continentals were killed, wounded, or captured.

In early December 1777 the 11,000 Continental survivors left Whitemarsh, Pennsylvania. Short on rations and chilled to the bone from marching through sleet, they took a week to reach their winter headquarters only eleven miles away. One-fourth of them had worn out at least one shoe. On days when the roads froze, they suffered horribly. Washington later recalled, "You might have tracked the army from White Marsh to Valley Forge by the blood of their feet." As the British rested comfortably in Philadelphia, eighteen miles away, the Continentals stumbled around the bleak hills of Valley Forge and huddled, exhausted and hungry, in crude huts.

The army slowly regained its strength but still lacked training. The Saratoga victory had resulted from the Americans' overwhelming numbers, not their superior skill. Meeting Howe on an even basis, the Continentals had lost badly—twice. The key skills of marching and maneuvering were nonexistent. Then in February 1778 the Continental Army's fortunes rose when a German soldier of fortune and drillmaster, Friedrich von Steuben, reached Valley Forge and turned the army into a formidable fighting force.

Just how formidable became clear in June 1778. The British, now under General Henry Clinton, evacuated Philadelphia and marched toward New York. The Continentals caught up on June 28 at Monmouth Court House, New Jersey. The battle blazed for six hours, with the Continentals throwing back Clinton's best units. The British finally broke off and slipped away under cover of darkness.

The Battle of Monmouth ended the contest for the North. Clinton occupied New York, which the Royal Navy made safe from attack. Washington kept his army on watch nearby, while Whig militia hunted down the last few Tory guerrillas.

Frontier Campaigns

West of the Appalachians and along New York and Pennsylvania's western borders, a different kind of war unfolded. The numbers engaged along the frontier were small, but the stakes were enormous. In 1776 few Anglo-Americans had any clear idea of the country's western boundaries. By 1783 when the Peace of Paris concluded the war, the new nation would claim the Mississippi River as its western border. So although the frontier campaigns would not determine the war's outcome, they would significantly shape the future of the United States.

Frontier fighting first erupted in the South when Cherokees had begun attacking frontier settlements from Virginia to Georgia in 1776. Within a year retaliatory expeditions had forced the Cherokees to cede most of their lands in South Carolina and large tracts in North Carolina and Tennessee. Kentucky saw fierce fighting as rebels under Colonel George Rogers Clark established control of the Ohio River valley from Pittsburgh to the Mississippi after defeating both the British and Native Americans.

In the East pro-British Iroquois under the gifted Mohawk leader Joseph Brant devastated the New York and Pennsylvania frontiers in 1778. General John Sullivan led a Continental force, with Tuscarora and Oneida allies, against the Iroquois. Victorious at what is now Elmira, New York, in 1779, Sullivan and his forces burned two dozen Iroquois villages and destroyed a million bushels of corn. The Iroquois fled north to Canada, and hundreds starved to death. Sullivan had destroyed the heartland of the Iroquois; their population declined by one-third during the Revolutionary War. The Iroquois never recovered.

The War in the West, 1776–1779

George Rogers Clark's victory at Vincennes in 1779 gave the United States effective control of the Ohio Valley. Carolina militiamen drove attacking Cherokees far back into the Appalachians in 1776. In retaliation for raids on New York and Pennsylvania, John Sullivan inflicted widespread starvation on the Iroquois by burning their villages and winter food supplies in 1779.

Victory in the South

After 1778 the British focus shifted to the South. France and Spain's entry had embroiled Britain in an international struggle that raged from India to Gibraltar and from the West Indies to the North American mainland. If the British could secure the South, they could easily shuffle forces between the West Indies and the mainland. And the South looked like an easy target: in 1778, 3,500 British troops had taken Savannah, Georgia, without difficulty, and Clinton expected a southern invasion to tap a huge reservoir of loyalist support. The British planned to seize key southern ports and then move back north, pacifying one region after another.

The War in the South, 1778–1781

By 1780 Britain held the South's major cities, Charles Town and Savannah, but could not establish control over the backcountry because of resistance from Nathanael Greene's Continentals. By invading Virginia, Lord Cornwallis placed himself within striking distance of Washington's U.S. and French forces, a decision that rapidly led to the British surrender at Yorktown in October 1781.

At first the plan unfolded smoothly. Sailing from New York with 4,000 men, Clinton captured Charles Town, South Carolina, in May 1780. He then returned to New York, leaving the mop-up operation to Lord Charles Cornwallis.

Meanwhile, battles between British troops and Continental regulars led to a string of Continental defeats. America's worst loss of the entire war came at Camden, South Carolina, in August 1780. General Horatio Gates's combined force of professionals and militiamen faced Cornwallis's army. The militia-men fled after the first volley, and the badly outnumbered Continentals were overrun. Washington dispatched General Nathanael Greene, whose dogged resistance forced Cornwallis to abandon the Carolina back-country and to lead his battered troops into Virginia.

Still secure in New York, Clinton wanted Cornwallis to return to Charles Town, but Cornwallis had other plans. He established a base at Yorktown, Virginia, where the York and James Rivers empty into Chesapeake Bay. On August 30, 1781, a French fleet dropped anchor off the Virginia coast and landed troops near Yorktown. Lafayette joined them, and Washington led his Continental Army south to tighten the noose. Trapped and besieged at Yorktown, Cornwallis's 6,000 troops lasted three weeks against 8,800 Americans and 7,800 French. On October 19, 1781, they surrendered.

The Peace of Paris

"Oh God!" Lord North exclaimed on hearing of Yorktown. "It's all over." Indeed, Cornwallis's surrender had extinguished the overtaxed people's will to fight and forced the government to begin peace negotiations. Talks opened in Paris in June 1782, with John Adams, Benjamin Franklin, and John Jay as America's principal diplomats.

Military realities largely dictated the terms of the peace treaty. Britain recognized American independence and promised the evacuation of all royal troops from U.S. soil. Moreover, the British had little choice but to award the new nation the vast territory east of the Mississippi, for by 1783 20,000 Anglo-American settlers lived west of the Appalachians and George Rogers Clark's victories had given Americans control of the Northwest.

The Peace of Paris left some problems unresolved. In a separate treaty Britain transferred East and West Florida back to Spain, but the designated boundaries were ambiguous. Although the United States promised to urge state legislatures to compensate loyalists for property losses, several states would later refuse to comply. And no-

@ A Loyalist Widow Decries the Fate of Tory Exiles in Canada

tably missing from the treaty was any reference to the Native Americans, most of whom had supported the British. The treaty left them to deal with the new American republic on their own.

Independence carried a heavy price. At least 5 percent of free white males aged sixteen to forty-five had died in the war. If the present-day United States were to suffer comparable casualties, 2.5 million would die. And the peace left two important issues unsettled: what kind of society the United States would become and what sort of government it would possess.

Revolutionary Society

Two forces shaped the Revolution's social effects: the principles articulated in the Declaration of Independence and the dislocations caused by the war. These factors combined to change relationships between members of different classes, races, and genders momentously.

Egalitarianism

Between 1700 and 1760 social relations between elites and common people had grown more formal, distant, and restrained. Members of the colonial gentry lived sumptuously to emphasize their position. By the late 1760s, however, many in the upper class were wearing homespun clothing in support of boycotts of British goods. By 1776 visible distinctions of wealth had noticeably lessened.

The war accelerated the erosion of class differences by forcing gentry-officers to respect ordinary men serving as privates. Indeed, the soldiers demanded to be treated with consideration, especially in light of the ringing statement of the Declaration of Independence that "all men are created equal."

Soldiers who expected officers to recognize their worth as individuals carried their new self-esteem and insistence on respect back into civilian life. Personal pride gradually translated into political behavior and beliefs, and candidates took care not to scorn the common people. The war thus fundamentally democratized Americans' political assumptions. This egalitarianism did not extend to propertyless males, women, and nonwhites, but it did undermine the tendency to believe that wealth or family background conferred a special claim to public office.

In short, Revolutionary-generation Americans insisted that virtue and sacrifice, not wealth, defined worth. They came to see the "natural aristocracy"— those who demonstrated fitness for government service by their personal accomplishments—as ideal candidates for political office.

A Revolution for African-Americans

The condition of African-Americans contradicted the ideals of equality and justice for which Americans fought. About 500,000 black persons, composing one-fifth of the total population, inhabited the United States in 1776. All but 25,000 were slaves.

The war nevertheless presented new opportunities to African-Americans. Some slaves took advantage of the confusion of war to run off and pose as freemen. A 1775 ban on black soldiers was collapsing by 1777. All states but Georgia and South Carolina eventually recruited blacks. Approximately 5,000 African-Americans, mainly from the North, served in the Continental Army. Most were slaves serving with their masters' consent, usually in racially integrated units.

Manpower demands, not a white commitment to equal justice, largely opened these opportunities. In fact, until the mid-eighteenth century most in the Western world saw slavery as part of the natural order. By the 1760s, however, some American opposition to slavery had blossomed. The Quakers led the way; by 1779 most Quaker slave owners had freed their slaves. The Declaration of Independence's broad assertion of natural rights and human equality spurred a larger attack on slavery. By 1804 all the states from Pennsylvania north, except New Hampshire, had abolished slavery.

Although slavery gnawed at Whig consciences even in the South, no state south of Pennsylvania abolished slavery. Most, however, passed laws making it easier to free slaves. Between 1775 and 1790 the number of free blacks in Virginia and Maryland rose from 4,000 to 21,000, or about 5 percent of all African-Americans residing there.

These "free persons of color" faced a future of destitution and second-class citizenship. Most had used up their cash savings to purchase their freedom and were past their physical prime. They found few whites willing to hire them or to pay equal wages. Most free blacks remained poor laborers or tenant farmers. But a few became landowners or skilled artisans. Benjamin Banneker of Maryland, a self-taught mathematician and astronomer, served on the commission that designed Washington, D.C., and published a series of almanacs.

Free blacks relied on one another for help, generally through religious channels. Because many white congregations spurned them, and because racially separate churches provided mutual support, self-pride, and a sense of accomplishment, free blacks began founding their own Baptist and Methodist congregations after the Revolution. In 1787 Philadelphia blacks established the Methodist congregation that by 1816 would become the African Methodist Episcopal church.

Most states granted important civil rights to free blacks during and after the Revolution. For example, male free blacks who met property qualifications gained the right to vote everywhere by the 1780s. Most northern states repealed or stopped enforcing curfews and other restrictive laws; most also guaranteed free blacks equal treatment in court.

The Revolution neither ended slavery nor brought equality to free blacks, but it did begin a process by which slavery could be extinguished. In half the nation, public opinion no longer condoned human bondage, and southerners increasingly saw slavery as a necessary evil, implicitly admitting its immorality.

Women in the New Republic

Apart from some states' easing of women's difficulties in obtaining divorces, the Revolution had little effect on women's legal position. Women gained no new political rights. The assumption of women's natural dependence—on parents and then husbands—dominated discussions of the female role. Nevertheless, the Revolution's ideological currents emphasizing liberty and equality were significant for white American women.

Women greatly broadened their involvement in the cause, creating a wide range of support activities during the war. Female "camp followers," many of them soldiers' wives, cooked, laundered, and nursed the wounded for both sides. A few women disguised themselves as men and joined the fighting. Women who remained at home managed families, households, farms, and businesses on their own.

The revolutionary era witnessed a challenge to traditional attitudes toward women. American republicans increasingly recognized a woman's right to choose her husband rather than wait for an arranged marriage.

Overall, white women had fewer children than their mothers and grandmothers had had. Declining farm size and urbanization were incentives for smaller families, but just as clearly, women were finding some relief from the endless cycle of pregnancy and nursing that had consumed their forebears.

As women's roles expanded, so did republican ideas of male-female relations. A female author calling herself Matrimonial Republican denounced the word *obey* in the marriage service. "The obedience between man and wife," she wrote, "is, or ought to be, mutual." Lack of mutuality contributed to a rising number of divorce petitions submitted by women.

Gradually, the subordination of women became the subject of debate. In the essay "On the Equality of the Sexes," written in 1779, Massachusetts poet and essayist Judith Sargent Murray wrote that the genders had equal intellectual ability and deserved equal education. She hoped that "sensible and informed" women would improve their minds rather than rush into marriage and would instill republican ideals in their children. Like many of her contemporaries, Murray advocated "republican motherhood," which emphasized the importance of educating women in the values of liberty and independence in order to strengthen virtue in the new nation.

After 1780 the urban elite founded numerous private schools, or academies, for girls, providing American women their first widespread opportunity for advanced education. Massachusetts also established an important precedent in 1789 by forbidding any town to exclude girls from its elementary schools. However, republican egalitarianism faced a serious limitation: even an educated woman would be confined to being a virtuous wife and mother.

Native Americans and the Revolution

Revolutionary ideology held out at least abstract hope for African-Americans and women, but it made no provisions for the many Indians who sought to maintain political and cultural independence. Moreover, in an overwhelmingly agrarian society, the Revolution's promise of equal economic opportunity for all set the stage for territorial expansion beyond settled areas, thereby threatening Indian lands. Indians were all the more vulnerable because during the wars between 1754 and 1783, their population east of the Mississippi had fallen by about one-half and many villages had been uprooted.

In the face of these uncertainties, Native Americans continued to incorporate aspects of European culture into their lives. From the early colonial period, they had adopted European-made goods of cloth, metal, and glass while retaining some of their traditional clothing, tools, and weapons. Indians also participated in the American economy by occasionally working for wages or selling food, craft items, and other products. Yet despite these adaptations to white culture, Native Americans insisted on retaining their own lands and customs, a resolve that the new nation was not eager to accommodate.

Forging New Governments

During the war rebels recognized the need to establish government institutions to sustain the war and to buttress the American claim to independence. But the task of forging a national government proved arduous.

Tradition and Change

In establishing the Revolutionary state governments, the patriots relied heavily on the colonial experience. For example, most took the value of bicameral legislatures for granted. Colonial legislatures in the royal provinces had consisted of two houses: an appointed upper chamber (council) and an elected lower chamber (assembly). Despite the Revolution's democratic tendencies, few questioned the long-standing practice of setting property requirements for voters and elected officials.

Americans generally agreed, too, that their elected representatives should exercise independent judgment rather than simply carry out the popular will. The idea of political parties as instruments for identifying and mobilizing public opinion was alien to the Revolutionary era, which equated parties with "factions"—selfish groups that advanced their interests at the expense of the public good.

In sum, the colonial experience provided no precedent for democratization. Yet the imperial crisis of the 1760s and 1770s had pulled political elites in a democratic direction. The assemblies, the most democratic parts of colonial government, had led the fight against British policy. Colonists had embarked on the Revolution dreading executive officeholders and convinced that they could not trust even elected governors. Their recent experience seemed to confirm the view that those in power tended to become corrupt or dictatorial.

But Revolutionary leaders described themselves as republicans, not democrats. These words had strongly charged meanings in the eighteenth century. At worst, democracy suggested mob rule; at best, it meant the concentration of power in an uneducated people. In contrast, republicanism presumed that government would be entrusted to capable leaders, elected for their talent and wisdom. For republicans, the ideal government would balance the interests of different classes to prevent any group's gaining absolute power. Most Whigs believed that a republic could not include a hereditary aristocracy or even a monarchy. Yet by rejecting these institutions, Whigs created a problem: how to maintain balance in government amid a pervasive distrust of executive power.

Reconstituting the States

The state governments organized during the Revolution reflected a struggle between democratic elements and elites. Eleven of the thirteen states set up bicameral legislatures. In most states the majority of officeholders continued to be appointed. The most radical constitution, Pennsylvania's, tried to establish election districts roughly equal in population so that a minority of voters could not elect a majority of legislators. Nine states reduced property requirements for voting, but none abolished them.

The persistence of these features should not obscure the pathbreaking nature of the state constitutions. First, their adoption required ratification by the people. Second, they could be changed only by popular vote. Above all, counter to the British view of a constitution as a body of customary practices, the state constitutions were *written* compacts that defined and limited rulers' powers. As a final check on government power, the Revolutionary constitutions contained bills of rights outlining fundamental freedoms beyond government control.

The state constitutions strictly limited executive power. In most states the governor became an elected official. Stripped of the veto and most appointive powers, governors became figureheads.

Having weakened the executive branch and vested more power in the legislatures, the state constitutions also made the legislatures more responsive to the will of the people. The Whigs' assault on executive power reflected bitter memories of arbitrary royal governors and underscored the influence of oppositionist ideologues who had warned against executives' usurpation of authority (see Chapter 5).

During the 1780s, however, elites gradually reasserted their desires for centralized authority and the political prerogatives of wealth. The Massachusetts constitution of 1780, which established stiff property qualifications for voting and holding office, created state senate districts apportioned according to property values, and increased the governor's powers of veto and appointment, signaled a general trend.

Troubled far less by differences among social classes and restrictions on the expression of popular will than by the prospect of tyranny, elites nevertheless feared that deep-seated and permanent social divisions could jeopardize republican liberty. Although more committed to liberty than equality, some republicans did use state government legislation to im-

The Northwest, 1785–1787

The Ordinance of 1785 provided for surveying land into townships, each supporting four families on a 160-acre plot (approximately twenty-five people per square mile). In 1787 the Northwest Ordinance stipulated that states would ultimately be created in the region.

plement major social changes. In Virginia between 1776 and 1780, Thomas Jefferson drafted a series of bills to promote equality. He also attacked two legal bastions of the British aristocracy, primogeniture and entail. Primogeniture required that the eldest son inherit all property if there was no will; entail dictated that an heir and his descendants keep an estate intact—that is, neither sell nor divide it. Jefferson hoped that this legislation would prevent an aristocracy from arising in America.

These years also witnessed the end of most state-established churches. Religiously conservative New Hampshire, Connecticut, and Massachusetts resisted this reform until 1817, 1818, and 1833, respectively, but in every state where the Anglican church was established, such status was abolished by 1786. Jefferson's Statute for Religious Freedom (1786) resoundingly defended religious freedom. "Truth is great," he proclaimed, "and will prevail if left to itself."

In 1782 Thomas Paine wrote that the American Revolution was intended to ring in "a new era and give a new turn to human affairs." In this ambitious declaration, Paine expressed the heart of the republican ideal: that *all* political institutions would be judged by whether they served the public good, not the interests of a powerful few. More than anything else, this way of thinking made American politics revolutionary.

The Articles of Confederation

Americans' first national government reflected their fears of centralized authority. In 1776 John Dickinson drafted a proposal for a national government, and in 1777 Congress sent a weakened version of this document, the Articles of Confederation, to the states for ratification. The Articles reserved to each state "its sovereignty, freedom and independence" and made Americans citizens of their states first and of the United States second.

Under the Articles, the national government consisted of a unicameral congress, elected by the state legislatures, in which each state had one vote. Congress could request funds from the states but could not tax without every state's approval, nor could it regulate interstate or overseas commerce. The Articles provided for no executive branch. Rather, congressional committees oversaw financial, diplomatic, and military affairs. Nor was there a judicial system by which the national government could compel allegiance to its laws.

All thirteen states had to approve the Articles. Maryland refused to sign them until states claiming lands north of the Ohio River turned them over to the national government. Maryland lawmakers wanted to keep Virginia and New York from dominating the new nation. As individual states gradually abandoned their northwestern claims, Maryland relented, and the Articles became law in March 1781.

Finance Under the Confederation

Perhaps the greatest challenge facing the Confederation was putting the nation on a sound financial footing. Winning the war cost $160 million, far more than taxes covered. The government borrowed from abroad and printed paper money, called Continentals. But from 1776 to 1791 lack of public faith in the government destroyed 98 percent of the Continentals' value—an inflationary disaster.

Congress turned to Robert Morris, a wealthy Philadelphia merchant who became the nation's superintendent of finance in 1781. Morris proposed a national import duty of 5 percent to finance the congressional budget and to guarantee interest payments on the war debt, but the duty failed to pass.

When peace came in 1783, Morris found it impossible to fund the government adequately. After New York blocked another congressional tax measure sent to the states, state contributions to Congress fell steadily. By the late 1780s the states lagged 80 percent behind in providing the funds that Congress requested.

The Confederation and the West

The postwar settlement and administration of western lands posed another formidable challenge to the new government. Settlers and speculators were determined to possess these lands, and Native Americans were equally determined to keep them out.

After the states surrendered claims to more than 160 million acres north of the Ohio River, Congress, in the Ordinance of 1785, established uniform procedures for surveying the region. The law made the basic unit of settlement a township six miles square, subdivided into thirty-six sections of 640 acres each, with one section reserved as a source of income for public schools. A subsequent law, the Northwest Ordinance of 1787, defined the land north of the Ohio River as the Northwest Territory, provided for its later division into states, and forbade slavery in the territory. The Northwest Ordinance outlined three steps for admitting states to the Union. First, Congress would appoint a territorial governor and judges. Second, as soon as 5,000 adult males lived in a territory, the people would write a temporary constitution and elect a legislature. Third, when the population reached 60,000, the settlers would write a state constitution, which Congress would approve before granting statehood.

@ **Township and Range Map of Old Northwest Territory**

The Ordinance of 1785 and the Northwest Ordinance became the Confederation's major contributions to American life. They set the principles for surveying the frontier, allowed territorial self-government at an early stage of settlement, and provided reasonable standards for statehood. They became models for organizing territories west of the Mississippi River and established precedents for banning slavery from certain territories.

The Northwest Territory offered enough rich land to guarantee future citizens landownership, thus satisfying the republican belief that opening the West would prevent the rise, east of the Appalachians, of a large class of tenant farmers and poor laborers lacking the property needed to vote.

In the anticipated westward push by whites, Jefferson and other republicans hoped to avoid conflict with Indians by assimilating them into white society.

However, because Native Americans had no desire to abandon their own cultures, the opening of western lands to whites made war inevitable.

The British encouraged Native American resistance and refused to abandon seven northwestern forts. Despite the efforts of leaders such as Joseph Brant, the inability of the Indians to unite undermined their cause.

The Confederation also faced problems in the Southeast, where Spain and its Indian allies worked to block American encroachment on their land. The Spanish found an ally in the shrewd Creek diplomat Alexander McGillivray, who was determined to regain surrendered Creek territory. McGillivray negotiated a secret treaty with Spain that promised the Creeks weapons to protect themselves "from the Bears and other fierce Animals." In 1786 he launched an attack on occupants of disputed lands. He offered a cease-fire after winning his objective.

The Spanish further attempted to prevent American infiltration by denying western settlers permission to ship crops down the Mississippi River to New Orleans. After the Spanish closed New Orleans to Anglo-American commerce in 1784, John Jay went to Spain to negotiate trading privileges at New Orleans. Although he failed to win concessions, he returned with a treaty that opened Spanish markets to eastern merchants at the price of relinquishing American export rights through New Orleans. In 1786 Congress rejected this Jay-Gardoqui Treaty, but westerners and southerners, whose interests seemed to have been sacrificed to benefit northern commerce, felt betrayed.

Shays's Rebellion

Had not violence erupted in Massachusetts, the Confederation might have lasted indefinitely. In 1786 the state legislature had imposed high taxes to pay off its Revolutionary debt rapidly. British creditors and Massachusetts bankers and tax collectors demanded payment in specie (gold and silver coin). Thousands of small farmers, accustomed to paying local creditors with goods and services, often over a period of years, found the idea of paying all debts in hard currency not only alien but also impossible. As they had more than a decade earlier, farmers held rallies to discuss "the Supressing of tyrannical government." This time, however, tyranny stemmed from the state house in Boston, not Parliament in London. Late in 1786 Daniel Shays, a Revolutionary War officer and hard-pressed farmer, led 2,000 angry men in an attempt to shut down the courts and to prevent foreclosures and tax auctions. Although routed by the state militia, Shays's followers won control of the Massachusetts legislature in 1787, cut taxes, and secured a pardon for Shays.

Although Shays's Rebellion caused little bloodshed and never raised a serious threat of anarchy, critics of the Confederation painted it and similar, less radical movements elsewhere as a taste of the disorder to come under the weak national government. Meanwhile, rumors that Spain had offered westerners export rights at New Orleans if they would secede from the Union sowed fears that the United States was on the verge of coming apart.

The mid-Atlantic and southern states, emerging from the depression that still gripped New England, generally did not share this alarm about the Confederation's fragility. However, a growing minority was dissatisfied. Urban artisans wanted a strong government that could impose high tariffs to protect their products. Merchants and shippers desired a government powerful enough to secure trading privileges for them, and land speculators and westerners wanted a strong government that would pursue aggressive anti-Indian policies.

Shortly before Shays's Rebellion, delegates from five states, meeting at Annapolis, Maryland, had called for a convention to propose amendments to the Articles of Confederation. Accepting their suggestions, Congress asked the states to send delegates to meet in Philadelphia.

The Philadelphia Convention

In May 1787 fifty-five delegates, from every state but Rhode Island, began gathering at the Pennsylvania State House (later called Independence Hall) in Philadelphia. Among them were men of established reputation—George Washington, Benjamin Franklin, Robert Morris—as well as talented newcomers such as Alexander Hamilton and James Madison. Most were wealthy, were in their thirties or forties, and had legal training. Nineteen owned slaves. Most important, they shared a "continental" or "nationalist" perspective. Thirty-nine had served in Congress and knew firsthand the weaknesses of the Articles. They were convinced that without a strong national government, the country would fall victim to foreign aggression or simply disintegrate.

Two basic issues confronted the convention. First, should the delegates merely tinker with the Articles, or should they draw up a new frame of government? Second, how could any government balance the conflicting interests of large and small states? Thirty-six-year-old James Madison of Virginia proposed answers to both questions.

Madison's Virginia Plan boldly called for a national government, not a confederation of states. It gave Congress virtually unrestricted rights of legislation and taxation, power to veto state laws, and authority to use military force against states. The Virginia Plan specified a bicameral legislature and made representation in both houses of Congress proportional to each state's population. The voters would elect the lower house, which would then choose delegates to the upper house from nominations submitted by the state legislatures. The houses would jointly name the country's president and judges. But opposition to Madison's plan surfaced immediately, particularly his call for proportional representation, which favored Virginia, the largest state.

On June 15 William Paterson of New Jersey offered a counterproposal that, like Madison's plan, strengthened the national government at the states' expense. The New Jersey Plan featured a unicameral legislature in which each state had one vote, just as under the Articles.

The New Jersey Plan exposed the convention's greatest problem: the question of representation. The Virginia Plan gave the four largest states—Virginia, Massachusetts, New York, and Pennsylvania—a majority in both houses. The New Jersey Plan allowed the seven smallest states, with only 25 percent of the U.S. population, to control Congress. By early July the convention was stalemated. To end the impasse, the delegates appointed a "grand committee" dedicated to compromise. This panel adopted a proposal by the Connecticut delegation: an equal vote for each state in the upper house and proportional representation in the lower house. The convention accepted the compromise on July 17 and in two months overcame the remaining hurdles.

As approved on September 17, 1787, the Constitution of the United States was an extraordinary document. Besides reconciling the interests of large and small states, it balanced the delegates' desire for a strong national government against their fear of tyranny. It increased national authority in several ways. It vested in Congress the authority to levy and collect taxes, to regulate interstate commerce, and to conduct diplomacy. Under the Constitution, all acts and treaties of the United States would become "the supreme law of the land." State officials would have to uphold the Constitution, even against acts of their own states. The national government could use military force against any state.

The Constitution's framers restrained the new national government in two key ways. First, they established three distinct branches within the new government—the legislative, the executive, and the judicial. Second, they designed a system of checks and balances to prevent one branch from dominating the others. States' equal representation in the Senate offset proportional representation by population in the House, and each chamber could block hasty measures demanded by the other. Further, the president could veto acts of Congress, but to prevent capricious use of the presidential veto, a two-thirds majority in each house could override a veto. The president would conduct diplomacy, but only the Senate could ratify treaties. The president appointed his cabinet, but only with Senate approval. Congress could, by joint vote, remove the president and his appointees from office, but only for "high crimes," not for political disagreements.

To further guarantee the independence of each branch, the Constitution provided that the members of one branch would not choose those of another, except judges, whose independence was protected by lifetime appointments. For example, an electoral college, composed of members chosen by the various state legislatures, would select the president. State legislatures would also elect senators, whereas popular vote would determine delegates to the House of Representatives.

In addition to checks and balances, the Constitution embodied a novel form of federalism—a system of shared power and dual lawmaking by the state and national governments—to limit central authority. Not only did the state legislatures have a key role in electing the president and senators, but the Constitution could be amended by the votes of three-fourths of the state legislatures. Federalism assumed that the national government would limit its activities to foreign affairs, national defense, regulation of commerce, and coining of money. Most other political matters were left to the states.

The Philadelphia Convention faced a dilemma concerning slavery: were slaves property or persons? In general, southern states regarded slaves as property; however, since slaves made up much of the southern population, southern delegates wanted to count them as persons in determining representation in the lower house. Many northern delegates from the states that were abolishing slavery hesitated to give southern states a political edge by counting as persons slaves who had neither civil nor political rights. At the same time, northern delegates, themselves property owners, balked at questioning southern notions of property rights. Thus they agreed to allow three-fifths of all slaves to be counted for congressional representation and forbade any state's people to prevent the return of runaway slaves to another state. The Constitution did limit slavery by not repudiating the Northwest Ordinance's restrictions on slavery and by permitting Congress to ban the importation of slaves after 1808.

Although leaving much authority to the states, the Constitution established a national government clearly superior to the states in several spheres and abandoned the notion of a confederation of virtually independent states. Having thus strengthened national authority, the convention faced the issue of ratification. Two factors argued against submitting the Constitution to the state legislatures for ratification. First, the state legislatures would probably reject the Constitution, which shrank their power relative to the national government. Second, most of the framers believed that the government had to rest on the consent of the American people themselves. The Constitution's opening words—"We the People of the United States"—embodied this view. In the end the Philadelphia Convention provided for the Constitution's ratification by special state conventions composed of delegates elected by the people. Approval by nine such conventions would enable the new government to operate.

Thus, the Constitution recognized the American people as the ultimate source of political legitimacy. By making the Constitution flexible and amendable and by dividing political power among competing branches of government, the framers made it possible for the national government to be slowly democratized.

Ratification

At first the Constitution had little popular support. To quiet fears of centralized national authority, the Constitution's supporters shrewdly dubbed themselves Federalists, a term implying that the Constitution successfully balanced the relationship between state and national governments.

The Constitution's opponents became known as Antifederalists, a negative-sounding name that conveyed little of their fears that the Constitution *did not* balance the power of the state and national governments.

Antifederalist arguments reflected the deep-seated Anglo-American suspicion of any concentration of power, a suspicion that had driven events from the Stamp Act Congress through the War of Independence. Antifederalists feared that a national government separated from most of its citizens by long distances would be far less responsive to the popular will than state governments would be. They doubted that the untried scheme of checks and balances would work. The Constitution contained no guarantees that the new government would protect the liberties of individuals or the states. The absence of a bill of rights prompted Madison's nationalist ally and fellow Virginian George Mason, the author of the first state bill of rights in 1776, to oppose the Constitution.

The Antifederalists confronted several major disadvantages. For one thing, the Federalists included most of the country's wealthiest and most honored men, including Washington and Franklin. In addition, the majority of newspapers were Federalist and did not hesitate to bias their reporting. Finally, the Antifederalists, largely drawn from state and local leaders, lacked their opponents' contacts and experience at the national level. Ultimately, however, Federalist superiority in funds and political organizing proved decisive.

Federalist delegates prevailed in eight state conventions between December 1787 and May 1788, in all cases but one by margins of two-thirds or more. Such lopsided voting in favor of the Constitution reflected Federalist aggressiveness more than popular support.

But unless the large states of Virginia and New York ratified, the new government would be unworkable. Antifederalism ran high in both, especially among small farmers, who believed that the Constitution favored city dwellers and monied interests. Prominent Antifederalists included New York's governor George Clinton and Virginia's Richard Henry Lee, George Mason, Patrick Henry, and future president James Monroe.

On June 21, 1788, the Constitution became the law of the land when the ninth state, New Hampshire, ratified. Debate continued in Virginia, where the Federalists won wide support from settlers in the western part of the state who wanted a strong national government capable of ending Indian raids along the Ohio River. Western Virginians' votes, combined with Madison's logic and tidewater planters' support, ruled the day. On June 25 the Virginia delegates ratified by a narrow 53 percent majority.

The struggle was even hotter in New York. Antifederalists controlled the state convention and probably would have voted down the Constitution had not news arrived of New Hampshire's and Virginia's ratification. A number of Antifederalists switched sides and New York ratified on July 26 by a 30–27 vote.

Despite the defeat, the Antifederalists left an important legacy. At Antifederalist insistence, the Virginia, New York, and Massachusetts conventions ratified the Constitution with requests that the new charter be amended to include a bill of rights protecting Americans' basic freedoms. Widespread support for a bill of rights made it a major item on the new government's agenda.

Antifederalists in New York also stimulated one of the greatest works of political analysis ever written: *The Federalist*, a series of eighty-five newspaper articles by Alexander Hamilton, James Madison, and John Jay. Although *The Federalist* papers did little to influence the New York vote, they provided a glimpse of the framers' intentions in designing the Constitution and thus powerfully shaped the American philosophy of government. The Constitution, insisted *The Federalist*'s authors, had two main purposes: to defend minority rights against majority tyranny and to prevent a stubborn minority from blocking measures necessary for the national interest. There was no reason to fear that the Constitution would allow a single economic or regional interest to dominate. In the most profound essay in the series, *Federalist* No. 10, Madison argued that the nation's size and diversity would neutralize the attempts of factions to steer unwise laws through Congress.

Madison's analysis was far too optimistic, however. The Constitution did indeed afford enormous scope for special interests to influence government. The great challenge for Madison's generation would be maintaining a government that provided equal benefits to all but special privileges to none.

CHRONOLOGY

1776   British troops evacuate Boston.
British defeat American forces under George Washington in fighting around New York City.
American victory in Battle of Trenton.

1777   American victory in Battle of Princeton.
British surrender at Saratoga.
Battle of Brandywine Creek; British occupy Philadelphia.
Congress approves Articles of Confederation.

1778	France formally recognizes the United States. France declares war on Britain. Philadelphia evacuated by British; Battle of Monmouth Court House (New Jersey). British occupy Savannah. Joseph Brant leads Iroquois attacks in western Pennsylvania and New York.	1783	Peace of Paris.

1778   France formally recognizes the United States.
France declares war on Britain.
Philadelphia evacuated by British; Battle of Monmouth Court House (New Jersey).
British occupy Savannah.
Joseph Brant leads Iroquois attacks in western Pennsylvania and New York.

1779   Spain declares war on Britain.
George Rogers Clark's recapture of Vincennes.
John Sullivan leads U.S. raids on Iroquois.
Judith Murray, "On the Equality of the Sexes" (published in 1790).

1780   British seize Charles Town.
Dutch Republic declares war on Britain.

1781   Articles of Confederation become law.
Battle of Yorktown; British general Charles Cornwallis surrenders.

1782   Paris peace negotiations begin.

1783   Peace of Paris.

1784   Spain closes New Orleans to American trade.

1785   Ordinance of 1785.

1786   Congress rejects Jay-Gardoqui Treaty.
Joseph Brant organizes Indian resistance to U.S. expansion.
Virginia adopts Thomas Jefferson's Statute for Religious Freedom.

1786–   Shays's Rebellion in Massachusetts.
1787

1787   Northwest Ordinance.
Philadelphia Convention; federal Constitution signed.

1788   Alexander Hamilton, James Madison, and John Jay, *The Federalist*.
Federal Constitution becomes law.

FOR FURTHER READING

Edward Countryman, *The American Revolution* (1985). An excellent introduction to developments from the Revolution through ratification of the Constitution.

Jack P. Greene, ed., *The American Revolution: Its Character and Limits* (1987). Leading scholars' analysis of how Americans dealt with the problem of applying their political ideals to an imperfect society without endangering the nation's survival.

Robert Middlekauff, *The Glorious Cause: The American Revolution, 1763–1789* (1982). A comprehensive account of military and political developments through the Philadelphia Convention.

Mary Beth Norton, *Liberty's Daughters: The Revolutionary Experience of American Women, 1750–1800* (1980). A wide-ranging study of changes in the lives and roles of women during the revolutionary era.

Benjamin Quarles, *The Negro in the American Revolution* (1961). An authoritative study of blacks' role in the Revolution and its consequences for them.

Charles Royster, *A Revolutionary People at War: The Continental Army and American Character* (1980). An illuminating analysis of how revolutionary Americans created and fought in an army.

Gordon Wood, *The Creation of the American Republic, 1776–1787* (1969). Comprehensive treatment of the evolution of American political thought from the first state governments to the Philadelphia Convention.

7

Launching the New Republic, 1789–1800

The Fragile New Nation

Constitutional Government Takes Shape

National Economic Policy and
Its Consequences

The United States in a Hostile World

Battling for the Nation's Soul

Deferring Equality

The Fragile New Nation

The postwar years brought problems, not prosperity, to many Americans. Restrictions on export markets and the Confederation's default on the national debt brought financial hardships. Conflicting regional interests and clashes with Native Americans on the frontier made the state of the new nation still more precarious.

The West and the South

Most U.S. territory from the Appalachians to the Mississippi River belonged to Native Americans. Divided into more than eighty tribes numbering perhaps 150,000 people in 1789, Indians struggled to preserve their way of life. During the Revolutionary War patriot forces had dealt the Iroquois and Cherokees punishing blows, but most Indians, though bloodied, had continued to hold their land.

Confronting the inland Indians were about 200,000 frontier settlers, many of them isolated and vulnerable. By 1786 Indian war parties had spread death, destruction, and panic from Pennsylvania to Georgia. Fifteen hundred of Kentucky's 74,000 settlers were captured or killed in Indian raids from 1784 to 1790, a casualty rate twice that of the Revolutionary War.

Massive military force—enough to raze Indian villages, destroy food supplies, and threaten starvation—represented the key to whites' conquering the Indians. The situation clearly called for federal forces. But in 1789 the U.S. Army's total strength stood at 672 soldiers, less than one-half the number of warriors in the northwestern Indian confederation. Despairing frontier settlers concluded that the United States had forfeited their loyalty.

Nevertheless, militia raids gradually forced Miamis, Shawnees, and Delawares to evacuate southern Indiana and Ohio. In spring 1788 fifty New Englanders sailed down the Ohio in a bullet-proof barge christened the *Mayflower* to found the town of Marietta. Later that year Pennsylvanians and New Jerseyites established Cincinnati.

Westerners felt a special bitterness toward the British, whose continued occupation of seven northwestern forts seemed the mainspring of the endless border fighting. British complaints about American failure to compensate the loyalists were a fig leaf for slowing U.S. expansion until Britain could establish an Indian buffer state south of the Great Lakes and annex the region to Canada.

Spain, unable to prevent American settlers' occupation of land it claimed in the Southeast, sought their allegiance by offering citizenship—and bribes. Most westerners who accepted the gold doled out by Spanish officials meant only to pocket badly needed cash in return for vague promises of goodwill.

Meanwhile, southerners watched with concern as Anglo-American fortunes in the West deteriorated. Many southern citizens had acquired a stake in trans-Appalachian affairs when Virginia and North Carolina had awarded revolutionary soldiers with western land. Many planters (including George Washington) hoped to make a quick fortune in land speculation. They had borrowed heavily to buy frontier land, but uncertainty about the West's future endangered their investments. By 1789 a potent combination of small farmers and landed gentry in the South were enraged at foreign barriers to expansion.

Regional Economies

The failure of tobacco and rice to regain their prewar export levels intensified the frustrations of southern planter-speculators. In 1770 the South had produced two-thirds of the mainland colonies' exports; by 1790 this portion had shrunk to less than half. Southerners' attempts to diversify their crops had had little effect.

In the mid-Atlantic region New York and Pennsylvania benefited from a steady demand for foodstuffs and quickly recovered from the Revolution's ravages.

New England enjoyed less fortune. A short growing season and poor soil kept farm yields low. Farmers barely produced enough grain for local consumption. New Englanders faced both high taxes to repay Revolutionary debts and tightened credit that spawned countless lawsuits against debtors. And economic depression only aggravated the region's chronic overpopulation. Moreover, British restrictions on West Indian trade hit New England hard.

Entrepreneurs, Artisans, and Wage Earners

After 1783, however, ambitious businessmen reduced northern dependence on farming by investing their profits in factories, ships, government bonds, and banks. Convinced that American strength required a balancing of agriculture with banking, manufacturing, and commerce, they sought to limit U.S. dependence on British manufacturers.

These entrepreneurs' innovative business ventures pointed toward the future. In the 1780s the country's first private banks appeared in Philadelphia, Boston, and New York. In 1787 Philadelphia merchants created the Pennsylvania Society for the Encouragement of Manufactures and the Useful Arts. Among the English artisans whom the society encouraged to bring their knowledge of industrial technology across the Atlantic was Samuel Slater, who helped to establish an early cotton mill in Rhode Island in 1793 (see Chapter 9). In 1791 New York and Philadelphia investors founded the Society for the Encouragement of Useful Manufactures, and New York merchants organized America's first association for trading government bonds, which evolved into the New York Stock Exchange.

Yet in 1789 northeastern cities lacked large factories. Half the work force consisted of "mechanics," or master artisans and journeymen, who produced handmade goods. Mechanics lived in close-knit neighborhoods and drank, marched, and "mobbed" together. Facing stiff competition from British manufacturers using laborsaving machinery and cheap unskilled labor, they supported a national tariff to raise the price of imported goods and wanted a strong, assertive national government.

In 1789 virtually all politically conscious Americans—urban mechanics and frontier settlers, nationalists and Antifederalists, northerners and southerners—expressed their hopes for the nation's future in terms of republican ideals. These lofty goals of selfless service had helped leaders to rally public resistance to the British since the 1760s. Republican ideology had shaped Antifederalist doctrines as well as state constitutions and the new federal Constitution.

Constitutional Government Takes Shape

The First Congress began assembling in the new national capital, New York, in March 1789. The new leaders had to reach decisions on critical questions that the Constitution's framers had left unresolved, including the extent of the president's powers, the organization of the federal courts, and the rights of citizens.

Defining the Presidency

No office in the new government aroused more suspicion than the presidency. Many feared that the president's powers could make him a king. The 1789 election of George Washington as president checked public apprehension, and Washington himself tried to calm fears of unlimited executive power.

The Constitution mentioned the executive departments of the federal government only in passing, required Senate approval of presidential nominees to head these bureaus, and made all executive personnel liable to being impeached or to being charged with wrongdoing in office. Otherwise, Congress was free to establish the organization and accountability of what became known as the cabinet. The first cabinet consisted of four departments, headed by the secretaries of state, treasury, and war and by the attorney general. A proposal to forbid the president's dismissal of cabinet officers without Senate approval was defeated. This outcome reinforced presidential authority; it also separated executive and legislative powers beyond what the Constitution required and made the president a more equal partner of Congress.

To reassure the public that he was above favoritism and conflicts of interest, Washington balanced his cabinet with southerners and northeasterners. When Secretary of State Thomas Jefferson opposed policies of Secretary of the Treasury Alexander Hamilton, Washington implored Jefferson not to resign, even though the president supported Hamilton.

"He is polite with dignity, affable without familiarity, distant without haughtiness, grave without austerity, modest, wise, and good." So Abigail Adams, the wife of Vice President John Adams, described Washington. The nation's first president genuinely sought to understand the hopes of the two groups that dominated American society—southern planters and northeastern merchants and entrepreneurs. Like most republican leaders, he believed that the proper role for ordinary citizens was not to set policy through elections but to choose well-educated men to make laws in the people's best interest, independently of direct popular influence.

National Justice and the Bill of Rights

The Constitution authorized Congress to establish federal courts below the level of the Supreme Court but provided no plan for their structure. The absence of a comprehensive bill of rights, moreover, had led several delegates at Philadelphia to refuse to sign the Constitution and had been a major Antifederalist point of attack. The task of dealing with these gaps fell to Congress.

In 1789 many citizens feared that the new federal courts would ride roughshod over local customs. However, the Judiciary Act of 1789, which created the federal court system, quieted popular apprehensions by establishing in each state a federal district court that operated according to local procedures. As the Constitution stipulated, the Supreme Court exercised final jurisdiction. Congress's compromise respected state traditions while offering wide access to federal justice.

Behind the movement for a bill of rights lay Americans' long-standing fear that a strong central government would lead to tyranny. Antifederalists saw strong state governments as the best safeguard against this. From the House of Representatives, James Madison battled to preserve a powerful national government. He played the leading role in drafting the ten amendments that became known as the Bill of Rights when ratified in December 1791.

Madison insisted that the first eight amendments guarantee personal liberties, not strip the national government of authority. The First Amendment safeguarded the most fundamental freedoms of expression—religion, speech, press, and political activity. The Second Amendment ensured that each state could form its own militia. Like the Third Amendment, it sought to protect citizens from what Americans saw as the most sinister embodiment of tyranny: standing armies. The Fourth through the Eighth Amendments limited the police powers of the states by guaranteeing fair treatment in legal and judicial proceedings. The Ninth and Tenth Amendments reserved to the people or to the states powers not allocated to the federal government, but Madison headed off proposals to limit federal power more explicitly.

National Economic Policy and Its Consequences

With Washington absorbed in diplomacy and military affairs, Secretary of the Treasury Alexander Hamilton emerged as the country's most dynamic statesman. Undaunted by debt and financial disorder, he put forward a sweeping program for national economic development.

Hamilton and His Policies

Hamilton's financial policies had two goals: to strengthen the nation against foreign enemies and to lessen the threat of disunion. The possibility of war with Britain, Spain, or both presented the most immediate danger. To finance a war, the Republic would have to borrow, but because Congress under the Articles had failed to redeem or pay interest on the Revolutionary debt, the nation had little credit.

Hamilton feared that the Union might disintegrate because he believed that Americans tended to think first of local loyalties. To him, the

Constitution represented a close victory of national over state authority. Now he worried that the states might reassert power over the new government. If they succeeded, he doubted whether the nation could prevent ruinous trade discrimination between states, deter foreign aggression, and avoid civil war.

His view of human nature and his service in the Continental Army shaped Hamilton's political beliefs. He shared the conviction of many nationalists that the vast majority of the Republic's population would never display the degree of self-sacrifice that he had shown. Hamilton concluded that the federal government's survival depended on building support among influential citizens through a direct appeal to their financial interests. Private ambitions would then serve the national welfare.

Charming and brilliant, vain and handsome, a notorious womanizer, thirsty for fame and power, Hamilton exemplified the worldly citizens whose fortunes he hoped to link to the Republic's future. To his opponents, however, Hamilton embodied the dark forces luring the Republic to doom—a man who, Jefferson wrote, believed in "the necessity of either force or corruption to govern men."

Report on the Public Credit

In 1789 Congress directed the Treasury Department to evaluate the Revolutionary debt. Hamilton seized the opportunity to devise policies to strengthen the nation's credit, enable it to defer paying its debt, and entice the upper class to place its prestige and capital at the nation's service. In January 1790 Congress received his Report on the Public Credit.

Hamilton recommended that the federal government "fund" the national debt by raising $54 million in new securities to honor the Revolutionary debt. The report proposed that the federal government use the same means to pay off state debts remaining from the Revolution.

A deeper motive lay behind Hamilton's argument that the failure of some states to honor their obligations would undermine American credit overseas. Hamilton saw the federal assumption of state debts as a chance for the national government to win the gratitude and loyalty of state creditors.

Hamilton exhorted the government to use the money earned by selling federal lands in the West to pay off the $12 million owed to Europeans as soon as possible, but he suggested that the remaining $42 million owed to Americans be made a permanent debt, with annual interest payments made to the holders of the bonds.

Hamilton believed such a debt would tie the economic fortunes of the nation's creditors to the government. In an age of notoriously risky investments, the federal government would protect the savings of wealthy bond holders through conservative policies. The guarantee of future interest payments would link the interests of the moneyed class to those of the nation.

Hamilton's proposals provoked controversy. Many members of Congress objected that those least deserving reward would gain the most. The original owners of more than 60 percent of the debt certificates issued by the Continental Congress had long since sold at a loss, often out of dire necessity. Wealthy speculators, anticipating Hamilton's intentions, had snapped up large holdings at the expense of the original owners and would reap huge gains.

To Hamilton's surprise, James Madison became a chief opponent of reimbursing current holders at face value. Sensing disapproval of the plan in Virginia, Madison tried but failed to obtain compensation for original owners who had sold their certificates.

Opposition to assuming the state debts also ran high, especially in the South. But Hamilton saved his proposal by exploiting Virginians' desire to relocate the national capital in their region. They hoped that moving the capital would keep Virginia the nation's largest, most influential state. Essentially, Hamilton traded the votes necessary to locate the capital along the Potomac for enough votes to win his battle for assumption.

Enactment of the Report on the Public Credit rescued the nation's fiscal standing. By 1792 some U.S. bonds sold at 10 percent above face value.

Reports on the Bank and Manufactures

In December 1790 Hamilton presented Congress with his Report on a National Bank. Having restored full faith in greatly undervalued certificates, Hamilton had in effect expanded the capital available for investment. Now he intended to direct that money toward projects to diversify the national economy through a federally chartered bank.

The proposed bank would raise $10 million through a public stock offering. Fully four-fifths of the control of the bank would fall to private hands. Private investors could purchase shares by paying for three-quarters of their value in government bonds. In this way the bank would capture a substantial portion of the recently funded debt and make it available for loans; it would also receive steady interest payments from the Treasury.

Hamilton argued that the Bank of the United States would cost taxpayers nothing and greatly benefit the nation. It would provide a safe place for federal deposits, make inexpensive loans to the government when taxes fell short, and relieve the scarcity of hard cash by issuing paper notes. Further, the bank would regulate the business of state banks and, above all, provide much-needed credit for economic expansion.

Hamilton also called for American economic self-sufficiency. An admirer of the way that factory expansion had stimulated British wealth, he wanted to encourage industrialization in the United States. His Report on Manufactures of December 1791 advocated protective tariffs on imports to foster domestic manufacturing, which would in turn attract immigrants and create national wealth.

Hamilton's Challenge to Limited Government

To many, Hamilton's plan to establish a permanent national debt violated the principle of equality among citizens by favoring the interests of public creditors. Some detractors also denounced the national bank as a dangerous scheme that gave a small elite leverage over the government.

The bank controversy drew Thomas Jefferson into the ranks of Hamilton's opponents. To Jefferson, the bank represented "a machine for the corruption of the legislature [Congress]."

Constitutional issues presented the bank's opponents with their strongest argument. The Constitution did not authorize Congress to issue charters of incorporation. Unless Congress adhered to a "strict interpretation" of the Constitution, critics argued, the central government might oppress the states and trample individual liberties.

Congress approved the bank by only a thin margin. Dubious about its constitutionality, Washington consulted Hamilton, who urged him to sign the bill. Because Article I, Section 8, of the Constitution specified that Congress could enact all measures "necessary and proper," Hamilton contended that the only unconstitutional activities were those *forbidden* to the national government. Washington accepted this "loose interpretation" of the Constitution, and in February 1791 the Bank of the United States obtained a twenty-year charter.

Hamilton's proposal to use protective tariffs to encourage industry met with strong opposition from Jefferson and Madison. Such protection, they thought, constituted an unfair subsidy promoting uncompetitive industries. The beneficiaries would be individuals shielded from overseas competition and the institutions, such as the bank, that lent them money.

Congress ultimately refused to approve a high protective tariff. Hamilton nevertheless succeeded in setting higher duties on goods brought in by non-American than by American ships.

Hamilton's Legacy

Hamilton built a political base by appealing to people's economic self-interest. His "rescue" of the national credit provided enormous gains for speculators, merchants, and others who by 1790 possessed most of the Revolutionary debt. Moreover, federal assumption of state debts liberated taxpayers from crushing burdens in New England, New Jersey, and South Carolina, while Hamilton's promotion of industry, commerce, and shipping won favor with the Northeast's budding entrepreneurs and hard-pressed artisans.

Supporters of Hamilton's policies called themselves Federalists in order to associate themselves with the Constitution. But they actually favored a centralized ("consolidated") national government,

not a truly federal system that left substantial power to the states.

Hamilton's economic program sowed dissension in areas where it provided little advantage. Southerners especially detested it. Southern states had generally paid off their Revolutionary debts, and few southerners still held Revolutionary certificates.

Hamilton's plan for commercial expansion and industrial development appeared similarly irrelevant to the West, where agriculture promised high profits once the right of export through New Orleans was guaranteed. Resentment of a supposedly national program that benefited eastern "moneyed men" and debt-ridden Yankees gradually united westerners, southerners, and many people in the mid-Atlantic into a political coalition. Challenging the Federalists for control of the government, these opponents called for a return to true republicanism.

The Whiskey Rebellion

Hamilton's program helped to ignite a civil insurrection called the Whiskey Rebellion, the young Republic's first serious crisis.

To augment national revenue, Hamilton had proposed an excise tax on domestically produced whiskey. Western Pennsylvanians found the new tax especially burdensome. Unable to ship their crops to world markets through New Orleans, most local farmers were distilling their rye or corn into alcohol, which could be carried across the Appalachians at a fraction of the price charged for bulky grain. Hamilton's excise tax, equal to 25 percent of whiskey's retail value, would wipe out frontier farmers' profit. And because the law specified that federal courts would try all cases of alleged tax evasion, any western Pennsylvanian indicted for noncompliance would have to travel 300 or so miles to Philadelphia to face a jury of unsympathetic easterners.

In a scene reminiscent of colonial protests against Britain, large-scale resistance erupted in July 1794. One hundred men attacked a U.S. marshal serving delinquent taxpayers with summonses to appear in court in Philadelphia. A crowd of 500 burned the chief revenue officer's house following a shootout with federal soldiers. Roving bands torched buildings, assaulted tax collectors, and raised a flag symbolizing an independent country that they hoped to create from six western counties.

The frontier turmoil alarmed the Washington administration. Washington concluded that a federal failure to respond strongly would encourage outbreaks in other frontier areas where lax enforcement had allowed distillers to escape paying taxes. The president accordingly summoned 12,900 militiamen to march west under his command, but opposition evaporated once the troops reached the Appalachians. Of 150 suspects later seized, 20 were sent in irons to Philadelphia.

The Whiskey Rebellion was a milestone in determining the limits of public opposition to federal policies. In the early 1790s many Americans assumed that it was still legitimate to protest unpopular laws by using the methods that they had employed against British policies. By firmly suppressing the first major challenge to national authority, President Washington served notice that citizens could change the law only through constitutional procedures.

The United States in a Hostile World

The United States faced a particularly hostile international environment in the 1790s. European powers restricted American trade, supported Indian trouble along the frontier, strengthened and expanded their North American empires, and maintained garrisons on U.S. soil.

Foreign Powers and Native Americans in the West

Spain held much territory in North America, but its rivals were formidable—Russia and Britain on the Pacific coast and the United States and Britain in the Mississippi Valley. To counter these twin threats, Spain flung colonists and missionaries northward

along the California coast from San Diego to Sonoma (north of San Francisco). Meanwhile, Spain strengthened its position in the southwest by making peace with the Comanches, the Navajos, and most of the Apache nations that threatened its settlements.

Revitalized by these western successes, Spain joined Britain and Native Americans as a formidable barrier to U.S. aims in the Mississippi Valley. In the 1790s the Spanish bribed many well-known political figures in Tennessee and Kentucky, including James Wilkinson, one of Washington's former generals.

President Washington tried to keep tight control of foreign policy. Recognizing that the complex western problems would not easily yield, he pursued patient diplomacy to "preserve the country in peace if I can, and to be prepared for war if I cannot." The prospect of peace improved in 1789 when Spain unexpectedly opened New Orleans to U.S. commerce.

Washington then moved to weaken Spanish influence in the West by neutralizing Spain's most important ally, the Creek Indians. Under terms of the 1790 Treaty of New York, American settlers could occupy the Georgia piedmont but not other Creek territory. Washington insisted that Georgia restore to the Chickasaws and Choctaws, Creek allies, a vast area along the Mississippi River that Georgia had already begun selling off to land speculators.

Hoping to conclude a similar agreement with Britain's Indian allies, the United States sent an envoy to the Great Lakes tribes. The Miamis responded by burning a captured American to death. Two military campaigns, in 1790 and 1791, failed to force peace and cost the United States 1,100 men.

The Washington administration tried to pacify the Indians through a benevolent policy. It formally recognized Indian title as secure and inalienable except by the "free consent" of the Indians themselves. To reinforce this policy, Congress passed laws to prohibit trespassing on Indian lands, to punish crimes committed there by non-Indians, to outlaw alcohol, and to regulate trade.

However, the United States continued to pressure Indians to sell their lands and to move farther west. Washington's frontier policy became a wreck. Not only had two military expeditions suffered de-

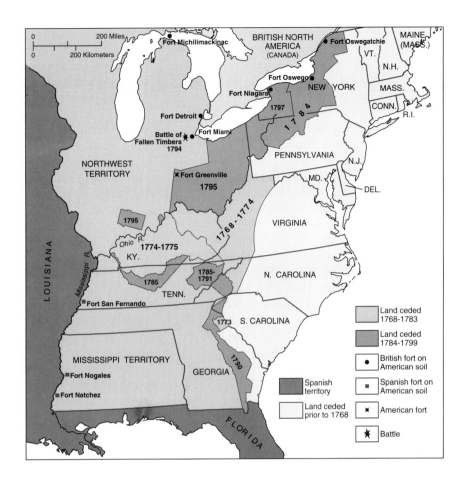

Indian Land Cessions, 1768–1799

Between 1768 and 1775 western Indians sold off vast territories, mostly hunting grounds in mountainous regions. The upheavals of the Revolutionary War, followed by conflicts with U.S. military forces from 1784 to 1799, led to large cessions of inhabited Indian lands.

feat in the Northwest, but in 1792 the Spanish had persuaded the Creeks to renounce their treaty with the federal government and to resume hostilities.

France and Factional Politics

One of the most momentous events in history, the French Revolution, began in 1789. Americans watched sympathetically as the French abolished nobles' privileges, wrote a constitution, and repelled invading armies. In 1793, after becoming a republic, France proclaimed a war of all peoples against all kings and assumed that the United States would eagerly enlist.

Enthusiasm for a pro-French foreign policy burned brightest in the South and along the frontier.

A slave uprising in France's Caribbean colony of Saint Domingue (later renamed Haiti), in which Britain became involved, aroused passionate anti-British sentiment in the South. White southerners grew alarmed for slavery's future and their own lives as terrified French planters fled to the United States from Saint Domingue with vivid accounts of how British invaders in 1793 had supported the rebellious slaves.

After 1790 economics led to sharp differences between northern and southern reactions to the French Revolution. Growing antagonism toward France among northern merchants reflected their basic conservatism and their awareness that their prosperity depended on good relations with Britain.

Southerners had no such reasons to favor Britain. They perceived American reliance on British commerce as a menace to national self-determination and wished to divert most U.S. trade to France.

After declaring war with Spain and Britain in 1793, France sought to enlist the United States in the war and to strengthen the treaty of alliance between the two nations. France dispatched Edmond Genet as minister to the United States with orders to recruit American mercenaries to conquer Spanish territories and to attack British shipping. Much to France's disgust, President Washington issued a proclamation of neutrality on April 22, 1793.

Meanwhile, Citizen Genet found numerous southern volunteers for his American Foreign Legion despite official U.S. neutrality. Genet also outfitted privateers, whose crews were paid from captured plunder. By summer 1793 nearly 1,000 Americans were at sea in a dozen ships flying the French flag. These privateers seized over eighty British ships.

The British Crisis

Although Washington swiftly closed the nation's harbors to Genet's buccaneers, the episode provoked an Anglo-American crisis. Britain decided that only a massive show of force would deter U.S. aggression. On November 6, 1793, Britain's Privy Council issued orders confiscating foreign ships trading with the French islands in the Caribbean. The Royal Navy seized more than twenty-five American ships, a high price for Genet's mischief making.

Meanwhile, the U.S. merchant marine suffered another indignity—the drafting of its crewmen into the Royal Navy. Thousands of British sailors had fled to U.S. ships looking for an easier life than the tough, poorly paying British system. In late 1793 British naval officers began inspecting American crews for British subjects, whom they then impressed (forcibly enlisted) as the king's sailors. Impressment struck a raw nerve in most Americans.

Next the British challenged the United States for control of the West. In February 1794 at an Indian council, Canada's governor denied U.S. claims north of the Ohio River and urged his listeners to destroy every white settlement in the North-

west. Britain soon erected Fort Miami near Toledo, Ohio.

Hoping to halt the drift toward war, Washington launched a desperate diplomatic initiative, sending Chief Justice John Jay to Great Britain and Thomas Pinckney to Spain. The president also authorized General Anthony Wayne to negotiate a treaty with the Indians of the Ohio Valley.

The Indians scoffed at Washington's peace offer until "Mad Anthony" Wayne led 3,000 regulars and militiamen deep into their homeland, ravaging every village in reach. On August 20, 1794, Wayne's troops routed 2,000 Indians at the Battle of Fallen Timbers, two miles from Britain's Fort Miami. In August 1795 twelve northeastern tribes signed the Treaty of Greenville, which opened most of Ohio to white settlement.

Wayne's success allowed John Jay a major diplomatic victory in London: a British promise to withdraw troops from American soil. Jay also gained American access to West Indian markets, but only by bargaining away U.S. rights to load cargoes of sugar, molasses, and coffee from the Caribbean.

Jay's Treaty left Britain free not only to violate American neutrality but also to restrict U.S. trade with French ports during wartime. Moreover, Jay did not succeed in ending impressment. In 1795 the Federalist-dominated Senate ratified the unpopular treaty by just one vote.

Jay's Treaty probably represented the most that a weak, politically divided United States could extract from Britain. It defused an explosive crisis, ended British occupation of U.S. territory, and provided for arbitration to settle both American and British claims for compensation. Jay's Treaty also stimulated American trade as British governors in the West Indies used the treaty's ratification as an excuse to open their harbors to U.S. ships.

On the heels of Jay's Treaty came an unqualified diplomatic triumph engineered by Thomas Pinckney. Ratified in 1796, the Treaty of San Lorenzo (also called Pinckney's Treaty) with Spain gave westerners unrestricted, duty-free access to world markets via the Mississippi River.

By 1796 the Washington administration had defended U.S. territorial integrity, restored peace to the frontier, opened the Mississippi for western exports, reopened British markets to U.S. shipping, and kept the nation out of a European war.

Battling for the Nation's Soul

After 1796 the U.S. political scene was the site of a battle over the future of representative government. The election of 1800 would determine whether the political elite could accommodate demands from ordinary citizens for more influence in determining policy. No issue was more hotly argued than that of officeholders' accountability to their constituents.

Ideological Confrontation

The French Revolution led many Americans to reassess their political values. The Revolution's radical turn in 1793–1794, which sent thousands to the guillotine, polarized public opinion, generally along regional lines.

Conservative and religiously oriented, New Englanders detested the French government's disregard for civil rights and its adoration of reason over the worship of God. Middle Atlantic businessmen, less religious but no less conservative, condemned French leaders as evil radicals who incited the poor against the rich.

Federalists trembled at the thought of "mob rule" in the nation's future. They took alarm when artisans in New York and Philadelphia bandied the French revolutionary slogan "Liberty, Equality, Fraternity" and exalted pro-French political leaders such as Jefferson. Citizen Genet's recruitment of hundreds of Americans to fight for France reinforced their fears.

By the mid-1790s Federalist leaders had concluded that it was dangerous to involve the public deeply in politics. The people were undependable, too easy a prey for rabble-rousers like Genet. They argued that citizens need not be presented with policy choices during elections. Thus Federalists favored a representative government in which elected officials would rule in the people's name, independently of direct popular influence.

Federalist measures alienated many Americans, including Jefferson and Madison, who held a different view of republican ideology. Antifederalist sentiment ran high in the South, where republican ideology stressed the corruption inherent in a powerful government dominated by a few highly visible men. Southern Republicans insisted that only the distribution of power among virtuous, independent citizens would protect liberty. Further, many southern planters had absorbed Enlightenment ideals, and they saw the French as fellow republicans, carrying on a revolution for liberty, equality, and brotherhood. With their own labor force consisting of enslaved blacks, not free wage workers, southern elites did not fear popular participation in politics.

Self-interest also drove Jefferson, Madison, and like-minded Americans to rouse ordinary citizens' concerns about civic affairs. If the public held elected officials accountable, Federalists would think twice before enacting measures opposed by the majority; or if they persisted in advocating such policies, they would be removed from office.

In October 1791 organized efforts to turn public opinion against the Federalists began with the publication of the *National Gazette*. Then in 1793–1794 popular dissatisfaction with government policies led to the formation of several dozen Democratic (or Republican) societies. Their membership ranged from planters and merchants to artisans and sailors.

Federalists interpreted the societies' emotional appeals to ordinary people as demagoguery and denounced their followers as "democrats, mobocrats, & all other kinds of rats." They feared that the societies would become revolutionary organizations.

The Republican Party

Neither Jefferson nor Madison belonged to a Democratic society. However, the clubs' criticism of the administration galvanized into political activity many who would later support Jefferson and Madison's Republican party.

In 1794 party development reached a decisive stage. Shortly after Washington aligned himself with Federalist policies, supporters of Jefferson who had begun to call themselves Republicans won a slight majority in the House of Representatives. The election signaled their transformation into a broad-based party, the Republican party, capable of coordinating national political campaigns.

Federalists and Republicans alike used the press to mold public opinion. American journalism came of age in the 1790s as the number of newspapers multiplied from 92 to 242. By 1800 newspapers had perhaps 140,000 subscribers (about one-fifth of eligible voters), and their secondhand readership probably exceeded 300,000. Newspapers of both camps, libelous and irresponsible, cheapened public discussion through constant fear mongering and character assassination. Yet newspaper warfare stimulated citizens to become politically active.

Underlying the inflammatory rhetoric was the Republican charge that the Federalists were bent on enriching the wealthy at taxpayers' expense. Although wrong in claiming that opponents wanted to introduce aristocracy and monarchy, the Republicans correctly identified the Federalists' fundamental assumption: that citizens' worth could be measured in terms of their money.

Accusations that he secretly supported a plot to establish a monarchy enraged Washington. He was alarmed by the furor over Jay's Treaty and dreaded the nation's polarization into hostile factions. Stung by Republican abuse, he decided in 1796 to retire after two terms and called on Hamilton to give a sharp political twist to a farewell address.

In the farewell message Washington vigorously condemned political 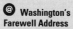 **Washington's Farewell Address** parties. Partisan alignments, he insisted, endangered the republic's survival, especially if they became entangled in foreign policy disputes. Aside from fulfilling existing treaty obligations and maintaining foreign commerce, the United States had to avoid "political connection" with Europe and its wars. Washington evoked a vision of a United States virtuously isolated from foreign intrigue and power politics, an ideal that would remain a potent inspiration until the twentieth century.

Washington left the presidency in 1797 amid a barrage of criticism. The nation's political division into Republicans and Federalists meanwhile hard-

ened. Each party consolidated its hold over particular states and groups of voters, leaving the electorate almost equally divided.

The Election of 1796

As the election of 1796 approached, the Republicans cultivated a large, loyal body of voters, the first time since the Revolution that the political elite effectively mobilized ordinary Americans.

Immigrants became a prime target for Republican recruiters. During the 1790s the United States absorbed 20,000 French refugees from Saint Domingue and 60,000 Irish.

In 1796 the presidential candidates were Vice President John Adams, whom the Federalists supported, and the Republicans' Jefferson. Republican strength in the South offset Federalist strength in New England, leaving Pennsylvania and New York as crucial "swing" states where the Irish vote might tip the scales. In the end Jefferson carried Pennsylvania but not New York and lost the presidency by three electoral votes. The Federalists kept control of Congress. But Jefferson became vice president under the constitutional provision (soon changed by the Twelfth Amendment) that the candidate receiving the highest number of electoral votes would become president and the candidate amassing the next-highest number would become vice president.

President Adams was a paradoxical figure. His brilliance, insight, and idealism have seldom been equaled among American presidents. He was more comfortable, however, with ideas than with people, more theoretical than practical, and rather inflexible. As Benjamin Franklin observed, Adams was "always an honest man, often a wise one, but sometimes, and in some things, absolutely out of his senses." He was utterly unsuited to unify the country.

The French Crisis

To Adams's initial good fortune, French provocations produced a sharp anti-Republican backlash. France interpreted Jay's Treaty as an American attempt to assist the British in their war against

France. Learning of Jefferson's defeat, the French ordered the seizure of American ships; within a year they had plundered more than 300 U.S. vessels.

Seeking to avoid war, Adams dispatched a peace commission to France. The French foreign minister, Charles de Talleyrand, refused to meet with the Americans, instead promising through three unnamed agents ("X, Y, and Z") that talks could begin after he received $250,000 and France obtained a $12 million loan. This barefaced demand for a bribe became known as the XYZ Affair. Outraged Americans adopted the battle cry "Millions for defense, not one cent for tribute."

The XYZ Affair discredited Republican foreign policy views. The party's leaders compounded the damage by refusing to condemn French aggression and opposing Adams's call for defensive measures. Federalists rode a wave of patriotism to an enormous victory in the 1798 congressional elections.

Congress responded to the XYZ Affair by arming fifty-four ships to protect U.S. commerce. The new warships joined what became known as the Quasi-War—an undeclared Franco-American naval conflict in the Caribbean from 1798 to 1800, during which U.S. forces seized ninety-three French privateers at the loss of just one ship.

Despite Adams's misgivings, the Federalist Congress tripled the regular army to 10,000 men in 1798. The risk of a land war with France was minimal. What Federalists actually wanted was a strong military force ready in case of a civil war, for the crisis had produced near-hysterical fears that French and Irish malcontents were hatching treasonous conspiracies.

The Alien and Sedition Acts

The Federalists insisted that the possibility of war with France demanded stringent legislation to protect national security. In 1798 the Federalist Congress accordingly passed four measures known collectively as the Alien and Sedition Acts.

The least controversial of the four laws, the Alien Enemies Act, was designed to prevent wartime espionage or sabotage. It outlined procedures for determining whether a hostile country's citizens, when staying in America, posed a threat to the United States; if so, they would be deported or jailed.

The second of the laws, the Alien Friends Act, enforceable in peacetime until June 25, 1800, authorized the president to expel foreign residents whose activities he considered dangerous. It required no proof of guilt. Republicans maintained that the law's real purpose was to deport immigrants critical of Federalist policies. Republicans also denounced the third law, the Naturalization Act. This measure increased the residency requirement for U.S. citizenship from five to fourteen years to reduce Irish voting.

Finally came the Sedition Act, the only one of these measures enforceable against U.S. citizens. Although its alleged purpose was to distinguish between free speech and attempts to encourage a revolution, the act defined criminal activity so broadly that it blurred distinctions between sedition and legitimate political discussion. Thus it forbade an individual or a group "to oppose any measure or measures of the United States"—wording that could be interpreted to ban any criticism of the party in power. Another clause made it illegal to speak, write, or print any statement that would bring the president "into contempt or disrepute."

The real target of all this Federalist repression was the opposition press. Four of the five largest Republican newspapers were charged with sedition just as the election of 1800 was getting under way. The attorney general used the Alien Friends Act to drive the Irish journalist John Daly Burk underground. After failing to deport Scottish editor Thomas Callender, an all-Federalist jury sent him to prison for criticizing the president. Federalist leaders intended that a small number of highly visible prosecutions would intimidate journalists and candidates into silence during the election.

Shocked Republicans realized that with the Federalists in control of all three branches of government, neither the Bill of Rights nor the system of checks and balances protected individual liberties. In this context the doctrine of states' rights was advanced as a way to prevent the national government from violating freedoms.

James Madison and Thomas Jefferson anonymously wrote two manifestos on states' rights that the assemblies of Virginia and Kentucky endorsed in 1798. Madison's Virginia Resolutions and Jefferson's Kentucky Resolutions proclaimed that state legislatures retained both their right to judge the constitutionality of federal actions and an authority called interposition, which enabled them to protect the liberties of their citizens. A set of Kentucky Resolutions adopted in November 1799 added that states could "nullify" objectionable federal laws.

The Election of 1800

In 1800 the Republicans rallied around Thomas Jefferson for president and New York politician Aaron Burr for vice president. The Federalists became mired in wrangling between Adams and the "High Federalists" who looked to Hamilton for guidance. That the nation survived the election of 1800 without a civil war owed much to the good sense of moderates in both parties.

High Federalists called for war on France and were outraged when Adams responded to overtures for peace in 1799. Adams's negotiations with France did not achieve a settlement until 1801, but the expectation of normal relations prevented Federalists from exploiting charges of Republican sympathy for the enemy. With the immediate threat of war removed, voters grew resentful that in just two years taxes had soared 33 percent to support an army that had done virtually nothing.

Two years after triumphing in the 1798 elections, Federalists found their support badly eroded. Republicans successfully mobilized voters in Philadelphia and New York who were ready to forsake the Federalists. Voter turnouts more than doubled those of 1788.

Adams lost the presidency by just eight electoral votes, but Jefferson's election was not assured. Because all seventy-three Republican electors voted for both their party's nominees, the electoral college deadlocked in a Jefferson-Burr tie. The election went to the House of Representatives, where, after thirty-five ballots, Jefferson won the presidency by history's narrowest margin.

Deferring Equality

After 1800 government policies would be judged by Jefferson's standard of "equal rights for all, special privileges for none." Yet Native Americans had no redress when their lands were trespassed, and African-Americans were denied basic rights and held in bondage.

Indians in the New Republic

By 1795 most eastern Indian tribes had suffered severe reductions in population and territory, owing to battle, famine, and disease. Settlers crowded Indians onto reservations (often illegally), liquor dealers and criminals trespassed on Indian lands, and government agents and missionaries pressured Indians to abandon their lands and cultures.

Demoralized and unable to strike back, Indians often consumed enormous amounts of whiskey and became violent. A social and moral crisis gripped tribes threatened by whites' expansion.

Beginning in 1799 a Seneca prophet, Handsome Lake, led his people in a creative effort to resolve the crisis. He tried to end alcoholism among Indians by appealing to their religious traditions. He welcomed Quaker missionaries and federal aid earmarked for teaching Euro-American agricultural methods to Iroquois men in search of new livelihoods after the collapse of the fur trade and the loss of most of their lands.

Redefining the Color Line

The Republic's first years marked the high tide of African-Americans' Revolutionary-era success in bettering their lot. Although racism persisted, Jefferson's eloquent words "all men are created equal" awakened many white consciences. In 1790, 8 percent of African-Americans enjoyed freedom. By 1800, 11 percent were free. Most states had outlawed the Atlantic slave trade by 1794.

Hesitant measures to ensure free blacks' legal equality appeared in the 1780s and early 1790s. Most states dropped restrictions on their freedom of movement, protected their property, and allowed them to enroll in the militia. All but three states either permitted free blacks to vote or made no specific attempts to exclude them. But before the 1790s ended, the trend toward lessening the social and legal distances between the races ended. Abolitionist sentiment ebbed, slavery became more entrenched, and whites demonstrated reluctance to accept free blacks as fellow citizens.

Federal law led the way in restricting the rights of African-Americans. An especially revealing symptom of changing attitudes occurred in 1793 when Congress passed the Fugitive Slave Law. The law required judges to award possession of a runaway slave on a formal request by a master or his representative. Accused runaways were denied jury trials and sometimes were refused permission to present evidence. Slaves' legal status as property disqualified them from claiming these constitutional privileges, but the Fugitive Slave Law denied even *free* blacks the legal protections guaranteed to them under the Bill of Rights. White Americans clearly found it easy to forget that the Constitution had not limited citizenship to their race.

The bloody slave revolt on Saint Domingue undermined the trend toward abolition, reinforced the kind of fears that spawned racism, and helped to transform the image of blacks from that of victims of injustice to one of potential menaces. In August 1800 a planned insurrection of more than 1,000 slaves in Richmond, Virginia, kindled smoldering white fears. The militia put down the conspiracy and executed 35 slaves, including the leader, Gabriel Prosser.

Isolated uprisings occurred in the United States for years after "Gabriel's Rebellion," and rumors persisted that a massive revolt was brewing. Antislavery sentiment diminished rapidly. The antislavery movement would not recover from the damage inflicted by the Saint Domingue revolt until the early 1830s.

Another development would strengthen slavery. In the 1790s demand in the British textile industry stimulated the cultivation of cotton in coastal South Carolina and Georgia. Here the soil and climate were ideal for growing long-staple cotton, whose fibers could be separated easily from its seed. In the South's upland and interior regions, however, only short-staple cotton thrived. Its seed clung tenaciously to the fibers and defied cleaning. It was as if southerners had discovered gold but could not mine it. In 1793 a Connecticut Yankee, Eli Whitney, rescued the South by inventing a cotton gin that efficiently cleaned short-staple cotton. Improved by others, Whitney's machine removed a major obstacle to cotton cultivation, gave plantation slavery a new lease on life, and undermined the doubts of those who considered slavery economically outmoded. Thus by the time Thomas Jefferson became president in 1801, free blacks had suffered a subtle erosion of their political gains, and slaves stood no closer to freedom.

CHRONOLOGY

1789 First Congress convenes in New York.
George Washington sworn in as first president.
Judiciary Act of 1789.
French Revolution begins.

1790 Alexander Hamilton submits his Report on the Public Credit and Report on a National Bank to Congress.

1791 Bank of the United States is granted a twenty-year charter.
Bill of Rights ratified.
Slave uprising begins in French colony of Saint Domingue.
Hamilton submits his Report on Manufactures to Congress.

1792   Washington reelected president.

1793   Fugitive Slave Law.
Large-scale exodus of French planters from Saint Domingue to the United States.
Washington's Neutrality Proclamation.
Citizen Genet arrives in United States.
Democratic societies established.

1794   Whiskey Rebellion.

1795   Treaty of Greenville.
Jay's Treaty with Britain ratified.

1796   Treaty of San Lorenzo (Pinckney's Treaty) ratified.
Washington's Farewell Address.
John Adams elected president.

1798   XYZ Affair.
Alien and Sedition Acts.

1798–   Virginia and Kentucky Resolutions.
1799

1798–   United States fights Quasi-War with France.
1800

1800   Gabriel's Rebellion in Virginia.
Thomas Jefferson elected president.

FOR FURTHER READING

Joyce Appleby, *Capitalism and a New Social Order: The Republican Vision of the 1790s* (1984). A brief, penetrating analysis of Jeffersonian ideology.

Stanley Elkins and Eric McKitrick, *The Age of Federalism: The Early American Republic, 1788–1800* (1993). A magisterial account of politics and diplomacy through the decisive election of 1800.

Richard Hofstadter, *The Idea of a Party System: The Rise of Legitimate Opposition in the United States, 1780–1840* (1969). A classic account of how and why America's founders, originally fearing political parties, came to embrace them.

Drew R. McCoy, *The Elusive Republic: Political Economy in Jeffersonian America* (1980). An insightful portrayal of the influence of economic considerations on early national political thought.

James M. Smith, *Freedom's Fetters: The Alien and Sedition Laws and American Civil Liberties*, rev. ed. (1966). The most comprehensive study of the country's first great crisis in civil rights.

Laurel Thatcher Ulrich, *A Midwife's Tale: The Life of Martha Ballard, Based on Her Diary, 1785–1812* (1990). A Pulitzer Prize–winning study of a woman's life in rural America.

Anthony F. C. Wallace, *The Death and Rebirth of the Seneca* (1969). An anthropologist's masterful account of the Senecas' devastation during the Revolution and their remarkable cultural recovery afterward.

Jeffersonianism and the Era of Good Feelings

responsive to popular will. Popular liberty required popular virtue, he believed, virtue being the disposition to place public good above private interest and to exercise vigilance in keeping government under control. To Jefferson, the most virtuous people were educated farmers, accustomed to acting and thinking with sturdy independence. Least vigilant were the inhabitants of cities, which he saw as breeding grounds for mobs and as menaces to liberty.

The Age of Jefferson

To admirers, Jefferson was an aristocrat who trusted the people and defended popular liberty; to detractors, he was an infidel and a radical. Jefferson had so many facets that misunderstanding him was easy. Trained in law, he had spent much of his life in public service—as governor of Virginia, Washington's secretary of state, Adams's vice president. He designed his own neoclassical mansion, Monticello; studied the violin and numerous languages (including several Native American tongues); and served twenty years as president of the American Philosophical Society, America's oldest and most important scientific organization. Although he saw himself as a humanitarian, he owned more than 200 slaves.

To prevent the United States from sinking into tyranny, Jefferson advocated that state governments retain great authority because they were immediately

Jefferson's "Revolution"

Jefferson described his election as a revolution, but the revolution he sought was to restore the liberty and tranquillity that (he thought) the United States had enjoyed in its earliest years and to reverse what he saw as a drift into despotism. The $10 million growth in the national debt under the Federalists alarmed Jefferson and his secretary of the treasury, Albert Gallatin. They rejected Alexander Hamilton's argument that debt strengthened the government by giving creditors a stake in its health.

Jefferson and Gallatin asked Congress to repeal most internal taxes, and they slashed expenditures by closing some embassies and reducing the army. The navy was a different matter because of the Barbary pirates. For centuries rulers in North Africa (the "Barbary Coast") had tried to solve their own budget problems by engaging in piracy and demanding ransom for captured seamen. Jefferson refused to meet their demands for tribute: he calculated that war would be cheaper than giving in to such bribery. In 1801 he dispatched a naval squadron to the Barbary Coast. After the navy had bombarded several ports and the marines had landed at Tripoli, in 1805 the United States concluded a peace treaty with the Barbary rulers. The military solution had cost less than half the annual bribe!

Jefferson and the Judiciary

In his first inaugural address Jefferson reminded Americans that their agreements were more basic than their disagreements. "We have called by different name brothers of the same principle," he said. "We are all republicans; we are all federalists."

In theory, both Jefferson and the Federalists believed that talent and virtue, not political affiliation, were the primary qualifications for judgeships. In practice, Federalists had found neither talent nor virtue among Republicans, and in 1800 not a single Republican sat on the federal bench. For Republicans, the crowning blow was the Federalist-sponsored Judiciary Act, passed in February 1801. Ostensibly nonpartisan, the act created sixteen new federal judgeships to relieve Supreme Court justices of circuit-riding responsibilities but reduced the number of justices from six to five. This latter provision threatened to strip Jefferson of his first opportunity to appoint a justice—and threatened also to perpetuate Federalist domination of the judiciary.

The act confirmed Jefferson's fears that the Federalists would use the judiciary as a stronghold from which "all the works of Republicanism are to be beaten down and erased." Outgoing president John Adams strengthened Jefferson's suspicions when he made last-minute "midnight appointments" installing Federalists in the new positions.

Although Jefferson rejected the radical view that judges should be elected rather than appointed, the Federalists seemed bent on turning the judiciary into an arm of their party. Ironically, an unfinished "midnight appointment" prompted Jefferson to seek repeal of the Judiciary Act of 1801. On his last day in office, Adams appointed William Marbury justice of the peace in the District of Columbia but failed to deliver Marbury's commission. When Jefferson's secretary of state, James Madison, refused to release the commission, Marbury petitioned the Supreme Court for a writ of mandamus* ordering Madison to make the delivery. Chief Justice Marshall then called on Madison to show cause why he should not be compelled to deliver the commission.

Chief Justice John Marshall was a Virginian, but his service in the Revolution had instilled in him a burning attachment to the Union rather than to any state. In 1803 Marshall's long-awaited decision in *Marbury* v. *Madison* came down. It would be immensely important in the evolution of the Constitution, for in this decision Marshall declared an act of Congress unconstitutional for the first time in American history. He denied Marbury's petition for a writ of mandamus to force Madison to deliver the commission on the grounds that when Congress had granted the Court authority to issue such a writ in 1789, it had exceeded its constitutional authority. By overturning an act of Congress, the justices set an important precedent and solidified the role of the Court as a third, coequal branch of the federal government.

President Jefferson, like most Republicans, believed that the Court possessed the right of judicial review (the right to declare acts of Congress unconstitutional), but he did not believe that the Supreme Court alone had the power of judicial review. Instead, he believed that all branches of the government had the right to decide the constitutionality of measures before them.

Even before the Court handed down *Marbury*, Republicans had taken the offensive against the Federalist judiciary by moving to impeach two Federalist judges. One of them, John Pickering of the New Hampshire District Court, was an insane alcoholic given to bizarre behavior in court. The other, Samuel Chase of the Supreme Court, was a notoriously partisan Federalist, the devil incarnate to Republicans.

Although the details clearly differed, the two cases raised the same issue. Under the Constitution, impeachment was the only way to remove federal

---

*Mandamus: an order from a higher court commanding that a specified action be taken.

judges, but it could be considered only in cases of "Treason, Bribery and other high Crimes and Misdemeanors." Was impeachment an appropriate way to get rid of mad or partisan judges? On March 12, 1804, the Senate convicted Pickering, despite some senators' misgivings. Although the House voted to indict Chase that same day, John Randolph, a Jefferson supporter, botched the prosecution so badly that he failed to obtain the two-thirds majority necessary to convict.

Chase's acquittal ended Jefferson's skirmishes with the judiciary. Unlike his radical followers, Jefferson objected neither to judicial review nor to an appointed judiciary; he merely challenged Federalist use of judicial power for political goals. Yet there was always a gray area between law and politics. To Federalists, there was no conflict between protecting the Constitution and advancing their party's cause. Nor did Federalists use their domination of the courts to undo Jefferson's "revolution" of 1800; the Marshall court, for example, upheld the constitutionality of the repeal of the Judiciary Act of 1801. In turn, Jefferson never proposed impeaching Marshall.

The Louisiana Purchase

Jefferson's goal of avoiding foreign entanglements would remain beyond reach as long as European powers held large territories in North America. In the Treaty of San Ildefonso (1800), a weakened Spain had returned the vast Louisiana Territory to France, which, under Napoleon Bonaparte, was emerging as Europe's strongest military power. Jefferson was appalled.

The president had long imagined that the inevitable expansion of a free and virtuous American people would create an "empire of liberty." Spain was no obstacle, but Napoleonic France posed a real danger; Bonaparte's capacity for mischief was boundless, and American fears were great.

Bonaparte dreamed of re-creating a French New World empire bordering the Caribbean and the Gulf of Mexico. The island of Santo Domingo (modern Haiti and the Dominican Republic) would be the fulcrum of the empire and Louisiana its breadbasket. Before this dream could become reality, however, the French would have to subdue Santo Domingo, where a bloody slave rebellion had led to the creation of a

government under the black statesman Toussaint L'Ouverture. Napoleon accordingly dispatched an army to reassert French control and to reestablish slavery, but yellow fever and fierce resistance by the former slaves doomed the French forces.

As a slaveholder, Jefferson tacitly approved Napoleon's attempted reconquest of Santo Domingo; as a nationalist, he continued to fear the French presence in Louisiana. This fear turned to alarm when the Spanish colonial administrator in New Orleans prohibited the deposit of American produce in that city for transshipment to foreign lands. Because American farmers west of the Appalachians depended on access to the sea via New Orleans, the Spanish order was a major provocation. Most Americans assumed (wrongly) that the order had come from Napoleon, who had not yet taken formal possession of Louisiana.

The combination of France's failure to subdue Santo Domingo and the termination of the American right of deposit at New Orleans led to the American purchase of Louisiana. First, Jefferson nominated James Monroe and Robert R. Livingston to negotiate with France for the purchase of New Orleans and as much of the Floridas as possible. Meanwhile, Napoleon had concluded that his Caribbean empire was not worth the cost. In addition, he planned to resume war in Europe and needed cash—so he decided to sell *all* of Louisiana. The American commissioners and the French government settled on a price of $15 million. Thus the United States bought this immense, uncharted territory. No one knew its exact size, but the Louisiana Purchase virtually doubled the area of the United States.

The Lewis and Clark Expedition

Louisiana dazzled Jefferson's imagination. Americans knew virtually nothing about the immense territory, not even its western boundary.

Jefferson had long planned an exploratory expedition to Louisiana. He had chosen Lieutenant Meriwether Lewis, his personal secretary, as commander and had sent him to Philadelphia for a crash course in zoology, astronomy, and botany.

> @ **Jefferson Seeks Funding for Exploration of Louisiana**

> @ **The President's Instructions to Meriwether Lewis**

The Louisiana Purchase and the Exploration of the West   *The explorations of Lewis and Clark demonstrated the vast extent of the area purchased from France.*

Lewis was to trace the Missouri River to its source, cross the western highlands, and follow the best water route to the Pacific. Although Jefferson stressed commercial possibilities in requesting congressional funding for the expedition, he probably cared more about advancing scientific knowledge. His instructions to Lewis focused on obtaining accurate measurements of latitude and longitude, gathering information about Native American languages and customs, and studying climate, volcanoes, and plant and animal life.

Leaving St. Louis in May 1804, Lewis; his second-in-command, William Clark; and about fifty others followed the Missouri and then the Snake and Columbia Rivers. After reaching the Pacific in November 1805, the expedition returned to St. Louis. The explorers had collected vast amounts of scientific information, including the disturbing fact that more than 300 miles of mountains separated the Missouri from the Columbia.

@ **Animated Map of the Lewis & Clark Expedition**

@ **President's Instruction to Meriwether Lewis**

The Election of 1804

The main threat to Jefferson's reelection in 1804 was not the Federalists, who were dispirited and lacked a popular national issue, but Aaron Burr, his own vice president, who had tried to take advantage of a tie in the electoral college to gain the presidency in 1800. The Republicans dispensed with the threat by unceremoniously dumping him from the ticket in 1804 in favor of George Clinton. In the election the Federalist nominees, Charles C. Pinckney and Rufus King, carried only two states. Jefferson's overwhelming victory brought his first term to a fitting close; between 1801 and 1804 the United States had doubled its territory, started to pay off its debt, and remained at peace. President Jefferson basked in the sun of success.

@ Jefferson Campaign Poster

The Gathering Storm

But the sky was not cloudless for long. The renewed Napoleonic Wars between 1803 and 1814 turned the United States into a pawn in a foreign chess game. Internal squabbling weakened the Republicans, making Jefferson's second term far less successful than his first.

Jefferson's Coalition Fragments

The election of 1804 temporarily eliminated the Federalists as a force in national politics. Intraparty factionalism, however, provided trouble enough for the Republicans. Aaron Burr, dropped from the 1804 ticket, began to intrigue with a faction of extreme, or High, Federalists who were scheming to form a "Northern Confederacy" that would include Nova Scotia, New England, New York, and Pennsylvania. To advance their plot, the Federalists helped Burr to gain the Federalist nomination for governor of New York. Alexander Hamilton, who had thwarted Burr's grab for the presidency in 1800 by supporting Jefferson, now foiled Burr a second time by making known his "despicable opinion" of Burr. After his defeat in the New York election, Burr challenged Hamilton to a duel and mortally wounded him at Weehawken, New Jersey, on July 11, 1804.

Indicted in two states for murdering Hamilton, Burr next hatched a scheme so audacious that not even his opponents could believe that he was capable of such treachery. Burr allied himself with General James Wilkinson, the military governor of the Louisiana Territory, who had been taking Spanish money since the 1780s. Their plot had several dimensions: they would create an independent confederacy of western states, conquer Mexico, and invade West Florida. The scheming duo presented the plot imaginatively. To westerners, they said that it had the covert support of the Jefferson administration; to the British, that it was a way to attack Spanish lands; and to the Spanish, that it would open the way to dividing up the United States.

In fall 1806 Burr and some sixty followers made their way down the Ohio and Mississippi Rivers to join Wilkinson at Natchez. Wilkinson was not there. Recognizing that Jefferson was ready to move against Burr and that the British were not interested in supporting the plot, Wilkinson had double-crossed Burr, reporting the conspiracy in a letter to Jefferson.

In October 1806 Jefferson denounced the conspiracy. Burr panicked and tried to flee, but was captured and returned to Richmond to stand trial for treason. Chief Justice John Marshall presided and advised the jury that the prosecution had to prove actual treasonable acts—an impossible task because the conspiracy had never reached fruition. The jury returned a "not proved" verdict, which Marshall entered as "not guilty."

The Suppression of American Trade

Foreign affairs posed even sharper challenges to the second Jefferson administration. As Britain and France resumed their war, the United States prospered at Britain's expense by carrying sugar and coffee from French and Spanish Caribbean colonies to Europe.

American prosperity rested on the reexport trade, which created conflicts with Britain. According to the British Rule of 1756, any trade closed during peacetime could not be opened during war. For example, France usually restricted the sugar trade to French ships during peacetime and thus could not open it to American ships during war. The U.S. response to the Rule of 1756 was the "broken voyage," by which U.S. ships would carry French sugar or coffee to American ports, unload it, pass it through customs, and then reexport it as *American* produce. Britain tolerated this dodge for nearly a decade but in 1805 initiated a policy of total war toward France, including the strangulation of French trade. In the *Essex* case (1805), a British court declared broken voyages illegal.

Next came a series of British trade decrees ("Orders in Council"), through which Britain intended to blockade part of continental Europe and thus staunch the flow of any products that might aid the French war effort. French counterdecrees, proclaiming the British Isles blockaded, followed. In effect, if Americans obeyed the British regulations, they would violate the French rules, and vice versa. In total war, however, there was no room for neutrality, so both Britain and France seized U.S. ships.

Impressment

To these provocations the British added impressment. At issue was Britain's seizing purported Royal Navy deserters from American merchant ships and subsequently forcing them back into service. Discipline on the Royal Navy's "floating hells" was often brutal, and the pay low; sailors on American ships earned up to five times more than those on British ships. Consequently, at a time when war raised the demand for sailors, the Royal Navy suffered a high rate of desertion to American ships.

Impressment was galling to American pride, for even though many deserters had become U.S. citizens, the British impressed them anyway. The British also impressed U.S.-born seamen, including those who could prove their American birth; between 1803 and 1812, 6,000 Americans were impressed.

The *Chesapeake* incident heightened British-American tensions. In June 1807 a British warship,

HMS *Leopard*, attacked an American frigate, the USS *Chesapeake*, just off Virginia. The British boarded the vessel and seized four supposed deserters. One, an actual deserter, was later hanged; the other three, former Britons, had "deserted" only from impressment and were now U.S. citizens. Public outrage mounted; Jefferson claimed that he had not seen so belligerent a spirit in America since 1775. Yet while making some preparations for a possible war, Jefferson sought peace, first by engaging in fruitless negotiations with Britain to gain redress for the *Chesapeake* and then by steering the Embargo Act through Congress in December 1807.

The Embargo Act

By far the most controversial legislation of Jefferson's presidency, the Embargo Act prohibited vessels from leaving American harbors for foreign ports. Technically, it prohibited only exports, but it stopped imports as well, for few foreign ships would enter American ports if they had to leave empty.

Jefferson defended the embargo as "peaceable coercion," a way of forcing France and, especially, Britain to respect American neutrality. But it did not work. Although British trade with the United States plummeted, the British opened new markets in South America. France's Napoleon, for his part, treated the act as a joke, seizing American ships and then informing the United States that he was only helping to enforce the embargo.

The United States itself felt the harshest effects. Thirty thousand seamen lost their jobs, hundreds of merchants went bankrupt, and debtors swelled the jail population. Unable to export produce or to sell it at a decent price in the cities, farmers suffered as well. New England's hardships were greatest; in Massachusetts, which accounted for a third of foreign trade, the embargo was a calamity.

Yet there were benefits. Unable to export goods, merchants used their capital to begin manufacturing. In 1808 the United States had only fifteen cotton textile mills; by the end of 1809 eighty-seven more had been built. But merchants already ruined or seamen driven to soup kitchens took little comfort. Nor could New Englanders forget that the source of their misery was one of the "Virginia lordlings," "Mad Tom" Jefferson, who knew little about New England and loathed cities, the foundation of the region's prosperity.

The Election of 1808

With Jefferson's blessing, the Republicans nominated James Madison and George Clinton for the presidency and vice-presidency in 1808. The Federalists renominated Charles C. Pinckney and Rufus King, the same ticket that had failed in 1804. In 1808 the Federalists staged a modest comeback, but Madison handily won the presidency, and the Republicans continued to control Congress.

The Failure of Peaceable Coercion

To some contemporaries, "Little Jemmy" Madison, five feet four inches tall, seemed a weak, shadowy figure compared to Jefferson. In fact, Madison's intelligence and capacity for systematic thought equaled Jefferson's. Like Jefferson, Madison believed that American liberty rested on the virtue of the people and that virtue was critically tied to the growth and prosperity of agriculture. Madison also recognized that agricultural prosperity depended on trade—farmers needed markets. The British West Indies, dependent on the United States for much lumber and grain, struck Madison as both a natural trading partner and a tempting target. By embargoing its own trade with the Indies, Madison reasoned, the United States could force Britain to its knees before Americans would suffer severe losses.

The U.S. embargo, however, was coercing no one. Increased trade between Canada and the West Indies ruined Madison's plan to pressure Britain. On March 1, 1809, Congress replaced the Embargo Act with the weaker, face-saving Non-Intercourse Act, which opened U.S. trade to all nations except Britain and France and authorized the president to restore trade if those nations stopped violating neutral rights. But neither nation complied. Meanwhile, U.S. shippers kept up their profitable trade with the British and French, despite the restrictions. In May 1810 Congress substituted a new measure, Macon's Bill No. 2, for the Non-Intercourse Act. This legislation reopened trade with both belligerents, France and Britain, and then offered a clumsy and unsuccessful bribe to each: if either nation repealed its restrictions on neutral shipping, the United States would halt all trade with the other.

Madison now faced not only a hostile Britain and France but also militant Republicans demanding more aggressive policies. Primarily southerners and westerners, the militants were infuriated by insults to the American flag. The election of 1810 brought several young militants, christened "war hawks," to Congress. Led by Henry Clay of Kentucky, who preferred war to the "putrescent pool of ignominious peace," the war hawks included John C. Calhoun of South Carolina, Richard M. Johnson of Kentucky, and William R. King of North Carolina—all future vice presidents. Clay was elected Speaker of the House.

Tecumseh and the Prophet

Pugnaciously nationalistic, the war hawks called for expelling Britain from Canada and Spain from the Floridas. Their demands merged with westerners' fears that the British in Canada were recruiting Indians to halt U.S. settlement. These fears, groundless but plausible, intensified when the Shawnee Indian chief Tecumseh and his half-brother, the Prophet, tried to unite several Ohio and Indiana tribes against westward-moving settlers. Demoralized by the continuing loss of land and by alcoholism's ravages on Native American society, Tecumseh and the Prophet (a recovered alcoholic) tried to unite their people and to revive traditional values.

The Shawnee leaders were on a collision course with the governor of the Indiana Territory, William Henry Harrison. In the Treaty of Fort Wayne (1809), Harrison had purchased much of central and western Indiana from the Miami and the Delaware tribes for a paltry $10,000. After Tecumseh's Shawnees refused to sign the treaty, Harrison saw the charismatic leader as an enemy and even as a British cat's-paw. Accordingly, in September 1811 Harrison led an army against a Shawnee encampment at the junction of the Wabash and Tippecanoe Rivers. Two months later when the Prophet prematurely attacked Harrison (Tecumseh was away recruiting Creek Indians), Harrison won a decisive victory. Ironically, the Battle of Tippecanoe, which made Harrison a national hero, accomplished what it had been designed to prevent: it prompted Tecumseh to join with the British.

Congress Votes for War

By spring 1812 President Madison had concluded that war with Britain was inevitable, and he sent a war message to Congress on June 1. Ironically, an economic slump prompted Britain to repeal its Orders in Council on June 23, but by then Congress had declared war.

The war hawks constituted a Senate minority, so the key to the declaration of war was the support of Republicans from populous states such as Pennsylvania, Virginia, and Maryland. Southern Federalists joined their northern counterparts in opposition to the war, while northern Republicans supported it. In short, the vote for war followed party, rather than sectional, lines.

Madison, in his war message, listed impressment, the presence of British ships in U.S. waters, and British violation of neutral rights as wrongs that justified war. None of these complaints fully explains why America declared war in 1812. Neither do continuing Indian problems (blamed on the British) along the frontier. A more important underlying cause for the war was the economic recession that affected the South and West after 1808. Finally, the fact that Madison, rather than Jefferson, was president was vitally important. Unlike Jefferson, who thought that once the war in Europe ended, the provocations would stop, Madison held that Britain's real motive was to strangle American trade and thus to eliminate the United States as a trading rival.

The War of 1812

Although Americans unfurled the slogan "Free Trade and Sailors' Rights" in summer 1812, they marched, rather than sailed, to war; Canada, not the Royal Navy, was the principal target. Madison considered Canada a key prop of the British Empire and a main component of the British plan to strangle American trade. Moreover, an attack on Canada was also more practical. Republican emphasis on economy had shrunk both the national debt—from $83 million to $27.5 million—and the navy, which was down to six frigates, three sloops, and a number of smaller vessels.

Canada seemed an easy target. The United States was much more populous than its northern neighbor and had vastly larger armies and militias. Further, the British army was occupied with Napoleon, and 60 percent of Canadians were Americans by birth, lured north by cheap land. To Jefferson, the conquest of Canada seemed "a mere matter of marching." Yet he failed to reckon on the strength of Britain's Native American allies and the lack of discipline among the American state militias.

On to Canada

The American offensive opened in the West, largely for political reasons. In July 1812 the sixty-year-old general William Hull led an American army from Detroit into Canada, but Tecumseh cut his supply lines. Unnerved, Hull retreated to Detroit. The British commander played on Hull's fears by warning that he might not be able to control the Indians, and Hull promptly surrendered 2,000 men to 1,300 British and Native American troops.

In two other thrusts in 1812, the United States fared no better. A mixed force of regulars and New York militia was ordered into Canada north of Niagara Falls, but the militia refused to leave the state and watched as the British crushed the American regulars at the Battle of Queenston (October 13, 1812). In November General Henry Dearborn, en route to Montreal, had marched twenty miles north of Plattsburgh, New York, when the militia refused to advance. Dearborn retreated to Plattsburgh.

Renewed U.S. offensives and subsequent reverses in 1813 convinced the Americans that they could not retake Detroit while the British controlled Lake Erie. During winter 1812–1813 U.S. captain Oliver

Hazard Perry constructed a little fleet out of green wood and outfitted it with captured cannon and supplies dragged across the snow from Pittsburgh to his headquarters at Presqu'ile (Erie). On September 10, 1813, the homemade American fleet destroyed a British squadron at Put-in-Bay on the western end of Lake Erie; "we have met the enemy, and they are ours," Perry triumphantly reported. The British then pulled out of Detroit, but American forces under General William Henry Harrison overtook and defeated a combined British-Indian force at the Battle of the Thames on October 5. Tecumseh, a legend among whites, died in the battle.

The Naval War

The American navy, although small, boasted three of the largest, fastest frigates afloat—the *Constitution*, the *United States*, and the *President*. In 1812 the *Constitution* destroyed two British warships, HMS *Guerrière* in the mid-Atlantic and HMS *Java* off Brazil, but these victories had no military significance. By 1814 superior British naval strength had clamped a blockade along the American coast and trapped the frigates in harbor.

The British Offensive

Britain's military fortunes crested in spring 1814. Defeated in Europe, Napoleon abdicated in April, and Britain began moving regulars from Europe to North America.

Britain's main offensive thrust was meant to split the New England states, which were skeptical of the war, from the rest of the country. General Sir George Prevost headed a force of 10,000 British veterans, the largest and best-equipped British force ever sent to North America. They advanced readily down Lake Champlain until reaching the entrenched American forces at Plattsburgh; after his fleet met defeat on September 11, Prevost abandoned the campaign.

Ironically, Britain's most spectacular success began as a diversion from Prevost's offensive. A British army that had come up from Bermuda entered Chesapeake Bay and on August 24, 1814, met a larger American force (mainly militiamen) at Bladensburg, Maryland. The Battle of Bladensburg deteriorated into the "Bladensburg Races" as the American troops fled, virtually without firing a shot. The British then descended on Washington, D.C. Madison fled into the Virginia hills. His wife, Dolley, loaded her silver, a bed, and a portrait of Washington onto her carriage before joining her husband. British troops ate the supper prepared for the Madisons and then burned the presidential mansion and other public buildings in the capital. Beyond embarrassing and angering Americans, the Washington raid accomplished little, for after a failed attack on Baltimore, the British broke off the operation.

The Treaty of Ghent

English and American commissioners began peace negotiations at Ghent, Belgium, in August 1814. Napoleon's abdication had made Britain's primary goal a lasting European peace, and thus the British had little to gain by prolonging a minor war in America. The treaty, signed on Christmas Eve, 1814, restored the *status quo ante bellum*:* the United States neither gained nor lost territory. The fixing of the Canadian-American border was referred to a joint commission for future settlement. Impressment was left hanging, but the end of the European war made neutral rights a dead issue.

Ironically, America's most dramatic victory came on January 8, 1815, two weeks after the treaty had been signed but before word of it had reached America. A British force had descended on New Orleans. U.S. troops commanded by General Andrew ("Old Hickory") Jackson, legendary as a fierce Indian fighter, shredded the line of advancing redcoats, inflicting more than 2,000 casualties while suffering only 13 of their own.

The Hartford Convention

Although it meant nothing in terms of the war, the Battle of New Orleans proved devastating for the Federalist party. U.S. setbacks in the War of 1812

***Status quo ante bellum:* Latin for "the state of affairs before the war."

had allowed the Federalists to attack Madison and to denounce a decade of Republican misrule at New England's expense. The Louisiana Purchase, constitutionally dubious, had reduced the importance of New England, the Embargo Act had nearly destroyed the region's commerce, and "Mr. Madison's War" had brought fresh misery in the form of the British blockade. A few New England Federalists had begun to talk of secession from the Union.

In late 1814 a special Federalist convention met in Hartford, Connecticut. Although some supported secession, moderates took control and passed a series of resolutions expressing New England's grievances. Convinced that New England was becoming a permanent minority in a nation dominated by southern Republicans who failed to understand the region's commercial interests, the convention leaders proposed a series of constitutional amendments: to abolish the three-fifths clause, which allowed southerners to count slaves as a basis for representation; to require a two-thirds vote of Congress to declare war and to admit new states into the Union; and to prohibit the election of two successive presidents from the same state. These proposals were as bold as their timing was disastrous. News of the peace and of Jackson's victory at New Orleans dashed Federalist hopes of gaining popular support, while the states' rights emphasis of the convention smelled of treason to many delegates. In the presidential election of 1816, James Monroe, Madison's handpicked successor and another Virginia Republican, swept the nation over negligible Federalist opposition. Four years later he would receive every electoral vote but one. The Federalists were finished in national politics.

The Awakening of American Nationalism

The War of 1812 had three major political consequences. First, it eliminated the Federalists as a national political force. Second, it went far toward convincing the Republicans that the nation was strong and resilient, capable of fighting a war while maintaining liberty. Third, with political rivals removed, the Republicans began to embrace some Federalist ideas. Both President Madison and Henry Clay became advocates of federal support for internal improvements, tariff protection for new industries, and the creation of a new national bank; Clay christened these ideas the American System and proclaimed that they would make the nation economically self-sufficient. In 1816 Congress chartered the Second Bank of the United States and enacted a moderate tariff, but federally supported internal improvements were more difficult. Madison vetoed an internal improvements bill in 1817, believing that a constitutional amendment was necessary to authorize such improvements.

As Republicans adopted positions they once had disdained, an "Era of Good Feelings" dawned. Coined by a Boston newspaper editor, the term describes both of James Monroe's presidential administrations. Compared to Jefferson and Madison, Monroe was neither brilliant, polished, nor wealthy, but he wanted to heal America's political divisions, and he tried to avoid political controversies. Yet the good feelings were paper-thin. The embargo, the War of 1812, and the continuation of slavery had aroused sectional animosities that no phrase could paper over. Not surprisingly, the postwar consensus unraveled rapidly.

John Marshall and the Supreme Court

In 1819 Jefferson's old antagonist John Marshall, still chief justice, issued two opinions that stunned Republicans. The first case, *Dartmouth College* v. *Woodward*, focused on New Hampshire's attempt to transform a private corporation, Dartmouth College, into a state university. Marshall concluded that Dartmouth's original charter was a contract and thus was protected under the constitutional prohibition against state interference in contracts. Marshall's ruling had enormous implications. In effect, Marshall said that once a state had chartered a college or business, that state surrendered its power to alter the charter and, in large measure, its authority to regulate the beneficiary. Buttressed by Marshall's decision, businesses and colleges increasingly sought the legal privileges of a charter or an act of incorporation.

A few weeks later the chief justice handed down an even more momentous decision in *McCulloch v. Maryland*. At issue was whether the state of Maryland had the power to tax a national corporation, specifically the Baltimore branch of the Second Bank of the United States. Marshall focused on two issues. First, did Congress have the power to charter a national bank? The Constitution, Marshall conceded, did not explicitly grant this power, but the broad sweep of enumerated powers implied the power to charter a bank. This was a clear enunciation of a broad, or "loose," construction (interpretation) of the Constitution. The second issue revolved around whether a state could tax an agency of the federal government that was located within its borders. Marshall argued that any power of the national government was supreme within its sphere. States could not interfere with the exercise of federal power; thus Maryland's attempt to tax the bank was plainly unconstitutional.

Marshall's decision in *McCulloch* dismayed many Republicans. For one thing, it placed the unpopular bank beyond the regulatory power of any state government. Far more important, the *McCulloch* decision attacked state sovereignty. The Constitution, Marshall said, was the creation not of state governments but of the people of *all* the states and thus overrode state laws. Like Jefferson, most Republicans considered the Union a compact among states and saw state governments as the guarantors of popular liberty. In Republican eyes, the *Dartmouth* and *McCulloch* cases hobbled state governments and thus threatened liberty.

The Missouri Compromise

The fragility of the Era of Good Feelings again became apparent in a two-year-long controversy over the territory of Missouri. In February 1819 the House of Representatives considered a bill to admit Missouri as a slave state. A New York Republican, James Tallmadge Jr., offered an amendment that prohibited the further introduction of slaves into Missouri and provided for the emancipation, at age twenty-five, of all slave offspring born after Missouri joined the Union. Following rancorous debate, the House accepted the amendment and the Senate rejected it. Both chambers voted along sectional lines.

Sectional differences had long troubled American politics, but the issues had been primarily economic. The Missouri question now thrust slavery into the center of this long-standing sectional conflict. The matter of slavery surfaced at this time for a number of reasons. In 1819 the Union had eleven slave and eleven free states; the admission of Missouri as a slave state would upset this balance, to the South's advantage. Noting that every president since John Adams had been a Virginian, Federalists painted the admission of Missouri as part of a conspiracy to perpetuate the rule of Virginia slaveholders. Republicans, pointing to the sudden emergence in the House of Representatives of a vocal antislavery block, began to see all efforts to restrict slavery as a Federalist plot to regain power by dividing northern and southern Republicans. In sum, by 1819 the slavery issue had become intertwined with party and sectional rivalries.

Virtually every issue that would wrack the Union in the next forty years was present in the Missouri controversy: southern charges that the North was conspiring to destroy the Union and to end slavery; northern accusations that southerners were conspiring to extend slavery.

A series of congressional agreements known collectively as the Missouri Compromise resolved the crisis in 1820. To balance the number of slave states and free states, Congress admitted Maine as a free state and Missouri as a slave state; to forestall a further crisis, it also prohibited slavery in the remainder of the Louisiana Purchase north of 36°30', Missouri's southern border.

The Missouri Compromise was widely viewed as a southern victory. The South had gained admission of Missouri, whose acceptance of slavery was controversial, while the North had merely gained Maine, whose rejection of slavery sparked no controversy. However, the South had allowed slavery to be banned from a vast territory north of 36°30', an area that would not long remain a wilderness. The Missouri Compromise also reinforced the principle that Congress could prohibit slavery in some territories.

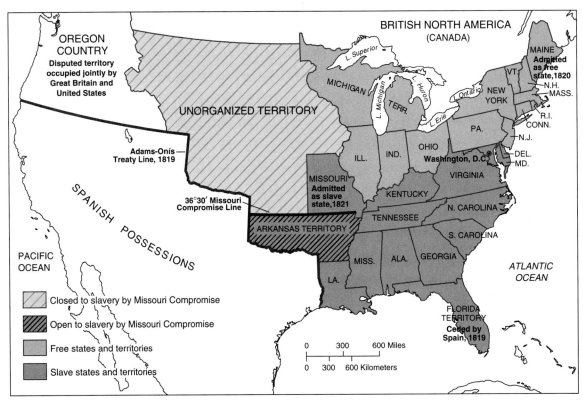

The Missouri Compromise, 1820–1821

The Missouri Compromise temporarily quelled controversy over slavery by admitting Maine as a free state and Missouri as a slave state and by prohibiting slavery in the remainder of the Louisiana Purchase north of 36°30'.

Foreign Policy Under Monroe

"Good feelings" also characterized American foreign policy from 1816 to 1824. The end of the War of 1812 and of the Napoleonic Wars had removed most Federalist-Republican disagreements over foreign policy. Moreover, President Monroe had as his secretary of state an extraordinary diplomat, John Quincy Adams, a tough negotiator and an ardent nationalist.

Adams moved quickly to strengthen the peace with Great Britain. During his term the Rush-Bagot Treaty of 1817 demilitarized the Great Lakes and the British-American Convention of 1818 fixed the Canadian-American boundary and restored U.S. fishing rights off Newfoundland.

Adams was equally successful with the Spanish, who still owned East Florida and claimed West Florida. It had never been clear whether the Louisiana Purchase included West Florida. Acting as if it did, the United States in 1812 had simply added a slice of West Florida to the state of Louisiana and another piece to the Mississippi Territory. Using the pretext that it was a base for Seminole Indian raids and a refuge for fugitive slaves, Andrew Jackson, now a military commander in the South, invaded West Florida in 1818 and captured Spanish forts. Although Jackson had acted without explicit orders, Adams supported the raid, guessing correctly that it would panic the Spanish into further concessions. In 1819 Spain agreed to the Adams-Onís (or Transcontinental) Treaty, ceding East Florida to the United States, renouncing all claims to West Florida, and agreeing to a border that ran north along the Sabine River (separating Spanish Texas from Louisiana), then west along the Red and Arkansas Rivers to the Rockies, and then along the forty-second parallel to the Pacific. Finally, the United States had a legitimate claim to the Pacific coast.

The Monroe Doctrine

Spain had even more pressing concerns in the New World than the fate of its North American territories. Anticolonial revolutions had erupted in South America, and the failing inperial power sought European aid in crushing the revolts. Britain's foreign minister, George Canning, now proposed a joint U.S.-British statement opposing European interference in South America and pledging that neither nation would annex any part of Spain's New World empire.

John Quincy Adams shared Canning's opposition to European intervention in the New World, but rejected his insistence on a joint Anglo-American pledge never to annex any of Spain's former territories. The U.S. secretary of state believed God and nature had ordained that the United States would eventually span the North American continent, and he wanted to keep open the possibility of annexing Texas or Cuba.

This was the background of the Monroe Doctrine, as President Monroe's message to Congress on December 2, 1823, became known. Largely written by Adams, the message announced three key principles: that U.S. policy was to avoid European wars unless American interests were involved, that the "American continents" were not "subjects for future colonization by any European power," and that the United States would construe any European attempt at colonization as an "unfriendly act."

Europeans widely derided the Monroe Doctrine as a unilateral pronouncement by a United States that could not enforce it. Fear of Britain's Royal Navy, not the Monroe Doctrine, prevented European intervention in South America. Nonetheless, the doctrine had two major implications. First, in pledging not to interfere in European wars, the United States in effect declined to support any future revolutionary movements in Europe. Second, by keeping open options to annex territory in the Americas itself, the United States was claiming for itself a preeminent position in the New World.

CHRONOLOGY

1800–1801	John Adams's midnight appointments.
1802	The repeal of the Judiciary Act of 1801. American right of deposit at New Orleans revoked.
1803	*Marbury* v. *Madison*. Conclusion of the Louisiana Purchase.
1804	Judge John Pickering convicted by the Senate. Impeachment of Justice Samuel Chase. Aaron Burr kills Alexander Hamilton in a duel. Jefferson elected to a second term.
1804–1806	Lewis and Clark expedition.
1805	Start of the Burr conspiracy. Chase acquitted by the Senate. *Essex* case.
1806	British government issues the first Order in Council.
1807	Burr acquitted of treason. *Chesapeake* affair. Embargo Act passed.
1808	James Madison elected president.
1809	Non-Intercourse Act passed; Embargo Act repealed.
1811	Battle of Tippecanoe.
1812	Orders in Council revoked. United States declares war on Britain. Madison reelected to a second term. General William Hull surrenders at Detroit. Battle of Queenston.
1813	Battle of Lake Erie (Put-in-Bay).

1814	Battle of Bladensburg.	**1818**	British-American Convention of 1818.
	British burn Washington, D.C.		Andrew Jackson invades West Florida.
	Battle of Plattsburgh.	**1819**	Adams-Onís (Transcontinental) Treaty.
	Hartford Convention.		*Dartmouth College v. Woodward.*
	Treaty of Ghent signed.		*McCulloch v. Maryland.*
1815	Battle of New Orleans.	**1820**	Monroe reelected to a second term.
1816	James Monroe elected president.	**1820–**	Missouri Compromise.
	Second Bank of the United States chartered.	**1821**	
1817	Rush-Bagot Treaty.	**1823**	Monroe Doctrine.

FOR FURTHER READING

Henry Adams, *History of the United States During the Administrations of Jefferson and Madison*, 9 vols. (1889–1891). A classic study by the great-grandson of John Adams.

Drew R. McCoy, *The Last of the Fathers: James Madison and the Republican Legacy* (1989). The best recent book on Madison.

Forrest McDonald, *The Presidency of Thomas Jefferson* (1976). A lively overview.

Dumas Malone, *Jefferson and His Time*, vols. 4 and 5 (1970, 1974). An extremely comprehensive biography.

Merrill Peterson, *Thomas Jefferson and the New Nation: A Biography* (1970). The best one-volume biography of Jefferson.

Marshall Smelser, *The Democratic Republic, 1801–1815* (1968). A thorough general work.

J. C. A. Stagg, *Mr. Madison's War: Politics, Diplomacy, and Warfare in the Early Republic* (1983). An important reinterpretation of the causes of the War of 1812.

G. Edward White, *The Marshall Court and Cultural Change, 1815–1835* (1991). A seminal reinterpretation of the Supreme Court under John Marshall.

9

The Transformation of American Society, 1815–1840

Westward Expansion and the Growth of the Market Economy

Buffeted by unforeseen social and economic forces, U.S. settlers moved westward in a series of waves. Americans leapfrogged the Appalachians after 1791 to bring four new states into the Union by 1803: Vermont, Kentucky, Tennessee, and Ohio. From 1816 to 1821 momentum carried settlers farther west, even across the Mississippi River, and six more states entered: Indiana, Mississippi, Illinois, Alabama, Maine, and Missouri. Ohio's population soared from 45,000 in 1800 to more than 1.5 million by 1840 and Michigan's from 5,000 in 1810 to 212,000 in 1840.

Exploration carried some Americans even farther west. Zebulon Pike explored the Spanish South-

west in 1806, sighting the Colorado peak later named after him. By 1811, in the wake of Lewis and Clark, the New York merchant John Jacob Astor had founded a fur-trading post at the mouth of the Columbia River in the Oregon Country. At first whites relied on Native Americans for furs, but in the 1820s such "mountain men" as Kit Carson and Jedediah Smith penetrated beyond the Rockies.

The mountain men, though celebrated, were not themselves typical westward migrants. For most pioneers, the West meant the area between the Appalachians and the Mississippi River, and their goal was stability, not adventure.

Western Society and Customs

Pioneers usually migrated in family groups. To reach markets with their produce, most settled along navigable rivers, particularly the great Ohio-Mississippi system. Not until the coming of canals and then railroads did westerners venture far from rivers. Settlers often clustered with people from the same eastern region; when New Englanders found southerners well entrenched in Indiana, they pushed on to Michigan.

These new westerners craved sociability. Men met for games that tested strength and agility: wrestling, lifting weights, pole jumping (for distance, not height), and hammer throwing. Women often combined work and play in quilting and sewing bees, carpet tackings, and even goose and chicken pluckings. At "hoedowns" and "frolics," the settlers danced to a fiddler's tune.

Western farm households usually practiced a clear gender division of labor. Men performed the heavy work such as cutting down trees and plowing fields. Women cooked, spun and wove, sewed, milked, and tended their large families. They also often helped with the butchering.

The Federal Government and the West

The federal government's growing strength spurred westward expansion. Under the Articles of Confederation, several states had ceded western lands to the national government, creating a bountiful public domain. The Land Ordinance of 1785 had provided for the survey and sale of these lands, and the Northwest Ordinance of 1787 had established a mechanism for transforming them into states. The Louisiana Purchase had brought the entire Mississippi River under U.S. control, and the Adams-Onís Treaty had wiped out the remnants of Spanish control east of the Mississippi. Six million acres of public land had been promised to volunteers during the War of 1812. The National Road, a highway begun in 1811, stretched westward, reaching Wheeling, Virginia, in 1818 and Vandalia, Illinois, by 1838.

The same governmental strength that aided whites brought misery to the Indians. Virtually all the foreign policy successes of the Republicans worked to the Native Americans' disadvantage. The Louisiana Purchase and Adams-Onís Treaty had stripped them of Spanish protection, and the War of 1812 had deprived them of British protection.

The Removal of the Indians

Westward-moving white settlers found in their path sizable numbers of Native Americans, especially in the South, home to the "Five Civilized Tribes"— the Cherokees, Creeks, Choctaws, Chickasaws, and Seminoles. Years of commercial dealings and intermarriage with Europeans had created in these tribes influential minorities of mixed-bloods who had embraced Christianity and agriculture. The Cherokees had adopted Anglo-American culture to a greater extent than any other tribe. Among them were farmers, millers, and even slave owners; they had a written form of their language, written laws, and their own bilingual newspaper, the *Cherokee Phoenix*.

While welcoming such signs of "civilization" among the Indians, whites did not hesitate to push the tribes out of their way. Whites' demands for Native American lands reached the boiling point in the 1820s. Andrew Jackson of Tennessee embodied the new militancy of those who rejected piecemeal and tribe-by-tribe treaties. Disdainful of Native Americans, Jackson argued that treaties were unnecessary because Indian tribes were not independent nations. They were thus subject to the laws of their state of residence.

@ **Jackson's Second Annual Message to Congress**

In 1830 Jackson secured from a divided Congress the Indian Removal Act, authorizing him to exchange public lands in the West for Indian lands in the East. The Creeks of Georgia and Alabama had started moving west in the late 1820s. In 1836 the Georgia militia attacked those still in the state, and when starving Creeks raided white settlements for food, federal troops finished the job begun by the militia. In 1836, 15,000 Creeks, most of the Creek nation, were removed—many in chains— and resettled west of the Mississippi River.

@ **The Removal of the Southern Tribes to the West**

The other southern "civilized" tribes suffered a similar fate. Chickasaws and Choctaws were removed by the early 1830s. Of the Seminoles, more than half were removed from Florida in 1842 after seven years of bitter warfare.

The Cherokees, however, pursued peaceful resistance by seeking an injunction from the Supreme Court against Georgia's attempts to extend its laws over them and to confiscate their lands. In *Worcester v. Georgia* (1832), Chief Justice John Marshall ruled that the Cherokees were entitled to federal protection of their lands against Georgia's claims and that Georgia laws were not valid in Cherokee territory.

President Andrew Jackson reportedly sneered, "John Marshall has made his decision; now let him

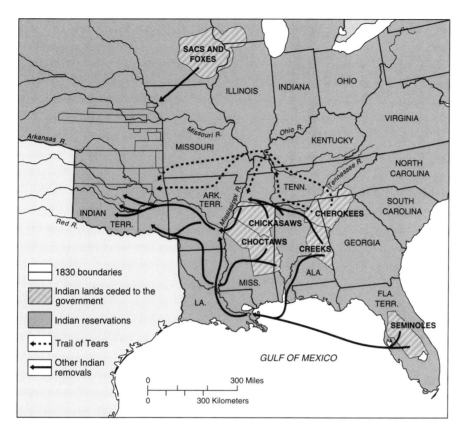

The Removal of the Native Americans to the West, 1820–1840
The so-called Trail of Tears, followed by the Cherokees, was one of several routes along which various tribes migrated on their forced removal to reservations west of the Mississippi.

enforce it," and ignored the ruling. Then in 1835 the U.S. government negotiated the fraudulent Treaty of New Echota with a handful of unauthorized individuals. It ceded most remaining Cherokee lands to the United States for $5.6 million and the Indians' transportation west. Sixteen thousand Cherokees straggled west to the Indian Territory between 1835 and 1838 along the so-called Trail of Tears. A total of perhaps 4,000 died along the trail itself and within a year of the initial roundup and hard journey.

Indians in the Northwest Territory fared no better after they signed land-cession treaties. Two uprisings marked their westward removal. The first was quickly crushed, but the second, led by a Sac and Fox chief, Black Hawk, raged along the frontier in Illinois until federal troops and state militiamen virtually annihilated the Indians in 1832. After Black Hawk's

@ Little Chief's World

defeat, the other northwestern tribes agreed to removal. Between 1832 and 1837 the United States acquired nearly 190 million acres of Indian land in the Northwest for $70 million.

The Agricultural Boom

In clearing the Indians from their territory, the federal government was responding to whites' pressures for land. Depleted soil and overcrowding had long driven farmers west, but after the War of 1812 soaring agricultural commodity prices and rising demand for western foodstuffs sharpened the land hunger. With produce prices skyrocketing, western farmers took advantage of the Ohio-Mississippi River system to ship their grain to foreign markets through New Orleans. In short, federal Indian policy, although devastating to Native Americans, made farming possible in the West, and high prices and high demand made it attractive.

Cotton, and Eli Whitney's cotton gin, provided the impetus for settlement of the Old Southwest, especially Alabama and Mississippi. Indeed, the explosive westward thrust of southern farmers and planters after the War of 1812 resembled a gold rush. By 1817 land prices had shot up from $30 to $50 an acre. By 1820 Alabama and Mississippi produced half the nation's cotton. With a seemingly unlimited British market for raw cotton, production tripled between 1816 and 1831. Between 1831 and 1836 the value of cotton exports rose 300 percent, and cotton accounted for two-thirds of U.S. exports.

American farmers, used to growing enough food for their families (subsistence farming) and some grain or cotton for sale (commercial farming for the "market economy"), pursued national and foreign markets with zeal after the War of 1812. But the new commercial farmers encountered serious problems, including wildly fluctuating markets. They also routinely had to borrow money to cover the often long interval between harvest and sale. Thus commercial farmers were forced to accept short-term debt in hope of reaping long-term profits.

The Panic of 1819

In 1819 the land boom collapsed like a house of cards, the victim of a financial panic. State banks' loose practices played a major role in causing the panic. These state banks issued their own bank notes, little more than a promise to pay the bearer a certain amount of specie (gold and silver coin) on demand. Also, many farmers took out loans to buy more land and plant more crops. And as American farmers were becoming more dependent on agricultural exports to repay their debts, bumper crops in Europe combined with an economic slump in England to trim foreign demand for U.S. crops.

The result was a cascade of economic catastrophes. In summer 1819 the Bank of the United States, holder of large amounts of state bank paper, began to insist that the state banks redeem this paper in specie. To pay these debts, state banks demanded

that farmers and land speculators repay their loans—in specie.

Land speculators suffered as credit dried up and land prices tumbled. Land prices plummeted from $69 an acre to $2 an acre as the credit squeeze drove down commodity prices. Hard-pressed farmers could not pay their debts, speculators could not collect their money, and land values collapsed.

The panic had three major consequences for Americans. First, they came to despise banks, especially the Bank of the United States. Second, they recognized how vulnerable American factories were to foreign competition and began to favor higher tariffs. Third, farmers recognized how deeply they depended on distant markets and began to look for better and cheaper ways to transport their products to these markets.

The Transportation Revolution: Steamboats, Canals, and Railroads

The transportation systems available in 1820 had serious weaknesses. The great rivers west of the Appalachians ran primarily north to south and hence could not by themselves connect western farmers to eastern markets. Roads were expensive to maintain, and horse-drawn wagons were slow and limited in range. Consequently, after 1820 attention and investment shifted to the development of waterways.

In 1807 Robert R. Livingston and Robert Fulton introduced the steamboat *Clermont* on the Hudson River. They soon gained a monopoly from the New York legislature to run a New York–New Jersey ferry service. Spectacular profits lured competitors, who secured a license from Congress and then filed suit to break the Livingston-Fulton monopoly. In 1824 Chief Justice John Marshall handed down his decision in what was known as the *Gibbons v. Ogden* case. Marshall ruled that Article I, Section 8, of the Constitution, which empowered Congress to regulate interstate commerce, applied to navigation as well. The power of Congress had to prevail over the power of New York; thus the Livingston-Fulton monopoly was void. Marshall's decision not only opened the way for rapid expansion of steamboat traffic but also forcefully reasserted the supremacy of national power over that of the states.

Steamboats assumed a vital role along the Mississippi-Ohio River system. They were far more useful than rafts, which journeyed only one way, or keelboats, which took up to four months to travel upstream from New Orleans to Louisville; in 1817 a steamboat made the identical trip in just twenty-five days. The development of long, shallow hulls permitted navigation of the Mississippi-Ohio system even when hot, dry summers lowered the river level.

While steamboats proved their value, canals replaced roads and turnpikes as the focus of popular enthusiasm and financial speculation. Although the cost of canal construction was mind-boggling, canals offered the possibility of connecting the Mississippi-Ohio system with the Great Lakes and even the East Coast.

The first major canal project was the Erie Canal, completed in 1825. Ten times longer than any existing canal in North America, it stretched 363 miles from Buffalo to Albany, linking Lake Erie to the Hudson River, New York City, and the Atlantic Ocean. A succession of other canals were soon built.

The canal boom slashed shipping costs. The Erie dramatically cut freight charges, which in the period 1817–1830 dropped from nineteen cents to two cents a ton per mile between Buffalo and New York City. Similar reductions prevailed nationwide.

Railroads soon were competing with canals and gradually overtook them. In 1825 the first railroad for general transportation began operation in England. The new technology quickly reached the United States, and by 1840 there were 3,000 miles of railroad track, equal to the total canal mileage. Faster, cheaper to build, and able to reach more places, railroads had clear advantages over canals, but Americans realized their potential only slowly.

Unlike canals, most railroads were built by private companies that tended to skimp on costs, as a result producing lines requiring constant repair. In contrast, canals needed little maintenance. Shipping bulky commodities such as iron, coal, and grain long remained cheaper by canal than by rail.

The Growth of Cities

The transportation revolution accelerated the growth of towns and cities. The forty years before the Civil War, 1820 to 1860, saw the most rapid urbanization in U.S. history. In that time the percentage of people living in places of 2,500 or more inhabitants rose from 6.1 percent to nearly 20 percent.

Urban growth was particularly fast in the West. The War of 1812 stimulated manufacturing and transformed villages into towns, as did the agricultural boom and the introduction of steamboats after 1815. Virtually all the major western cities were river ports. Of these, Pittsburgh, Cincinnati, Louisville, and New Orleans were the largest and most prominent. Pittsburgh was a manufacturing center, but the others were basically commercial hubs flooded by people eager to make money.

What the transportation revolution gave, it could also take away. The completion of the Erie Canal gradually shifted the center of western economic activity away from the river cities and toward the Great Lakes; Buffalo, Cleveland, Detroit, Chicago, and Milwaukee were the ultimate beneficiaries of the canal. In 1830 nearly 75 percent of western city dwellers lived in the river ports of New Orleans, Louisville, Cincinnati, and Pittsburgh, but by 1840 the proportion had dropped to 20 percent.

The Rise of Manufacturing

Although Americans in the early nineteenth century continued to think of themselves as a nation of farmers, industrialization was gradually taking hold. Multiple domestic and foreign factors stimulated industrialization. The Era of Good Feelings saw general agreement that the United States needed tariffs; once protected from foreign competition, American cloth production rose by an average of 15 percent *every year* from 1815 to 1833. At the same time, the transportation revolution enlarged markets and demand. Americans began to prefer factory-made products to homemade ones.

Immigration was also vital. Five million people emigrated from Europe to the United States between

1790 and 1860, most of them to pursue economic opportunity. British immigrants were most important to industrialization. That process in Britain was a generation ahead of the United States, and British immigrants understood the workings of machines. For example, immigrant Samuel Slater had learned the "mystery" of textile production as an apprentice in England. Although British law forbade emigration by skilled "mechanics" such as Slater, he disguised himself and brought his knowledge of machines and factories to eager Americans.

Americans also freely experimented with various machines and developed their own technologies. With labor scarce in the early Republic, manufacturers sought to cut costs by replacing expensive workers with machines. Eli Whitney borrowed the European idea of interchangeable parts and employed unskilled (and thus cheap) workers to make 10,000 muskets for the U.S. Army. The use of interchangeable parts became so common in the United States that Europeans and Americans alike called it the American system of manufacturing.

New England Industrializes

New England became America's first industrial region. The trade wars leading up to the War of 1812 had devastated the Northeast's traditional economy and stimulated capital investment in manufacturing. New England's many swift-flowing rivers were ideal sources of waterpower for mills. The westward migration of New England's young men, unable to wrest a living from rocky soil, left a surplus of young women, who supplied cheap industrial labor.

Cotton textiles led the way. Samuel Slater arrived in Pawtucket, Rhode Island, in 1790 and helped to design and build a mill that used Richard Arkwright's spinning frame to spin cotton yarn. His work force quickly grew from nine to one hundred, and his mills multiplied. In what was still essentially "cottage" manufacturing, the yarn produced in Slater's mills was woven into cloth by women working in their homes.

The establishment of the Boston Manufacturing Company in 1813 opened a new chapter in U.S. manufacturing. Backed by ample capital, the Boston Company built textile mills in the Massachusetts towns of Lowell and Waltham; by 1836 the company employed more than 6,000 workers.

Unlike Slater's mills, the Waltham and Lowell factories turned out finished products, thus elbowing aside Slater's cottage industry. Slater had tried to preserve tradition by hiring entire families to work at his mills. In contrast, 80 percent of the workers in the Lowell and Waltham mills were unmarried women fifteen to thirty years old. Hired managers and company regulations, rather than families, provided discipline. The workers ("operatives") boarded in factory-owned houses or licensed homes, observed a curfew, attended church, and accepted the "moral police of the corporations."

Manufacturing in New York City and Philadelphia

In the 1830s and 1840s New York, Philadelphia, and other cities witnessed a different kind of industrialization. Instead of building factories with complex machinery, New York and Philadelphia manufacturers hired large numbers of unskilled workers and paid them low wages. A worker would perform one simple hand operation such as stitching cloth or soling shoes. Such subdivision of tasks (performed without machines) and specialization of labor characterized much early industrialization.

The skilled artisans of New York City and Philadelphia tried to protect their interests by forming trade unions and "workingmen's" political parties. Initially, they sought to restore privileges and working conditions that artisans had once enjoyed, but gradually they joined forces with unskilled workers. The emergence of organized worker protests underscored the mixed blessings of economic development. Where some people prospered, others found their economic position deteriorating. By 1830 many Americans were questioning whether their nation was truly a land of equality.

@ Philadelphia Mechanics Respond to New Pressures

Equality and Inequality

The gap between rich and poor continued to widen in the first half of the nineteenth century. Although striking inequalities separated rich and poor farmers, the inequalities were far greater in the cities, where a small fraction of the people owned a huge share of the wealth. In Boston the richest 4 percent of the people owned almost 70 percent of the wealth by 1848, whereas 81 percent of the population owned only 4 percent of the wealth.

Although commentators celebrated the self-made man and his rise "from rags to riches," few actually fit this pattern. Less than 5 percent of the wealthy had started life poor; almost 90 percent of well-off people had been born rich. Clearly, the old-fashioned way to wealth was to inherit it, to marry more of it, and to invest it wisely.

The rich built their splendid residences close to one another. In New York half the city's wealthy families lived on only eight streets, and they belonged to the same clubs. French nobleman Alexis de Tocqueville, an astute observer of the social scene, noted these facts in his classic *Democracy in America* (1835, 1840). He also remarked that the rich feigned respect for equality, at least in public. They rode in ordinary carriages, brushed elbows with the less privileged, and avoided the conspicuous display of wealth.

At the opposite end of the social ladder were the poor. By today's standards most antebellum Americans were poor; they lived at the edge of destitution, depended on their children's labor to meet expenses, had little money for medical care or recreation, and suffered frequent unemployment. In 1850 an estimated three out of eight males over twenty owned little more than their clothing.

As some Americans convinced themselves that success lay within everyone's grasp, they also tended to believe that the poor were responsible for their own poverty. Ironically, even as many Americans blamed the poor for being poor, discrimination mired some groups in enduring poverty. Among the chief victims were northern free blacks.

Free Blacks in the North

Prejudice against African-Americans was deeply ingrained in white society throughout the nation. Although slavery had largely disappeared in the North by 1820, discriminatory laws remained. The voting rights of African-Americans were severely restricted; for example, New York eliminated property requirements for whites but kept them for blacks. There were attempts to bar free blacks from migrating. And segregation prevailed in northern schools, jails, and hospitals. Most damaging of all to free blacks was the social pressure that forced them into unskilled, low-paying jobs throughout the northern cities. Although a few free blacks accumulated moderate wealth, free blacks in general were only half as likely as other city dwellers to own real estate.

The "Middling Classes"

Most antebellum Americans were neither fabulously rich nor grindingly poor but part of the "middling classes." Even though the wealthy owned an increasing proportion of wealth, per capita income grew at 1.5 percent annually between 1840 and 1860, and the standard of living rose after 1800.

Americans applied the term *middling classes* to farmers and artisans, who held the ideal of self-employment and were considered steady and dependable. Often, however, farmers and artisans led lives considerably less stable than this ideal.

Like the poor, the middling class was transient. When debt-burdened farmers hoping to get out of debt exhausted land quickly by their intense cultivation of cash crops, they simply moved on. Artisans, increasingly displaced by machines, found that skilled jobs were seasonal, and so they, too, moved from place to place to survive.

The multiplying risks and opportunities that confronted Americans both widened the gap between social classes and increased the psychological burdens on individuals.

The Revolution in Social Relationships

The growth of interregional trade, commercial agriculture, and manufacturing disrupted traditional social relationships and forged new ones. Americans began to question traditional forms of authority and to embrace individualism.

The Attack on the Professions

An intense criticism of lawyers, physicians, and ministers exemplified the assault on and erosion of traditional authority. Between 1800 and 1840 the wave of religious revivals known as the Second Great Awakening (see Chapter 10) sparked fierce attacks on the professions. Revivalists blasted the clergy for creating complex theologies, drinking expensive wines, and fleecing the people.

These attacks on the learned professions peaked between 1820 and 1850. Samuel Thomson led a successful movement to eliminate all barriers to entry into the medical profession, including educational requirements. By 1845 every state had repealed laws requiring licenses or education to practice medicine. In religion ministers found little job security as finicky congregations dismissed clergymen whose theology displeased them.

The increasing commercialization of the economy led to both more professionals and more attacks on them. In 1765 America had one medical school; by 1860 there were sixty-five. The newly minted doctors and lawyers had neither deep roots in the towns where they practiced nor convincing claims to social superiority.

This questioning of authority was particularly sharp on the frontier. Easterners sneered that every man in the West claimed to be a "judge," "general," "colonel," or "squire." In a society in which *every* person was new, titles were easily adopted and just as readily challenged. Would-be gentlemen substituted an exaggerated sense of personal honor for legal or customary claims of authority. These "gentlemen" could react testily to the slightest insult, and consequently duels were common on the frontier.

The Challenges to Family Authority

Meanwhile, children quietly questioned parental authority. The era's economic change offered some young people the option of leaving their parents'

home to work in urban industries. The desire for independence fueled westward migration as well, with restless single men leading the way.

As young Americans tried to escape close parental supervision, courtship and marriage patterns also changed. No longer dependent on parents for land, young people wanted to choose their own mates. Romantic love, rather than parental preference, increasingly determined marital decisions.

One clear sign of lessening parental control over courtship and marriage was the number of women marrying out of their birth order. Traditionally, fathers had wanted their daughters to marry in the order of their birth to avoid suspicion that there was something wrong with any of them. Another mark of the times was the popularity of long engagements; young women were reluctant to tie the knot, fearing that marriage would snuff out their independence. Equally striking was the increasing number of young women who chose not to marry.

Thus young people lived more and more in a world of their own. Moralists reacted with alarm and flooded the country with books of advice to youth, all of which stressed the same message: that the newly independent young people should develop rectitude, self-control, and "character." The self-made adult began with the self-made youth.

Wives, Husbands

Another class of advice books counseled wives and husbands about their rights and duties. These books were a sign that relations between spouses were also changing. Young men and women accustomed to making their own decisions would under- 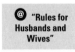 stand ably approach marriage as a compact among equals. Although inequalities within marriage remained—especially the legal tradition that married women could not own property—the trend was toward a form of equality.

One source of change was the rise of the doctrine of separate spheres. The traditional view of women as subordinate in all ways yielded to a separate-but-equal doctrine that portrayed men as superior in making money and governing the world and women as superior in exerting moral influence on family members. Most important was the shift of responsibility for child rearing from fathers to mothers.

The idea of a separate women's sphere blended with the image of 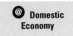 family and home as secluded refuges from a disorderly society. Popular culture painted an alluring portrait of the pleasures of home in such sentimental songs as "Home, Sweet Home" and poems such as "A Visit from St. Nicholas." But reality diverged far from this ideal. Ownership of a quiet single-family home lay beyond the reach of most Americans, even much of the middle class. Farm homes, far from tranquil, were beehives of activity, and city dwellers often had to sacrifice privacy by taking in boarders to supplement family income.

Nevertheless, these intertwined ideas—separate spheres for men and women and the home as a sanctuary—were virtually the only ones projected in antebellum magazines. Although ideals, they intersected with the real world at points. The decline of cottage industry and the growing number of men (merchants, lawyers, brokers) who worked outside the home gave women more time to lavish on children. Married women found these ideals sources of power: the doctrine of separate spheres subtly implied that women should control not only the discipline but also the number of children.

In 1800 the United States had one of the highest birthrates ever recorded. Statistically, the average woman bore 7.04 children. Children were valuable for the labor they provided and for their ability to take care of aging parents. However, the growth of the market economy raised questions about children's economic value. Unlike a farmer, a merchant or lawyer could not send his children to work at the age of seven or eight. The birthrate gradually dropped, especially in towns and cities, so that statistically, by 1900 the average woman would bear 3.98 children.

Abstinence, *coitus interruptus* (the withdrawal of the penis before ejaculation), and abortion were common birth-control methods. Whatever the method, husbands and wives jointly decided to limit family size. Husbands could note that the economic value of children was declining; wives, that having fewer children would give them more time to nurture each one and thereby to carry out their womanly duties.

Horizontal Allegiances and the Rise of Voluntary Associations

As some forms of authority weakened, Americans devised new social structures. The antebellum era witnessed the widespread substitution of *horizontal* allegiances for *vertical* allegiances. In vertical allegiances, authority flows from the top down, and people in a subordinate position identify their interests with those of superiors rather than others in the same subordinate roles. The traditional patriarchal family is an example of vertical allegiance, as is the traditional apprentice system. When social relationships assumed a horizontal form, new patterns emerged. Vertical relationships remained but became less important. New relationships linked those who were in a similar position: for example, in the large textile mills, operatives realized they had more in common with one another than with their supervisors. Wives tended to form associations that bound them with other married women, and young men developed associations with other young men.

Voluntary (and horizontal) associations proliferated in the 1820s and 1830s. Tocqueville described Americans as "a nation of joiners." At the most basic level these organizations promoted sociability by providing contact with people who shared similar interests, experiences, or characteristics. Beyond that, voluntary associations allowed members to assert their influence at a time when traditional forms of authority were weakening. Women joined maternal associations to exchange ideas about child rearing; temperance associations to work for abstinence from alcoholic beverages; and moral-reform societies to combat prostitution.

Temperance and moral-reform societies also enhanced women's power over men. Temperance advocates assumed that intemperance was a male vice, and moral reformers attributed prostitution to men who, unable to control their passions, exploited vulnerable girls. These organizations represented collective action by middle-class women to increase their influence in society.

CHRONOLOGY

1790   Samuel Slater begins designing his first Rhode Island mill.

1793   Eli Whitney invents the cotton gin.

1807   Robert R. Livingston and Robert Fulton introduce the steamboat *Clermont* on the Hudson River.

1811   Construction of the National Road begins at Cumberland, Maryland.

1819   Economic panic, ushering in four-year depression.

1820–   Growth of female moral-reform societies.
1850

1820s   Expansion of New England textile mills.

1824   *Gibbons v. Ogden.*

1825   Completion of the Erie Canal.

1828   Baltimore and Ohio Railroad chartered.

1830   Indian Removal Act passed by Congress.

1831   Alexis de Tocqueville begins visit to the United States to study American penitentiaries.

1832   *Worcester v. Georgia.*

1835–   Trail of Tears.
1838

1840   System of production by interchangeable parts perfected.

FOR FURTHER READING

William L. Anderson, ed., *Cherokee Removal: Before and After* (1991). An anthology containing the latest research on Cherokee relocation.

Rowland Berthoff, *An Unsettled People: Social Order and Disorder in American History* (1971). A stimulating interpretation of American social history.

Ray A. Billington, *Westward Expansion: A History of the American Frontier* (1949). The standard study of westward movement and settlement.

Carl Degler, *At Odds: Women and the Family in America from the Revolution to the Present* (1980). A fine overview of the economic and social experiences of American women.

Gary Nash, *Forging Freedom: The Formation of Philadelphia's Black Community, 1720–1840* (1988). An imaginative reconstruction of the emergence of a semi-autonomous African-American community.

Harry N. Scheiber, *The Ohio Canal Era: A Case Study of Government and the Economy, 1820–1861* (1969). An analysis that speaks volumes about economic growth in the early Republic.

George R. Taylor, *The Transportation Revolution, 1815–1860* (1951). The standard general study of the development of canals, steamboats, highways, and railroads.

Sean Wilentz, *Chants Democratic: New York City and the Rise of the American Working Class, 1788–1850* (1983). A stimulating synthesis of economic, social, and political history.

10

Politics, Religion, and Reform in Antebellum America

> The Transformation of American
> Politics, 1824–1832
>
> The Bank Controversy and the
> Second Party System
>
> The Rise of Popular Religion
>
> The Age of Reform

The Transformation of American Politics, 1824–1832

After 1824 American leaders had to adapt to the rising notion that politics should be an expression of the will of the common people rather than an activity that gentlemen conducted on the people's behalf. Democratizing forces in politics took several forms. One was the abolition of the requirement that voters own property; no western states had such a requirement, and eastern states gradually liberalized their laws. Moreover, written ballots replaced the custom of voting aloud, which had enabled elites to influence others at the polls. And appointive offices became elective. The selection of members of the electoral college shifted gradually from state legislatures to the voters, and by 1832 only South Carolina followed the old custom.

@ Election Day at the State House

The fierce tug of war between Republicans and Federalists in the 1790s and early 1800s had taught both parties to court voters and listen to their will. At grand party-run barbecues from Maine to Maryland, potential voters washed down free clams and oysters with free beer and whiskey.

The Election of 1824

Sectional politics shattered the harmony of the Era of Good Feelings. In 1824 five candidates, all Republicans, battled for the presidency. John Quincy Adams emerged as the New England favorite. John C. Calhoun and William Crawford fought to represent the South. Henry Clay of Kentucky assumed that his leadership in promoting the American System would endear him to the East as well as to his native West. Tennessean Andrew Jackson stunned the four by emerging as a favorite of frontier people, southerners, and some northerners as well.

Jackson won the popular and electoral vote but failed to win the majority electoral vote required by the Constitution. When the election went to the House of Representatives, Clay threw his support, and thus the presidency, to Adams; Adams then promptly appointed Clay secretary of state. Jackson's

@ Presidential Election, 1824

supporters raged that a "corrupt bargain" had cheated their candidate, "Old Hickory," of the presidency.

John Quincy Adams as President

Failing to understand the changing political climate, Adams made several other miscalculations that would cloak his presidency in controversy. For example, he proposed federal support for internal improvements, although Old Republicans had continued to attack them as unconstitutional. Adams then infuriated southerners by proposing to send American delegates to a conference of newly independent Latin American nations. Southerners opposed U.S. participation because it would imply recognition of Haiti, the black republic created by slave revolutionaries. Adams alienated his supporters by appointing his opponents to high office and wrote loftily, "I have no wish to fortify myself by the support of any party whatever." Idealistic though his view was, it guaranteed him a single-term presidency.

The Rise of Andrew Jackson and Martin Van Buren

As Adams's popularity fell, Andrew Jackson's rose. His victory over the British at the Battle of New Orleans made him a national hero, and southerners admired him as a Tennessee slaveholder and a renowned Indian fighter. Too, southerners praised Jackson's demand that they be allowed a free hand in pushing the Indians westward as a noble application of Jeffersonian ideals of states' rights—and a way to satisfy their land hunger.

By 1826 towns and villages across the country buzzed with political activity. Because supporters of Jackson, Adams, and Clay all still called themselves Republicans, few realized that a new political system was being born. The man most alert to the new currents was Martin Van Buren, who would be Jackson's vice president and then president.

Van Buren exemplified a new breed of politician. A tavernkeeper's son, he had worked his way up through New York politics and created a powerful statewide machine, the Albany Regency, composed

of men like himself from the middling and lower ranks. A genial man who befriended even his political rivals, Van Buren loved the game of politics and possessed an uncanny ability to sense which way the political winds were shifting.

The election of 1824 had convinced Van Buren of the need for two-party competition. The country would be well served, he thought, by reducing the shades of political opinion to just two so that parties could clash and a clear winner emerge. Jackson was the logical leader, and presidential nominee, of one new party, becoming known as the Democratic party; its opponents, calling themselves National Republicans, nominated Adams.

The Election of 1828

The 1828 campaign was a vicious, mudslinging affair. The National Republicans attacked Jackson as a murderer, a drunken gambler, and an adulterer. He had in fact killed several men in duels and had several more executed militarily; and in 1791 he had married Rachel Robards, erroneously believing that her divorce from her first husband had become final. Jackson supporters retaliated that Adams was rich and in debt, had tried to gain favor with the Russian tsar by providing him with a beautiful American prostitute, and—perhaps worst of all to westerners— wore silk underwear.

The Adams supporters' charges that Jackson was an illiterate backwoodsman backfired and endeared "Old Hickory" to ordinary people. Jackson's mudslingers, moreover, had better aim. They declared that Jackson was the common man incarnate—his mind unclouded by learning, his morals true, his will fierce and resolute. Adams, in contrast, was an aristocrat, a scholar whose learning obscured the truth, a man who could write but not fight.

The election swept Jackson into office with twice Adams's electoral votes. The popular vote, much closer, reflected the strong sectional bases of the new parties. Adams doubled Jackson's vote in New England, while Jackson doubled Adams's vote in the South and nearly tripled it in the Southwest.

@ Presidential Election, 1828

Jackson in Office

For all the furor, the campaign had revealed little about Jackson's position on major issues. On such key questions as federal aid for internal improvements and the tariff, Jackson had sent out conflicting signals. He would, as president, use the office to express the will of the majority.

Jackson's first policy on assuming office was to support "rotation in office," the removal of officeholders of the rival party. Rotation in office (popularly known as the spoils system) was fundamentally democratic, he argued. Officeholders' duties were so plain and simple that any intelligent man could perform them. By moving people into and out of office at will, Jackson hoped to prevent the emergence of an elite bureaucracy unresponsive to the will of the people.

Like most southerners, Jackson believed that federal support for internal improvements was simply a lavish giveaway. He thought that such funding violated the Constitution, which stated that Congress could appropriate money only for national purposes, not for the benefit of particular sections or interests. Accordingly, in 1830 Jackson vetoed a bill to provide federal support for a road in Kentucky between Maysville and Lexington.

The Maysville Road Bill veto and the almost simultaneous Indian Removal Act enhanced Jackson's popularity in the South. The tariff issue, however, would test southern loyalty. In 1828 while Adams was still president, Congress passed a high protective tariff favorable to western agriculture and New England manufacturing. Southerners fumed at the tariff, which raised the prices they paid for manufactured goods and also created the threat of retaliatory tariffs against southern cotton exports.

Nullification

The 1828 tariff, the "Tariff of Abominations," laid the foundation for a split between Jackson and his vice president, John C. Calhoun. Although he had entered Congress as a "war hawk" and had championed nationalism early in his career, Calhoun had gradually become a states' rights sectionalist. He had supported the tariff of 1816 but would fiercely oppose that of 1828.

Calhoun also burned with ambition to be president. Jackson had stated that he would serve only one term and as vice president Calhoun assumed that he would succeed Jackson. To do so, he needed to maintain the support of the South, which was increasingly taking an anti-tariff stance.

Calhoun accepted the Virginia and Kentucky Resolutions of 1798–1799, which defined the Union as a compact among the states, an association conferring limited powers on the central government. Calhoun, a South Carolinian, expressed his views on states' rights anonymously in the widely circulated *South Carolina Exposition and Protest* (1828), which argued not only that the 1828 tariff was unconstitutional but also that states had the right to nullify that tariff within their borders.

More was at stake than the price of manufactured goods. Southerners feared that a government capable of passing tariffs favoring one section over another might also pass laws meddling with slavery. Although Jackson himself was a slaveholder, South Carolina's whites were edgy about slavery's future. African-Americans composed a majority of their state's population, the slave Nat Turner's bloody rebellion in Virginia in 1831 raised fears of a similar threat to South Carolina, and William Lloyd Garrison's new newspaper, *The Liberator*, advocated immediate abolition. To South Carolinians, these were ominous signs warning that a line had to be drawn against tariffs and possible future interference with slavery.

Jackson Versus Calhoun

Like Calhoun, Jackson was strong-willed and proud. Unlike Calhoun, he already was president and the leader of a national party that included supporters of the tariff. To mollify both pro-tariff and anti-tariff forces, he devised two policies.

First, he distributed surplus federal revenue, largely derived from the tariff duties, to the states, hoping to remove the taint of sectional injustice from the tariff. Second, he tried to ease tariffs down from the sky-high 1828 rates, and Congress passed slight reductions in 1832. But these measures did little to satisfy Calhoun and the South Carolinians.

By the time the lower tariff was passed, other issues had ruptured relations between the president and vice president. Jackson learned that in 1818, then–Secretary of War Calhoun had urged that Jackson be punished for his unauthorized raid into Spanish Florida. Combined with the snubbing by Calhoun's wife, Floride, of Peggy Eaton, the scandal-tainted spouse of Jackson's ally and secretary of war, John H. Eaton, this news convinced Jackson that he had to "destroy [Calhoun] regardless of what injury it might do me or my administration."

The stage was set for the president and the vice president to clash over nullification. In November 1832 a South Carolina convention, citing Calhoun's states' rights doctrine, nullified the tariffs of 1828 and 1832 and forbade the collection of customs duties within the state. Jackson reacted quickly. Rejecting nullification as an "abominable doctrine" that would reduce the government to anarchy, he sent arms to Unionists in South Carolina and issued a proclamation that lambasted nullification as unconstitutional. The Constitution, he emphasized, had established "a single nation," not a league of states.

In March 1833 the crisis eased as President Jackson signed "the olive branch and the sword," in one historian's words. The Compromise Tariff of 1833, the olive branch or peace offering, provided for a gradual but significant lowering of tariff duties from 1833 to 1842. The Force Bill, the sword, authorized the president to use arms to collect customs duties in South Carolina. Although South Carolina did not abandon the principle of nullification—in fact, it petulantly nullified the Force Bill—it accepted the Compromise Tariff and rescinded its nullification of the tariffs of 1828 and 1832.

The Bank Veto

One reason that Jackson signed Clay's Compromise Tariff into law was that he had no strong convictions on the subject of tariffs. The same could not be said of his attitude toward banks. Owing to disastrous financial speculations early in his career, Jackson was

deeply suspicious of all banks, all paper money, and all monopolies. On each count the Bank of the United States was guilty.

The Bank of the United States had received a twenty-year charter from Congress in 1816. As a creditor of state banks, the Bank of the United States in effect restrained their printing and lending of money by its ability to demand the redemption of state notes in specie (gold or silver coin).

Many other aspects of the Bank of the United States made it controversial. For example, it was widely blamed for the Panic of 1819. Second, it was a privileged institution at a time when privilege was coming under fierce attack. Third, as the official depository for federal revenue, the bank had far greater lending capacity than state banks and thus dominated them. Fourth, although chartered by the federal government, the bank was controlled by its stockholders, who were private citizens—"moneyed capitalists" in Jackson's view. Finally, its location in Philadelphia, rather than Washington, symbolized the bank's independence of supervision by the national government. The bank's president, the aristocratic Nicholas Biddle, saw himself as a public servant duty-bound to keep the bank above politics.

After Jackson questioned "both the constitutionality and the expediency" of the Bank of the United States in his first annual message to Congress, Biddle sought an early rechartering of the bank. He was urged on by Henry Clay, who hoped to ride the probank bandwagon into the White House in 1832. Congress passed, and Jackson promptly vetoed, the recharter bill. The president denounced the bank as a private and privileged monopoly that drained the West of specie, was immune to taxation by states, and made "the rich richer and the potent more powerful."

@ **Veto of the Bank of the United States**

The Election of 1832

By 1832 Jackson had made clear his views on major issues. He was simultaneously a strong defender of states' rights *and* a staunch Unionist. Although he cherished the Union, Jackson believed the states far too diverse to accept strong direction from the federal government.

Throwing aside earlier promises to retire, Jackson ran for the presidency again in 1832, with Martin Van Buren as his running mate. Henry Clay ran on the National Republican ticket, stressing his American System of protective tariffs, national banking, and federal support for internal improvements. Jackson's overwhelming personal popularity swamped Clay, 219 to 49 electoral votes. Secure in office for another four years, Jackson was ready to finish dismantling the Bank of the United States.

The Bank Controversy and the Second Party System

Jackson could have allowed the Bank of the United States, "the monster," as he termed it, to die a natural death when its charter expired, but he and his followers believed that if the bank escaped with a breath of life, "it will soon recover its wonted strength . . . and all hope of its destruction must forever be renounced." When Biddle began calling in bank loans and contracting credit to forestall further moves by Jackson, Jacksonians saw their darkest fears confirmed. The bank, Jackson said, "is trying to kill me, but I will kill it." So the president began removing federal deposits from the Bank of the United States and putting them in state banks.

@ **Jackson's Farewell Address**

In turn, this policy raised new problems. State banks that were depositories for federal funds could use these moneys as the basis for issuing more notes and extending more loans. Jackson could not stem the rapid economic expansion fueled by paper money and by foreign specie flowing in to purchase cotton. In 1836 the president thus reluctantly signed the Deposit Act, increasing the number of deposit banks and lessening federal control over them.

The Democratic party split between advocates of soft money (paper) and hard money (specie). The two Democratic camps agreed that the Bank of the United States was evil, but for different reasons. Soft-money Democrats, especially strong in the West, resented the bank's restriction of credit and wanted more paper money. Hard-money Democrats, typically wage-earning urban workers, disliked the speculative economy based on paper money and easy credit, and they deeply feared inflation.

The Rise of Whig Opposition

During Jackson's second term the National Republicans changed their name to the Whig Party and broadened their base of support in both the North and the South. As Jackson's policies became clearer and sharper, the opposition attracted people alienated by his positions.

For example, Jackson's crushing of nullification led some southerners to the Whigs in order to oppose Jackson. Jackson's war against the Bank of the United States and his opposition to federal aid for internal improvements alienated other southerners. Most of the South remained Democratic, but the Whigs made substantial inroads nonetheless. Northern reformers also joined the Whigs, who were far more willing than the Democrats to effect social change by government intervention. And supporters of Henry Clay's American System joined advocates of public education and temperance in seeking a more interventionist national government.

By 1836 the Whigs had become a national party with widespread appeal. Whigs everywhere assailed Andrew Jackson as an imperious dictator, "King Andrew I"; and the name "Whigs" evoked memories of the American patriots who had opposed George III in 1776.

The Election of 1836

As the election of 1836 approached, the Whigs lacked a national leader. Henry Clay came close, but he carried political scars and a reputation for spending his days at the gaming table and his nights in brothels. In the end four sectional candidates ran with Whig support. Some Whigs hoped that the four would draw enough votes to prevent the Democratic candidate, Martin Van Buren, from gaining a majority of electoral votes, but Van Buren captured 170 electoral votes to his opponents' 124. Still, the

Whigs made substantial gains in the South—a clear sign of trouble ahead for the Democrats.

The Panic of 1837

Hailed as "the greatest man of his age," Jackson left office in 1837 in a sunburst of glory. Yet he bequeathed to his successor a severe depression, the legacy of the bank war.

In the speculative boom of 1835 and 1836, born of Jackson's policy of placing federal funds in state banks, the total number of banks doubled, the value of bank notes in circulation nearly tripled, and both commodity and land prices soared skyward. But the overheated economy began to cool rapidly in May 1837 as prices tumbled and as bank after bank suspended specie payments. After a short rally, 1839 saw a second crash as banks across the nation again suspended specie payments.

Van Buren, known as "the sly fox" and "the little magician" for his political craftiness, would need those skills to confront the depression, which was battering ordinary citizens and the Democratic party alike. The president called for the creation of an independent treasury that would hold government revenues and keep them from the grasp of corporations. When Van Buren finally signed the Independent Treasury Bill into law on July 4, 1840, his supporters hailed it as a second Declaration of Independence.

The Independent Treasury reflected the basic Jacksonian suspicion of an alliance between the federal government and banking. However, the Independent Treasury Act failed to address banking on the state level, where newly chartered state banks—more than 900 in number by 1840—lent money to farmers and businessmen, fueling the speculative economy feared by Jacksonians.

The Election of 1840

Despite the depression, the Democrats renominated Van Buren. Avoiding the mistake of 1836, the Whigs nominated a single candidate, Ohio's William Henry Harrison, and ran John Tyler of Virginia for vice president. The Whigs chose Harrison, sixty-seven years old, largely because he had few enemies.

Early in the campaign the Democrats made a fatal mistake, ridiculing Harrison as "Old Granny" who desired only to spend his declining years in a log cabin sipping cider. In so doing, they handed the Whigs the most famous campaign symbol in American history. The Whigs saluted Harrison as a rugged frontiersman, the hero of the Battle of Tippecanoe, and a defender of all those people who lived in log cabins. Disdaining a platform, the Whigs ran a "hurrah" campaign using log cabins for headquarters, singing log cabin songs, and ladling out log cabin cider. They trumpeted, "Tippecanoe and Tyler, too!" and attacked Van Buren as an aristocrat who lived in "regal splendor."

Harrison was elected in a clear victory. The depression would have made it difficult for any Democrat to win, and Van Buren lacked the halo of military glory that gleamed around Jackson and Harrison.

The strong contrasts between the two parties and the sharp choices they presented in the 1840 election jolted the U.S. electorate. Nearly 2.4 million people voted in 1840, up an astonishing 60 percent from 1836. Most of that change was in the number of people who chose to vote; prior to 1840 the proportion of white males who voted had ranged from 55 to 58 percent; in 1840 it rose to 80 percent.

The second party system reached a high plateau in 1840 and remained there over a decade. The gradual hardening of the line between the two parties piqued popular interest in politics.

The Rise of Popular Religion

Just as Americans demanded that politics be accessible to average people, they insisted ministers preach doctrines that appealed to ordinary men and women. Increasingly, Americans put individuals in charge of their own religious destiny, thrusting aside Calvinist predestination in favor of the belief that heaven itself was democratic.

The Second Great Awakening

The Second Great Awakening first flared in Connecticut in the 1790s, and during the following half century it set ablaze one section of the nation after another. As the revivals moved westward, they underwent striking changes, typified by the rise of camp meetings. Here the members of several denominations gathered together in sprawling open-air camps to hear revivalists proclaim that the Second Coming of Jesus was near and that the time for repentance was now. Although these early frontier revivals challenged traditional religious customs—indeed, the most successful preachers were farmers and artisans who had experienced powerful conversions and scorned those whose religion came from books—the revivalists promoted law, order, and morality.

Methodists, the most successful frontier denomination, became the largest American Protestant denomination, soaring from 70,000 members in 1800 to more than 1 million in 1844. The Methodists emphasized that religion was a matter of the heart rather than the head and relied on itinerant circuit riders, young, unmarried men who traveled ceaselessly and preached in houses, open fields, or wherever else listeners would gather. After the Methodist circuit riders left, their converts held weekly "classes" to provide mutual encouragement and to chastise members for drunkenness, fighting, gossiping, fornication, and even shrewd business practices.

Eastern Revivals

By the 1820s the Second Great Awakening had begun to shift back to the East. The hottest revival fires blazed in an area of western New York known as the Burned-Over District. It was a fertile field of high expectations and bitter discontent. The man who harnessed these anxieties to religion was Charles Grandison Finney, a lawyer-turned-Presbyterian minister.

Finney's innovations justified his reputation as the "father of modern revivalism." First, he pioneered in generating cooperation among Protestants, and all denominations participated in his revivals. In addition, he introduced such novelties as the "anxious seat," a bench where those ready for conversion could be made objects of special prayer, and the "protracted meeting," which ran nightly for a week or more. Finally, although a Presbyterian, Finney rejected the Calvinist doctrine of total depravity, humankind's irresistible inclination to sin. Instead, he

proclaimed, sin was a voluntary act, and those who willed themselves to sin could just as readily will themselves not to sin.

Originally controversial, Finney's ideas came to dominate "evangelical" Protestantism, which focused on the need for an emotional religious conversion. He succeeded because he told people what they wanted to hear: that their destinies were in their own hands. Finney multiplied his success by emphasizing the role of women, who outnumbered male converts nearly two to one.

The Rise of Mormonism

Far more controversial than Finney were the Mormons and their church, the Church of Jesus Christ of Latter-day Saints, another new denomination of the 1820s. Joseph Smith, its founder, grew up in the heart of the Burned-Over District.

Smith claimed that an angel had led him to a buried book of revelation and to special stones for use in translating it. The Book of Mormon, which Smith translated, tells the story of an ancient Hebrew prophet, Lehi, whose descendants migrated to America and created a prosperous civilization. Jesus had appeared and performed miracles in the New World, but Lehi's descendants had departed from the Lord's ways and quarreled among themselves. God had cursed some of these defectors with dark skin; these were the American Indians, who had long since forgotten their history.

Smith quickly gathered followers. Mormonism's appeal lay partly in its placing America at the center of Christian history and partly in its resolving the conflicting claims within Protestantism by additional revelations beyond those in the Bible. The Mormons moved steadily west, both to escape persecution and to draw closer to the Indians, whom they wished to convert. Smith's claim of a new revelation guaranteed a hostile reception for the Mormons wherever they went because it undermined the authority of the Bible, which, along with the Constitution, contained the ideals on which the American Republic rested.

In 1843 Smith added fuel to the fire by proclaiming yet another revelation, this one sanctioning polygyny, the practice of taking multiple wives. Smith's claims that he was a prophet, the "Second Mohammed," also intensified the controversy that boiled around Mormonism. In 1844 the state of Illinois charged him with treason and jailed him in the town of Carthage. There, in June 1844, a mob murdered Smith and his brother.

Although deprived of a founder, Mormonism grew rapidly in the next three decades; by 1870 it boasted 200,000 believers. Brigham Young, who assumed leadership after Smith's murder, led the Mormons westward into Utah, at the time still under Mexican control. There he established the independent republic of Deseret, and the Mormons prospered. They transformed the Great Salt Lake Valley into a rich oasis and continued to dominate Utah after it became part of the United States.

The Age of Reform

During the 1820s and 1830s unprecedented numbers of men and women joined organizations aimed at improving society. The abolition of slavery, women's rights, temperance, better treatment of criminals and the insane, public education, and even the establishment of perfect, utopian communities were on the various reformers' agendas.

Religious revivalism intensified the righteousness of reformers, who believed that they were on God's side of any issue. Abolitionists and temperance reformers tended to come from evangelical backgrounds, and even those who were unsympathetic to revivalism tended to borrow evangelical preachers' language and psychology by painting drunkenness, ignorance, and inequality as sins calling for immediate repentance and change.

The War on Liquor

Agitation for temperance (either total abstinence from alcoholic beverages or moderation in their use) intensified during the second quarter of the nineteenth century. Alcohol abuse was a growing problem: per capita consumption of rum, whiskey, gin, and brandy had risen steadily until it exceeded seven gallons per year by 1830, nearly triple today's rate. Reformers saw alcohol excess as a male indulgence whose bitter consequences (for example, spending money on liquor instead of food) fell on women and children. Not surprisingly, millions of women marched behind the temperance banner.

The movement took off in 1825 when the popular evangelist Lyman Beecher, in six widely acclaimed lectures, thundered against all use of alcohol. Evangelical Protestants established the American Temperance Society the following year, and by 1834 it enjoyed some 5,000 state and local affiliates. The American Temperance Society demanded total abstinence and flooded the country with tracts denouncing the "amazing evil" of strong drink.

The laboring class became a chief target for temperance reformers. Passing a jug around the workplace every few hours had been a time-honored way to relieve on-the-job fatigue, but large factories demanded a more disciplined, sober work force. Manufacturers quickly supported the evangelical temperance reformers.

As temperance won new supporters, the crusaders shifted their emphasis from the individual drinker to the entire community and demanded that towns and even states ban all traffic in liquor. By the late 1830s prohibition was scoring victories, especially in New England. The steady rise of alcohol consumption halted in the early 1830s and then began to fall; by the 1840s the rate of consumption was less than half that in the 1820s.

Public-School Reform

Like temperance crusaders, school reformers worked to encourage orderliness and thrift in the common people. Reformers insisted that schools had to equip children for the emerging competitive and industrial economy. In 1837 Horace Mann of Massachusetts, the most articulate and influential of the reformers, became the first secretary of his state's newly created board of education. He presided over sweeping reforms to transform schools from loose organizations into highly structured institutions that occupied most of a child's time and energy. Mann's goals included shifting financial support of schools from parents to the state, compelling attendance, extending the school term, introducing standardized textbooks, and grading schools (that is, classifying students by age and attainment).

School reformers sought to spread uniform cultural values as well as to combat ignorance. Requiring students to arrive at a set time would teach punctuality, and matching children against their peers would stimulate the competitiveness needed in an industrializing society. Children would read the same books and absorb the same moral lessons. The McGuffey readers, which sold 50 million copies between 1836 and 1870, preached industry, honesty, sobriety, and patriotism.

Mann's reforms took root primarily in the North, despite challenges from farmers satisfied with the district school, from Catholics objecting to anti-Catholic and anti-Irish barbs in the textbooks, and from the working poor, who widely saw compulsory education as a menace to families dependent on children's wages. He and other school reformers prevailed by attracting influential allies, including urban workers, manufacturers, and women.

School reform also appealed to native-born Americans alarmed by the swelling tide of immigration. The public school became a vehicle for forging a common American culture out of an increasingly diverse society. However, few reformers stressed the integration of black and white children. When black children got any schooling, it was usually in segregated schools; black children in integrated schools encountered such virulent prejudice that African-American leaders in northern cities often preferred segregated schools.

Abolitionism

Antislavery sentiment had flourished among whites during the Revolutionary era but faded in the early nineteenth century. The American Colonization Society, founded in 1817, was the main antislavery organization of this period. It proposed gradual emancipation, compensation for slave owners when slaves became free, and the shipment to Africa of freed blacks. Although these proposals attracted some support from slave owners in the Upper South, they were unrealizable. The growing cotton economy had made slavery more attractive than ever to most southerners, and few owners would have freed their slaves, even if compensated. The U.S. slave population soared in the early nineteenth century, from 1.2 million in 1810 to more than 2 million by 1830, but only 1,400 blacks migrated to Africa, and most were already free.

In 1821 Benjamin Lundy, a white Quaker, began a newspaper, the *Genius of Universal Emancipation*, that trumpeted repeal of the Constitution's three-fifths clause, the outlawing of the internal slave trade, and the abolition of slavery in U.S. territories. Seven years later Lundy hired a young New Englander, William Lloyd Garrison, as an editorial assistant. The prematurely bald, bespectacled Garrison looked like a genial schoolmaster, but he would become a potent force in the antislavery movement.

In 1831 Garrison launched a newspaper, *The Liberator*, to spread his radical antislavery message. "I am in earnest," he wrote. "I will not equivocate—I will not excuse—I will not retreat a single inch—AND I WILL BE HEARD." His battle cry was "immediate emancipation"; his demand, civil and legal equality for African-Americans.

Black abolitionists supported Garrison; in its early years three-fourths of *The Liberator*'s subscribers were African-American. Other blacks were emerging as powerful writers and speakers. Frederick Douglass, an escaped slave, could rivet an audience with an opening line: "I appear before the immense assembly this evening as a thief and a robber. I stole this head, these limbs, this body from my master, and ran off with them."

Relations between white and black abolitionists were often stormy. Many white abolitionists called for legal, but not civil and social, racial equality; preferred light-skinned to dark-skinned blacks; and hesitated to admit African-Americans to antislavery societies. And widespread white prejudice made the life of any abolitionist precarious. Mobs attacked abolitionists often; one angry crowd, in Alton,

Illinois, murdered abolitionist editor Elijah Lovejoy in 1837.

As if external hostility were not enough, abolitionists differed passionately with one another. The largest group, the American Anti-Slavery Society, founded in 1833, was split by disagreements over whether abolitionists should form their own political party and about what role women should play in antislavery. Abolitionists from the Midwest and the Burned-Over District, most with ties to Charles Grandison Finney, formed the antislavery Liberty party in 1840 and ran a presidential slate. In contrast, Garrison increasingly rejected *all* laws and government. Embracing the doctrine of "nonresistance," he established the New England Non-Resistance Society in 1838. Like slavery, Garrison and his followers argued, all government depended on force, and because force was the opposite of Christian love, Christians should refuse to vote, to hold office, or to have anything to do with government.

Equally divisive to the abolitionist cause were questions over the role of women in the movement. In 1837 Angelina and Sarah Grimké, the daughters of a South Carolina slaveholder, made an antislavery lecture tour of New England. The Grimké sisters were controversial because they spoke to audiences of both men and women at a time when it was thought indelicate for women to address male audiences. Clergymen chastised the Grimké sisters for lecturing men rather than obeying them.

Such criticism backfired, turning the Grimkés and others to the cause of women's rights. In 1838 Sarah wrote *Letters on the Condition of Women and the Equality of the Sexes;* Angelina penned her equally classic *Letters to Catharine E. Beecher* (a militant opponent of female equality). Many male abolitionists tried to dampen the feminist flames. Even Theodore Dwight Weld, who married Angelina Grimké, wanted to subordinate women's rights to antislavery. Garrison, welcoming the controversy, promptly espoused women's rights and urged that women be given positions equal to men in the American Anti-Slavery Society.

One of the most disruptive abolitionist tactics was to flood Congress with petitions calling for an end to slavery in the District of Columbia. Lacking time to consider the petitions, Congress in effect deprived citizens of their right to have the petitions heard. Then in 1836 southerners secured passage of the "gag rule," which automatically tabled abolitionist petitions and thus prevented congressional discussion of them. In the ensuing battle over the gag rule, congressmen with little sympathy for abolition attacked southerners for suppressing the constitutional right of petition. Ex-president John Quincy Adams, at the time a representative from Massachusetts, led the struggle against the gag rule until it was lifted in 1845.

Women's Rights

Women occupied a paradoxical position in the 1830s. They could not vote and, if married, had no right to own property or to keep their own wages. At the same time, reform movements gave women unprecedented opportunities for public activity within their own "sphere."

The argument that women were natural guardians of family life was double-edged. It justified reform activities on behalf of the family but undercut women's demands for legal equality. So deeply ingrained was sexual inequality that most women came reluctantly to the issue of women's rights as a result of their experience in other reform movements, especially abolitionism. Among the early women's rights advocates who started their reform careers as abolitionists were the Grimké sisters, Lucretia Mott, Lucy Stone, and Abby Kelley.

Like abolitionism, the women's rights cause revolved around the conviction that differences of race and gender were unimportant. "Men and women," wrote Sarah Grimké, "are CREATED EQUAL! They are both moral and accountable beings, and whatever is *right* for a man to do, is *right* for woman."

The discrimination within the abolition movement infuriated women and drove them to make women's rights a separate cause. When Lucretia Mott and other American women attended the World Anti-Slavery Convention in London in 1840, they were relegated to a screened-off section. The incident made a deep impression on Mott and on Elizabeth Cady Stanton. In 1848 they organized a women's rights convention at Seneca Falls, New York. The convention issued a Declaration of Sentiments

@ **Declaration of Sentiments**

that began, "All men and all women are created equal." The participants passed a series of resolutions, including a call for the right of women to vote, which would become the centerpiece of women's rights activity after the Civil War.

Women's rights had less immediate impact than most other reforms. Temperance and school reform were far more popular, and antislavery created more commotion. Women would not secure the right to vote throughout the nation until 1920, fifty-five years after the Thirteenth Amendment had abolished slavery.

Penitentiaries and Asylums

Beginning in the 1820s, reformers tried to combat poverty, crime, and insanity by establishing regimented institutions, themselves the products of bold new assumptions about the causes of deviancy. As poverty and crime had increased and become more visible in the early nineteenth century, alarmed investigators had concluded that indigence and deviant behavior resulted not from defects in human nature, as colonial Americans had thought, but from drunken fathers and broken homes. In light of the growing belief that the moral qualities of the individual could be changed, reformers turned their energies to finding the right combination of moral influences and structured environments to improve human nature.

Reformers created, for example, highly ordered and disciplined penitentiaries as substitutes for failed parental discipline. Sincere reformation, rather than simple incarceration, became the goal. Solitary confinement was widely adopted in the belief that it would purge offenders' violent habits.

Antebellum America also witnessed a transformation in the treatment of the poor. The infirm poor crowded into almshouses, while the able-bodied poor entered workhouses. Idealistic reformers argued that

taking the poor from demoralizing surroundings and putting them into such highly regimented institutions could change them into virtuous, productive citizens. But in practice such institutions were often crowded and dismal.

Many of the insane were confined in prisons. In 1841 an idealistic Unitarian schoolteacher, Dorothea Dix, discovered insane people kept in an unheated room at the East Cambridge, Massachusetts, jail. After visiting other jails and almshouses, an appalled Dix reported that the insane were confined "in *cages, closets, cellars, stalls, pens! Chained, naked, beaten with rods, and lashed into obedience.*" Supported by Horace Mann and other reformers, she encouraged legislatures to create separate insane asylums, and by 1860, twenty-eight states, four cities, and the federal government had built public mental institutions.

Utopian Communities

The belief in the perfectibility of human nature and conduct found its most extreme expression in the "utopian" communities that flourished during the reform years. Most of these, founded by intellectuals, were meant to be alternatives to the

@ **Oneida Sisters Comment on Love and Labor**

prevailing competitive economy and models whose success would inspire others.

American interest in utopian communities began in the 1820s. In 1825 British industrialist Robert Owen founded the New Harmony community in Indiana. As a mill owner, Owen had improved his workers' living conditions and educational opportunities; he was convinced that

@ **Robert Owen's Alternative to Industrial Degradation**

the problems of the early industrial age were social, not political. Vice and misery would vanish if social arrangements were perfected, he thought.

New Harmony was to provide a model for the United States; by 1827, Owen predicted, northern states would embrace its principles. Unfortunately, by 1827 there was little left to embrace, for the community, a magnet for idlers and fanatics, had fallen apart. However, Owen's belief that environment shaped character and that cooperation was superior to competition survived and influenced urban workers in particular throughout the nineteenth century.

Experimental communities with hopeful names such as Fruitlands, Hopedale, and Brook Farm proliferated amid the economic chaos of the late 1830s and 1840s. The most controversial of the antebellum experiments in communitarian utopianism, the Oneida community in New York State, es-

@ **Orestes Brownson Views Brook Farm as an Expression of American Egalitarianism**

@ **John H. Noyes Discusses Free Love, As Practiced at Oneida**

tablished in 1848, challenged conventional notions of religion, property, dress, and, most of all, sex—each Oneidan was allowed to have several sexual partners. Contemporaries dismissed its founder, John Humphrey Noyes, as a licentious crackpot, but Oneida achieved considerable economic prosperity and attracted new members long after less radical utopian experiments such as Brook Farm had collapsed. Although widely derided as fit only for cranks, utopian communities exemplified in an extreme form the idealism and hopefulness that permeated reform in the Jacksonian era.

CHRONOLOGY

1817   American Colonization Society founded.

1824   John Quincy Adams elected president by the House of Representatives.

1825   New Harmony community founded.

1826   American Temperance Society organized.

1828   Andrew Jackson elected president.
Congress passes the "Tariff of Abominations."
John Calhoun anonymously writes *South Carolina Exposition and Protest.*

1830   Jackson's Maysville Road Bill veto.
Indian Removal Act.

1830–1831   Charles G. Finney's revival in western New York.

1831   William Lloyd Garrison starts *The Liberator.*

1832   Jackson vetoes recharter of the Bank of the United States.
Jackson reelected president.
South Carolina Nullification Proclamation.

1833   Force Bill.
Compromise Tariff.

American Anti-Slavery Society founded.
South Carolina nullifies the Force Bill.

1834   Whig party organized.

1836   Congress imposes the gag rule.
Martin Van Buren elected president.

1837   Economic depression sets in.
Elijah Lovejoy murdered by proslavery mob.

1838   Garrison's New England Non-Resistance Society founded.
Publication of Sarah Grimké's *Letters on the Condition of Women and the Equality of the Sexes* and Angelina Grimké's *Letters to Catharine E. Beecher.*

1840   Independent Treasury Act passed.
William Henry Harrison elected president.

1841   Dorothea Dix begins exposé of prison conditions.

1848   Seneca Falls Convention.
Oneida community founded.

FOR FURTHER READING

Lee Benson, *The Concept of Jacksonian Democracy: New York as a Test Case* (1961). A major revisionist interpretation of the period.

William W. Freehling, *Prelude to Civil War* (1966). A major study of the nullification crisis.

Richard P. McCormick, *The Second American Party System: Party Formation in the Jacksonian Era* (1966). An influential work stressing the role of political leaders in shaping the second party system.

Edward Pessen, *Jacksonian America: Society, Personality, and Politics*, rev. ed. (1979). A comprehensive interpretation of the period, emphasizing the lack of real democracy in American society and politics.

Robert V. Remini, *Henry Clay: Statesman for the Union* (1991). An important new biography of the leading Whig statesman of the period.

Arthur M. Schlesinger Jr., *The Age of Jackson* (1945). A classic study, now dated in some of its interpretations but still highly readable.

Fred Somkin, *Unquiet Eagle: Memory and Desire in the Idea of American Freedom, 1815–1860* (1967). A penetrating study of American political values.

Ronald G. Walters, *American Reformers, 1815–1860* (1978). A balanced study that addresses the negative as well as the positive aspects of nineteenth-century reform.

Chilton Williamson, *American Suffrage: From Property to Democracy, 1760–1860* (1960). The standard study of changing requirements for voting.

Life, Leisure, and Culture,
1840–1860

Technology and Economic Growth

To optimistic Americans, technology—the use of scientific principles to transform the practical conveniences of life—was both democratic and progressive. Machines would advance civilization because they could perform the work of ten people without needing food or clothing, Daniel Webster contended.

The technology that transformed life in antebellum America included the steam engine, the cotton gin, the reaper, the use of interchangeable parts in manufacturing, the sewing machine, and the telegraph. Sadly, these advances did not benefit everyone. The cotton gin, for example, riveted slavery firmly in place by intensifying southern dependence on cotton.

@ Eli Whitney's Cotton Gin

Agricultural Advancement

Although few settlers ventured onto the treeless, semiarid Great Plains before the Civil War, settlement edged west after 1830 from the woodlands of Ohio and Kentucky into parts of Indiana, Michigan, and Illinois where flat grasslands (prairies) alternated with forests. The prairies' matted soil was difficult to break for planting, but in 1837 John Deere invented a steel-tipped plow that halved the labor required to clear prairie for planting.

Wheat quickly became the Midwest's major cash crop. Technology eased the task of harvesting wheat. The traditional hand sickle consumed enormous amounts of time and labor and collecting and binding the cut wheat, even more. Experiments with horse-drawn machines to replace sickles had failed until Cyrus McCormick of Virginia developed the mechanical reaper. The McCormick reaper, which harvested grain seven times faster than traditional methods with half the labor force, guaranteed that wheat would dominate the midwestern prairies.

@ The McCormick Reaper

Although Americans generally remained wasteful farmers—abundant cheap land made it more "practical" to move west than to try to improve played-out soil—a movement for more efficient cultivation developed before the Civil War, primarily in the East. Because eastern soils could not compete with fertile western lands, eastern farmers had little choice. For example, some farmers in Orange County, New York, fed their cattle only clover and bluegrass; combining better feed with an emphasis on cleanliness in processing dairy products, they could then charge twice as much as others for the superior butter they marketed.

@ **An Anonymous Endorsement of Scientific Agriculture**

Technology and Industrial Progress

The early growth of U.S. manufacturing relied primarily on imported technology. That dependence lessened during the 1830s as American industries became more innovative.

Eli Whitney had pioneered in the application of interchangeable parts in the United States in 1798, but the manufacture of guns and other products using interchangeable parts still required a great deal of handwork before the components could be fitted together. By the 1840s, however, American factories had eliminated the need for hand-fitting by improving the quality of machine tools. In 1853 the superintendent of the Springfield, Massachusetts, armory staged a spectacular demonstration of interchangeable parts for a British commission investigating American technology. Rifles that had been produced in ten consecutive years were stripped and their parts easily reassembled at random.

@ **A Trade Journal Outlines Technology's Impact on the Work Process**

The American system of manufacturing offered multiple advantages. Damaged machines no longer had to be discarded but could be repaired by installing new parts. Improved machine tools allowed entrepreneurs to mass-produce new inventions rapidly, and the speed of production attracted investors.

@ **American Technology as an Influence Abroad**

Americans were eager to use technology to conquer time and space. An impatient people inhabiting a huge area, they seized enthusiastically on Samuel F.B. Morse's invention of the telegraph in 1844. By 1852 more than 15,000 miles of lines connected cities as far-flung as Quebec, New Orleans, and St. Louis. And in 1857 a transatlantic cable linked New York and London for four months before snapping. (A new cable had to wait until 1867, after the Civil War.)

The Railroad Boom

The desire to conquer time and space also drove antebellum Americans to make an extraordinary investment in railroads. Even more than the telegraph, the railroad embodied progress through advances in technology.

The swift, comfortable transportation that American railroads provided for the common person dramatized technology's democratic promise. U.S. railroads offered only one class of travel, in contrast to the several classes on European railroads.

Between 1840 and 1860 the size of the rail network and the power and convenience of trains underwent stunning transformations. Railroad track went from 3,000 to 30,000 miles (more track than all the rest of the world), flat-roofed coaches replaced open cars, kerosene lamps made night travel possible, and increasingly powerful engines let trains climb even the steepest hills. Fifty thousand miles of telegraph wire enabled dispatchers to communicate with trains en route and thus to reduce delays.

@ **Expansion of the Railroads**

Railroads spearheaded the second phase of the transportation revolution. Canals remained in use, but railroads, both faster and less vulnerable to winter freezes, gradually overtook them, first in passengers and then in freight. By 1860 the value of goods transported by railroads greatly exceeded that carried by canals.

Most important, the railroads crossed the Appalachian Mountains to link the East and the Midwest. By 1860 rail routes ran from Buffalo to Cleveland, Toledo, and Chicago; from Pittsburgh to Fort Wayne; and from Wheeling to Cincinnati and St. Louis.

Chicago's growth illustrates the impact of these rail links. In 1849 it was a village of a few hundred people with virtually no rail service. By 1860 it had become a metropolis of 100,000, served by eleven railroads. Farmers in the upper Midwest no longer had to send their grain and livestock down the Mississippi to New Orleans; they could now ship their products directly east. Chicago supplanted New Orleans as the interior's main commercial hub.

Enabling farmers to speed their produce to the East, the east-west rail lines stimulated the settlement and agricultural development of the Midwest. By 1860 Illinois, Indiana, and Wisconsin had replaced Ohio, Pennsylvania, and New York as the leading wheat-growing states.

As the nation's first big business, railroads transformed the conduct of business, particularly in finance. The dramatic expansion of the rail network in the 1850s required new sources of financing, and the railroads turned to the capital market in New York City. The railroad boom helped to make Wall Street the nation's greatest capital market, as the securities of all the leading railroads were traded on the floor of the New York Stock Exchange. New York also became the center of modern investment firms.

@ **A Senate Report the Railroads' Significance**

Rising Prosperity

Technology also improved life by lowering prices. Clocks that cost $50 to make by hand in 1800 could be produced for 50¢ by 1850. Widespread use of steam power led to a 25 percent rise in the average worker's real income (purchasing power) between 1840 and 1860; unlike water wheels, steam engines could run in all seasons, and so workers did not have to face long winter layoffs.

The growth of towns and cities also contributed to the upward trend in average annual wages. In contrast to rural farming areas, with their heavily seasonal labor, urban settings offered year-round opportunities for jobs. Towns and cities also provided women and children—who seldom were paid for farm labor—new opportunities for paid work. Children's wages played an important role in family finances for working-class families.

@ **The Lady Shoemakers' Strike**

The Quality of Life

Subtle but critical changes in the quality of daily life accompanied the large-scale transformations in transportation, production, and income in the two decades before the Civil War.

Housing

During the early 1800s the unattached and distinctive wood-frame houses dotting colonial urban skylines yielded to quickly constructed, uniform-looking brick row houses. Where some praised the row houses as democratic, others condemned "their extreme uniformity—when you have seen one, you have seen all." The typical row house was narrow and long, fifteen to twenty feet across and thirty to forty feet from front to back. Most had open spaces in the rear for gardens, pigs, privies (outhouses), and cisterns (water-storage vessels).

@ **American Woman's Home: Floorplan**

As land values soared (as much as 750 percent in Manhattan between 1785 and 1815), renting, rather than owning, homes became common. By 1815 more than half of the homes in large cities were rented. Skyrocketing land values also led to the subdivision of row houses for occupancy by several families. The worst of these, known as tenements, were the usual habitats of Irish immigrants and free blacks.

In rural areas the quality of housing depended as much on the date of settlement as on social class. In recently settled areas the standard dwelling was a one-room log cabin with split-log floors that allowed in drafts, roofs that let in snow, crude chimneys made of sticks and clay, and windows covered by oiled paper or cloth. As rural communities matured, log cabins gave way to frame houses of two or more rooms with glass windows and better insulation.

Home Furniture

Furniture also revealed the widening gap between the prosperous and the poor. Families in the middle and upper classes increasingly decorated their parlors with a style of furniture known as rococo. Such furniture was ornate and featured elaborately carved wooden frames supporting heavily upholstered backs and seats topped with medallions; vines, leaves, and flowers covered both wooden and upholstered surfaces.

Such highly ornamental furniture marked its possessors as people of substantial wealth. The rise of mass-produced furniture brought rococo style within the reach of the middle class, which could not afford to import furniture from France, as the wealthy did.

Heating, Cooking, and Diet

The transportation and industrial revolutions also affected heating, cooking, and diet. Iron foundries took advantage of distant markets by specializing in the production of cast-iron stoves, which had displaced open hearths in urban areas by the late 1840s. The discovery of high-grade hard coal in eastern Pennsylvania guaranteed a steady supply of fuel.

Coal burned longer and hotter than wood and reduced the time and expense of acquiring fuel. The drawbacks of using coal, among them its sooty residue and the ever-present danger of carbon monoxide poisoning, paled beside its benefits, which included ease of cooking.

Meanwhile, better transportation brought a greater variety of foodstuffs to urban markets, particularly fresh vegetables. Preserving any kind of food was a problem, for few homes had iceboxes—the forerunners of refrigerators—before 1860. Housewives could bury meat in the snow to keep it from spoiling, but salt remained the most widely used preservative. Americans ate far more pork than beef because salt affected the taste of pork less.

Water and Sanitation

Rural homes rarely had running water. Instead, water was brought in from wells, springs, or cisterns; once used, it was carried outside and dumped. But antebellum cities had begun constructing public waterworks to deal with threats to well water posed by leakage from outdoor privies. By 1860 sixty-eight public water systems were operating in the United States.

Although public waterworks were engineering marvels, their impact was uneven. Most smaller cities had no waterworks before the Civil War, and even in New York less than a tenth of the city's population were customers of the water system. Most families carried water from street hydrants into their homes. Because hot running water was rare, the water had to be heated on the stove before one could take a bath. Not surprisingly, people rarely bathed.

Infrequent baths meant pungent body odors, but they mingled with a multitude of strong scents. Even fashionable residential streets contained stables backed by mounds of manure. Street cleaning was left to private contractors, who often discharged their duties casually, and so urban Americans relied on hogs, which they let roam freely to scavenge, for cleaning public thoroughfares. Outdoor privies added to the stench.

Disease and Health

Despite the slowly rising living standard, Americans remained vulnerable to disease. Epidemic disease swept through antebellum American cities and felled thousands. Yellow fever and cholera killed one-fifth of New Orleans's population in 1832–1833, and cholera alone killed 10 percent of St. Louis's population in 1849.

Ironically, the transportation revolution increased the danger of epidemic diseases. The cholera epidemic of 1832, the first truly national epidemic, followed shipping routes: one branch of the epidemic ran from New York City up the Hudson River, across the Erie Canal to Ohio, and down the Ohio River to the Mississippi and New Orleans; the other branch followed shipping up and down the East Coast from New York.

The inability of physicians to explain epidemic diseases led to general distrust of the medical profession and to the making of public health a low-priority issue (see Chapter 9). No one understood that bacteria caused cholera and yellow fever. Doctors speculated that diseases were spread by touch or by poisonous gases emitted from swamps and rotten organic matter.

Although epidemic disease baffled antebellum physicians, the discovery of anesthesia opened the way for remarkable advances in surgery. Crawford Long, a Georgia physician, employed sulfuric ether during surgery in 1842. Long did not follow up his discovery, but four years later William T.G. Morton, a dentist, successfully employed sulfuric ether during an operation at Massachusetts General Hospital. Within a few years ether was widely used.

The discovery of anesthesia improved the public image of surgeons, who had long been viewed as brutes hacking away at agonized patients. It also permitted longer and thus more careful operations. However, the failure of most surgeons to recognize the importance of clean hands and sterilized instruments partially offset the value of anesthesia. Operations remained as dangerous as the conditions they tried to heal. The mortality rate for amputations hovered around 40 percent, and during the Civil War 87 percent of soldiers who suffered abdominal wounds died from them.

Doubtful of medicine and skeptical of the benefits of public health, antebellum Americans turned to various therapies that promised a longer, healthier life. Hydropathy, the "water cure," offered "an abundance of water of dewy softness and crystal transparency, to cleanse, renovate, and rejuvenate the disease-worn and dilapidated system."

Sylvester Graham, a temperance reformer turned health advocate, popularized dietary changes as the way to better health. He urged Americans to eat less; to substitute vegetables, fruits, and whole-grain bread (called Graham bread) for meat; to abstain from spices, coffee, tea, and alcohol; and to avoid sexual "excess" (by which he meant most sex).

Democratic Pastimes

Between 1830 and 1860 technology transformed recreation into a commodity that could be purchased in the form of cheap newspapers and novels and equally cheap tickets to plays, museums, and lectures. These new democratic pastimes won a vast audience.

Newspapers

In 1830 the typical American newspaper was four pages long, with the front and back pages filled almost completely with advertisements. The interior pages contained editorials, reprints of political speeches, notices of political events, and information about shipping. Even the most prominent papers had a daily circulation of only 1,000 to 2,000; subsidies from political parties or factions supported them.

In the 1830s technology began to transform newspapers. Cheaper paper and steam-driven presses drastically lowered production costs, and enterprising journalists, among them James Gordon Bennett, saw the implications: slash prices, boost circulation, and reap vast profits. In 1833 New York's eleven daily newspapers had a combined daily circulation of only 26,500. Two years later the combined circulation of the three largest "penny" newspapers had soared to 44,000. From 1830 to 1840 national newspaper circulation rose from 78,000 to 300,000, and the number of weekly newspapers more than doubled.

The penny press also revolutionized the marketing and format of newspapers. Newsboys hawked the penny papers on busy street corners, and reporters filled the papers with gripping news stories designed to attract readers.

Some penny papers were little more than scandal sheets, but others, such as Bennett's *New York Herald* and Horace Greeley's *New York Tribune*, pioneered modern financial and political reporting. The *Herald* featured a daily "money article" that analyzed and interpreted financial events. The relentless snooping by the *Tribune's* Washington reporters outraged politicians. In 1841 *Tribune* correspondents were temporarily barred from the House of Representatives for reporting that an Ohio representative ate his lunch in the House chamber, picked his teeth with a jackknife, and wiped his greasy hands on his pants and coat.

The Popular Novel

Novels became affordable and enormously popular between 1830 and 1860. In the 1830s technology and transportation began to lower the price of novels, and in the 1840s cheap paperbacks selling for as little as seven cents flooded the national market. Serial versions appeared in newspapers devoted mainly to printing novels.

Sentimental novels dominated the fiction market in the 1840s and 1850s. The tribulations of orphans and deaths of children filled the pages of these tearjerkers. Both the authors and the audience of sentimental novels were overwhelmingly female.

A major theme in these novels was that women could conquer any obstacle. They challenged stereotypes of men as trusty providers and of women as delicate dependents. Instead, men were portrayed as liars, drunken lechers, and vicious misers and women as resourceful and strong-willed. A typical plot featured a female orphan or a spoiled rich girl thrown on hard times. Each learned to master her life. The moral was clear: women could overcome trials and make the world a better place.

The Theater

During the 1850s popular novelists such as Charles Dickens and Harriet Beecher Stowe were as well known through dramatizations of their work as through sales of their books. Antebellum theaters were large and crowded; cheap seats drew a democratic throng of lawyers and merchants and their wives, artisans and clerks, sailors and noisy boys, and a sizable body of prostitutes. Theater audiences were notoriously rowdy: they stamped their feet, hooted at villains, and threw garbage at the stage when they disliked the characters or the acting.

The plays themselves were as diverse as the audiences. Melodramas, whose plots resembled those of sentimental novels, were popular; vice was punished and virtue was rewarded. Yet the single most popular dramatist was William Shakespeare. In 1835 Philadelphia audiences witnessed sixty-five productions of his plays. Shakespeare himself might not have recognized some of these performances, adapted as they were for popular audiences. Theatrical managers highlighted swordfights and assassinations, cut long speeches, and changed tragic endings to happy ones. Producers arranged for short performances between acts. In the middle of *Macbeth*, the audience might see an impersonation of Tecumseh or of Aaron Burr, jugglers and acrobats, a drummer beating twelve drums at once, or a three-year-old who weighed one hundred pounds.

Minstrel Shows

The minstrel shows that Americans flocked to see in the 1840s and 1850s forged enduring stereotypes that buttressed white Americans' sense of superiority by diminishing blacks. The shows arose in northern cities in the 1840s as blackfaced white men took the stage to present an evening of songs, dances, and humorous sketches.

Although the performances featured elements of African-American culture, especially dance steps, most of the songs were from white culture. Stephen Foster's "Camptown Races" and "Massa's in the Cold, Cold Ground," first performed in minstrel shows, reflected whites' notions of how blacks sang, not authentic black music. The images of blacks projected by minstrelsy catered to the prejudices of the working-class whites who dominated the audiences. Minstrel troupes depicted blacks as stupid, clumsy, and obsessively musical and emphasized their Africanness. At a time of intensifying political conflict over race, minstrel shows planted images and expectations about blacks' behavior through stock characters such as Uncle Ned, the tattered, humble slave; and Zip Coon, the arrogant urban free black who paraded around in a high hat and long-tailed coat and lived off his girlfriends' money.

P. T. Barnum

No one understood better than P.T. Barnum how to turn the public's craving for entertainment into a profitable business. He was simultaneously a hustler who cheated his customers before they could cheat him and an idealist who founded a newspaper to attack wrongdoing.

After moving to New York City in 1834, Barnum began his career as an entrepreneur of entertainment. His first venture exhibited an African-American woman, Joyce Heth, whom Barnum billed as the 169-year-old former slave nurse of George Washington. In Barnum's mind, the truth or falsehood of the claim was irrelevant. What mattered was that people would pay.

In 1841 Barnum purchased a run-down museum in New York City, rechristened it the American

Museum, and opened a new chapter in the history of popular entertainment. Avoiding the educational slant of other museums, Barnum concentrated on curiosities and faked exhibits; he wanted to interest people, not to educate them. The American Museum included ventriloquists, magicians, albinos, a five-year-old midget named Tom Thumb, and the "Feejee Mermaid," a shrunken oddity "taken alive in the Feejee Islands."

Barnum's success rested on more than people's curiosity, however. A temperance advocate, he provided lectures on the evils of alcohol and gave the place a reputation as a center for safe family amusement. In addition, Barnum tapped the public's insatiable appetite for natural wonders. At a time when each year brought new technological marvels, Americans would believe in anything, even the Feejee Mermaid.

The Quest for Nationality in Literature and Art

Apart from the world of popular culture, a group of American writers and artists labored to build a national literature and art. "The American Scholar," an address by Ralph Waldo Emerson in 1837, constituted an intellectual Declaration of Independence. Americans had too long deferred to European precedents, he proclaimed. The democratic spirit of the age had made Americans more self-reliant, and the time had come for them to break free of European standards and to trust themselves. In addition, Emerson's address adopted romanticism, the major intellectual movement of the first half of the nineteenth century, which celebrated the nation and the individual. Rejecting the idea of universal standards, romantics first in Europe and then in the United States insisted that great literature had to reflect both the national character and the author's emotions.

The transcendentalism of Emerson and his colleagues formed a uniquely American romanticism. Transcendentalists argued that knowledge went beyond, or transcended, the intellect. Like sight, it was

an instantaneous, direct perception of truth. Intuition and emotion could provide knowledge as accurately as intellect could. Emerson concluded that learned people had no special advantage in the pursuit of truth. Rather, truth itself was democratic—all could see the truth if only they would trust the promptings of their hearts.

Many reputations that burned brightly in nineteenth-century America have dimmed, but the genius of seven writers continues to gleam: Cooper, Emerson, Thoreau, Whitman, Hawthorne, Melville, and Poe. Cooper and Emerson were the only writers who basked in public esteem in their day; neither Hawthorne nor Poe gained the audience that each believed he deserved, and the antebellum public largely ignored Thoreau and Whitman. Melville's light works were popular, but his serious fiction received little acclaim. Creativity, not popularity, linked these seven writers. Each challenged existing literary conventions and created new ones.

James Fenimore Cooper and the Stirrings of Literary Independence

Until well after 1800 British literature dominated American literary taste. Sir Walter Scott's historical novel *Waverly* (1814) had catapulted the British author to enduring fame in America and created a demand for historical novels. Born in 1789, James Fenimore Cooper, called the American Scott because he wrote historical novels, introduced American characters and themes to literature. In his frontiersman Natty Bumppo, "Leatherstocking," Cooper created an American archetype. Natty first appears in *The Pioneers* (1823) as an old man, a former hunter, who blames the farmers for wantonly destroying upstate New York's game and turning the silent and majestic forests into deserts of tree stumps. As a spokesman for nature against the march of civilization, Natty became a highly popular figure, and his life unfolded in several other enormously popular novels, such as *The Last of the Mohicans* (1826), *The Pathfinder* (1840), and *The Deerslayer* (1841).

The success of James Fenimore Cooper and other early-nineteenth-century writers was the first step in the development of an American literature. Americans still read British novels, but more and more they enjoyed American authors. In 1800 American authors had accounted for a negligible proportion of the output of American publishers, but by 1830, 40 percent of the books published in the United States were written by Americans and by 1850, 75 percent.

Emerson, Thoreau, and Whitman

Ralph Waldo Emerson's advocacy of a national literature extended beyond "The American Scholar." In his own writing he tried to capture the brisk language of the common people, and he also encouraged younger writers, among them Thoreau and Whitman. Whitman, extravagantly patriotic, contrasted sharply with Emerson and Thoreau, who criticized the materialism and aggressiveness of their compatriots. But all three shared a common trait: their uniquely American work emphasized the spontaneous and vivid expression of personal feeling rather than learned analysis.

Born in 1803, Emerson had served briefly as a Unitarian minister before fashioning a career as a public lecturer. Published as essays, his lectures won a wide readership. The true scholar, he stressed, must be independent: "Let him not quit his belief that a popgun is a popgun, though the ancient and honorable of the earth affirm it to be the crack of doom." A transcendentalist who believed that knowledge reflected the voice of God within every person and that truth was inborn and universal, Emerson relied not on a systematic analysis of the world around him but on vivid and arresting—although unconnected—assertions. Listening to Emerson, someone said, was like trying to see the sun in a fog; one could see light but never the sun.

In addition to dazzling his audiences, Emerson had a magnetic attraction for young intellectuals ill at ease in conventional society. Henry David Thoreau, born in 1817, typified the younger Emersonians. Unlike Emerson, whose adventurousness was largely intellectual, Thoreau was both a thinker and a doer. At one point he went to jail rather than pay poll taxes that would support the Mexican War, a conflict that he saw as part of a southern conspiracy to extend slavery. The experience of jail led Thoreau to write *Civil Disobedience* (1849), in which he defended disobedience of unjust laws.

In spring 1845 Thoreau moved a few miles from Concord into the woods near Walden Pond. He constructed a simple cabin on land owned by Emerson and spent the next two years providing for his wants away from civilization. Thoreau's stated purpose for his retreat to Walden was to write a book about a canoe trip that he had taken, but he soon undertook a much more important book. *Walden* (1854), although it abounded with descriptions of nature and wildlife, carried a larger, transcendentalist message. Thoreau proclaimed that his woodland retreat had taught him that only a few weeks' work was needed to satisfy material needs; most of the year could be used to examine life's purpose. The problem with Americans, he wrote, was that they turned themselves into "mere machines" to acquire wealth without asking why.

Emerson sympathized with personalities as dissimilar but distinctively American as Thoreau and Walt Whitman—the former was eccentric, reclusive, and critical, the latter was self-taught, exuberant, outgoing, and in love with everything American except slavery. A journalist and fervent Democrat, Whitman had an intimate, affectionate knowledge of ordinary Americans. His reading of Emerson nurtured his belief that the United States would be the cradle of a new citizen in whom natural virtue would flourish. The threads of Whitman's early career came together in his major work, *Leaves of Grass*, a book of poems first published in 1855.

Leaves of Grass shattered existing poetic conventions. Whitman composed in free verse, and his blunt, lusty words assailed "delicacy." He wrote of "the scent of these armpits finer than prayer" and "winds whose soft-tickling genitals rub against me." Whitman was the subject as well as the writer of his poems, especially in "Song of Myself." He saw himself—crude, plain, self-taught, passionately democratic—as the personification of the American people.

Hawthorne, Melville, and Poe

Emerson's call on American writers to create a democratic literature by comprehending "the near, the low, the common" had a negligible impact on the major fiction writers during the 1840s and 1850s: Nathaniel Hawthorne, Herman Melville, and Edgar Allan Poe. Hawthorne, for example, set *The Scarlet Letter* (1850) in New England's Puritan past, *The House of the Seven Gables* (1851) in a mansion haunted by memories of the past, and *The Marble Faun* (1859) in Rome. Poe set several of his short stories in Europe; and Melville's novels *Typee* (1846), *Omoo* (1847), and *Mardi* (1849) took place in the exotic South Seas, and his masterpiece, *Moby-Dick* (1851), aboard a whaler.

In part, these three writers felt that American life lacked the materials for great fiction. Hawthorne bemoaned the difficulty of writing about a country "where there is no shadow, no antiquity, no mystery, no picturesque and gloomy wrong." Psychology, not society, fascinated these writers. Each probed the depths of the human mind rather than the intricacies of social relationships, and each demonstrated an underlying pessimism about the human condition.

Pessimism led them to create characters obsessed by pride, guilt, a desire for revenge, or a quest for perfection and then to set their stories along the byways of society, where the authors could freely explore the complexities of human motivation without the jarring intrusions of everyday life. For example, in *The Scarlet Letter* Hawthorne returned to the Puritan era in order to examine the psychological and moral consequences of the adultery committed by Hester Prynne and the minister Arthur Dimmesdale. Melville, in *Moby-Dick,* created the frightening Captain Ahab, whose relentless pursuit of a white whale fails to fill the chasm in his soul and brings death to all his crew except the narrator. Poe, too, channeled his pessimism into creative work of the first rank. In his short story "The Fall of the House of Usher" (1839), he interwove the symbol of a crumbling mansion with the mental agony of a crumbling family.

Although these three authors ignored Emerson's call to write about the everyday experiences of their fellow Americans, they fashioned a distinctively American fiction. Their works, preoccupied with analysis of moral dilemmas and psychological states, fulfilled Tocqueville's prediction that writers in democratic nations, while rejecting traditional sources of fiction, would explore the abstract and universal questions of human nature.

American Landscape Painting

American painters between 1820 and 1860 also sought to develop nationality in their work. Lacking a mythic past of gods and goddesses, they subordinated historical and figure painting to landscape painting. The American landscape, though barren of the "poetry of decay" that Europe's ruined castles provided, was fresh and relatively unencumbered by the human imprint. These conditions posed a challenge to the painters of the Hudson River school, which flourished from the 1820s to the 1870s. Its best-known representatives—Thomas Cole, Asher Durand, and Frederic Church—painted scenes of the unspoiled region around the Hudson River.

The Hudson River painters did more than preserve a vanishing wilderness; they also emphasized emotional effect. Cole's rich colors; billowing clouds; massive, gnarled trees; towering peaks; and deep chasms so heightened the dramatic impact of his paintings that poet William Cullen Bryant compared them to "acts of religion."

Like Cole, George Catlin tried to preserve a vanishing America through his art. His goal was to paint as many Native Americans as possible in their pure and "savage" state. By 1837 he had created 437 oil paintings and thousands of sketches of faces and customs from nearly fifty tribes. Catlin's romantic view of the Indians as noble savages was a double-edged sword. His admirers delighted in his dignified portrayals of Indians but shared his foreboding that the march of progress had already doomed these noble creatures to oblivion.

The Diffusion of Knowledge

Just as Emerson contended that the democratizing spirit of his age would encourage Americans to discover their cultural identity, many of his contemporaries argued that the educated had a duty to "diffuse," or spread, enlightenment among the common people.

Advocates of systematic popular instruction turned to both public schools and lyceums, local organizations that sponsored public lectures on topics as diverse as astronomy, biology, physiology, geology, memory, Iceland, the true mission of women, and the domestic life of the Turks. After 1840 the spread of railroads contributed to the rise of a group of nationally known lecturers, including Ralph Waldo Emerson.

Not only railroads but also the growth of public education and the advent of low-priced newspapers and books helped to bring audiences and lecturers together. Originating in New England, lyceums expanded across the northern states and made inroads into the South. By 1840, 3,500 towns had lyceums, yet in that year's presidential election, the Whigs' log cabin campaign blasted Democratic candidate Martin Van Buren for displays of refinement. Americans were clearly of two minds on the subject of learning. Nowhere was this ambivalence sharper than in the West. Westerners prided themselves on their rough ways, but eastern missionaries swarmed across the West to build not only lyceum halls but also academies and colleges. In 1800 there was only one college in what is now the Midwest; by 1850 there were nearly seventy, more than in any other region. Audiences flocked to listen to emissaries of eastern refinement.

CHRONOLOGY

1823	Philadelphia completes the first urban water-supply system.
1826	Josiah Holbrook introduces the idea for lyceums. James Fenimore Cooper, *The Last of the Mohicans*.
1832	A cholera epidemic strikes the United States.
1833	The *New York Sun*, the first penny newspaper, is established.
1834	Cyrus McCormick patents the mechanical reaper.
1835	James Gordon Bennett establishes the *New York Herald*.
1837	Ralph Waldo Emerson, "The American Scholar."
1839	Edgar Allan Poe, "The Fall of the House of Usher."

1841	P. T. Barnum opens the American Museum.
1844	Samuel F. B. Morse patents the telegraph.
1846	W. T. G. Morton successfully uses anesthesia.
1849	Second major cholera epidemic.
1850	Nathaniel Hawthorne, *The Scarlet Letter*.
1851	Hawthorne, *The House of the Seven Gables*. Herman Melville, *Moby-Dick*.
1854	Henry David Thoreau, *Walden*.
1855	Walt Whitman, *Leaves of Grass*.
1857	Baltimore–St. Louis rail service completed.

FOR FURTHER READING

Carl Bode, *The Anatomy of American Popular Culture, 1840–1861* (1959). A useful general survey.

Mary Kupiec Cayton, *Emerson's Emergence: Self and Society in the Transformation of New England* (1989). A sensitive interpretation of the major figure in the American Renaissance.

William Cronon, *Chicago and the Great West* (1991). Analysis emphasizing environmental factors in the emergence of Chicago as the dominant city in the mid-nineteenth-century West.

Ann Douglas, *The Feminization of American Culture* (1977). An analysis of the role of the middle-class women and liberal ministers in the cultural sphere during the nineteenth century.

Siegfried Giedion, *Mechanization Takes Command* (1948). An interpretive overview of the impact of technology on Europe and America.

Barbara Novak, *Nature and Culture: American Landscape Painting, 1825–1875* (1982). An insightful study of the relationships between landscape painting and contemporary religious and philosophical currents.

Gwendolyn Wright, *Building the Dream: A Social History of Housing in America* (1981). An exploration of the ideologies and policies that have shaped American housing since Puritan times.

12

The Old South and Slavery, 1800–1860

King Cotton

In 1790 the South was essentially stagnant. Tobacco, its primary cash crop, had lost its economic vitality even as it had depleted the once-rich southern soils, and neither rice nor cotton could replace tobacco's economic importance. Three out of four southerners still lived along the Atlantic seaboard, specifically in the Chesapeake and the Carolinas. One of three resided in Virginia alone.

The contrast between that South and the dynamic South of 1850 was stunning. By 1850 southerners had moved south and west—now only one of seven southerners lived in Virginia—and cotton reigned as king, shaping this new South. The growth

of the British textile industry had created a huge demand for cotton, while Indian removal had made way for southern expansion into the "Cotton Kingdom," a broad swath of land that stretched from South Carolina, Georgia, and northern Florida in the east through Alabama, Mississippi, central and western Tennessee, and Louisiana, and from there on to Arkansas and Texas.

A warm climate, wet springs and summers, and relatively dry autumns made the Lower (or Deep) South ideal for cultivating cotton. A cotton farmer needed neither slaves nor cotton gins nor the capital required for sugar cultivation. Indeed, perhaps 50 percent of farmers in the "cotton belt" owned no slaves, and to process their harvest, they could turn to the widely available commercial gins. In short, cotton profited everyone; it promised to make poor men prosperous and rich men kings.

Yet large-scale cotton cultivation and slavery grew together as the southern slave population nearly doubled between 1810 and 1830. Three-fourths of all southern slaves worked in the cotton economy in 1830.

Cotton offered an added advantage: it was compatible with corn production. Corn could be planted either earlier or later than cotton and harvested before or after. Because the cost of owning a slave remained the same regardless of whether he or she was working, corn production allowed slaveholders to shift slave labor between corn and cotton. By 1860 the acreage devoted to corn in the Old South actually *exceeded* that devoted to cotton. Economically, corn and cotton gave the South the best of two worlds. Intense demand in Britain and New England kept cotton prices high and money flowing into the South.

Ties Between the Lower and Upper South

Two giant cash crops, sugar and cotton, dominated agriculture in the Lower South. The Upper South, a region of tobacco, vegetable, hemp, and wheat growers, depended far less on the great cash crops. Nevertheless, a common dependence on slavery unified the Upper and the Lower South and made the Upper South identify more with the Lower South than with the nation's free states.

A range of social, political, and psychological factors promoted this unity. First, many settlers in the Lower South had come from the Upper South. Second, all white southerners benefited from the Constitution's three-fifths clause, which let them count slaves as a basis for congressional representation. Third, abolitionist attacks on slavery stung all southerners and bound them together. Fourth, economic ties linked the two Souths. The profitability of cotton and sugar increased the value of slaves throughout the South. The sale of slaves from the declining plantation states of the Upper South to the booming Lower South was a huge business.

The North and South Diverge

The changes responsible for the dynamic growth of the South widened the distance between it and the North. The South remained predominantly rural as the North became more and more urban.

Lack of industry kept the South rural; by 1850 it had one-third of the U.S. population but accounted for only a tenth of the nation's manufacturing. In 1850 the industrial output of the entire South was less than a third that of Massachusetts alone.

Some southerners advocated and created factories in the South, but they were a minority. By 1860 cotton-textile mills were scattered throughout the South, and Richmond boasted the nation's fourth-largest producer of iron products, the Tredegar Iron Works. Despite these successes, industrial output in the South trailed far behind that of the New England and Middle Atlantic states.

Slavery posed a major obstacle to southern industrialization, but not because slaves were unfit for factories; the Tredegar Iron Works was among many factories that employed slaves. However, the prospect of industrial slavery troubled slaveholders. Away from the strict discipline and supervision possible on a plantation, slaves sometimes behaved as if they were free, shifting jobs, working overtime, and even negotiating better working conditions.

But the chief brake on southern industrialization was money, not labor. To raise the capital needed to build factories, planters would have had to sell their slaves. They seldom did. As long as southerners believed that the cash-crop economy remained profitable, they had little reason to plunge into the uncertainties of industrialization.

Thus the Old South was not economically backward—it was merely different. Cotton was a wonderful crop, and southerners could hardly be blamed for making it their ruler. As a southern senator wrote in 1858, "You dare not make war upon cotton; no power on earth dares to make war upon it. Cotton is king."

In education, as in industry, the South lagged behind the North. Where northerners recognized the benefits of an educated work force for their growing manufacturing economy, agriculturally oriented southerners rejected compulsory education and were reluctant to tax property to support schools. They abhorred the thought of educating slaves, and southern lawmakers made it a crime to teach slaves to read. For most whites, the only available schools were private. White illiteracy thus remained high in the South as it declined in the North.

Social Relations in the White South

There was wide diversity within and between the South's slaveholding and nonslaveholding classes. Although some planters owned hundreds of slaves and lived lavishly, most lived more modestly. In 1860, one-fourth of all white families in the South owned slaves; nearly half of those owned fewer than five slaves, and three-fourths had fewer than ten slaves. Only 12 percent owned twenty or more slaves, and only 1 percent a hundred or more. Nonslaveholders were equally diverse, ranging from the owners of family farms to squatters in the pine barrens or piney woods.

Planters, small slaveholders, family farmers, and pine-barrens folk composed the South's four main white groups. Many southerners—lawyers, physicians, merchants, and artisans—did not fall into any of these four, but they tended to identify their interests with one or another of the agricultural groups.

Planters and Plantation Mistresses

The plantation, with its porticoed mansion and fields teeming with slaves, stands at the center of the popular image of the Old South. This romanticized view, reinforced by novels and movies such as *Gone with the Wind,* is not entirely false, for the South did contain plantations that travelers found "superb beyond description." Most planters counted their wealth not in grand mansions and elegant furnishings but in the value of their slaves. A field hand was worth as much as $1,700 in the 1850s, and few planters sold their slaves to buy luxuries.

 @ Aiken House, Slave Quarters

@ The Hermitage, Slave Quarters

But in their constant worry about profit, planters enjoyed neither repose nor security. High fixed costs—housing and feeding slaves, maintaining cotton gins, hiring overseers—led them to search for better land and higher efficiency. Because cotton prices tended to fluctuate seasonally, planters often assigned their cotton to commercial agents in cities, who held the cotton until the price was right. The agents extended credit so that the planters could pay their bills before the cotton was sold. Indebtedness became part of the plantation economy and intensified the planters' quest for profitability. Psychological strains compounded economic worries. Frequent moves disrupted circles of friends and relatives, particularly as migration to the Southwest (Alabama and Mississippi) carried families into less settled, more desolate areas.

Planters and their wives found various ways of coping with their isolation. Employing overseers to run the plantation, some lived in cities; in 1850 one-half the planters in the Mississippi Delta lived in New Orleans or Natchez. Most planters acted as their own overseers, however, and dealt with the problems of harsh living conditions by opening their homes to visitors. The responsibility for such hospitality fell heavily on wives, who might have to entertain as many as fifteen people for breakfast and attend to the needs of visitors who stayed for days. Plantation wives also bore the burdens of raising their children, supervising house slaves, making clothes and carpets, looking after smokehouses and dairies, planting gardens, and, often, keeping the plantation accounts.

Among the heaviest sorrows of some plantation mistresses was the presence of mulatto children, constant reminders of their husbands' infidelities. Charlestonian Mary Boykin Chesnut, a famous diarist, observed tartly, "Any lady is ready to tell you who is the father of all the mulatto children in everybody's household but her own. These, she seems to think, drop from clouds." Southern men insisted on sexual purity for white women but allowed themselves a looser standard.

@ A Slave Perspective on Family Ties

The Small Slaveholders

In 1860, 88 percent of all slaveholders owned fewer than twenty slaves, and most possessed fewer than ten. One out of every five slaveholders worked outside of agriculture, as a lawyer, physician, merchant, or artisan.

Small slaveholders experienced conflicting loyalties and ambitions. In upland regions they absorbed the outlook of the more numerous yeomen (non-slave-owning

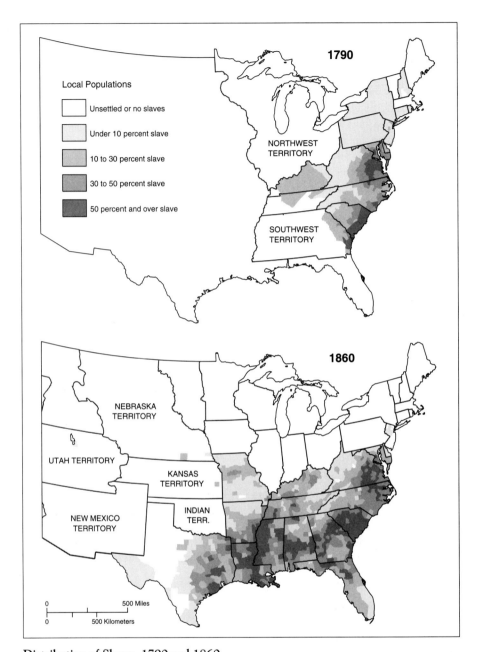

Distribution of Slaves, 1790 and 1860

In 1790 the majority of slaves resided along the southeastern seaboard. By 1860, however, slavery had spread throughout the South, and slaves were most heavily concentrated in the Deep South states.

SOURCE: Reprinted with permission of the McGraw-Hill Companies, from *Ordeal by Fire: The Civil War and Reconstruction*, Second Edition, by James M. McPherson. Copyright © 1992 by the McGraw-Hill Companies.

small farmers); they owned only a few slaves and rarely aspired to become large planters. In contrast, in the plantation-dominated low country and delta regions, small slaveholders often aspired to planter status. There someone with ten slaves could realistically look forward to owning thirty. And ambitious, acquisitive individuals equated success with owning more slaves.

The social structure of the deltas was fluid. In the early antebellum period large planters had been reluctant to risk transporting their hundreds of valuable slaves in a still turbulent region. It was small slaveholders who led the initial westward push into the cotton belt in the 1810s and 1820s. Gradually, large planters, too, moved westward, buying land developed by small slave owners and turning the region from Vicksburg to Natchez into large plantations. Small slave owners took the profits from selling their land, bought more slaves, and moved on.

The Yeomen

Nonslaveholding family farmers, or yeomen, composed the largest single group of southern whites. Most owned land, and many hired slaves to help at harvest. In areas of poor soil, such as eastern Tennessee, yeomen were typically subsistence farmers, but most yeomen grew some cash crops. Their landholdings were comparatively small, ranging from 50 to 200 acres. Yeomen generally inhabited uplands far from the rich coastal plains and deltas, such as the piedmont of the East or the hilly upcountry of the Southwest.

Above all, the yeomen valued self-sufficiency. Unlike planters, who were driven to acquire more land and to plant more cash crops, the yeomen devoted much of their acreage to subsistence crops such as corn, sweet potatoes, and oats. The planter's ideal was profit with modest self-sufficiency; the yeoman's goal, self-sufficiency with modest profit. Unlike planters, yeomen marketed their cash crops locally, trading cotton, wheat, and tobacco for goods and services from nearby artisans and merchants.

The People of the Pine Barrens

Independent whites of the wooded "pine barrens" were one of the most controversial groups in the Old South. About 10 percent of southern whites, they usually squatted on the land; put up crude cabins; cleared some acreage, where they planted corn between tree stumps; and grazed hogs and cattle in the woods. They neither raised cash crops nor engaged in the daily routine of orderly work that characterized family farmers. With their ramshackle houses and handful of stump-strewn acres, they appeared lazy and shiftless.

Abolitionists cited the pine-barrens people as proof that slavery degraded whites, but southerners responded that, while the pine-barrens folk were poor, they could at least feed themselves, unlike the paupers of northern cities. The people of the pine barrens were both self-sufficient and fiercely independent.

Conflict and Consensus in the White South

Planters tangled with yeomen on several issues. With extensive economic dealings and need for credit, planters inclined toward the Whig party, which generally supported economic development. The independent yeomen, cherishing their self-sufficiency, tended to be Democrats. Yet conflicts between these two groups were mild, softened by an underlying political concord.

The white South's political structure was sufficiently democratic to prevent any one group from gaining exclusive control over politics. Planters dominated state legislatures, but they owed their election to the popular vote. And the democratic currents that had swept northern politics between 1815 and 1860 had affected the South as well; newer southern states entered the Union with democratic constitutions that included universal white manhood suffrage—the right of all adult white males to vote.

Conflict over Slavery

Nevertheless, considerable *potential* existed for conflict between slaveholders and nonslaveholders. The southern white carpenter who complained in 1849 that "unjust, oppressive, and degrading" competition from slave labor depressed his wages surely had a point. Between 1830 and 1860 the slaveholding class shrank in size in relation to the total white population, but its share of total wealth increased.

Yet although pockets of opposition dotted the South, slavery did not create profound or lasting divisions between slaveholders and nonslaveholders. For example, antagonism to slavery flourished in parts of Virginia up to 1860, but proposals for emancipating the slaves dropped from the state's political agenda after 1832.

The rise and fall of pro-emancipation sentiment in the South raises a key question: as most white southerners were nonslaveholders, why did they not attack slavery more consistently? To look ahead, why were so many southerners willing to fight ferociously and to die bravely during the Civil War in defense of an institution in which they apparently had no real stake? There are several reasons. First, some non-slaveholders hoped to become slaveholders. Second, most southerners accepted the racist assumptions on which slavery rested; they dreaded the likelihood that emancipation would encourage "impudent" blacks to entertain ideas of social equality with whites. Slavery appealed to whites as a legal, time-honored, and foolproof way to enforce the social subordination of blacks. Third, no one knew where the slaves, if freed, would go or what they would do. Colonizing freed blacks in Africa was unrealistic, southerners concluded, but they also believed that without colonization, emancipation would lead to a race war.

The Proslavery Argument

Between 1830 and 1860 southerners constructed a defense of slavery as a positive good rather than a necessary evil. St. Paul's injunction that servants obey their masters became a biblical justification for some. Others looked to the classical past to argue that slavery was both an ancient and classical institution; the slave society of Athens, they said, had produced Aristotle and Plato, and Roman slaveholders had laid the foundations of Western civilization. A third proslavery argument, advanced particularly by George Fitzhugh of Virginia, contrasted the plight of the northern "wage slaves," callously discarded when they became too ill or 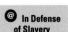 @ **In Defense of Slavery**

too old to work, with the lot of southern slaves, cared for by masters who attended to their health, their clothing, and their discipline.

The rise of the proslavery argument coincided with a shift in the position of southern churches on slavery. During the 1790s and early 1800s some Protestant ministers had assailed slavery as immoral, but by the 1830s most clergymen had convinced themselves that slavery was entirely compatible with Christianity. Slavery, they proclaimed, provided the opportunity to display Christian responsibility toward one's inferiors, and it helped African-Americans to develop Christian virtues such as humility and self-control. In 1837 southerners and conservative northerners had combined forces to drive antislavery New School Presbyterians out of that denomination's main body, in 1844 the Methodist Episcopal Church split into northern and southern wings, and in 1845 Baptists formed a separate Southern Convention. In effect, southern evangelicals seceded from national church organizations long before the South seceded from the Union.

Honor and Violence in the Old South

To the northern eye, southerners seemed to run to extremes. One minute they were hospitable and gracious, full of courtly gestures; the next, savagely violent. In the 1760s a minister described backcountry Virginians "biting one anothers Lips and Noses off, and gowging one another—that is, thrusting out anothers Eyes, and kicking one another on the Cods [genitals], to the great damage of many a Poor Woman." Mike Fink, a legendary southern fighter and hunter, boasted that he was so mean in infancy that he refused his mother's milk and howled for whiskey. Yet beneath the folklore lay the reality of violence that gave the Old South a murder rate as much as ten times higher than that of the North.

The Code of Honor and Dueling

At the root of most violence in the white South lay intensified feelings of personal pride that reflected the inescapable presence of slaves. White southerners saw slaves degraded, insulted, and powerless to resist. In turn, whites reacted violently to even trivial insults to demonstrate that they had nothing in common with slaves.

Among gentlemen this exaggerated pride took the form of a code of honor, with honor defined as an extraordinary sensitivity to one's reputation. In the honor culture of the Old South, even the slightest insult, as long as it was perceived as intentional, could become the basis for a duel.

Formalized by French and British officers during the Revolutionary War, dueling gained a secure niche in the Old South as a means by which gentlemen dealt with affronts to their honor. Seemingly trivial incidents—a harmless brushing against the side of someone at a public event, a hostile glance—could trigger a duel. Gentlemen viewed dueling as a refined alternative to the random violence of lower-class life. Instead of leaping at his antagonist's throat, a gentleman remained cool, settled on a weapon with his opponent, and agreed to a meeting place. In the interval, friends of the parties negotiated to clear up the "misunderstanding" that had provoked the challenge.

Although dueling was as much a way of settling disputes peacefully as of ending them violently, the ritual could easily end in death or maiming. Dueling bypassed the court system, which would have guaranteed a peaceful result; in disputes involving honor, recourse to the law struck many southerners as cowardly and shameless.

The Southern Evangelicals and White Values

With its emphasis on the personal redress of grievances and its inclination toward violence, the ideal of honor conflicted with the values preached by the southern evangelical churches, notably the Baptists, Methodists, and Presbyterians. These denominations stressed humility and self-restraint, virtues that sharply contrasted with the culture of display that buttressed the extravagance and violence of the Old South.

Before 1830 most southern gentlemen looked down on the evangelicals as uncouth fanatics. But the evangelicals shed their backwoods image by founding colleges such as Randolph Macon and Wake Forest and by exhorting women (two-thirds of the average congregation) to make every home "a sanctuary, a resting place, a shadow from the heats, turmoils, and conflicts of life." By the 1860s the South counted many gentlemen like the Bible-quoting Presbyterian general Thomas J. "Stonewall" Jackson, fierce in a righteous war but a sworn opponent of strong drink, gambling, and dueling.

Life Under Slavery

Slavery changed significantly between 1700 and 1830. In 1700 the typical slave was a man in his twenties, recently arrived from Africa or the Caribbean, who worked on an isolated small farm. Drawn from different regions of Africa, few slaves spoke the same language. Because slave ships carried twice as many men as women, and because slaves were widely scattered, blacks had difficulties finding partners and creating a semblance of family life. Without continuing importations, the number of slaves in North America would have declined between 1710 and 1730.

@ **Main Sources of African Slaves**

In contrast, by 1830 the typical North American slave was as likely to be female as male, had been born in America, spoke English, and worked beside numerous other slaves on a plantation. The rise of plantation agriculture in the eighteenth century was at the heart of the change. Plantation slaves found mates more easily than slaves on scattered farms. The native-born slave population soared after 1750. The importation of African slaves declined, and in 1808 Congress banned it.

Work and Discipline of Plantation Slaves

In 1850 the typical slave worked on a large farm or plantation with at least ten other slaves. Almost three-quarters of all slaves belonged to masters with ten or more slaves, and just over one-half lived in units of twenty or more slaves.

An hour before sunrise, a horn or a bell awakened the slaves. After a sparse breakfast, they marched to the fields, where slave men and women worked side by side. Those female slaves who did not labor in the fields remained busy. Plantations never lacked tasks for slaves of either gender. In any season the slave's day stretched from dawn to dusk. When darkness made field work impossible, slaves toted cotton bales to the ginhouse, gathered wood for supper fires, and fed the mules. Weary from their labors, they slept in log cabins on wooden planks.

Although virtually all antebellum Americans worked long hours, no others experienced the combination of long hours and harsh discipline that slave field hands endured. Northern factory workers did not live in fear of drivers walking among them with a whip. Repulsive brutality pervaded American slavery. The barbaric discipline twinged the consciences of many masters, but most justified it as their Christian duty to ensure the slaves' proper "submissiveness."

Despite the system's brutality, some slaves advanced—not to freedom but to semiskilled or skilled indoor work. Some became blacksmiths, carpenters, or gin operators, and others served as cooks, butlers, and dining-room attendants. These house slaves became legendary for their disdain of field hands and poor whites.

Slave Families

Masters thought of slaves as naturally promiscuous and flattered themselves into thinking that they alone held slave marriages together. Masters had powerful incentives to encourage slave marriages: bringing new slaves into the world and discouraging slaves from running away.

Slavery itself posed the keenest challenge to slave families. The law provided neither recognition of nor protection for the slave family. Masters reluctant to break slave marriages by sale could neither bequeath their reluctance to heirs nor avoid economic hardship that might force them to sell slaves. The reality, one historian has calculated, was that on average a slave would see eleven family members sold during his or her lifetime.

@ **Human Cattle for Sale**

Inevitably, the buying and selling of slaves disrupted attempts to create a stable family life. Even couples who were allowed to remain together saw their family life disrupted by other aspects of slavery. The marriage of a slave woman did not protect her against the sexual demands of her master or, indeed, of any white. Field work kept slave mothers from their children, who were cared for by the elderly or by the mothers of other children.

@ **The Price of a Prime Male Slave in New Orleans**

Despite these enormous obstacles, relationships within slave families were often intimate and, where possible, long lasting. Given the opportunity, slaves solemnized their marriages before members of the clergy. White clergymen who accompanied Union armies into Mississippi and Louisiana during the Civil War conducted thousands of marriage rites for slaves who had long viewed themselves as married and desired a formal ceremony and registration.

Broad kinship patterns—close ties between children and grandparents, aunts, and uncles as well as parents—had marked West African cultures, and they were reinforced by the separation of children and parents that routinely occurred under slavery. In addition, slaves often created "fictive" kin networks, naming friends as their uncles, aunts, brothers, or sisters. In this way they helped to protect themselves against the disruption of family ties and established a broader community of obligation.

The Longevity, Health, and Diet of Slaves

Of the 10 million to 12 million Africans imported to the New World between the fifteenth and nineteenth centuries, North America received only 550,000 of them (about 5 percent), whereas Brazil received 3.5 million (nearly 33 percent). Yet by 1825, 36 percent of all slaves in the Western Hemisphere lived in the United States, and only 31 percent in Brazil. The reason for this difference is that slaves in the United States reproduced faster and lived longer than those in Brazil and elsewhere in the Western Hemisphere.

Several factors account for U.S. slaves' longer lives and higher rates of reproduction. First, with the gender ratio among slaves equalizing more rapidly in North America, slaves there married earlier and had more children. Second, because raising corn and livestock was compatible with growing cotton, the Old South produced plentiful food. Slaves generally received a peck of cornmeal and three to four pounds of fatty pork a week, which they often supplemented with vegetables grown on small plots and with catfish and game.

Slaves enjoyed greater immunity from malaria and yellow fever than whites but suffered more from cholera, dysentery, and diarrhea. Lacking privies, slaves usually relieved themselves behind bushes, and consequently urine and feces contaminated the sources of their drinking water. Slave remedies for stomach ailments, though commonly ridiculed by whites, often worked.

Nonetheless, slaves experienced a higher mortality rate than whites. The very young suffered most; infant mortality among slaves was double that among whites, and one in three African-American children died before age ten.

Slaves off Plantations

Greater freedom from supervision and greater opportunities awaited slaves who worked off plantations in towns and cities. Most southern whites succumbed to the lure of cotton and established small farms; the resulting shortage of white labor created a steady demand for slaves outside the plantation economy. Driving wagons, working as stevedores on the docks, manning river barges, and toiling in mining and lumbering gave slaves an opportunity to work somewhere other than the cotton fields.

The draining of potential white laborers from southern cities also provided opportunity for slaves to become skilled artisans. In the eighteenth century Charleston, Savannah, and other cities had a large class of highly skilled slave blacksmiths and carpenters, and the tradition endured into the nineteenth century.

Despite slavery's stranglehold, urban African-Americans in the South enjoyed opportunities denied their counterparts in the North. Generally, slaves who worked in factories, mining, or lumbering were hired out by their masters rather than owned by their employers. If working conditions for hired-out slaves deteriorated badly, masters would refuse to provide employers with more slaves. Consequently, working conditions for slaves off the plantation generally stayed at a tolerable level.

Life on the Margin: Free Blacks in the Old South

Free blacks were likelier than southern blacks in general to live in cities. In 1860 one-third of the free blacks in the Upper South and more than half in the Lower South were urban.

Urban specialization allowed free blacks the chance to become carpenters, coopers (barrel makers), barbers, and small traders. Most of the meat, fish, and produce in an antebellum southern market was prepared for sale by free blacks. Urban free blacks formed their own fraternal orders and churches; in New Orleans free blacks also had their own opera and literary journals.

Despite such successes, free blacks were vulnerable in southern society. They continued to increase in absolute numbers (a little more than 250,000 free people of color lived in the South in 1860), but the rate of growth of the free black population slowed radically after 1810. Fewer masters freed their slaves after that time, and following the Nat Turner rebellion in 1831, states legally restricted the liberties of free blacks. Every southern state forbade free blacks to enter, and in 1859 Arkansas ordered all free blacks to leave.

> @ **Black Recollections of Freedom's Impact**

Many free blacks were mulattos, the product of white masters and black women, and looked down on "darky" field hands and laborers. But as discrimination against free people of color intensified during the late antebellum period, many free blacks realized that whatever future they had was as blacks, not whites. Feelings of racial solidarity increased during the 1850s, and after the Civil War, the leaders of the ex-slaves were usually blacks who had been free before the war.

Slave Resistance

Fear of slave insurrection haunted the Old South. In lowland and delta plantation areas slaves often outnumbered whites. In the cities free blacks could have provided leadership for rebellions. Rumors of slave conspiracies flew within the southern white community, and all whites knew of the massive black revolt that had destroyed French rule in Santo Domingo.

Yet only three organized rebellions occurred in the Old South during the nineteenth century. Taken together, they say more about the futility than the possibility of slave rebellion. In 1800 the Virginia slave Gabriel Prosser's planned rebellion was betrayed by other slaves, and Prosser and his followers were executed. That same year Denmark Vesey, a South Carolina slave, used $1,500 won in a lottery to buy his freedom. Purchasing a carpentry shop in Charleston, Vesey preached at the city's African Methodist Episcopal church and built a sizable African-American following. In 1822 he and his loyalists devised a plan to attack Charleston and seize the city's arms and ammunition; betrayed by other slaves, they were captured and executed.

The Nat Turner rebellion, which occurred in 1831 in Southampton County, Virginia, was the only slave insurrection to lead to white deaths. Gloomy and introspective by nature, the slave Nat Turner taught himself to read and write in childhood. He became an electrifying preacher and gained a reputation for prophecy, including visions of white and black angels warring in the sky.

In 1831 Turner's anger over slavery's injustice boiled over. In August he and a handful of slaves set out, armed with axes and clubs. Gathering recruits as they moved from plantation to plantation, Turner and his followers killed all whites whom they encountered, men, women, and children alike. Before the rebellion was suppressed, fifty-five whites and more than a hundred blacks had died.

Turner's rebellion stunned the South. Coupled with the slave uprising of the 1790s on Santo Domingo, it convinced white southerners that a slave insurrection constituted an ever-present threat. Yet the Nat Turner rebellion, like the Prosser and Vesey conspiracies, never had a chance of success. During the Turner rebellion several slaves alerted their masters to the threat, less from loyalty than

from a correct assessment of Turner's chances. Despite constant fears of slave rebellion, the Old South experienced far fewer threats than the Caribbean or South America.

Several factors explain this apparent tranquillity. First, although slaves formed a majority in South Carolina and a few other areas, they did not constitute a *large* majority in any state. Second, unlike Caribbean slave owners, most southern masters lived on their plantations; they possessed armed force and were willing to use it. Third, family ties among U.S. slaves made them reluctant to risk death and thereby to orphan their children. Finally, slaves who ran away or plotted rebellion had no allies. Southern Indians routinely captured runaway slaves and claimed rewards for them; some Indians even owned slaves.

Unable to rebel, many slaves tried to escape to freedom in the North. Some light mulattos who passed as whites succeeded. More often, slaves borrowed, stole, or forged passes from plantations or obtained papers describing them as free. Frederick Douglass borrowed a sailor's papers to make his escape from Baltimore to New York City. Some former slaves, including Harriet Tubman and Josiah Henson, returned to the South to assist others to escape. Despite legends of an "Underground Railroad" of abolitionists helping slaves to freedom, fugitive slaves owed little to abolitionists. The "safe houses" of white sympathizers in border states were better known to slave catchers than to runaways. Probably fewer than a thousand slaves actually escaped to the North.

@ **Runaway Slave Advertisements**

Despite poor prospects for permanent escape, slaves could disappear for prolonged periods into the free-black communities of southern cities. Slaves enjoyed a fair degree of practical freedom to drive wagons to market and to come and go when they were off plantations. This kind of practical freedom did not change slavery's underlying oppressiveness, but it did give slaves a sense of having certain rights, and it helped to channel slave resistance into activities that were furtive and relatively harmless rather than open and violent. Theft, for example, was so common that planters kept tools, smokehouses, and closets under lock and key. Overworked field hands might leave tools out to rust, feign illness, or simply refuse to work. Indeed, not all furtive resistance was harmless. Arson and poisoning, both common forms of vengeance in African culture, flourished in the Old South. So did fear. Masters afflicted by dysentery never knew for sure that they had not been poisoned.

Arson, poisoning, theft, work stoppage, and negligence acted as alternatives to violent rebellion, but their goal was not freedom. Their object was merely to make slavery bearable. Most slaves would have preferred freedom but settled for less.

The Emergence of African-American Culture

Enslaved blacks combined elements of African and American culture to create a distinctive culture of their own.

The Language and Religion of Slaves

Before slaves could develop a common culture, they needed a common language. During the colonial period African-born slaves, speaking a variety of languages, had developed a "pidgin"—that is, a language that has no native speakers but in which people with different native languages can communicate.

Like all pidgins, English pidgin was a simplified language. Slaves usually dropped the verb *to be* (which had no equivalent in African tongues) and ignored or confused genders. Instead of saying "Mary is in the cabin," they typically said, "Mary, he in cabin." They substituted *no* for *not*, as in "He no wicked." Some African words, among them *banjo*, moved from pidgin to standard English, and others, such as *goober* (peanut), entered southern white slang.

Religion played an equally important role in forging an African-American culture. Africa contained rich and diverse religious customs and beliefs. Despite the presence of a few Muslims and Christians in the early slave population, most of the slaves brought from Africa followed one of many native African religions. Most of these religions drew little distinction between the spiritual and natural worlds—storms, illnesses, and earthquakes were all assumed to stem from supernatural forces. God, spirits that inhabited woods and waters, and ancestor spirits all constituted these supernatural forces.

However, African religions did not unify American slaves. African religions differed greatly, and the majority of slaves in the colonial period were young men who had not absorbed this religious heritage. Remnants of African religion remained, however, in part because before the 1790s whites made few attempts to convert slaves to Christianity. When whites' conversion efforts increased, dimly remembered African beliefs may have aided Christian missionaries in influencing slaves to accept Christianity. Evangelical Christianity, like African religions, drew few distinctions between the sacred and the worldly. Just as Africans believed that droughts and plagues resulted from supernatural forces, revivalists knew in their hearts that every drunkard who fell off his horse and every Sabbath breaker struck by lightning had experienced a deliberate, direct punishment from God.

Christian blacks' experience in the Old South illustrates the contradictions of life under slavery. Urban blacks often had their own churches, but rural blacks and slaves worshiped in the same churches as whites. Although African-Americans sat in segregated sections, they heard the same service as whites. Churches became the most interracial institutions in the Old South, and biracial churches sometimes disciplined whites for abusing black Christian members. But Christianity was not a route to black liberation. Ministers went out of their way to remind slaves that spiritual equality was not the same as civil equality.

However, slaves listening to the same sermons as whites often came to different conclusions. For example, slaves drew parallels between their captivity and that of the Jews, the Chosen People. Like the Jews, slaves concluded, they were "de people of de Lord." If they kept the faith, they would reach the Promised Land. The "Promised Land" could refer to Israel, to heaven, or to freedom. Whites agreed that Israel and heaven were the only permissible meanings,

@ **Religion as Social Control**

but some African-Americans thought of freedom as well.

Masters argued that slavery was a benign and divinely ordained institution, but Christianity told slaves that the institution was an affliction, a terrible and unjust system that God had allowed in order to test their faith. For having endured slavery, he would reward slaves. For having created it, he would punish masters.

African-American Music and Dance

African-American culture expressed blacks' feelings. Long after white rituals had grown sober and sedate, the congregation in African-American religious services shouted "Amen" and let their body movements reflect their feelings. Slaves also expressed their emotions in music and dance. Southern law forbade them to own "drums, horns, or other loud instruments, which may call together or give sign or notice to one another of their wicked designs and intentions." Instead, slaves made rhythmical clapping, called "patting juba," an indispensable accompaniment to dancing. Slaves also played an African instrument, the banjo, and beat tin buckets as substitutes for drums. Slave music was tied to bodily movement; slaves expressed themselves in a dance African in origin, emphasizing shuffling steps and bodily contortions rather than quick footwork and erect backs as in whites' dances.

Whether at work or prayer, slaves liked to sing. Work songs usually consisted of a leader's chant and a choral response. Masters encouraged such songs, believing that singing induced slaves to work harder and that the innocent content of work songs proved that slaves were happy. However, Frederick Douglass, recalling his own past, observed that "slaves sing most when they are most unhappy. The songs of the slave represent the sorrows of his heart; and he is relieved by them, only as an aching heart is relieved by its tears."

African-Americans also sang religious songs, later known as spirituals, which reflected the powerful emphasis that slave religion placed on deliverance from earthly travails. Whites took a dim view of spirituals and tried to make slaves sing "good psalms and hymns" instead of "the extravagant and nonsensical chants, and catches, and hallelujah songs of their own composing." But enslaved blacks clung to their spirituals, drawing hope from them that "we will soon be free, when the Lord will call us home," as one spiritual promised.

CHRONOLOGY

1790s	Methodists and Baptists start to make major strides in converting slaves to Christianity.
1793	Eli Whitney invents the cotton gin.
1800	Gabriel Prosser leads a slave rebellion in Virginia.
1808	Congress prohibits external slave trade.
1816–1819	Boom in cotton prices stimulates settlement of the Southwest.
1822	Denmark Vesey's conspiracy is uncovered in South Carolina.
1831	William Lloyd Garrison starts *The Liberator.* Nat Turner leads a slave rebellion in Virginia.
1832	Virginia legislature narrowly defeats a proposal for gradual emancipation.
1837	Economic panic begins, lowering cotton prices.
1844–1845	Methodist and Baptist churches split over slavery into northern and southern wings.
1849	Sugar production in Louisiana reaches its peak.
1849–1860	Period of high cotton prices.

FOR FURTHER READING

John B. Boles, *Black Southerners, 1619–1869* (1983). An excellent synthesis of scholarship on slavery.

Wilbur J. Cash, *The Mind of the South* (1941). A brilliant interpretation of southern history.

Bruce Collins, *White Society in the Antebellum South* (1985). A very good, brief synthesis of southern white society and culture.

William J. Cooper, *Liberty and Slavery: Southern Politics to 1860* (1983). A valuable synthesis and interpretation of recent scholarship on the antebellum South in national politics.

Robert W. Fogel, *Without Consent or Contract: The Rise and Fall of American Slavery* (1989). A comprehensive reexamination of the slaves' productivity and welfare.

Robert W. Fogel and Stanley L. Engerman, *Time on the Cross: The Economics of American Negro Slavery* (1974). A controversial book that uses mathematical models to analyze the profitability of slavery. (Fogel won the Nobel Prize in Economics in 1993.)

Lacy K. Ford, *Origins of Southern Radicalism: The South Carolina Upcountry, 1800–1860* (1988). An important recent study that underscores the commitment of poorer whites in the hill regions to their personal independence and to widespread property ownership.

Eugene D. Genovese, *Roll, Jordan, Roll: The World the Slaves Made* (1974). The most influential work on slavery in the Old South written during the last twenty-five years; a penetrating analysis of the paternalistic relationship between masters and slaves.

Peter Kolchin, *Unfree Labor: American Slavery and Russian Serfdom* (1987). A comparative study that sets American slavery within the context of unfree labor in the early nineteenth century.

James Oakes, *The Ruling Race: A History of American Slaveholders* (1982). An important attack on the ideas of Eugene D. Genovese.

James Oakes, *Slavery and Freedom: An Interpretation of the Old South* (1990). A study stressing slavery's development in the context of liberal capitalism.

U. B. Phillips, *American Negro Slavery* (1918) and *Life and Labor in the Old South* (1929). Works marred by racial prejudice but containing a wealth of information about slavery and the plantation system.

Kenneth M. Stampp, *The Peculiar Institution: Slavery in the Antebellum South* (1956). A standard account of the African-American experience under slavery.

13

Immigration, Expansion, and Sectional Conflict,

1840–1848

Newcomers and Natives

Although a desire for religious freedom drew some immigrants to U.S. shores, hopes of economic betterment lured the majority. Travelers' accounts and relatives' letters assured Europeans that America was an ideal world, a utopia. Yet typically, emigrants faced hard times.

Cities, rather than farms, attracted most antebellum immigrants; by 1860 German and Irish newcomers constituted half or more of the population of St. Louis, New York, Chicago, Cincinnati, Milwaukee, Detroit, and San Francisco. These fast-growing cities needed people with strong backs willing to work for low wages. Irish construction gangs built the houses, streets, and aqueducts that were changing the face of urban America and dug the canals and railroads that linked these cities.

The Germans

German immigrants spanned a wide spectrum of class and occupation. Most were farmers, but professionals, artisans, and tradespeople made up a sizable minority.

A common language transcended the differences among German immigrants and bound them together. They clustered in the same neighborhoods, formed their own militia and fire companies, and established German-language parochial schools and newspapers. Native-born Americans simultaneously admired German industriousness and resented German self-sufficiency, which they interpreted as clannishness.

The Irish

There were three waves of Irish immigration. Between 1815 and the mid-1820s, most Irish immigrants were Protestants, small landowners and tradespeople drawn by enthusiastic veterans of the War of 1812 who reported that America was a paradise where "all a man needed was a gun and sufficient ammunition to be able to live like a prince." From the mid-1820s to the mid-1840s, Irish immigration became both more Catholic and poorer, primarily comprising tenant farmers evicted by Protestant landlords as "superfluous." Rich or poor, Protestant or Catholic, nearly a million Irish crossed the Atlantic to the United States between 1815 and 1845.

Then, between 1845 and the early 1850s the character of Irish immigration changed dramatically. In Ireland blight destroyed harvest after harvest of potatoes, the staple food of the peasantry, and triggered one of the most gruesome famines in history. The Great Famine killed a million people. To escape death, 1.8 million Irish migrated to the United States in the decade after 1845.

Overwhelmingly poor and Catholic, these newest Irish immigrants entered the work force at the bottom. Paddy with his pickax and Bridget the maid were at once stereotypes and realities. While Irish men dug streets and canals and railroads, Irish women worked as maids and textile workers.

It sometimes seemed that no matter what the Irish did, they clashed with other Americans. The poorer Irish who dug canals, took in laundry, or worked as domestics competed with equally poor free blacks. The result was Irish animosity toward blacks and Irish hatred of abolitionists. At the same time, the Irish who secured skilled or semiskilled jobs clashed with native-born white workers.

Anti-Catholicism, Nativism, and Labor Protest

In the 1840s swelling Catholic immigration led to a Protestant counterattack in the form of nativist (anti-immigrant) societies. Many nativist societies began as secret or semisecret fraternal orders but developed political offshoots; for example, the Order of the Star-Spangled Banner evolved into the "Know-Nothing" party, a major political force in the 1850s.

An explosive mixture of fears and discontents fueled nativism. Protestants generally saw their doc-

trines such as the responsibility of each individual to interpret scripture as far more democratic than Catholicism, which made doctrine the province of the pope and the hierarchy. Native-born artisans and journeymen, already hard pressed by the subdivision of tasks and the aftermath of the Panic of 1837, feared that desperately poor Catholic immigrants represented threats to their jobs.

Demands for land reform joined nativism as a proposed solution to workers' economic woes. Americans had long believed that abundant land guaranteed security against a permanent class of "wage slaves." Land reformers argued that workers in an industrial economy abandoned all possibility of economic independence; their only hope lay in claiming land and becoming farmers.

Labor unions appealed to workers left cold by the promises of land reformers. For example, desperately poor Irish immigrants, refugees from an agricultural society, believed that they could gain more through unions and strikes than through farming.

Probably the most important development for workers in the 1840s was a state court decision. In *Commonwealth* v. *Hunt* (1842), the Massachusetts Supreme Court ruled that labor unions were not illegal monopolies that restrained trade. However, because less than 1 percent of the work force at that time belonged to unions, their impact was sharply limited.

Ethnic and religious tensions also split the antebellum working class during the 1830s and 1840s. Friction between native-born and immigrant workers inevitably became intertwined with the political divisions of the second party system.

Labor Protest and Immigrant Politics

Few immigrants had voted before reaching America, and even fewer had fled political persecution. Once settled in the United States, however, many immigrants became politically active. They discovered that urban political organizations could help them to find housing and jobs—in return for votes. Both the Irish and the Germans identified overwhelmingly with the Democratic party.

Immigrants' fears about jobs partly explained their widespread Democratic support. Former president Andrew Jackson had given the Democratic party an antiprivilege, anti-aristocratic coloration, making the Democrats seem more sympathetic than the Whigs to the common people. In addition, antislavery was linked to the Whig party, and the Irish loathed abolitionism because they feared that freed slaves would become their economic competitors.

The West and Beyond

As late as 1840 the American West meant the area between the Appalachian Mountains and the Mississippi River or just beyond. West of 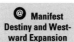 that lay the inhospitable Great Plains. A semiarid treeless plateau, the Plains sustained huge buffalo herds and the nomadic Indians who lived off the buffalo. Because the Great Plains presented wouldbe farmers with formidable obstacles, public interest shifted toward the Far West, the fertile region beyond the Rockies.

By the Transcontinental (or Adams-Onís) Treaty of 1819, the United States had relinquished to Spain its claims to Texas west of the Sabine River and in return had received Spanish claims to the Oregon Country north of California. Two years later the Mexican Revolution had brought Mexico independence from Spain and possession of all North American territory claimed by Spain—Texas, California, and the southwest quadrant of the continent. In 1824 and 1825 Russia yielded its claims to Oregon south of Alaska, and in 1827 the United States and Great Britain revived an earlier agreement for the joint occupation of the Oregon Territory.

Despite these agreements and treaties, the American line of settlement reached only to Missouri, a 2,000-mile trek (allowing for mountains) from the West Coast.

Far Western Trade

After sailing around South America and up the Pacific coast, early merchants had established American and British outposts on the West Coast. The California trade generated little friction with Mexico. Californians were as eager to buy as the traders were to sell. Traders who settled in California learned to speak Spanish and became assimilated into Mexican culture.

Also during the 1820s, trading links developed between St. Louis and Santa Fe. Each spring, midwesterners loaded wagon trains with tools, clothing, and household sundries and rumbled westward to Santa Fe, where they traded their goods for mules and silver. Mexico welcomed the trade. The Mexican people of New Mexico and California depended on U.S. trade for manufactured goods, and the Mexican government in both provinces needed revenues from customs duties.

Yet despite the mutually beneficial relations between Mexicans and Americans, the potential for conflict was always present. Spanish-speaking, Roman Catholic, and accustomed to a hierarchical society, the Mexicans formed a striking contrast to the Protestant, individualistic Americans. Furthermore, glowing reports from U.S. traders about the fertility and climate of Mexico's northern provinces prompted U.S. settlers to move into eastern Texas, where ties to Mexico's government were fraying.

Mexican Government in the Far West

Spain, and later Mexico, recognized that the key to controlling their frontier provinces lay in promoting settlement there by Spanish-speaking people—Spaniards, Mexicans, and Indians who had embraced Catholicism and agriculture. Thus by the early nineteenth century, Spanish missions, which had long been the chief instrument of Spanish expansion, stretched up the California coast as far as San Francisco and into the interior of New Mexico and Texas. The Franciscan priests who ran the missions tried to convert Native Americans and settle them on mission lands. By 1823 more than 20,000 Indians lived on the twenty-one California missions.

In the late 1820s the mission system began to decline, the victim of Mexican independence and the new government's decision to secularize the missions by distributing their lands to ambitious government officials and private ranchers. Most mission Indians returned to their nomadic ways and joined with Indians who had resisted the missions. During the 1820s and 1830s these "barbaric Indians"—notably the Comanches, Apaches, Navajos, and Utes—terrorized the Mexican frontier, carrying off women and children as well as livestock.

Overofficered and corrupt, the Mexican army had little taste for frontier fighting and less for protecting settlers. Consequently, few people ventured into the undeveloped, lawless territories, and most of the Mexican empire remained underpopulated. In 1836 New Mexico contained 30,000 settlers of Hispanic culture; California, about 3,200; and Texas, 4,000. Separated by vast distances from an uncaring government in Mexico City, and dependent on U.S. traders for the necessities of civilization, the frontier Mexicans constituted a frail barrier against the advance of Anglo-American settlement.

American Settlements in Texas

Unlike the provinces of New Mexico and California, the Mexican state known as Coahuila-Texas had neither mountains nor deserts to protect its boundaries. By 1823, 3,000 Americans had drifted into eastern Texas, some in search of cotton lands, others in flight from creditors. In 1824 the Mexican government began to encourage American colonization of Texas as a way to bring in manufactured goods and to gain protection against the Indians. The government bestowed generous land grants on agents known as *empresarios* to recruit peaceful American settlers for Texas. Stephen F. Austin, the most successful of the *empresarios*, had brought in 300 families by 1825. By 1830, 7,000 Americans lived in Texas, more than double the Mexican population there.

This large number of Americans proved a mixed blessing. Unlike the assimilated traders of California, the American settlers in Texas were generally farmers living in their own communities, far from the Mexican settlements to the west. Although naturalized Mexican citizens and nominal Catholics, the American settlers distrusted the Mexicans and complained constantly about the creaking, erratic Mexican judicial system.

Mexican policies in the early 1830s quickly eroded the American settlers' allegiance to the Mexican government. In 1830 the government closed Texas to further U.S. immigration and forbade the introduction of more slaves to Texas, a troubling matter because many American settlers were slaveholders. But Mexico could not enforce its decrees, and between 1830 and 1834 the number of Americans in Texas doubled. Austin secured repeal of the prohibition against American migration in 1834; within a year an estimated 1,000 Americans a month were entering Texas. In 1836 Texas counted some 30,000 white Americans, 5,000 black slaves, and 4,000 Mexicans.

At the same time, the Mexican government grew more and more erratic. When Antonio López de Santa Anna became president of Mexico in 1834, he restricted the power of the individual states, including Coahuila-Texas. His actions ignited a series of rebellions in the Mexican states, the most important of which became the Texas Revolution.

The Texas Revolution

At first the insurgent Anglo-Texans sought the restoration of the liberal Constitution of 1824 and greater autonomy for Texas, not independence. But Santa Anna's brutal treatment of the rebels alarmed the initially moderate Austin and others. When Santa Anna invaded Texas in fall 1835, Austin cast his lot with the radicals who wanted independence.

Santa Anna's armies met with initial success. In February 1836, 4,000 of his men laid siege to San Antonio, where 200 rebels had retreated into an abandoned mission, the Alamo. On March 6—four days after Texas had declared its independence, although they did not know about it—the defenders of the Alamo were overwhelmed by Mexican troops. Under Santa Anna's orders, the Mexican army killed all the Alamo's defenders, including the wounded. A few weeks later Mexican troops massacred 350 Texas prisoners at Goliad.

Meanwhile, the Texans had formed an army with Sam Houston at its head. A giant man of extensive military experience, Houston retreated east to pick up recruits, many of them Americans who crossed the

Sabine River border to fight Santa Anna. On April 21, 1836, Houston's army turned and surprised the complacent Mexican forces under Santa Anna, which had encamped on a prairie just to the east of what is now the city of Houston. Shouting "Remember the Alamo!" Houston's army of 1,200 tore through the Mexican lines, killing nearly half of Santa Anna's men in fifteen minutes and capturing the general himself. This engagement, the Battle of San Jacinto, gave Texas its independence from Mexico, although the Mexican government never ratified the treaty that Santa Anna signed. However, Texas became an independent republic, not the American state that most had envisioned.

American Settlements in California, New Mexico, and Oregon

Before 1840 California and New Mexico, both less accessible than Texas, exerted only a mild attraction for American settlers. That year a mere 100 Americans lived in New Mexico and perhaps 400 in California. During the 1840s, however, Americans streamed into the Sacramento Valley, lured by favorable reports of the region and welcomed by the Hispanic population as a way to encourage economic development.

To the north, Oregon's abundant farmland beckoned settlers from the Mississippi Valley. By 1840 some 500 Americans had settled there, in what was described as a "pioneer's paradise" where "the pigs are running around under the great acorn trees, round and fat and already cooked, with knives and forks sticking in them so that you can cut off a slice whenever you are hungry."

The Overland Trail

Whether bound for California or Oregon, Americans faced a four-month ordeal crossing terrain little known in reality but vividly depicted in fiction as an Indian killing ground. Cautious pioneers stocked up on enough guns to equip an army in jump-off towns such as Independence and St. Joseph, Missouri. In fact, they were more likely to shoot one another than to be shot by the usually cooperative Indians and much more likely to be scalped by Missouri merchants selling their goods at inflated prices.

Along the Overland Trail the emigrants faced hardships and hazards: ornery mules that kicked, bit, and balked; oxen that collapsed from thirst; and overloaded wagons that broke down. Trails were difficult to follow and too often marked by the debris of broken wagons and the bleached bones of oxen.

Between 1840 and 1848, an estimated 11,500 pioneers trekked to Oregon, and some 2,700 reached California. Such small numbers made a difference, for the British did not settle Oregon at all and the Mexican population of California was small and scattered. By 1845 California was clinging to Mexico by the thinnest of threads.

The Politics of Expansion

During the 1840s opportunistic leaders thrust expansion-related issues to the top of the political agenda. Boundary conflicts with Mexico and the fate of slavery in the western territories were major issues in all three of the decade's presidential elections.

The Whig Ascendancy

The election of 1840 brought the Whig candidate William Henry Harrison to the presidency and installed Whig majorities in both houses of Congress. The Whigs proposed abolishing Van Buren's independent treasury and erecting revenue, not protective, tariffs.

The Whig program might well have breezed into law. But Harrison died after only a month in office, and his successor, John Tyler, a Virginia aristocrat put on the ticket for his southern appeal, proved a disaster for the Whigs. A former Democrat, Tyler continued to favor the Democratic philosophy of states' rights. As president, he used the veto to shred his new party's program.

Tyler's erratic course confounded and disrupted his party. In the congressional elections of 1842, the Whigs paid a heavy price for failing to enact their program; they lost control of the House to the Democrats. Now the nation had one party controlling the Senate, another controlling the House, and a president who appeared to belong to neither.

Tyler and Texas Annexation

Although disowned by his party, Tyler ardently desired a second term as president. Domestic issues offered him little hope of building a popular following, but foreign policy was another matter. Tyler reasoned that if he could annex Texas, he could build a national following.

The issue of slavery clouded every discussion of Texas. Antislavery northerners saw proposals to annex Texas as part of a southern conspiracy to extend American territory into Mexico, Cuba, and Central America and thus to create an unlimited number of new slave states.

Nevertheless, in summer 1843 Tyler launched a campaign for Texas annexation. He justified his crusade by reporting that he had learned of an attempt to make Texas a British, rather than an American, ally.

In spring 1844 Tyler submitted to the Senate a treaty annexing Texas. Accompanying the treaty was a letter from Secretary of State John C. Calhoun to the British minister in Washington defending slavery as beneficial to African-Americans, the only way to protect them from "vice and pauperism." Abolitionists now had evidence that the annexation of Texas was linked to a conspiracy to extend slavery. Consequently, both Whig and Democratic leaders came out in opposition to the annexation of Texas, and the treaty met a crushing defeat in the Senate.

The Election of 1844

Tyler's ineptitude turned the presidential campaign into a free-for-all. Lacking support as an independent, he dropped out of the race. Henry Clay had a secure grip on the Whig nomination, but Martin Van Buren's apparently clear path to the head of the Democratic ticket vanished as the issue of annexation split his party. A deadlocked Democratic party finally turned to James K. Polk of Tennessee, the first "dark-horse" nominee in American history.

Little known outside the South, the slaveholding Polk enjoyed broad southern support as the "bosom friend of [Andrew] Jackson, and a pure whole-hogged Democrat, the known enemy of banks and distribution." Jeering "Who is James K. Polk?" the Whigs derided the nomination. However, Polk, a wily campaigner, convinced many northerners that annexation of Texas would benefit them.

In contrast to the Democrats, whose position was clear, Clay and the Whigs wobbled. After several shifts Clay finally came out against annexation, but not until September. His wavering alienated his southern supporters and prompted some of his northern supporters to bolt the Whigs for the antislavery Liberty party, formed in 1840.

This divided opposition allowed Polk to win the electoral vote 170–105, although his margin in the popular vote was only 38,000 out of 2.6 million votes cast.

Manifest Destiny

The election of 1844 showed the strength of national support for the annexation of Texas. The surging popular sentiment for expansion reflected a growing conviction that America's natural destiny was to expand into Texas and all the way to the Pacific.

Americans needed only a phrase to capture this ebullient spirit. In 1845 John L. O'Sullivan, a New York Democratic journalist, supplied that phrase when he wrote of "our manifest destiny to overspread and to possess the whole of the continent which Providence has given us for the development of the great experiment of liberty and federated self-government entrusted to us."

> @ **Manifest Destiny**

Advocates of Manifest Destiny used lofty language and invoked God and nature to justify expansion. Because most champions of Manifest Destiny were Democrats who favored annexing Texas, northern Whigs dismissed Manifest Destiny as a smoke screen to conceal an evil intent to extend slavery. In fact, many expansionists supported neither slavery nor annexation. Most had their eyes not on Texas but on Oregon and California. Blaming the post-1837 depression on the failure of Americans to find markets for their agricultural surplus, they saw California and Oregon as solutions.

More than trade was at stake. To many, expansion presented an opportunity to preserve the agricultural character of the American people and thus to safeguard democracy. Fundamentally Jeffersonian, expansionists equated industrialization and urbanization with social stratification and class strife. To avoid the "bloated wealth" and "terrible misery" that afflicted Britain, the United States *had to* expand. Americans would continue to be farmers, and the foundations of the Republic would remain secure. This message, trumpeted by the penny press, made sense to the working poor, many of them Irish immigrants.

@ **The Texas Revolution, 1835–1836**

Polk and Oregon

The growing spirit of Manifest Destiny intensified the Oregon issue. To soften northern criticism of the pending annexation of Texas, the Democrats had included in their 1844 platform the assertion that American title "to the whole of the Territory of Oregon is clear and unquestionable." Taken literally, this statement, which Polk repeated in his inaugural address, pressed an American claim to the entire Oregon Territory between California and 54°40', a claim never before advanced.

Polk's position succeeded in rousing furious interest in the nation's acquiring the entire territory. Mass meetings adopted such resolutions as "The Whole or None!" Even John Quincy Adams, no supporter of the 54°40' boundary for Oregon, asserted that the United States was destined "to make the wilderness blossom as the rose, to establish laws, to increase, multiply, and subdue the earth."

In April 1846 Polk forced the issue by notifying Britain that the United States was terminating the joint British-American occupation of Oregon. In effect, this message was that the British could either go to war over the American claims to 54°40' or negotiate. They chose to negotiate. The ensuing treaty divided Oregon at the forty-ninth parallel, although Britain retained all of Vancouver Island and navigation rights on the Columbia River. On June 15, 1846, the Senate ratified the treaty, stipulating that Britain's navigation rights on the Columbia were temporary.

The Origins of the Mexican War

While Polk challenged Britain over Oregon, the United States and Mexico moved toward war. One long-standing grievance lay in the failure of the Mexican government to pay $2 million in debts owed to U.S. citizens. Bitter memories of the Alamo and of the Goliad massacre, moreover, reinforced American loathing of Mexico. Above all, the issue of Texas poisoned relations. Mexico still hoped to regain Texas or to keep it independent of the United States.

Polk's election increased the strength of the proannexationists, as his campaign had persuaded many northerners that Texas's annexation would bring national benefits. In February 1845 both houses of Congress responded to popular sentiment by passing a resolution annexing Texas. However, Texans balked, in part because some feared that union with the United States would provoke a Mexican invasion and war on Texas soil.

Polk moved rapidly. To sweeten the pot for Texans, he supported their claim that the Rio Grande constituted Texas's southern border, despite Mexico's contention that the Nueces River, 100 miles farther north, bounded Texas. Because the Rio Grande meandered west and north nearly 2,000 miles, it encompassed a huge territory, including part of modern New Mexico. The Texas that Polk proposed to annex thus was far larger than the Texas that had gained independence from Mexico. On July 4, 1845, reassured by Polk's support, Texas voted to accept annexation. Polk then ordered American troops under General Zachary Taylor to the edge of the disputed territory. Taylor deployed his army at Corpus Christi, south of the Nueces River, in territory still claimed by Mexico.

California and its fine harbors influenced Polk's actions, for he had entered the White House with the firm intention of extending American control over that province, too. If Mexico went to war with the United States over Texas, Polk's supporters claimed, "the road to California will be open to us."

Continued turmoil in Mexican politics further complicated the situation. In early 1845 a new Mexican government agreed to negotiate with the United States, and Polk decided to give negotiations a chance. In November 1845 he sent John Slidell to Mexico City with instructions to gain Mexican recognition of the annexation of Texas with the Rio Grande border. Polk also authorized Slidell to offer up to $25 million for California and New Mexico. However, by the time Slidell reached Mexico City, the government there had become too weak to make concessions to the United States, and its head, General José Herrara, refused to receive Slidell. Polk then ordered Taylor to move southward to the Rio Grande, hoping to provoke a Mexican attack and to unite the American people behind war.

The Mexican government, however, dawdled over taking the bait. Polk was about to send a war message to Congress when word finally arrived that Mexican forces had crossed the Rio Grande and attacked the U.S. army. *American blood has been shed on American soil!* Polk's followers jubilantly proclaimed. On May 11, 1846, Polk informed Congress that war "exists by the act of Mexico herself" and called for $10 million to fight the war.

Polk's disingenuous assertion that the United States was already at war provoked furious opposition in Congress. For one thing, the Mexican attack on Taylor's troops had taken place on land never before claimed by the United States. Equally grievous, in announcing that war already existed, Polk seemed to undercut congressional power to declare war. Polk had backed the Whigs into a corner. They could not afford to appear unpatriotic—they remembered vividly what opposition to the War of 1812 had cost the Federalists—so they swallowed their outrage and supported war.

The Mexican War

Most European observers expected Mexico to win the war. Its army was four times the size of the American forces, and it was fighting on home ground. The United States, having botched its one previous attempt to invade a neighbor, Canada in 1812, now had to sustain offensive operations in an area remote from American settlements. American expansion-

ists, however, hardly expected the Mexicans to fight at all. Racism and arrogance convinced many Americans that the Mexican people, degraded by their mixed Spanish and Indian population, were "as sure to melt away at the approach of [American] energy and enterprise as snow before a southern sun," as one newspaper publisher insisted.

In fact, the Mexicans fought bravely and stubbornly, although unsuccessfully. In May 1846 Taylor, "Old Rough and Ready," routed the Mexican army in Texas and pursued it across the Rio Grande, eventually to capture the major city of Monterrey in September. After taking Monterrey, Taylor, starved for supplies, halted and granted Mexico an eight-week armistice. Eager to undercut Taylor's popularity—the Whigs were already touting him as a presidential candidate—Polk stripped him of half his forces and reassigned them to General Winfield Scott. He was to mount an amphibious attack on Vera Cruz and proceed on to Mexico City. Events outstripped Polk's scheme, however, when Taylor defeated a far larger Mexican army at the Battle of Buena Vista, on February 22–23, 1847.

Farther north, American forces took advantage of the shakiness of Mexican rule to strip away New Mexico and California. In spring 1846 Colonel Stephen Kearny led an army from Fort Leavenworth, Kansas, toward Santa Fe. Having overcome immense natural obstacles to reach New Mexico, Kearny took the territory by a combination of bluff, bluster, and, perhaps, bribery.

California also fell easily into American hands. In 1845 Polk had ordered the Pacific Squadron under Commodore John D. Sloat to occupy California's ports in event of war. The president had also dispatched a courier overland with secret orders for one of the most colorful actors in the conquest of California, John C. Frémont. A Georgia-born adventurer, Frémont had taken advantage of his marriage to the daughter of a powerful senator to have accounts of his explorations in the Northwest published as official government documents, then basked in glory as "the Great Pathfinder." Polk's courier caught up with Frémont in Oregon. Instructed to proceed to California and "watch over the interests of the United States," Frémont interpreted his orders liberally. In June 1846 he rounded up some American insurgents, captured the town of Sonoma, and proclaimed the independent "Bear Flag Republic." The combined efforts of Frémont, Sloat, and Kearny (who had continued on to California after his successful New Mexico campaign) established U.S. control over California.

The war's final and most important campaign brought Winfield Scott to glory in the conquest of Mexico City itself. In March 1847 Scott carried out a successful amphibious landing near Vera Cruz, pounded the city into submission, and moved inland to attack Mexico City. On September 13, 1847, 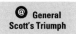 Mexico City fell to Scott, and he joined Zachary Taylor in the pantheon of new American heroes.

By the Treaty of Guadalupe-Hidalgo (February 2, 1848), Mexico ceded Texas with the Rio Grande boundary, New Mexico, and California to the United States; from the Mexican cession would come the states of New Mexico, California, Nevada, and Utah, most of Arizona, and parts of Colorado and Wyoming. In turn, the United States assumed the claims of U.S. citizens against the Mexican government and paid Mexico $15 million. On March 10, 1848, the Senate ratified the treaty by a vote of 38–10.

The Mexican War in the Popular Mind

Occurring amid the rise of the penny press and the popular novel, the Mexican War became the most fully reported war that the United States had yet fought and the first conflict in which war correspondents were employed. The extensive coverage given to battlefield victories fueled soaring nationalism and helped to submerge political divisions.

Romance as well as patriotism gripped the popular mind. Popular novelists portrayed the war as evidence that the noble streak in the American character could prevail over the grasping materialism of U.S. society.

Zachary Taylor became the main beneficiary of public infatuation with the war. "Old Rough and Ready" seemed to combine, in equal parts, military genius, a democratic bearing, and a conspicuously ordinary manner. In contrast to the more punctilious Winfield Scott ("Old Fuss and Feathers"), Taylor went into battle wearing a straw hat and plain brown coat. To a people searching for heroes, even his short, stocky stature seemed vaguely Napoleonic. The war made Taylor a hero, and the conflicts spinning out of that war would boost his political career.

Intensifying Sectional Divisions

Despite wartime patriotic enthusiasm, sectional conflict sharpened between 1846 and 1848. Territorial expansion generated the Polk administration's major battles. To Polk, it mattered little whether new territories were slave or free. Expansion would meet its purposes by dispersing the population, weakening dangerous tendencies toward centralized government, and ensuring the agricultural and democratic character of the United States. Polk saw the Missouri Compromise, prohibiting slavery north of 36°30', as a simple, permanent solution to the question of territorial slavery.

But many northerners were coming to see slavery in the territories as a profoundly disruptive issue that neither could nor should be solved simply by extending the 36°30' line. Abolitionist Whigs, who opposed any expansion of slavery on moral grounds, posed a lesser threat to Polk than northern Democrats who feared that extending slavery into New Mexico and California would deter free laborers from settling those territories.

The Wilmot Proviso

A young Democratic congressman from Pennsylvania, David Wilmot, galvanized these disaffected northern Democrats. In August 1846 he introduced an amendment to an appropriations bill. This amendment, which became known as the Wilmot Proviso, stipulated that slavery be prohibited in any territory acquired by the negotiations with Mexico.

The proviso raised unsettling constitutional questions. Calhoun and other southerners contended that because slaves were property, the Constitution protected slaveholders' right to carry their slaves wherever they chose. On the other side, many northerners cited the Northwest Ordinance of 1787, the Missouri Compromise, and the Constitution itself, which gave Congress the power to "make all needful rules and regulations respecting the territory or other property belonging to the United States," as justification for congressional legislation over slavery in the territories.

The Election of 1848

The Whigs watched in dismay as prosperity returned under Polk. But the Wilmot Proviso gave the Whigs a political windfall; originating in the Democratic party, it allowed the Whigs to portray themselves as the South's only true friends.

These considerations inclined the majority of Whigs toward Zachary Taylor. As a Louisiana slaveholder, he had obvious appeal to the South. As a political newcomer, he had no loyalty to a discredited American System. And as a war hero, he had broad national appeal. Nominating Taylor as presidential candidate in 1848, the Whigs presented him as an ideal man "without regard to creeds or principles" and ran him without any platform.

The Democrats faced a greater challenge because David Wilmot was one of their own. They could not ignore the issue of slavery in the territories, but if they embraced the positions of Wilmot or Calhoun, the party would split along sectional lines. When Polk declined to run for reelection, the Democrats nominated Lewis Cass of Michigan, who solved their dilemma by announcing the doctrine of "squatter sovereignty," or popular sovereignty as it was later called. Cass argued that Congress should let the question of slavery in the territories be decided by the people who settled there.

In the campaign both parties tried to avoid the issue of slavery in the territories, but neither succeeded. A pro-Wilmot faction of the Democratic party linked up with the abolitionist Liberty party and antislavery "Conscience" Whigs to form the Free-Soil party. Declaring their dedication to "Free Trade, Free Labor, Free Speech, and Free Men," the Free-Soilers nominated Martin Van Buren on a platform opposing any extension of slavery.

Zachary Taylor benefited from the opposition's alienation of key northern states over the tariff issue, from Democratic disunity over the Wilmot Proviso, and from his war-hero stature. He captured a majority of electoral votes in both North and South. Although it failed to carry any state, the Free-Soil party ran well enough in the North to demonstrate the grassroots popularity of opposition to the extension of slavery.

The California Gold Rush

When Wilmot had introduced his proviso, the issue of slavery in the West was more abstract than immediate, for Mexico had not yet ceded any territory. The picture quickly changed when an American carpenter discovered gold while building a sawmill in the foothills of California's Sierra Nevada only nine days before the Treaty of Guadalupe-Hidalgo was signed. By December 1848 pamphlets with such titles as *The Emigrant's Guide to the Gold Mines* had hit the streets of New York City, and the gold rush was on. Overland emigrants to California rose from 400 in 1848 to 44,000 in 1850.

The gold rush made the issue of slavery in the West an immediate, practical concern. The newcomers to California included Mexicans, free blacks, and slaves brought by southern planters. White prospectors loathed the idea of competing with these groups and wanted to drive them from the goldfields. Violence mounted, and demands grew for a strong civilian government to replace the ineffective military government left over from the war. The gold rush guaranteed that the question of slavery in the Mexican cession would be the first item on the agenda for Polk's successor.

CHRONOLOGY

1818   The United States and Britain agree on joint occupation of Oregon for a ten-year period.

1819   Transcontinental (Adams-Onís) Treaty.

1821   Mexico gains independence from Spain.

1822   Stephen F. Austin founds the first American community in Texas.

1824–   Russia abandons its claims to Oregon south
1825   of 50°40'.

1827   The United States and Britain renew their agreement on joint occupation of Oregon for an indefinite period.

1830   Mexico closes Texas to further American immigration.

1834   Antonio López de Santa Anna comes to power in Mexico.
        Austin secures repeal of the ban on American immigration into Texas.

1835   Santa Anna invades Texas.

1836   Texas declares its independence from Mexico.
        Fall of the Alamo.
        Goliad massacre.
        Battle of San Jacinto.

1840   William Henry Harrison elected president.

1841   Harrison dies; John Tyler becomes president.

1843   Tyler launches campaign for Texas annexation.

1844   Senate rejects treaty annexing Texas.
        James K. Polk elected president.

1845   Texas accepts annexation by the United States.
        Mexico rejects Slidell mission.

1846   Congress ends the joint occupation of Oregon.
        Zachary Taylor defeats the Mexicans in two battles north of the Rio Grande.
        The United States declares war on Mexico.
        John C. Frémont proclaims the Bear Flag Republic in California.
        Congress votes to accept a settlement of the Oregon boundary issue with Britain.
        Colonel Stephen Kearny occupies Santa Fe.
        Wilmot Proviso introduced.
        Taylor takes Monterrey.

1847   Taylor defeats Santa Anna at the Battle of Buena Vista.
        Vera Cruz falls to Winfield Scott.
        Mexico City falls to Scott.
        Lewis Cass's principle of "squatter sovereignty."

1848   Gold discovered in California.
        Treaty of Guadalupe-Hidalgo signed.
        Taylor elected president.

FOR FURTHER READING

Ray A. Billington, *The Far Western Frontier, 1830–1860* (1956). A comprehensive narrative of the settlement of the Far West.

William R. Brock, *Parties and Political Conscience: American Dilemmas, 1840–1850* (1979). An excellent interpretive study of the politics of the 1840s.

William H. Goetzmann, *When the Eagle Screamed: The Romantic Horizon in American Diplomacy, 1800–1860* (1966). A lively overview of antebellum expansionism.

Maldwyn A. Jones, *American Immigration* (1960). An excellent brief introduction to immigration.

Patricia Nelson Limerick, *Legacy of Conquest* (1987). A provocative interpretation of western history.

Charles G. Sellers, *James K. Polk: Continentalist, 1843–1846* (1966). An outstanding political biography.

Henry Nash Smith, *Virgin Land: The American West as Symbol and Myth* (1950). A classic study of westward expansion in the American mind.

14

From Compromise to Secession, 1850–1861

The Compromise of 1850

Ralph Waldo Emerson's grim prediction that a U.S. victory in the Mexican War would be like swallowing arsenic proved disturbingly accurate. When the war ended in 1848, the United States contained an equal number (fifteen each) of free and slave states, but the vast territory gained by the war threatened to upset this balance. Any solution to the question of slavery in the Mexican cession ensured controversy.

As the rhetoric escalated, events plunged the nation into crisis. Utah and then California, both acquired from Mexico, sought admission to the Union as free states. Texas, admitted to the Union as a slave state in 1845, aggravated matters by claiming the eastern half of New Mexico, thus potentially opening the door to slavery's extension into other newly acquired territory.

By 1850 other issues had become intertwined with territorial questions. Northerners had grown increasingly unhappy with slavery in the District of Columbia, within the shadow of the Capitol; southerners complained about lax enforcement of the Fugitive Slave Act of 1793. Any broad compromise would have to take both matters into account.

President Zachary Taylor believed that the South must not kindle the issue of slavery in the territories because neither New Mexico nor California was suited for slavery. His position differed significantly from the thinking behind the still controversial Wilmot Proviso, which proposed that Congress bar slavery in the territories ceded by Mexico. Taylor's plan, in contrast, left the decision to the states. He prompted California to apply for admission as a free state, bypassing the territorial stage, and hinted that he expected New Mexico (where the Mexican government had abolished slavery) to do the same.

Southerners rejected Taylor's plan. Not only would it yield the Wilmot Proviso's goal—the banning of slavery from the lands acquired from Mexico—but it rested on the shaky assumption that slavery could never take root in California or New Mexico. Southerners also protested the addition of two new free states.

Henry Clay Proposes a Compromise

Had Taylor held a stronger position in the Whig party, he might have blunted mounting southern opposition. But many leading Whigs had never

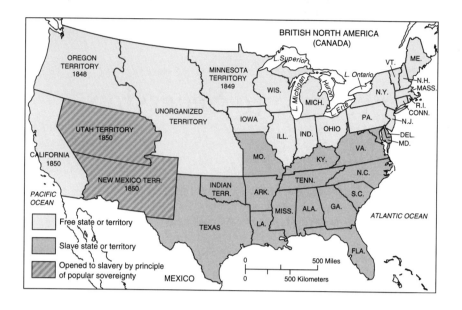

The Compromise of 1850

The Compromise of 1850 admitted California as a free state. Utah and New Mexico were left open to slavery or freedom according to the principle of popular sovereignty.

accepted this political novice, and in early 1850 Kentucky senator Henry Clay challenged Taylor's leadership by forging a compromise bill to resolve the whole range of contentious issues. Clay proposed (1) the admission of California as a free state; (2) the division of the remainder of the Mexican cession into two territories, New Mexico and Utah, without federal restrictions on slavery; (3) the settlement of the Texas–New Mexico boundary dispute on terms favorable to New Mexico; (4) as a pot-sweetener for Texas, an agreement that the federal government would assume the state's large public debt; (5) continuation of slavery in the District of Columbia but abolition of the slave trade; and (6) a more effective fugitive slave law.

Clay rolled all these proposals into a single "omnibus" bill. In the debates over the bill during late winter and early spring 1850, Daniel Webster argued for compromise, while strident voices from the proslavery and antislavery camps countered his efforts. The antislavery Whig William Seward of New York enraged southerners by talking of a "higher law than the Constitution"—namely, the will of God against the extension of slavery.

Even as the Union faced its worst crisis since 1789, events in summer 1850 eased the way toward resolution. Zachary Taylor celebrated too extravagantly on July 4 and died five days later of a stomach ailment. His successor, Millard Fillmore of New York, supported Clay's compromise. Finally, Senator Stephen A. Douglas of Illinois took over stewardship of the bill from the exhausted Clay and ingeniously secured its passage by chopping the bill into a series of individual measures. By summer's end Congress had passed each component of Clay's plan and the Compromise of 1850 had become reality.

Assessing the Compromise

Although President Fillmore hailed the compromise as a final settlement of sectional issues, it failed to bridge the underlying differences between North and South.

Each section could claim victories from the compromise. Northern victories were clear: admission of California and abolition of the slave trade in the District of Columbia. However, southern victories, such as the stricter fugitive slave law, were clouded by the legislators' failure to resolve the issue of congressional authority over slavery in territories outside the Mexican cession.

Enforcement of the Fugitive Slave Act

Northern moderates accepted the Fugitive Slave Act of 1850 as the price of saving the Union, but the law outraged antislavery northerners. It denied alleged fugitives the right of trial by jury, forbade them to testify at their own trial, and permitted their return to slavery merely on the testimony of a claimant. Above all, the law brought home to northerners the uncomfortable truth of their own complicity in slavery. By legalizing the activities of slave catchers on northern soil, the law reminded northerners that slavery was a national problem.

Efforts to catch and return runaways inflamed emotions in both North and South. In 1854 a Boston mob aroused by antislavery speeches killed a courthouse guard in an abortive effort to rescue fugitive slave Anthony Burns. President Franklin Pierce sent federal troops to escort Burns to the harbor, where a ship carried him back to slavery. As five platoons of troops marched Burns to the ship, 50,000 people lined the streets. One Bostonian hung from his window a black coffin bearing the words "THE FUNERAL OF LIBERTY." The Burns incident shattered the complacency of conservative supporters of the Compromise of 1850.

Northerners devised ways to hamper enforcement of the Fugitive Slave Act. "Vigilance" committees spirited endangered blacks to Canada, lawyers dragged out hearings to raise slave catchers' expenses, [@ Levi Coffin Remembers the Underground Railroad] and "personal liberty laws" hindered state officials' enforcement of the law. These obstructionist tactics convinced southerners that opposition to slavery boiled just beneath the surface of northern opinion.

Uncle Tom's Cabin

Harriet Beecher Stowe's novel *Uncle Tom's Cabin* (1852) drummed up wide northern support for fugitive slaves. Stowe, the daughter of famed evangelical Lyman Beecher, greeted the Fugitive Slave Act with horror. In one of the novel's most memorable scenes, she [@ Women and the Attack on Slavery] depicted the slave Eliza, clutching her infant son, bounding across ice floes on the Ohio River to freedom. Slavery itself was Stowe's main target. Much of her novel's power derives from its view that good intentions mean little in the face of so evil [@ Black Potential and the Key to *Uncle Tom's Cabin*] an institution. The good intentions of a kindly slave owner die with him, and Uncle Tom is sold to the vicious Yankee Simon Legree, who whips Tom to death. Stowe also played effectively to the emotions of her audience by demonstrating how slavery ripped slave families apart.

Three hundred thousand copies of *Uncle Tom's Cabin* were sold in 1852, and 1.2 million by summer 1853. Stage dramatizations reached perhaps fifty times as many people as [@ Promoting *Uncle Tom's Cabin*] the novel did. As a play, *Uncle Tom's Cabin* enthralled working-class audiences normally indifferent or hostile to abolitionism.

The Election of 1852

The Fugitive Slave Act fragmented the Whig party. Northern Whigs took the lead in defying the law, and southern Whigs had a difficult time explaining away the power of vocal free-soil Whigs.

In 1852 the Whigs' nomination of Mexican War hero General Winfield Scott as their presidential candidate widened the sectional split in the party. Although a Virginian, Scott owed his nomination to the northern free-soil Whigs.

The Democrats had their own problems. Substantial numbers of free-soilers who had left the party in 1848 gravitated to the Whig party in 1852. The Democrats nominated Franklin Pierce of New Hampshire, a dark-horse candidate whose chief attraction was that no faction of the party violently opposed him. Northern and southern Democrats alike rallied behind the Compromise of 1850 and the ideal of popular sovereignty, and Pierce won a smashing victory. In the most one-sided election since

1820, he carried twenty-seven of the thirty-one states and collected 254 of 296 electoral votes.

The Collapse of the Second Party System

Franklin Pierce became the last president of the nineteenth century to hold office under the second party system—Whigs against Democrats. The Whig party would soon disintegrate, to be replaced by two newcomers, the Republican party and the short-lived American (Know-Nothing) Party.

The Kansas-Nebraska Act

Signed in late May 1854, the Kansas-Nebraska Act shattered the already weakened second party system and triggered renewed sectional strife. The bill's roots lay in the seemingly uncontroversial desire of farmers to organize the large territory west of Iowa and Missouri. Railroad enthusiasts who dreamed of a rail line linking the Midwest to the Pacific also wanted the territory organized.

In January 1854 Democratic senator Stephen A. Douglas of Illinois proposed a bill to organize Nebraska as a territory. Two sources of potential conflict loomed. First, some southerners advocated a southern-based Pacific route rather than a midwestern one. Second, Nebraska lay north of the Missouri Compromise line in the Louisiana Purchase, a region closed to slavery. Under Douglas's bill, the South would lose the Pacific rail route *and* face the possibility of more free territory in the Union. To placate southerners, Douglas made two concessions. First, he proclaimed the Missouri Compromise now void, superseded by the Compromise of 1850 and its doctrine of popular sovereignty. Second, Douglas agreed to divide the territory into northern and southern parts, Nebraska and Kansas. Implicit in this, at least to southerners, was the idea that Nebraska would be free soil but Kansas would be open to slavery.

These modifications to Douglas's original bill outraged antislavery northerners and set off a storm of protest. Despite the uproar, Douglas guided the

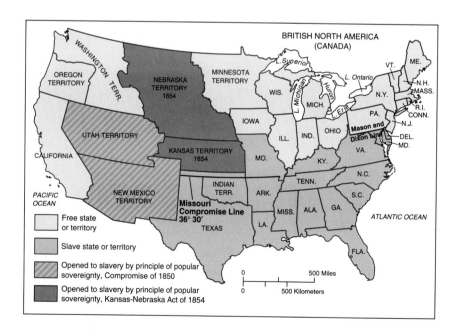

The Kansas-Nebraska Act, 1854

Kansas and Nebraska lay within the Louisiana Purchase, north of 36°30', and hence were closed to slavery until Stephen A. Douglas introduced his bills in 1854.

bill easily through the Senate. Matters were far more tumultuous in the House, where the bill passed by a narrow margin. Ominously, not a single northern Whig in the House voted for the bill, and northern Democrats split evenly.

The Surge of Free Soil

Amid the clamor over his bill, Douglas ruefully observed that he could now travel to Chicago by the light of his own burning effigies. Neither a fool nor a political novice, he was the victim of a political bombshell, free soil, that exploded under his feet.

Support for free soil united many who agreed on little else. Many free-soilers were racists who opposed allowing any African-Americans, slave or free, into the West. Others repudiated slavery on moral grounds and rejected racist legislation.

Although split over the morality of slavery, most free-soilers agreed that slavery impeded whites' progress. Most accepted Abraham Lincoln's portrayal of the North as a society of upwardly mobile farmers, artisans, and small-business operators. Because a slave worked for nothing, free-soilers claimed, no free laborer could compete with a slave. In any territory that allowed slavery, free labor would therefore vanish. Free-soilers also rejected the idea that slavery had natural limits. "Slavery is as certain to invade New Mexico and Utah, as the sun is to rise," insisted a free-soiler.

The Kansas-Nebraska Act, in free-soilers' opinion, was "a part of a continuous movement of slaveholders to advance slavery over the entire North." To free-soilers, a *pattern* of events—the Fugitive Slave Act, the repeal of the Missouri Compromise, and the division of Nebraska—demonstrated that a diabolical "Slave Power" was spreading its tentacles like an octopus.

The Ebbing of Manifest Destiny

The uproar over the Kansas-Nebraska Act embarrassed the Pierce administration. It also doomed Manifest Destiny, the one issue that had held the Democrats together in the 1840s.

Franklin Pierce had come to office championing Manifest Destiny, but increasing sectional rivalries sidetracked his efforts. In 1853 his emissary James Gadsden negotiated the purchase of a strip of land south of the Gila River (now southern Arizona and part of southern New Mexico), an acquisition favored by advocates of a southern railroad route to the Pacific. Fierce opposition to the Gadsden Purchase revealed mounting free-soilers' suspicions of expansion, and the Senate approved the treaty only after slashing 9,000 square miles from the purchase.

Cuba provided even more vivid proof of the change in public attitudes toward expansion. In 1854 a former Mississippi governor, John A. Quitman, planned a filibuster (an unofficial military expedition) to seize Cuba from Spain. Northerners denounced the filibuster as another manifestation of the Slave Power's conspiracy to grab more territory for the South's "peculiar institution."

Though northern opposition forced Pierce to repudiate Quitman's plan, southern expansionists kept the acquisition of Mexico and Cuba at the top of their agenda and won some support from northern Democrats. As late as 1859 James Buchanan, Pierce's successor, asked Congress to appropriate funds to purchase Cuba.

Although some southerners were against expansion—among them the Louisiana sugar planters who opposed acquiring Cuba because Cuban sugar would compete with their product—southern expansionists stirred up enough commotion to make antislavery northerners fear that the South aspired to establish a Caribbean slave empire. Like a card in a poker game, the threat of expansion southward was all the more menacing for not being played.

The Whigs Disintegrate

While straining Democratic unity, the Kansas-Nebraska Act wrecked the Whig party. Although Democrats lost ground in the 1854 congressional elections, the Whigs failed to benefit. No matter how furious the free-soil Democrats were at Douglas for introducing the act, they could not forget that southern Whigs had supported him. Northern Whigs split into two camps: antislavery "Conscience" Whigs, led by Senator William Seward of New York, and conservatives, led by former president Millard Fillmore.

This deep division within the Whig party repelled anti-slavery Democrats and prompted antislavery Whigs to look for an alternative party. In 1854 and 1855 many were drawn to the rising American, or Know-Nothing, party. Originally a semisecret society hostile to immigration, the Know-Nothings saw conspiracies on all sides. Many feared not only Catholicism and the pope but also a Slave Power conspiracy. Yet the issue of slavery soon divided the party, with proslavery southerners ranged against antislavery northerners. By 1856 the Know-Nothings' popularity had plummeted, and the Republicans emerged as the new antislavery party.

The Origins of the Republican Party

Born in the chaotic aftermath of the Kansas-Nebraska Act, the Republican party would become the main opposition to the Democratic party by 1856 and would win each presidential election from 1860 until 1884. In 1855, however, few might have predicted such a bright future. Although united in opposition to the Kansas-Nebraska Act, the fledgling party was host to conservatives who wanted to restore the Missouri Compromise, radicals who had been part of the Liberty party abolitionists, and a sizable middle of free-soilers.

The Republicans succeeded in some state elections in 1855 but lost ground as popular ire against the Kansas-Nebraska Act cooled. By the start of 1856 they were organized in only half the northern states and lacked any national organization. Salvation for the nascent party came in the form of violence in Kansas, which quickly became known as Bleeding Kansas. This violence united the party around its free-soil center, intensified antislavery feelings, and boosted Republican fortunes.

Bleeding Kansas

In the wake of the Kansas-Nebraska Act, Boston abolitionists had organized a company to send antislavery settlers into Kansas, but most of the territory's early settlers came from Missouri or other parts of the Midwest. Few of these opposed slavery on moral grounds. Some supported slavery; others wanted to keep all African-Americans out of Kansas.

Despite most settlers' racist leanings, Kansas became a battleground between proslavery and antislavery forces. In March 1855 thousands of proslavery Missouri "border ruffians" crossed into Kansas to vote illegally in the first elections for the territorial legislature. Drawing revolvers, they quickly silenced judges who challenged their right to vote in Kansas. Ironically, proslavery forces probably would have won an honest election. But the proslavery legislature established in 1855 in Lecompton, Kansas, operated under a cloud of fraud.

@ "Border Ruffians" Invading Kansas

The legislature's actions set off a chain reaction. In summer 1855 free-staters, including many aroused to oppose the Lecompton legislature, organized a rival government at Topeka. In May 1856 the Lecompton government dispatched a posse to Lawrence, where some free-staters were organizing a militia. The Lecompton posse, bearing banners emblazoned "SOUTHERN RIGHTS" and "LET YANKEES TREMBLE AND ABOLITIONISTS FALL," tore through Lawrence, burning buildings and destroying two printing presses. There were no deaths, but Republicans dubbed the incident "THE SACK OF LAWRENCE."

The next move belonged to John Brown, a Connecticut-born abolitionist with an overpowering sense of divinely ordained mission. The "sack" of Lawrence convinced Brown that God now beckoned him "to break the jaws of the wicked." In late May Brown led seven men, including his four sons and his son-in-law, toward Pottawatomie Creek near Lawrence. They shot to death one man associated with the Lecompton government and hacked four others to pieces with broadswords. Brown's "Pottawatomie Massacre" terrified southerners and transformed "Bleeding Kansas" into a battleground between North and South.

Popular sovereignty had failed in Kansas. Instead of resolving the issue of the extension of slavery, popular sovereignty had institutionalized the division over slavery by creating two rival governments. The Pierce administration compounded its problems, and

Kansas's, by denouncing the antislavery Topeka government and recognizing the proslavery Lecompton government, thus forcing northern Democrats into the awkward appearance of supporting the "Bogus Legislature" at Lecompton. Nor did popular sovereignty keep the slavery issue out of politics. On the day before the proslavery attack on Lawrence, Republican senator Charles Sumner of Massachusetts delivered a wrathful speech, "The Crime Against Kansas," in which he verbally lashed the Senate for its complicity in slavery. Sumner singled out Senator Andrew Butler of South Carolina for making "the harlot, slavery" his mistress. The speech stunned the Senate. Two days later a relative of Butler, Democratic representative Preston Brooks of South Carolina, strode into the Senate chamber and beat Sumner with a cane. The hollow cane broke after five or six blows, but Sumner took three years to recuperate. Brooks immediately became a hero in the South.

Now "Bleeding Kansas" and "Bleeding Sumner" united the North. The "sack" of Lawrence, President Pierce's recognition of the proslavery Lecompton government, and Brooks's actions seemed to clinch the Republican argument that an aggressive slaveocracy was in power and holding white northerners in contempt. By denouncing the Slave Power rather than slavery, the Republicans sidestepped the divisive question of slavery's morality. Not until the Civil War would Kansas enter the Union.

The Election of 1856

The presidential race of 1856 revealed the scope of the political realignment of the preceding few years. The Republicans, in their first presidential contest, nominated John C. Frémont, the "pathfinder" of California "Bear State" fame. Northern Know-Nothings also endorsed Frémont, while southern Know-Nothings nominated Millard Fillmore, the last Whig president. The Democrats dumped the battered Pierce for James Buchanan of Pennsylvania, who had been out of the country (as minister to Great Britain) during the Kansas-Nebraska furor.

The campaign became two separate races: Frémont versus Buchanan in the free states and Fillmore versus Buchanan in the slave states. Buchanan in effect was the only national candidate. Although Frémont attracted wide support in the North and Fillmore equal support in the South, Buchanan carried enough votes in both North and South to win the presidency.

The election of 1856 made three facts clear. First, the American party was finished as a major national force. Second, although in existence for barely a year, lacking any base in the South, and running a political novice, the Republican party did very well. A purely sectional party had nearly captured the presidency. Third, as long as the Democrats could unite behind a single national candidate, they would be hard to defeat.

The Crisis of the Union

No one ever accused James Buchanan of impulsiveness or fanaticism. Although a moderate who wished to avoid controversy, Buchanan would preside over one of the most controversy-ridden administrations in American history. The forces driving the nation apart were spinning out of control by 1856, and Buchanan could not stop them.

The Dred Scott Case

On March 6, 1857, two days after Buchanan's inauguration, the Supreme Court handed down its decision in *Dred Scott* v. *Sandford*, a case that promised to resolve the vexatious issue of slavery's extension.

In the 1830s his master had taken Dred Scott, a slave, from the slave state of Missouri into Illinois and the Wisconsin Territory, both closed to slavery. After his master's death, Scott sued for his freedom on the grounds of his residence in free territory.

The Court faced two key questions. Did Scott's residence in free territory during the 1830s make him free? Did Scott, again enslaved in Missouri, have the right to sue in the federal courts? The Supreme Court could have neatly sidestepped controversy by ruling that Scott had no right to sue, but it chose not to.

Instead, Chief Justice Roger B. Taney, a seventy-nine-year-old Marylander, handed down a sweeping decision that touched off another firestorm. First, Taney wrote, Scott, a slave, could not sue for his freedom. Further, no black, whether a slave or a free descendant of slaves, could become a U.S. citizen. Continuing his incendiary opinion, Taney ruled that even had Scott been entitled to sue, his residence in free territory did not make him free because the Missouri Compromise, whose provisions prohibited slavery in the Wisconsin Territory, was itself unconstitutional. The compromise, declared Taney, violated the Fifth Amendment's protection of property (including slaves).

The *Dred Scott* decision, instead of settling the issue of expansion of slavery, touched off another blast of controversy. The antislavery press flayed it as "willful perversion" filled with "gross historical falsehoods." Republicans saw it as further evidence that the fiendish Slave Power gripped the nation.

The Lincoln-Douglas Debates

Stephen A. Douglas, his presidential hopes still strong, faced a stiff challenge in the 1858 Illinois senatorial election. Of his Republican opponent, Abraham Lincoln, Douglas remarked: "I shall have my hands full. He is the strong man of his party—full of wit, facts, and dates—and the best stump speaker with his droll ways and dry jokes, in the West." Indeed, the campaign pitted the Republican party's rising star against the Senate's leading Democrat. Thanks to the railroad and the telegraph, it received unprecedented national attention.

Physically and ideologically, the two candidates presented a striking contrast. Tall and gangling, Lincoln possessed energy, ambition, and a passion for self-education that had carried him from the Kentucky log cabin where he was born into law and politics in his adopted Illinois. The New England–born Douglas stood a foot shorter than Lincoln, but to the small farmers who populated the Illinois flatlands, he was the "little giant," the personification of the Democratic party in the West.

Lincoln saw Douglas as a man who cared not whether slavery was voted up or down as long as the vote was honest. Opening his campaign with his famous "House Divided" speech ("this government cannot endure permanently half *slave* and half *free*"), Lincoln stressed the gulf between his free-soil position and Douglas's popular sovereignty. Douglas dismissed the house-divided doctrine as an invitation to secession. What mattered to him was not slavery but the continued expansion of white settlement.

The high point of the campaign came in a series of seven debates held from August to October 1858. Douglas used the debates to portray Lincoln as a virtual abolitionist and advocate of racial equality. Lincoln replied that Congress had no constitutional authority to abolish slavery in the South. He also asserted that "I am not, nor ever have been in favor of bringing about the social and political equality of the white and black man."

@ **Lincoln the Pragmatist Responds to Civil Disorder**

In the debate at Freeport, Illinois, Lincoln tried to make Douglas squirm by asking how popular sovereignty could be reconciled with the *Dred Scott* decision. Douglas responded that, although the Supreme Court had ruled that Congress could not exclude slavery from the territories, the voters in a territory could do so by refusing to enact laws that gave legal protection to slave property. Trying to move beyond debates on free soil and popular sovereignty, Lincoln shifted in the closing debates to attacks on slavery as "a moral, social, and political evil."

Neither man scored a clear victory in the debates, and the senatorial election, which Douglas won, settled no major issues. Yet the candidates' contest was crucial. It solidified the sectional split in the Democratic party and made Lincoln famous in the North—and infamous in the South.

John Brown's Raid

Although Lincoln explicitly rejected abolitionism, he called free soil a step toward the "ultimate extinction" of slavery. Many southerners ignored the differences between free soil and abolitionism, seeing them as inseparable components of a desperate and unholy alliance against slavery.

Nothing reinforced this image more than John Brown's raid on the federal arsenal at Harpers Ferry,

Virginia. Brown, the religious zealot responsible for the Pottawatomie massacre, seized the arsenal on October 16, 1859, hoping to ignite a slave rebellion throughout the South. Federal troops overpowered the raiders, and Brown, apprehended and convicted of treason, was hanged on December 2, 1859.

Had Brown been a lone fanatic, southerners might have dismissed the raid, but captured correspondence revealed that he enjoyed ties to prominent abolitionists. They had provided both moral and financial support for Brown's plan to "purge this land with blood." When the North responded to Brown's execution with memorial services and tolling bells, southerners saw proof positive of northern support for abolition and even for race war.

Brown's abortive raid also rekindled southern fears of a slave insurrection. Rumors flew around the South, and vigilantes turned out to battle conspiracies that existed only in their own minds.

Although fears of a slave insurrection proved groundless, they strengthened southern anxieties about abolitionism. More and more southerners concluded that the Republican party itself directed abolitionism and deserved blame for John Brown's plot as well. After all, had not influential Republicans assailed slavery, unconstitutionally tried to ban it, and spoken of an "irrepressible conflict" between slavery and freedom?

The South Contemplates Secession

Convinced that the menace to southern rights lay not just with eccentrics such as abolitionist editor William Lloyd Garrison but also with the Republican party that had swept two-thirds of the northern states in the election of 1856, some southerners saw secession from the United States as their only recourse. Most southerners, however, reached this conclusion gradually and reluctantly. In 1850, insulated from the main tide of immigration, southerners thought themselves the most American of Americans. The events of the 1850s led growing numbers of southerners to conclude that the North

had deserted the principles of the Union and had virtually declared war on the South by using such headline-grabbing phrases as "irrepressible conflict" and "a higher law." To southerners, the North, not slavery, was the problem.

Secession made no sense as a tactic to win concrete goals, but logic had yielded to emotion in much of the South. Fury at what southerners considered the irresponsible, unconstitutional course taken by Republicans in attacking slavery drove the talk of secession, and so did the belief that the North treated the South as inferior, even as a slave. "Talk of Negro slavery," wrote one angry southerner, "is not half so humiliating and disgraceful as the slavery of the South to the North."

As long as the pliant James Buchanan occupied the White House, southerners only talked of secession. However, once Buchanan declined to seek reelection, they anxiously awaited the next presidential election.

The Election of 1860

Republicans had done well in the elections of 1856 as a single-issue, free-soil party, but they had to broaden their base and develop an economic program in order to win in 1860. A severe economic slump following the Panic of 1857 provided them an opening. The depression shattered a decade of prosperity and thrust economic concerns to the fore. In response, the Republicans developed an economic program based on support for a protective tariff, federal aid for internal improvements, and grants to settlers of free 160-acre homesteads carved from public lands.

To broaden their appeal, the Republicans chose Abraham Lincoln as their presidential candidate over the better-known William H. Seward. Lincoln offered a greater chance of carrying key states such as Pennsylvania and his home state of Illinois and projected a more moderate image than Seward, whose penchant for phrases like "irrepressible conflict" and "higher law" made him appear radical. In contrast, Lincoln repeatedly had said that Congress had no constitutional right to interfere with slavery

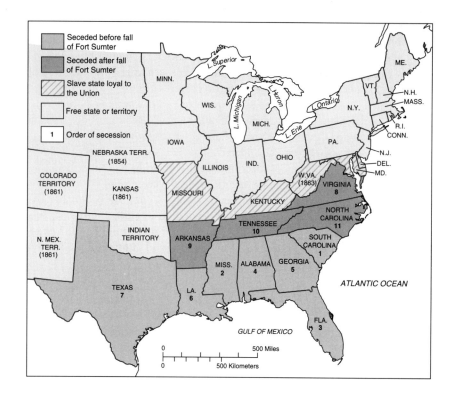

Legend:
- Seceded before fall of Fort Sumter
- Seceded after fall of Fort Sumter
- Slave state loyal to the Union
- Free state or territory
- 1 Order of secession

Secession

Four key states—Virginia, Arkansas, Tennessee, and North Carolina—did not secede until after the fall of Fort Sumter. The border slave states of Maryland, Delaware, Kentucky, and Missouri stayed in the Union.

in the South and had rejected the "higher law" doctrine.

The Democrats, still clinging to national party status, had to bridge their own sectional divisions. The *Dred Scott* decision and the conflict over Kansas had weakened northern Democrats and strengthened southern Democrats. While Douglas still desperately defended popular sovereignty, southern Democrats stretched *Dred Scott* to conclude that Congress now had to protect slavery in the territories.

The Democratic party's internal turmoil boiled over at its Charleston convention in spring 1860. Failing to win a platform guaranteeing the federal protection of slavery in the territories, delegates from the Lower South stormed out. The convention adjourned to Baltimore, where a new fight erupted over whether to seat the pro-Douglas delegates hastily chosen to replace the absent delegates from the Lower South. When the convention voted to seat these new delegates, representatives from Virginia and the Upper South walked out. What remained of the original Democratic convention nominated Douglas, but the seceders marched off to yet another hall in Baltimore and nominated Buchanan's vice president, John C. Breckinridge of Kentucky, on a platform calling for the congressional protection of slavery in the territories. The spectacle of two different Democratic candidates for the presidency signaled the complete disruption of the party.

In 1860 southern moderates joined former northern Whigs in the new Constitutional Union party. They nominated John Bell of Tennessee, a slaveholder who had opposed the Kansas-Nebraska Act. Calling for the Union's preservation, the new party took no stand on slavery's extension.

The four candidates presented a relatively clear choice. At one end of the spectrum, Lincoln conceded that the South had the constitutional right to preserve slavery, but he demanded that Congress prohibit its extension. At the other end, Breckinridge insisted that Congress had to protect slavery anywhere it existed. In the middle were Bell and Douglas, the latter still trying to salvage popular sovereignty. In the end Lincoln won 180 electoral votes; his three opponents, only 123. However, Lincoln's popular votes, 39 percent of the total, came almost completely from the North. Douglas, the only candidate to run in both sections, ran second in the popular vote but carried only Missouri. Bell won most of the Upper South, and Breckinridge took Maryland and the Lower South.

@ Preserving the Union?

The Movement for Secession

Southerners faced a dilemma. The president-elect was so unpopular in the South that his name had not even appeared on the ballot in many southern states. Lincoln's victory struck many southerners as a calculated insult. Few southerners believed that Lincoln would fulfill his promise to protect slavery in the South, and most feared that he would act as a tool for more John Browns.

@ Louisiana Newspapers Respond to Lincoln's Victory

Some southerners had threatened secession at the prospect of Lincoln's election, and now the moment of decision had arrived. On December 20, 1860, a South Carolina convention voted unanimously for secession; in short order Alabama, Mississippi, Florida, Georgia, Louisiana, and Texas followed. On February 4, 1861, delegates from these seven states met in Montgomery, Alabama, and established the Confederate States of America. But uncertainty colored the secession movement. Many southerners, even in the Deep South, had resisted the fire-eaters' call to leave the Union. Jefferson Davis, inaugurated in February 1861 as president of the Confederacy, was a reluctant secessionist who had remained in the Senate two weeks after his own state of Mississippi had seceded.

@ South Carolina Defines the Causes of Secession

At first the Upper South rejected secession completely. More economically dependent on the North, it had proportionately fewer slaves and more nonslaveholders, whose loyalty in case of secession

was dubious. Finally, if secession precipitated a war, the Upper South was the likely battleground. Consequently, the secession movement that South Carolina had begun so boldly in December 1860 seemed to be falling apart by March 1861.

The Search for Compromise

The lack of southern unity confirmed the view of most Republicans that the secessionists were more bluster than substance. This perception stiffened Republican resolve to resist compromise.

Lincoln's faith in a "loyal majority" of southerners exaggerated both their numbers and their dedication to the Union. Many southern opponents of the fire-eating secessionists sat on the fence, waiting for major concessions from the North; their allegiance to the Union thus was conditional.

The precipitous secession of the Lower South had changed the question that Lincoln faced. The issue no longer revolved around slavery's extension but around secession. The Lower South had left the Union in the face of losing a fair election. For Lincoln to cave in to such pressure would violate majority rule, the sacred principle on which the nation had been founded.

The Coming of War

By the time Lincoln took office in March 1861, only a spark was needed to set off a war. Lincoln pledged in his inaugural address to "hold, occupy, and possess" federal property in the states that had seceded, a statement that committed him to the defense of Fort Pickens in Florida and Fort Sumter in the harbor of Charleston, South Carolina. Accordingly, the president informed South Carolina's governor of his intention to supply Fort Sumter with provisions but neither reinforcements nor ammunition. Shortly before dawn on April 12, 1861, Confederate shore batteries bombarded the fort, which surrendered the next day.

Proclaiming an insurrection in the Lower South, Lincoln called for 75,000 militia to suppress the rebellion. The outbreak of hostilities ended fence-sitting in the Upper South. In quick succession Virginia, North Carolina, Arkansas, and Tennessee joined the Confederacy. Acknowledging that "I am one of those dull creatures that cannot see the good of secession," Robert E. Lee resigned from the U.S. Army rather than lead troops against his native Virginia.

The North, too, was ready for a fight, less to abolish slavery than to punish secession. Stephen Douglas, exhausted by his efforts to find a peaceable solution to the issue of slavery extension, assaulted "the new system of resistance by the sword and bayonet to the results of the ballot-box" and affirmed, "I deprecate war, but if it must come I am with my country, under all circumstances, and in every contingency."

CHRONOLOGY

1846 Wilmot Proviso.

1848 Treaty of Guadalupe-Hidalgo ends Mexican War.
Free-Soil party formed.
Zachary Taylor elected president.

1849 California seeks admission to the Union as a free state.

1850 Nashville convention assembles to discuss the South's grievances.
Compromise of 1850.

1852 Harriet Beecher Stowe, *Uncle Tom's Cabin*.
Franklin Pierce elected president.

1854 Kansas-Nebraska Act.

1854–1855 Republican party emerges.

1855 Proslavery forces steal the election for a territorial legislature in Kansas.
Proslavery Kansans establish a government in Lecompton.
Free-soil government established in Topeka, Kansas.

1856 The "sack" of Lawrence, Kansas.
John Brown's Pottawatomie massacre.
James Buchanan elected president.

1857 *Dred Scott* decision.
Panic of 1857.

1858 Congress refuses to admit Kansas to the Union under the Lecompton constitution.
Lincoln and Douglas debate.

1859 John Brown's raid on Harpers Ferry.

1860 Abraham Lincoln elected president.
South Carolina secedes from the Union.

1861 The remaining Lower South states secede.
Confederate States of America established.
Lincoln takes office.
Firing on Fort Sumter; Civil War begins.
Upper South secedes.

FOR FURTHER READING

Tyler Anbinder, *Nativism and Slavery: The Northern Know Nothings and the Politics of the 1850s* (1992). A study of the Know-Nothings' striking success in the North in the mid-1850s.

Eric Foner, *Free Soil, Free Labor, Free Men: The Ideology of the Republican Party Before the Civil War* (1970). An outstanding analysis of the thought, values, and components of the Republican party.

William W. Freehling, *The Road to Disunion: Secessionists at Bay, 1776–1854* (1990). A major study that traces the roots of secession.

William E. Gienapp, *The Origins of the Republican Party, 1852–1856* (1988). A major recent study of the party's formative period.

Michael F. Holt, *The Political Crisis of the 1850s* (1978). A lively reinterpretation of the politics of the 1850s.

Allan Nevins, *The Ordeal of the Union* (vols. 1–2, 1947). A very detailed, highly regarded account of the coming of the Civil War.

David Potter, *The Impending Crisis, 1848–1861* (1976). The best one-volume overview of the events leading to the Civil War.

15

Reforging the Union: Civil War, 1861–1865

Mobilizing for War

In Battle, 1861–1862

Emancipation Transforms the War

War and Society, North and South

The Union Victorious, 1864–1865

Mobilizing for War

Neither North nor South was prepared for war. In April 1861 most of the Union's small army, a scant 16,000 men, 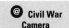 was scattered across the West. One-third of its officers had resigned to join the Confederacy. The Confederacy was even less prepared: it had no tax structure, no navy, only two tiny gunpowder factories, and poorly equipped, unconnected railroad lines. During the first two years of war, both sides would have to overcome these deficiencies, raise large armies, and finance the war.

Recruitment and Conscription

The Civil War armies were the largest organizations ever created in America; by the end of the war, more

@ **Civil War Camera**

than 2 million men had served in the Union army and 800,000 in the Confederate army.

At first the raising of armies was a local, rather than a national or state, effort. Regiments usually consisted of volunteers from the same locale. As casualties mounted, military demand exceeded the supply of volunteers. The Confederacy felt the pinch first and in April 1862 enacted the first conscription law in American history, requiring all able-bodied white men aged eighteen to thirty-five to serve in the military. (By war's end the limits would be seventeen and fifty.) The Confederacy's Conscription Act aroused little enthusiasm. A later amendment exempting owners or overseers of twenty or more slaves evoked complaints about "a rich man's war but a poor man's fight."

Once the army was raised, the Confederacy had to supply it. At first the South imported arms and ammunition from Europe or relied on weapons captured on the battlefield. Gradually, the Confederacy assigned contracts to privately owned factories such as the Tredegar Iron Works in Richmond, provided loans to establish new plants, and created government-owned industries such as the giant Augusta Powder Works in Georgia. The South lost few, if any, battles for want of munitions.

Supplying troops with clothing and food proved more difficult. Supply problems had several sources: railroads that fell into disrepair or were captured, an economy that grew more cotton and tobacco than food, and Union capture of the livestock and grain-raising districts of central Tennessee and Virginia. Close to desperation, the Confederate Congress in 1863 passed the Impressment Act, authorizing army officers to take food from reluctant farmers at prescribed rates. One provision, bitterly resented, empowered agents to impress slaves into labor for the army.

The industrial North more easily supplied its troops with arms, clothes, and food, but keeping a full army was another matter. When the initial tide of enthusiasm for enlistment ebbed, Congress turned to conscription with the Enrollment Act of March 1863. Every able-bodied white male citizen aged twenty to forty-five faced the draft.

The Enrollment Act provided some exemptions and offered two ways of escaping the draft: substitution, or paying another man to serve; and commutation, or paying a $300 fee to the government. Nevertheless, as in the Confederacy, the law stimulated volunteering: only 8 percent of all Union soldiers were draftees or substitutes.

Financing the War

The recruitment and supply of huge armies lay far beyond the capacity of American public finance at the start of the war. During the 1840s and 1850s federal spending had averaged only 2 percent of the gross national product.* During the war, however, as annual federal expenditures rose to 15 percent of the gross national product, the need for new sources of revenue became urgent. When neither additional taxes nor war bond sales produced enough revenue, the Union and the Confederacy began to print paper money. Early in 1862 President Lincoln signed into law the Legal Tender Act, authorizing the issue of $150 million in paper "greenbacks." To bolster confidence in the paper money, Union officials made the greenbacks legal tender (that is, acceptable in payment of most public and private debts).

---

*Gross national product (GNP): the sum, measured in dollars, of all goods and services produced in a given year. By contrast, in the 1980s the federal budget averaged about 25 percent of GNP.

In contrast, the Confederacy never made paper money legal tender, and so suspicions arose that the southern government had little faith in its own money. That the Confederacy raised little revenue from taxes compounded the problem. Northern invasions and poor internal transportation made collecting taxes difficult, and ultimately the South raised less than 5 percent of its wartime revenue from taxes (compared to 21 percent in the North).

Confidence in the Confederacy's paper money quickly evaporated, and the value of paper money in relation to gold plunged. The Confederate response—printing more paper money—merely accelerated inflation. Prices in the North rose 80 percent during the war, but those in the South soared more than 9,000 percent.

In the North, Republicans took advantage of the departure of southern Democrats to push through Congress a measure that they had long advocated: a national banking system. The National Bank Act of 1863 allowed banks to obtain federal charters and to issue national bank notes (backed by the federal government).

Political Leadership in Wartime

The Civil War pitted rival political systems as well as armies and economies against each other. The South entered the war with several apparent advantages. Lincoln's call for militiamen to suppress the rebellion had transformed southern waverers into secessionists. "Never was a people more united or more determined," wrote a New Orleans resident. "There is but one mind, one heart, one action." Jefferson Davis, the president of the Confederacy, possessed experience, honesty, courage, and what one commentator called "a jaw sawed in *steel*."

In contrast, the Union's list of political liabilities appeared lengthy. Loyal but contentious northern Democrats wanted no conscription, no National Bank, and no abolition of slavery. Even within the Republican party, Lincoln, with little national experience, had trouble commanding respect.

Lincoln's style of leadership both encouraged and disarmed opposition within the Republican party. Keeping his counsel to himself until ready to act, he met criticism with homespun anecdotes that threw his opponents off guard. Caught between Radicals and conservatives, Lincoln used his cautious reserve to maintain open communications with both wings of the party and to fragment his opposition. He also co-opted some opponents by bringing them into his cabinet.

In contrast, Jefferson Davis had a knack for making enemies. A West Pointer, he would rather have led the army than the government, and he used his sharp tongue to win arguments rather than friends. Davis's cabinet suffered frequent resignations; for example, the Confederacy had five secretaries of war in four years.

Ideological divisions nearly crippled the Confederacy. The Confederate Constitution explicitly guaranteed the sovereignty of the Confederate states and prohibited the government from enacting protective tariffs or supporting internal improvements. For many Confederate leaders, the Confederacy existed to protect slavery and to enshrine states' rights. For Davis, the overriding objective of the Confederacy was to secure the independence of the South from the North, if necessary at the expense of states' rights.

Lincoln believed that winning the war demanded increasing the central government's power; northern Democrats resisted centralization. Lincoln, more suited by temperament to reconciliation than Davis, was more effective in controlling his opponents.

Securing the Union's Borders

Even before large-scale fighting began, Lincoln moved to safeguard Washington, which was bordered by two slave states (Virginia and Maryland) and filled with Confederate sympathizers. He dispatched federal troops to Maryland and suspended the writ of habeas corpus;* federal troops could now arrest Marylanders without formally charging them with specific offenses. Both Maryland and Delaware, another border slave state, voted down secession.

---

*Habeas corpus: a court order requiring that the detainer of a prisoner bring the person in custody to court and show cause for his or her detention.

Next Lincoln authorized the arming of Union sympathizers in Kentucky, a slave state with a Unionist legislature and a secessionist governor. Lincoln also stationed troops just across the Ohio River from Kentucky, in Illinois, and when a Confederate army invaded Kentucky early in 1862, those troops drove it out. Officially, at least, Kentucky became the third slave state to declare for the Union. Four years of murderous fighting ravaged the fourth, Missouri, as Union and Confederate armies and bands of guerrillas clashed. Despite savage fighting and divided loyalties, Missouri never left the Union.

By holding the border slave states in the Union, Lincoln kept open his lines to the free states and gained access to the river systems in Kentucky and Missouri that led into the heart of the Confederacy.

In Battle, 1861–1862

The Civil War was the first war in which both sides relied extensively on railroads, the telegraph, mass-produced weapons, joint army-navy tactics, iron-plated warships, rifled guns and artillery, and trench warfare. In many ways it was the first modern war.

Armies, Weapons, and Strategies

Compared to the Confederacy's 9 million people, who included 3 million slaves, the Union had 22 million people in 1861. The North also enjoyed 3.5 times as many white men of military age, 90 percent of all U.S. industrial capacity, and two-thirds of its railroad track. But the North faced a daunting challenge: to force the South back into the Union. The South, in contrast, fought only for independence. To subdue the Confederacy, the North would have to sustain offensive operations over an area comparable in size to the part of Russia that Napoleon had invaded in 1812 with disastrous results.

Measured against this challenge, the North's advantages in population and technology shrank. The North had more men but needed them to defend long supply lines and to occupy captured areas. Consequently, it could commit a smaller proportion of its overall force to combat. The South, relying on slaves for labor, could assign a higher proportion of its white male population to combat. And although the Union had superior railroads, it had to move its troops and supplies huge distances, whereas the Confederacy could shift its troops relatively short distances within its defense area without railroads. The South's poor roads hampered the supply-heavy northern forces as well. Finally, southerners had an edge in morale, for Confederate troops usually fought on home ground.

The Civil War witnessed experiments with a variety of new weapons, including the submarine, the repeating rifle, and the multibarreled Gatling gun, the predecessor of the machine gun. Whereas smoothbore muskets had an effective range of 80 yards, the Springfield or Enfield rifles widely in use by 1863 were accurate at 400 yards. The rifle's development posed a challenge to long-accepted military tactics, which stressed the mass infantry charge. As the fighting wore on, both sides recognized the value of trenches, which offered defenders protection against withering rifle fire.

Much like previous wars, the Civil War was fought in a succession of battles during which ex-

The War in the East, 1861–1862

Union advances on Richmond were turned back at Fredericksburg and the Seven Days' Battles, and the Confederacy's invasion of Union territory was stopped at Antietam.

posed infantry traded volleys, charged, and counter-charged. The side that withdrew first from the battlefield was considered the loser, even though it often sustained lighter casualties than the "victor." The defeated army usually moved back a few miles to lick its wounds; the winners stayed in place to lick theirs. Not surprisingly, generals on both sides concluded that the best defense was a good offense.

What passed for long-range Union strategy in 1861 was the Anaconda plan, which called for the Union to blockade the southern coast and to thrust, like a huge snake, down the Mississippi River, thus sealing off the Confederacy. However, the lack of adequate ships and men to seize the Mississippi in 1861 prevented the implementation of this ambitious plan.

Early in the war the need to secure the border slave states, especially Kentucky and Missouri, dictated Union strategy in the West, sending northern armies plunging southward from Kentucky into Tennessee. The Appalachian Mountains tended to separate this western theater from the eastern theater. East of the mountains, the Confederates' decision to locate their capital in Richmond, Virginia, shaped Union strategy. "Forward to Richmond!" became the Union's first war cry.

Stalemate in the East

Before Union troops could reach Richmond, one hundred miles southwest of Washington, they would have to dislodge a Confederate army brazenly encamped at Manassas Junction, Virginia, only twenty-five miles from the Union capital. Lincoln ordered General Irvin McDowell to attack the rebel force. In the resulting First Battle of Bull Run (or First Manassas*), amateur armies clashed in bloody chaos under a blistering sun in July 1861 as well-dressed, picnicking Washington dignitaries watched the carnage. The Confederates routed the larger Union army.

After Bull Run, Lincoln appointed General George B. McClellan to replace McDowell as commander of the Union's Army of the Potomac.

*Because the North often named battles after local landmarks, usually bodies of water, and the South after the nearest town, some Civil War battles are known by two names.

McClellan, a master of administration and training, transformed a ragtag mob into a disciplined fighting force. His soldiers adored him, but Lincoln became disenchanted. To the president, the key to victory lay in launching simultaneous attacks on several fronts so that the North could exploit its advantages in manpower and communications. McClellan, a proslavery Democrat, hoped for a series of relatively bloodless victories followed by the readmission of southern states into the Union with slavery intact.

@ A Union Soldier's Opinion of the War

In spring 1862 McClellan got an opportunity to demonstrate the value of his strategy. After Bull Run, the Confederates had pulled back behind the Rappahannock River to block a Union march toward Richmond. McClellan decided to go around the southerners by transporting his troops down the Chesapeake Bay to the tip of the peninsula formed by the York and James rivers and then to attack Richmond from the rear.

At first McClellan's Peninsula Campaign unfolded smoothly. But after luring the Confederacy to the brink of defeat, he hesitated, refusing to launch the final attack without the reinforcements he expected. As McClellan delayed, General Robert E. Lee assumed command of the Confederacy's Army of Northern Virginia. An opponent of secession, a man so courteous that he seemed almost too gentle, Lee nevertheless was McClellan's opposite, bold and willing to accept casualties.

Lee immediately took the offensive, attacking the much larger Union forces in the Seven Days' Battles (June–July 1862). Raging through forests east of Richmond, the battles cost the Confederacy nearly twice as many men as the Union, but McClellan, not Lee, blinked. His panicky reports prompted Lincoln to order him back to Washington.

With McClellan out of the picture, Lee and his lieutenant, Stonewall Jackson, pushed north, routing a Union army at the Second Battle of Bull Run (Second Manassas) in August 1862. Lee followed up this victory with a typically bold stroke: he took his army across the Potomac and northward into Maryland, hoping that the fall harvest could provide him with desperately needed supplies. McClellan met Lee at the Battle of Antietam (Sharpsburg) on September 17, 1862. North and South together suffered 24,000 casualties in this bloodiest day of the entire war. Tactically, the battle was a draw, but strategically it constituted a major Union victory because it forced Lee to withdraw south of the Potomac. Most important, Antietam provided Lincoln the occasion to issue the Emancipation Proclamation, freeing all slaves under rebel control.

Lincoln complained that McClellan had "the slows" and faulted him for not pursuing Lee after Antietam. McClellan's replacement, General Ambrose Burnside, thought himself unfit for high command. He was right. In December 1862 he led 122,000 federal troops against 78,500 Confederates at the Battle of Fredericksburg (Virginia). Burnside captured the town but then sacrificed his army in futile charges up the heights west of the town.

Richmond remained, in the words of a southern song, "a hard road to travel." The war in the East had become a stalemate.

The War in the West

The Union fared better in the West, which also spawned new leadership in the person of an obscure Union general, Ulysses S. Grant. A West Point graduate with a reputation for heavy drinking, and a failed farmer and businessman, Grant soon proved one of the Union's best leaders.

In 1861–1862 Grant had stabilized control of Missouri and Kentucky and then moved south to attack Corinth, Mississippi, a major rail junction. In early April 1862 Confederate forces staged a surprise attack on Grant's army, encamped at Shiloh Church in southern Tennessee. Driven back on the first day, Union forces counterattacked on the second day and drove the Confederate army from the field. Of 77,000 men who fought at Shiloh, 23,000 were killed or wounded.

For the Corinth-Shiloh Campaign, the Confederacy had stripped New Orleans of its defenses, leaving its largest city guarded by only 3,000 militia. A combined land-sea force under Union general Benjamin Butler and Admiral David G. Farragut

@ **The Heat of Battle from the Southern Soldier's Perspective**

The War in the West, 1861–1862
By the end of 1862 the North held New Orleans and the entire Mississippi River except for the stretch between Vicksburg and Port Hudson.

took advantage of the weakened defenses and captured New Orleans in late April. Farragut continued up the Mississippi as far as Natchez. When a Union flotilla moved down the river in June and took Memphis, the North controlled the great river except for a 200-mile stretch between Port Hudson, Louisiana, and Vicksburg, Mississippi.

In 1862 Union and Confederate forces also clashed in the trans-Mississippi West, a vast region that stretched from the Midwest to the Pacific Coast. On the banks of the Rio Grande, Union volunteers and Mexican-American companies drove a Confederate army from Texas out of New Mexico. A thousand miles to the east, at Pea Ridge, Arkansas, in March 1862, northern troops scattered a Confederate force of 16,000.

These Union victories changed the trans-Mississippi war. As the rebel threat faded, western volunteers who had mobilized to crush Confederates turned to fighting Indians. After 1865 federal troops moved west to complete the rout of the Indians that had begun during the Civil War.

Ironclads and Cruisers: The Naval War

By plunging the navy into the Confederacy like a dagger, the Union exploited one of its clearest advantages. The North began the war with more than forty active warships—the South had none—and by 1865 northern industrial advantages had given the United States the largest navy in the world. Steamships could penetrate the South's river systems from any direction. Yet the Union navy faced an extraordinary challenge in its efforts to blockade the South's 3,500 miles of coastline. Sleek Confederate blockade runners darted in and out of southern harbors with little chance of capture early in the war. In 1861 almost 90 percent of blockade runners made it through, but by 1865 the blockade had tightened, and the rate had sunk to 50 percent.

Despite meager resources, the South made impressive efforts to offset the North's naval advantages. The Confederates raised a scuttled Union frigate, the *Merrimac*; sheathed its sides in iron; rechristened it the *Virginia*; and deployed it to attack wooden Union ships at Hampton Roads, Virginia. The *Virginia*'s success ended on March 9, 1862, when it tangled with the hastily built Union ironclad *Monitor* in the first battle ever fought between ironclads. The battle ended in a draw, but the South eventually lost the naval war because it could not build enough ships to overcome the northern lead.

The Diplomatic War

While armies and navies clashed in 1861–1862, conflict developed on a third front, diplomacy. At the war's start southerners had expected to gain swift diplomatic recognition for the Confederacy. They were sure of the support of Britain and France's upper classes and even more certain that Britain, dependent on the South for four-fifths of its cotton, would have to break the Union blockade.

The South fell far short of its diplomatic objectives. Neither Britain nor France ever recognized the Confederacy as a nation. Southerners had badly overestimated the leverage of "cotton diplomacy" and the power of King Cotton, exaggerating the impact of their threats to withhold raw cotton. Britain had a huge cotton surplus on hand when the war began and developed other sources of cotton during the war, especially in India and Egypt.

Lincoln's issuance of the Emancipation Proclamation, freeing the slaves, effectively preempted any British or French move toward recognition of the Confederacy. By transforming the war into a struggle about slavery, Lincoln won wide support among liberals and the working class in Britain.

Emancipation Transforms the War

The Union's policy on emancipation developed in several stages. As soon as northern troops invaded the South, questions arose about captured rebel property, including slaves. Generally, slaves who fled behind Union lines were considered "contraband"—enemy property liable to seizure—and were put to work for the Union army. In August 1861 Congress passed the first Confiscation Act, which authorized the seizure of all property, including slaves, used in military aid of the rebellion. This law did not free slaves, nor did it apply to those who had not worked for the Confederate army.

Several factors determined the Union's cautious approach. For one thing, Lincoln maintained that the South could not legally secede and thus argued that the Constitution's protection of property still applied. Second, Lincoln did not want to alienate slaveholders in the border states and proslavery Democrats. At the same time, however, the Radical Republicans pressured Lincoln to make the Civil War a second American Revolution, one that would abolish slavery.

Emancipation also took on military significance with each Union setback, as northerners began to recognize that slavery permitted the South to commit a higher percentage of its white men to battle. In July 1862 Congress therefore passed the second Confiscation Act, which authorized the seizure of property belonging to all rebels, stipulated that slaves who entered Union lines "shall be forever free," and authorized the use of blacks as soldiers.

Nevertheless, Lincoln continued to stall. "My paramount object in this struggle *is* to save the Union, and is *not* either to save or destroy slavery," he averred. But Lincoln, who had always loathed slavery, gradually came around to the view that the war had to lead to abolition. Reluctant to push the issue while Union armies reeled in defeat, he drafted a proclamation of emancipation and waited for the right moment to announce it. After the Union victory at Antietam, Lincoln issued the Preliminary Emancipation Proclamation (September 1862), which declared all slaves under rebel control free as of January 1, 1863. The final Emancipation Proclamation, issued on January 1, 1863, declared "forever free" all slaves in areas in rebellion.

The proclamation had limited practical impact. It applied only to areas in which it could not be enforced, those still in rebellion, and did not touch slavery in the border states. But the Emancipation Proclamation was a brilliant political stroke. By making it a military measure, Lincoln pacified northern conservatives, and by issuing the proclamation himself, he stole the initiative from the Radical Republicans. The proclamation also mobilized support for the Union among European liberals, pushed the border states toward emancipation (both Missouri and Maryland abolished slavery before the war's end), and increased slaves' incentives to escape as Union troops neared. Fulfilling the worst of Confederate fears, the proclamation also enabled African-Americans to join the Union army.

The Emancipation Proclamation did not end slavery everywhere or free all the slaves, but it changed the war. From 1863 on the war for the Union was also a war against slavery.

Crossing Union Lines

The attacks and counterattacks of the opposing armies turned many slaves into pawns of the war, free when Union troops overran their area, slaves again if the Confederates regained control.

Although in the first year of the war masters could retrieve slaves from Union armies, after 1862 slaves who crossed Union lines were considered free. However, the freedmen encountered fierce prejudice among Yankee soldiers, who widely feared that emancipation would propel blacks northward after the war. The best solution to the widespread "question of what to do with the darkies," wrote one northern soldier, "would be to shoot them."

But this was not the whole story. Contrabands who aided the Union as spies and scouts helped to break down bigotry. In March 1865 Congress established the Freedmen's Bureau to provide relief, education, and work for the former slaves. The same law also provided that forty acres of abandoned or confiscated land could be leased to each freedman or southern Unionist, with an option to buy after three years. This was the first and only time that Congress provided for the redistribution of confiscated Confederate property.

African-American Soldiers in the Union Army

During the first year of the war the Union had rejected African-American soldiers. Only after the Emancipation Proclamation did the large-scale enlistment of blacks begin. By the war's end 186,000 African-Americans had served in the Union army, one-tenth of all Union soldiers.

Even Union soldiers who held African-Americans in contempt eventually came to approve of "anything that will kill a rebel." Black recruitment offered opportunities for whites to secure commissions, for blacks served in separate regiments under white officers. For most of the war, black soldiers earned far less pay than

@ **Thomas Wentworth Higginson Assesses the Black Soldier**

whites. Not until June 1864 did Congress belatedly equalize the pay of black and white soldiers.

African-American soldiers also suffered a far higher mortality rate than whites. Seldom committed to combat, they were far more likely to die of disease in bacteria-ridden garrisons. The Confederacy refused to treat captured black Union soldiers as prisoners of war; instead they were sent back to the states from which they had come to be reenslaved or executed. In an especially gruesome incident, when Confederate troops captured Fort Pillow, Tennessee, in 1864, they massacred 262 blacks.

Slavery in Wartime

Anxious white southerners on the home front felt as if they were perched on a volcano. To maintain control over their 3 million slaves, they tightened slave patrols, spread scare stories among slaves, and sometimes even moved entire plantations to relative safety in Texas.

Some slaves remained faithful to their owners, hiding treasured belongings from Union soldiers. Others were torn between loyalty and desire for freedom; one body servant, for example, accompanied his master to war, rescued him when he was wounded, and then escaped on his master's horse. Given the chance to flee to Union lines, most slaves did. But the majority of southern slaves stayed on plantations under the nominal control of their masters. Despite the fears of southern whites, no general slave uprising occurred, and the Confederate war effort continued to utilize slave labor.

Whether slaves fled to freedom or merely stopped working, they effectively undermined the plantation system. Slavery disintegrated even as the Confederacy fought to preserve it. By 1864 a desperate Confederate Congress considered impressing slaves into the army in exchange for their freedom at the war's end. In March 1865 the Confederate Congress passed a bill to arm 300,000 slave soldiers, a plan that never took effect.

The Turning Point of 1863

In summer and fall 1863 Union fortunes improved dramatically in every theater of the war. However,

The War in the East, 1863
Victorious at Chancellorsville in May 1863, Lee again invaded Union territory but was decisively stopped at Gettysburg.

the spring had gone badly as General Joseph "Fighting Joe" Hooker, a windbag fond of issuing pompous proclamations to his troops, suffered a crushing defeat at Chancellorsville, Virginia, in May 1863. Reports from the West were no better: Grant was still unable to take Vicksburg, and the rebels clung to a vital 200-mile stretch of the Mississippi.

Union fortunes rose when Lee determined to invade the North. Lee needed supplies that war-racked Virginia could no longer provide. He also hoped that Lincoln would move troops from Vicksburg back into the eastern theater, and he believed that a major Confederate victory on northern soil could tip the balance to propeace northern Democrats and

The War in the West, 1863: Vicksburg
Grant first moved his army west of Vicksburg to a point on the Mississippi south of the town. Then he marched northeast, taking Jackson, and finally west to Vicksburg.

gain European recognition for the Confederacy. Lee led his 75,000 men into Maryland and then pressed forward into southern Pennsylvania.

Early in July 1863 Lee's offensive ground to a halt at a Pennsylvania road junction, Gettysburg. Confederates foraging for shoes in the town stumbled into Union cavalry, and both sides called for reinforcements. Thus began the war's greatest battle. The Union fielded 90,000 troops against Lee's 75,000, and the struggle raged for the first three days of July. On the afternoon of the third day, Lee ordered a direct frontal assault on the Union lines, and 15,000 men under General George E. Pickett charged across the open field, flags bright in the brilliant sunshine. Union rifles poured volley after volley into the onrushing Con-

@ The Home of the Rebel Sharpshooter

@ Incidents of War: A Harvest of Death, Gettysburg, July 1863

federates, whose line wavered and then broke. More than one-half of Pickett's force lay dead, dying, or captured. When Lee withdrew to Virginia the next day, July 4, he had lost seventeen generals and more than one-third of his army. Total Union and Confederate casualties numbered 50,000.

Almost simultaneously, the North won a strategically vital battle in the West, at Vicksburg. After arduous maneuvering, Grant had besieged Vicksburg, the key to the Mississippi. After six weeks, during which southern soldiers and civilians alike survived by eating mules and even rats, the Confederate commander surrendered his 30,000-man garrison to Grant on July 4. Port Hudson, the last Confederate stronghold on the Mississippi, soon surrendered. "The Father of Waters flows unvexed to the sea," Lincoln proclaimed.

Coming on the heels of reverses that had driven northern morale to its lowest point of the war, Union successes in the second half of 1863 stiffened the North's will to continue fighting. The South, however, was far from falling. Lee and his Army of Northern Virginia still defended Virginia and Richmond. Although the loss of Vicksburg had cut the Confederacy in half, southern states west of the Mississippi could still provide soldiers. And the heart of the Confederacy—the Carolinas, Georgia, Florida, Mississippi, and Virginia—remained in southern hands.

War and Society, North and South

The Civil War, engulfing two economies and societies, extended far beyond the battlefields. The North's superior resources enabled it to meet wartime demands more successfully than the South, but both sides confronted similar problems: labor shortages, inflation, and dissent.

The War's Economic Impact: The North

The war had a wildly uneven effect on the Union's economy. Deprived of southern markets, the shoe industry in Massachusetts declined; deprived of raw cotton, the textile industry went into a tailspin. But northern industries related to the war effort, such as the manufacture of arms and uniforms, benefited from huge government contracts. Railroads flourished. Now an overwhelming majority in Congress, the Republican party carried through a vigorous pro-business legislative agenda. Congress hiked the tariff in 1862 and again in 1864 to protect domestic industries. In 1862 it passed the Pacific Railroad Act to build a transcontinental railroad. The government chartered the Union Pacific and Central Pacific corporations and gave each large land grants and generous loans, a total of 60 million acres of land and $20 million. The issuance of greenbacks and the creation of a national banking system brought a measure of uniformity to the nation's financial system.

The Homestead Act (passed in May 1862), embodying the Republican party's ideal of "free soil, free labor, free men," granted 160 acres of public land to settlers after five years of residence on the land. By 1865, 20,000 homesteaders had occupied new land in the West under this act. To bring higher education within the reach of the common people, the Morrill Land Grant Act **@ Morrill Act** of July 1862 gave states proceeds from public land to establish universities emphasizing "such branches of learning as are related to agriculture and mechanic arts [engineering]."

Despite the idealism underlying such laws, the war benefited the wealthy more than the average citizen. Corrupt contractors grew rich by selling the government substandard merchandise such as the notorious "shoddy," clothing made from compressed rags, which quickly disintegrated. Speculators made millions in the gold market, profiting more from Union defeats than from Union victories.

Ordinary workers suffered. Protective tariffs, wartime excise taxes, and inflation bloated the price of finished goods, while wages lagged 20 percent or more behind cost increases.

The War's Economic Impact: The South

The war shattered the South's economy. In fact, if both regions are considered together, the war retarded *American* economic growth. For example, the U.S. commodity output, which had increased 51 percent and 62 percent in the 1840s and 1850s, respectively, rose only 22 percent during the 1860s. Even this modest gain depended wholly on the North, for during that same decade commodity output in the South *declined* 39 percent.

Multiple factors offset the South's substantial wartime industrial growth. For example, the war destroyed the South's railroads. Cotton production plunged from 4 million bales in 1861 to 300,000 in 1865. Southern food production also declined because of Union occupation and a shortage of manpower.

Part of the blame for the South's food shortage rested with the planters. Despite government pleas to grow more food, many planters continued to raise cotton. To feed its hungry armies, the Confederacy impressed food from civilians. Farms and plantations run by the wives of active soldiers provided the easiest targets for food-impressment agents, and the women sent desperate pleas to their husbands to return home. By late 1864, half the Confederacy's soldiers were absent from their units.

Dealing with Dissent

Both wartime governments faced mounting dissent and disloyalty. Within the Confederacy, dissent assumed two basic forms. First, a vocal group of states' rights supporters persistently attacked Jefferson Davis's government as a despotism. Second, loyalty to the Union flourished among the nonslaveholding small farmers who lived in the Appalachian region. On the whole, the South responded mildly to popular disaffection. In 1862 the Confederate Congress gave President Davis the power to suspend the writ of habeas corpus, but he used it sparingly.

Lincoln faced similar challenges in the North, where the Democratic minority opposed both emancipation and the wartime growth of centralized power. One faction, the "Peace Democrats" (called Copperheads by their opponents, after a species of easily concealed poisonous snakes), demanded a truce and a peace conference.

Strongest in the border states, the Midwest, and northeastern cities, the Democrats mobilized farmers of southern background and the urban working class, especially recent immigrants, who feared losing their jobs to free blacks. In 1863 this volatile mix of political, ethnic, racial, and class antagonisms exploded into antidraft protests in several cities. By far the most violent eruption occurred in July 1863 in New York City, where mobs of Irish working-class men and women roamed the streets for four days until federal troops suppressed them. The Irish loathed the idea of being drafted to fight a war on behalf of slaves who, once freed, might compete with them for jobs. They also bitterly resented the provision of the draft law that allowed the rich to purchase substitutes. The rioters lynched at least a dozen blacks, injured hundreds more, and burned draft offices and the homes of wealthy Republicans.

President Lincoln's speedy dispatch of federal troops to quash these riots typified his forceful response to dissent. Lincoln imposed martial law with far less hesitancy than Davis; he suspended the writ of habeas corpus nationwide in 1863 and authorized the arrest of rebels, draft resisters, and anyone engaged in "any disloyal practice."

Yet Lincoln did not unleash a reign of terror against dissent. In general, the North preserved freedom of the press, speech, and assembly. In 1864 the Union became the first warring nation in history to hold a contested national election.

The Medical War

The Union and the Confederacy alike witnessed remarkable wartime patriotism that propelled civilians, especially women, to work tirelessly to alleviate soldiers' suffering. The United States Sanitary Commission, organized to assist the Union's medical bureau, depended on women volunteers. Described by one woman as a "great artery that bears the people's love to the army," the commission raised funds, bought and distributed supplies, and ran special kitchens to supplement army rations.

Women also reached out to aid the battlefront through the nursing corps. Some 3,200 women served the Union and the Confederacy as nurses. Dorothea Dix, famed for her campaigns on behalf of the insane,

@ **The Women's War**

became head of the Union's nursing corps. The Confederacy also had extraordinary nurses, among them Belle Boyd, who served as both nurse and spy and once dashed through a field, waving her bonnet, to give Stonewall Jackson information.

Pioneered by British reformer Florence Nightingale in the 1850s, nursing was a new vocation for women. In the eyes of critics, it marked a brazen departure from women's proper sphere. But nurses were useful, and the sanitary reforms they helped bring about improved the practice of medicine. The widely held theory that disease was caused by noxious vapors also prompted doctors to adopt valuable sanitary measures. In partial consequence, the ratio of disease to battle deaths was much lower in the Civil War than in the Mexican War. Nonetheless, for every soldier killed during the Civil War, two died of disease. The germ theory of disease was unknown, and arm and leg wounds often led to gangrene or tetanus. Typhoid, malaria, diarrhea, and dysentery were rampant in army camps.

Prison camps posed a special problem. Both sides had far more prisoners than they could handle, and prisoners suffered gravely. The worst conditions plagued the southern camps. Squalor and insufficient rations turned the Confederate prison camp at Andersonville, Georgia, into a virtual death camp; 3,000 prisoners a month (out of a total of 32,000) were dying there by August 1864. After the war an outraged northern public demanded, and got, the execution of Andersonville's commandant. Union prison camps were only marginally better.

@ **An Enlisted Man Describes Life in a Confederate Prison Camp**

The War and Women's Rights

Nurses were not the only women to serve society in wartime. In North and South alike, women took over jobs vacated by men. In rural areas, where manpower shortages were most acute, women often plowed, planted, and harvested.

Northern women's rights advocates hoped that the war would yield equality for women as well as for slaves. A grateful North, they contended, should reward women for their wartime service and recognize the link between black rights and women's rights. In 1863 feminists Elizabeth Cady Stanton and Susan B. Anthony organized the National Woman's Loyal League to promote abolition and woman suffrage. Despite high expectations, the war did not bring women significantly closer to economic or political equality. Nor did it much change the prevailing definition of women's sphere.

This failure to win the vote for women by capitalizing on the rising sentiment for abolition keenly disappointed women's rights advocates. The North had compelling reasons to abolish slavery, but northern politicians saw little practical value in woman suffrage.

The Union Victorious, 1864–1865

Successes at Gettysburg and Vicksburg in 1863 notwithstanding, the Union stood no closer to taking Richmond at the start of 1864 than in 1861, and most of the Lower South remained under Confederate control. War weariness strengthened the Democrats and jeopardized Lincoln's reelection in 1864.

The Eastern Theater in 1864

Early in 1864 Lincoln made Grant the commander of all Union armies and promoted him to lieutenant general. At first glance, the stony-faced, cigar-puffing Grant seemed an unlikely candidate for so exalted a rank, held previously only by George Washington. But Grant's successes in the West had made him the Union's most popular general.

Grant shared Lincoln's belief that the Union had to coordinate its attacks on all fronts to exploit its numerical advantage. He planned a sustained offensive against Lee in the East while ordering Sherman to attack the rebel army in Georgia. Sherman's mission was "to break it [the Confederate army] up, and to get into the interior of the enemy's country . . . inflicting all the damage you can."

In early May 1864 Grant led 118,000 men against Lee's 64,000 in a forested area near Fredericksburg, Virginia, called the Wilderness. The Union army fought the Army of Northern Virginia in a series of bloody en-

gagements in May and June. These battles ranked among the war's fiercest; at Cold Harbor, Grant lost 7,000 men in one hour. Instead of recoiling from such an immense "butcher's bill," Grant pressed on, forcing Lee to pull back to trenches guarding Petersburg and Richmond. Once entrenched, Lee could not threaten the Union rear with rapid moves as he had done for three years.

@ **Wounded Escaping from the Burning Woods of the Wilderness**

Sherman in Georgia

While Grant and Lee grappled in the Wilderness, Sherman led 98,000 men into Georgia. Opposing him with 53,000 men (later reinforced to 65,000), General Joseph Johnston slowly retreated toward Atlanta, conserving his strength for a defense of the city. Dismayed by this defensive strategy, President Davis replaced Johnston with the adventurous John B. Hood. He gave Davis what he wanted, a series of attacks on Sherman, but Sherman pressed relentlessly forward against Hood's dwindling forces. Unable to defend Atlanta, Hood evacuated the city, which Sherman took on September 2, 1864.

The Election of 1864

Atlanta's fall came at a timely moment for Lincoln, in the thick of a tough campaign for reelection. Despite opposition from Radical Republicans, Lincoln's managers controlled the nomination by the time of the Republican convention. To isolate the Peace Democrats, the Republicans formed a temporary organization, the National Union party, and chose a southern Unionist, Democratic senator Andrew Johnson of Tennessee, for the vice-presidency. The Democrats nominated George B. McClellan, former commander of the Army of the Potomac, who advocated military victory and tried to distance himself from the Democratic platform, which called for peace without victory.

Lincoln doubted that he would be reelected, but the fall of Atlanta provided an enormous boost. With 55 percent of the popular vote and 212 out of 233 electoral votes, he swept to victory.

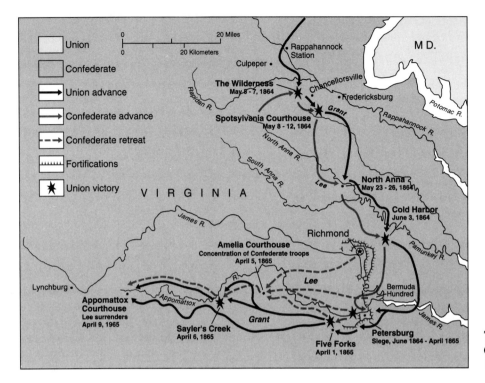

The Final Virginia Campaign, 1864–1865

Sherman's March Through Georgia

Meanwhile, Sherman gave the South a lesson in total war. Refusing to chase Hood back into Tennessee, he decided to abandon his own supply lines, to march his army across Georgia to Savannah, and to live off the countryside. He would break the South's will to fight, terrify its people, and "make war so terrible . . . that generations would pass before they could appeal to it again."

@ General Sherman Recalls the March Through Georgia

Sherman began by burning much of Atlanta and forcing the evacuation of its civilian population. Then he led the bulk of his army, 62,000 men, out of Atlanta toward Savannah. Four columns of infantry, augmented by cavalry squads and followed by thousands of jubilant slaves, moved on a front sixty miles wide and at a pace of ten miles a day, destroying everything that could aid the Confederacy—arsenals, railroads, munitions plants, cotton gins, crops,

and livestock. After taking Savannah in December 1864, Sherman's army wheeled north toward South Carolina and advanced unimpeded to Columbia, where fires set by looters, slaves, soldiers of both sides, and liberated Union prisoners razed the city. Sherman headed for North Carolina. By spring 1865 his army had left behind 400 miles of ruin. Other Union armies controlled the entire Confederacy, except Texas and Florida, and destroyed its wealth.

Toward Appomattox

While Sherman headed north, Grant renewed his assault on the entrenched Army of Northern Virginia. His main objective was Petersburg, a railroad hub south of Richmond. The fall of Atlanta and the devastation wrought by Sherman's army took a heavy toll on Confederate morale. Desertions reached epidemic proportions. Late in March 1865

Grant, reinforced by Sheridan, swung his army around the western flank of the Petersburg defenders. Lee could not stop him. On April 2 a courier brought the grim news to Jefferson Davis, attending church in Richmond: "General Lee telegraphs that he can hold his position no longer."

Davis left his pew, gathered his government, and fled. On the morning of April 3 Union troops entered Richmond, pulled down the Confederate flag, and raised the Stars and Stripes over the capital. Explosions set by retreating Confederates left the city "a sea of flames." On April 4 Lincoln toured the city and, for a few minutes, sat at Davis's desk with a dreamy expression on his face.

Lee led a last-ditch effort to escape westward to Lynchburg and its rail connections. But Grant and Sheridan choked off the route, and on April 9 Lee bowed to the inevitable. He asked for terms of surrender and met Grant in a private home in the village of Appomattox Courthouse, east of Lynchburg. The final surrender came four days later as Lee's troops laid down their arms between federal ranks. "On our part," wrote a Union officer, "not a sound of trumpet . . . nor roll of drum; not a cheer . . . but an awed stillness rather." Grant paroled Lee's 26,000 men and sent them home with the horses and mules "to work their little farms." Within a month the remnants of Confederate resistance collapsed.

On April 14 at Ford's Theater an unemployed pro-Confederate actor, John Wilkes Booth, entered Lincoln's box and shot him in the head. Assassination attempts on the secretary of state and vice president failed, and Booth escaped. Within two weeks Union troops hunted him down and shot him to death (or he shot himself). Four accused accomplices were hanged, and four more were imprisoned. On April 15 Lincoln died and Andrew Johnson became president. Six days later Lincoln's funeral train left Washington on its mournful journey to Springfield, Illinois. Crowds of thousands gathered at stations to weep as the black-draped train passed.

CHRONOLOGY

1861 President Abraham Lincoln calls for volunteers to suppress the rebellion (April).
Virginia, Arkansas, Tennessee, and North Carolina join the Confederacy (April–May).
Lincoln imposes a naval blockade on the South (April).
First Battle of Bull Run (July).
First Confiscation Act (August).

1862 Legal Tender Act (February).
George B. McClellan's Peninsula Campaign (March–July).
Battle of Shiloh (April).
Confederate Congress passes the Conscription Act (April).
David G. Farragut captures New Orleans (April).
Homestead Act (May).
Seven Days' Battles (June–July).
Pacific Railroad Act (July).
Morrill Land Grant Act (July).
Second Confiscation Act (July).
Second Battle of Bull Run (August).
Battle of Antietam (September).
Preliminary Emancipation Proclamation (September).
Battle of Fredericksburg (December).

1863 Emancipation Proclamation issued (January).
National Bank Act (February).
Congress passes the Enrollment Act (March).
Battle of Chancellorsville (May).
Battle of Gettysburg (July).
Surrender of Vicksburg (July).
New York City draft riots (July).

1864 Ulysses S. Grant given command of all Union armies (March).
Wilderness campaign (May–June).
Surrender of Atlanta (September).
Lincoln reelected (November).
William T. Sherman's march to the sea (November–December).

1865 Sherman moves through South Carolina (January–March).
Grant takes Richmond (April).
Robert E. Lee surrenders at Appomattox (April).
Lincoln dies (April).

FOR FURTHER READING

Iver Bernstein, *The New York Draft Riots: The Significance for American Society and Politics in the Age of the Civil War* (1990). An exploration of the social, economic, and political facets of the riots, and their ramifications.

Albert Castel, *Decision in the West: The Atlanta Campaign of 1864* (1992). A critical examination of William T. Sherman's legendary brilliance of command.

Catherine Clinton and Nina Silber, eds., *Divided Houses: Gender and the Civil War* (1992). Essays focusing on changes in women's roles and activities.

David H. Donald, *Lincoln* (1995). An impressive new biography of one of America's greatest presidents.

Alvin M. Josephy Jr., *The Civil War in the American West* (1993). A penetrating look at a relatively unexamined arena of the war.

Leon Litwack, *Been in the Storm So Long: The Aftermath of Slavery* (1979). A prize-winning examination of slaves'

responses to the process of emancipation, continuing into the Reconstruction era.

James M. McPherson, *Battle Cry of Freedom: The Civil War Era* (1988). An award-winning study of the war years, skillfully integrating political, military, and social history.

Philip Shaw Paludan, *The Presidency of Abraham Lincoln* (1994). An assessment of Lincoln as statesman, party leader, commander in chief, and emancipator.

Charles Royster, *The Destructive War: William Tecumseh Sherman, Stonewall Jackson, and the Americans* (1991). An insightful exploration of the meaning of violence and nationality in the Civil War era.

Emory M. Thomas, *The Confederate Nation, 1861–1865* (1979). An engaging narrative history, emphasizing the rise and fall of southern nationalism.

16

The Crises of Reconstruction,
1865–1877

Reconstruction Politics

The end of the Civil War offered multiple possibilities for chaos and vengeance. The federal government could have imprisoned Confederate leaders; former rebel troops could have become guerrillas; freed slaves could have waged a racial war against their former masters. None of this happened. Instead, intense *political* conflict dominated the postwar period. The political upheaval, sometimes attended by violence, produced new constitutional amendments, an impeachment crisis, and some of the most ambitious domestic legislation ever enacted by Congress, the Reconstruction Acts of 1867–1868. It culminated in something that few expected, the enfranchisement of African-American men.

@ Secession
and Reconstruction

Conflict over Reconstruction had begun even before the war ended. In December 1863 President Lincoln issued the Proclamation of Amnesty and Reconstruction, which allowed southern states to form new governments if at least 10 percent of those who had voted in the 1860 elections swore an oath of allegiance to the Union and accepted emancipation. This plan excluded most Confederate officials and military officers, who would have had to apply for presidential pardons. Lincoln hoped both to undermine the Confederacy and to build a southern Republican party.

Radical Republicans in Congress wanted a slower readmission process that would exclude even more ex-Confederates from political life. Lincoln's death foreclosed the possibility that he and Congress might draw closer to agreement, and Radicals now looked with hope to the new president, Andrew Johnson.

Presidential Reconstruction
Under Johnson

At first glance, Andrew Johnson seemed a likely ally for the Radicals. The only southern senator to remain in Congress when his state seceded, Johnson had taken a strong anti-Confederate stance and had served as military governor of Tennessee for two years. Self-educated, an ardent Jacksonian, a foe of the planter class, a supporter of emancipation— Johnson had his own political agenda, sharply different from that of the Radicals.

In May 1865, with Congress out of session, Johnson shocked Republicans by announcing his own program to bring the southern states still without Reconstruction governments—Alabama, Florida, Georgia, Mississippi, North Carolina, South Carolina, and Texas—back into the Union. Virtually all southerners who took an oath of allegiance would receive pardon and amnesty, and all their property except slaves would be restored to them. Confederate civil and military officers would still be disqualified, as would well-to-do former Confederates (anyone owning taxable property worth $20,000 or more). By purging the plantation aristocracy, Johnson claimed, he would aid "humble men, the peasantry and yeomen of the South, who have been decoyed . . . into rebellion." Oath takers could elect delegates to state conventions, which would call regular elections, proclaim secession illegal, repudiate Confederate debts, and ratify the Thirteenth Amendment, which abolished slavery.

This presidential Reconstruction took effect in summer 1865. Johnson handed out pardons liberally (some 13,000) and dropped his plans for the punishment of treason. By the end of 1865 all seven states had created new civil governments that in effect restored the *status quo ante bellum*. Confederate officers and large planters resumed state offices, and former Confederate congressmen and generals won election to Congress.

@ The Louisiana Black Code

Most infuriating to the Radicals, every state passed a "black code" intended to ensure a landless, dependent black labor force—to "secure the services of the negroes, teach them their place," in the words of one Alabamian. These codes, which replaced earlier slave codes, guaranteed the freedmen some basic rights—marriage, ownership of property, the right to testify in court against other blacks—but also harshly restricted their behavior. Most harmful, black codes included economic restrictions to prevent blacks from leaving the plantation, usually by establishing a system of labor contracts and then stipulating that anyone who had not signed a labor contract was subject to arrest as a vagrant. The black codes reflected white southern attitudes and showed what "home rule" would have been like without federal intervention.

When former abolitionists and Radical Republicans decried the black codes, Johnson defended them and his restoration program. Former Confederates should not become "a degraded and debased people," he said. To many northerners, both the black codes and the election of former Confederates to high office reeked of southern defiance. When the Thirty-ninth Congress convened in December 1865, it refused to seat the southern delegates and prepared to dismantle the black codes and to lock ex-Confederates out of power.

Congress Versus Johnson

Southern blacks' status became the major issue in Congress. With Congress split into four blocs—Democrats, and radical, moderate, and conservative Republicans—a politically adroit president could have protected his program. Ineptly, Johnson alienated the moderates and pushed them into the Radicals' arms.

In late 1865 Congress voted to extend the life of the Freedmen's Bureau for three more years. Staffed mainly by army officers, the bureau provided relief, rations, and medical care; built schools for former slaves; put them to work on abandoned or confiscated lands; and tried to protect their rights as laborers. In February 1866 Johnson vetoed the bill. Then in March 1866 Congress passed the Civil Rights Act of 1866, which made African-Americans U.S. citizens with the same civil rights as other citizens and authorized federal intervention to ensure African-Americans' rights in court. Johnson vetoed this measure also, arguing that it would "operate in favor of the colored and against the white race." In April Congress overrode his veto, and in July it enacted the Supplementary Freedmen's Bureau Act over another presidential veto.

Although the vetoes gained support for Johnson among northern Democrats, the president drove moderate and radical Republicans together toward their next step: the passage of a constitutional amendment to protect the new Civil Rights Act.

The Fourteenth Amendment

In April 1866 Congress adopted the Fourteenth Amendment, its most ambitious attempt to deal with the problems of Reconstruction and the freed slaves. In the first clause, the amendment proclaimed that all persons born or naturalized in the United States were citizens and that no state could abridge their rights without due process of law or deny them equal protection under the law. Second, the amendment guaranteed that if a state denied suffrage to any male citizen, its representation in Congress would be proportionally reduced. Third, the amendment disqualified from state and national offices *all* prewar officeholders who had supported the Confederacy. Finally, it repudiated the Confederate debt and maintained the validity of the federal debt. Beyond demonstrating widespread receptivity to the Radicals' demands, including African-American male suffrage, the Fourteenth Amendment represented the first national effort to limit the states' control of civil and political rights.

Passage of the amendment created a fire-storm. Abolitionists said that it did not go far enough to protect African-American voting rights, southerners blasted it as vengeful, and President Johnson denounced it. The president's unwillingness to compromise solidified the new alliance between moderate and Radical Republicans and transformed the congressional elections of 1866 into a referendum on the Fourteenth Amendment.

Republicans carried the congressional elections of 1866 in a landslide, winning nearly two-thirds of the House and three-fourths of the Senate. They had secured a mandate for the Fourteenth Amendment and their own Reconstruction program.

Congressional Reconstruction

The congressional debate over reconstructing the South began in December 1866 and lasted three months. Radical leaders, anxious to stifle a resurgence of Confederate power, called for African-American suffrage, federal support for public schools, confiscation of Confederate estates, and extended

military occupation of the South. Moderate Republicans accepted part of this plan. In February 1867, after complex political maneuvers, Congress passed the Reconstruction Act of 1867. Johnson vetoed it, and on March 2 Congress passed the law over his veto. Three more Reconstruction acts, passed in 1867 and 1868 over presidential vetoes, refined and enforced the first act.

The Reconstruction Act of 1867 divided the former Confederate states into five military districts. It provided that voters—all black men, plus whites not disqualified by the Fourteenth Amendment—could elect delegates who would write a new state constitution granting African-American suffrage. After congressional approval of the state constitution, and after the state legislature's ratification of the Fourteenth Amendment, Congress would readmit the state into the Union. The enfranchisement of African-Americans and disfranchisement of so many ex-Confederates made the Reconstruction Act of 1867 far more radical than Johnson's program. Even then, however, it provided only temporary military rule, made no provisions to prosecute Confederate leaders for treason, and neither confiscated nor redistributed property.

Congressional Reconstruction took effect in spring 1867, but Johnson impeded its implementation by replacing pro-Radical military officers with conservative ones. Furious and more suspicious than ever of the president, congressional moderates and Radicals again joined forces to block Johnson from further hampering Reconstruction.

The Impeachment Crisis

In March 1867, responding to Johnson's obstructionist tactics, Republicans in Congress passed two laws to restrict presidential power. The Tenure of Office Act prohibited the president from removing civil officers without Senate consent. Its purpose was to protect Secretary of War Edwin Stanton, a Radical ally needed to enforce the Reconstruction acts. The other law banned the president from issuing military orders except through the commanding general, Ulysses S. Grant, who could not be removed without the Senate's consent. Not satisfied with clipping the president's wings, Radicals also began to look for grounds for impeachment.

In August 1867 Johnson suspended Stanton and in February 1868 tried to remove him. The president's defiance of the Tenure of Office Act drove moderate Republicans back into alliance with the Radicals. The House approved eleven charges of impeachment, nine of them based on violation of the Tenure of Office Act.

Johnson's trial by the Senate, which began in March 1868, riveted public attention for eleven weeks. Johnson's lawyers maintained that he was merely seeking a court test of a law that he believed unconstitutional, the Tenure of Office Act, by violating it. The congressmen who served as prosecutors countered that impeachment was a political process, not a criminal trial, and that Johnson's "abuse of discretionary power" constituted an impeachable offense. Some Senate Republicans wavered, fearful that the removal of a president would destroy the balance of power within the federal government.

Intense pressure weighed on the wavering Republican senators. Ultimately, seven Republicans risked political suicide by voting with the Democrats against removal, and the Senate failed by one vote to convict Johnson. In so doing, the legislators set two critical precedents: in the future, no president would be impeached on political grounds, nor would he be impeached because two-thirds of Congress disagreed with him.

The Fifteenth Amendment

African-American suffrage was the linchpin of congressional Reconstruction. Only with the support of African-American voters could Republicans secure control of the southern states. The Fifteenth Amendment, drawn up by Republicans and approved by Congress in 1869, aimed both to protect black suffrage in the South and to extend it to the northern and border states, on the assumption that newly enfranchised African-Americans would gratefully vote Republican. The amendment prohibited the denial of suffrage by the states to anyone on account of race, color, or previous condition of servitude.

Democrats opposed the amendment on the grounds that it violated states' rights, but they did not control enough states to prevent its ratification. However, the new amendment did not guarantee African-American officeholding, nor did it prohibit restrictions on suffrage such as property requirements and literacy tests.

The debate over black suffrage drew new participants into the fray. Women's rights advocates had tried to promote both black suffrage and woman suffrage, but Radical Republicans rejected any linkage between the two, preferring to concentrate on black suffrage. Women's rights leaders Elizabeth Cady Stanton and Susan B. Anthony disagreed. If the Fifteenth Amendment did not include women, they emphasized, it would establish an "aristocracy of sex" and increase the disabilities under which women already labored.

By the time the Fifteenth Amendment was ratified in 1870, Congress could look back on five years of momentous achievement. Three constitutional amendments had broadened the scope of democracy by abolishing slavery, affirming the rights of citizens, and prohibiting the denial of suffrage on the basis of race. Congress had readmitted the former Confederate states into the Union. At the same time, momentum had slowed at the federal level. In 1869 the center of action shifted to the South, where tumultuous change was under way.

Reconstruction Governments

During the years of presidential Reconstruction, 1865–1867, the southern states faced formidable tasks: creating new governments, reviving war-torn economies, and dealing with the impact of emancipation. Racial tensions flared as freedmen organized political meetings to protest ill treatment and demand equal rights, and race riots erupted in major southern cities. In May 1866 white crowds attacked African-American veterans in Memphis and rampaged through African-American neighborhoods, killing forty-six people. Two months later in New Orleans, whites assaulted black delegates on their way to a political meeting and left forty people dead.

Congressional Reconstruction, supervised by federal troops, began in spring 1867 with the dismantling of existing governments and the formation of new state governments dominated by Republicans. The Reconstruction laws of 1867–1868 transformed the southern electorate by temporarily disfranchising 15 percent of potential white voters and by enfranchising more than 700,000 freed slaves. Black voters outnumbered whites by 100,000 overall and held voting majorities in five states.

This new electorate provided a base for the Republican party, which had never existed in the South. To scornful Democrats, the Republicans comprised three types of scoundrels: northern "carpetbaggers" who had come south for wealth and power; southern "scalawags," poor and ignorant, looking to profit from Republican rule; and hordes of uneducated freedmen, easily manipulated.

To northerners who moved south after the war, the former Confederacy was an undeveloped region, ripe with possibilities. The carpetbaggers included many former Union soldiers who hoped to buy land, open factories, build railroads, or simply enjoy the warmer climate. Wielding disproportionate political power—they held almost one in three state offices—carpetbaggers recruited African-American support through a patriotic society called the Union League, which urged African-Americans to vote and escorted them to the polls.

A handful of scalawags (white southerners who supported the Republicans) were old Whigs, but most were small farmers from the mountain regions of North Carolina, Georgia, Alabama, and Arkansas. Former Unionists who had owned no slaves and who felt no loyalty to the old plantation elite, they wanted to improve their economic position and cared little about black suffrage.

Freedmen, the backbone of southern Republicanism, provided eight out of ten Republican votes. They sought land, education, civil rights, and political equality and remained loyal Republicans. Although Reconstruction governments depended on African-

American votes, freedmen held at most one in five political offices and constituted a legislative majority only in South Carolina, whose population was more than 60 percent black. No African-Americans were elected governor, and only two served in the U.S. Senate. A mere 6 percent of southern members of the House were African-American, and almost 50 percent came from South Carolina.

Republican Rule

Large numbers of African-Americans participated in government for the first time in the state constitutional conventions of 1867–1868. The South Carolina convention had an African-American majority, and in Louisiana one-half the delegates were freedmen. In general, these conventions instituted democratic changes such as universal manhood suffrage and public-school systems but failed to provide either integrated schools or land reform.

Once civil power shifted to the new state governments, Republican administrations began ambitious public-works programs. Republican regimes also expanded state government and formed state militias in which African-Americans often were heavily represented. Finally, they created public-school systems, almost nonexistent in the antebellum South.

These reforms cost millions, and state debts and taxes skyrocketed. During the 1860s taxes rose 400 percent. Although northern tax rates still exceeded southern tax rates, southerners, particularly landowners, resented the new levies.

Opponents of Reconstruction viewed Republican rule as wasteful and corrupt, the "most stupendous system of organized robbery in history." Indeed, corruption did permeate some state governments, as in Louisiana and South Carolina. The main profiteers were government officials who accepted bribes and railroad promoters who doled them out. But neither group was exclusively Republican. In fact, corruption increasingly characterized government *nationally* in these years and was both more flagrant and more lucrative in the North.

Counterattacks

For ex-Confederates, African-American enfranchisement and the "horror of Negro domination" created nightmares. As soon as congressional Reconstruction began, it fell under attack. But Democrats delayed any political mobilization until the readmission of the southern states was completed. Then they swung into action, often calling themselves Conservatives to attract former Whigs.

Vigilante efforts to reduce black votes bolstered Democratic campaigns to win white ones. Antagonism toward free blacks, long present in southern life, grew increasingly violent. As early as 1865 Freedmen's Bureau agents itemized a variety of outrages against blacks, including shooting, murder, rape, arson, and "severe and inhuman beating." White vigilante groups sprang up in all parts of the former Confederacy, but one organization became dominant. In spring 1866 six young Confederate war veterans in Tennessee formed a social club, the Ku Klux Klan, distinguished by elaborate rituals, hooded costumes, and secret passwords. New Klan dens spread rapidly. By the election of 1868, when African-American suffrage had become a reality, the Klan had become a terrorist movement directed against potential African-American voters.

@ Southern Skepticism of the Freedmen's Bureau

The Klan sought to suppress black voting, to reestablish white supremacy, and to topple the Reconstruction governments. Some Democrats denounced Klan members as "cutthroats and riff-raff," but some prominent Confederate leaders, including General Nathan Bedford Forrest, were active Klansmen. Vigilantism united southern whites of different social classes and drew on the energy of many Confederate veterans.

Republican legislatures tried to outlaw vigilantism, but when state militias could not enforce the laws, state officials turned to the federal government for help. In response, between May 1870 and February 1871 Congress passed three Enforcement Acts. The First Enforcement Act protected African-American voters. The Second Enforcement Act provided for federal supervision of southern elections, and the Third Enforcement Act (also known as the Ku Klux Klan Act) authorized the use of federal troops and the suspension of habeas corpus. Although thousands were arrested under the Enforcement Acts, most terrorists escaped conviction.

By 1872 the federal government had effectively suppressed the Klan, but vigilantism had served its purpose. A large military presence in the South could have protected black rights, but instead troop levels fell steadily. Congress allowed the Freedmen's Bureau to die in 1869, and the Enforcement Acts became dead letters.

The Impact of Emancipation

"The master he says we are all free," a South Carolina slave declared in 1865. "But it don't mean we is white. And it don't mean we is equal." Yet despite the daunting handicaps they faced—illiteracy, lack of property, lack of skills—most former slaves found the exhilaration of freedom overwhelming.

@ A Freedman to His Old Master

Confronting Freedom

For the ex-slaves, mobility was often liberty's first fruit. Some left the slave quarters; others fled the plantation completely.

Emancipation stirred waves of migration within the former Confederacy. Some slaves headed to the Deep South, where desperate planters would pay higher wages for labor, but more moved to towns and cities. Urban African-American populations doubled and tripled after emancipation. The desire to find lost family members drove some migrations. Parents sought children who had been sold; husbands and wives who had been separated reunited; and families reclaimed children who were being raised in masters' homes.

@ Black Recollections of Freedom's Impact

Once reunited, freed blacks quickly legalized unions formed under slavery, sometimes in mass ceremonies of up to seventy couples. Legal marriage had a tangible impact on family life. In 1870 eight out of ten African-American families in the cotton-producing South were two-parent families, about the same proportion as white families. Men asserted themselves as household heads, and their wives and children often withdrew from the work force. However, by Reconstruction's end, many African-American women had rejoined the work force out of economic necessity, either in the fields or as cooks, laundresses, and domestic servants.

African-American Institutions

The freed blacks' desire for independence also led to the growth of African-American churches. The African Methodist Episcopal Church, founded by Philadelphia blacks in the 1790s, gained thousands of new southern members. Negro Baptist churches, their roots often in plantation "praise meetings" organized by slaves, sprouted everywhere.

The influence of African-American churches extended far beyond religion. They provided relief, raised funds for schools, and supported Republican policies. African-American ministers assumed leading political roles. Even after southern Democrats excluded most freedmen from political life at Reconstruction's end, ministers remained pillars of authority within African-American communities.

Schools, too, played a crucial role for freedmen as the ex-slaves sought literacy for themselves and above all for their children. At emancipation, African-Americans organized their own schools, which the Freedmen's Bureau soon supervised. In 1869 the bureau reported more than 4,000 African-American schools in the former Confederacy. Within three more years each southern state had a public-school system, at least in principle, generally with separate schools for blacks and whites. The Freedmen's Bureau and others also helped to establish Howard, Atlanta, and Fisk Universities in 1866–1867 and Hampton Institute in 1868. Nonetheless, African-American education remained limited.

Not only school segregation but also other forms of racial separation were taken for granted. Whether by law or by custom, segregation continued on street-cars and trains as well as in churches, theaters, and restaurants. In 1875 Congress passed the Civil Rights Act, banning segregation except in schools, but in the 1883 *Civil Rights Cases*, the Supreme Court threw the law out. The Fourteenth Amendment did not prohibit discrimination by individuals, the Court ruled, only by the state.

Land, Labor, and Sharecropping

"The sole ambition of the freedman," a New Englander wrote from South Carolina in 1865, "appears to be to become the owner of a little piece of land, there to erect a humble home, and to dwell in peace and security, at his own free will and pleasure." Indeed, to free blacks everywhere, "forty acres and a mule" promised emancipation from plantation labor, white domination, and cotton, the "slave crop." Landownership signified economic independence.

But the freedmen's visions of landownership failed to materialize, for large-scale land reform never occurred. Proposals to confiscate or to redistribute Confederate property failed. By the end of Reconstruction, only a fraction of former slaves owned working farms. Without large-scale land reform, barriers to African-American landownership remained overwhelming.

Three obstacles impeded African-American landownership. Freedmen lacked capital to buy land or tools. Furthermore, white southerners generally opposed selling land to blacks. Most important, planters sought to preserve a cheap labor force and forged laws to ensure that black labor would remain available on the plantations.

The black codes written during presidential Reconstruction were designed to preserve a captive labor force. Under labor contracts in effect in 1865–1866, freedmen received wages, housing, food, and clothing in exchange for fieldwork. But cash was scarce, and wages often became a small share of the crop, typically one-eighth or less, to be divided among the entire work force.

Southerners began trying out new labor schemes, including the division of plantations into small

@ Black Testimony on the Aftermath of Enslavement

tenancies. Sharecropping was the most widespread arrangement. Under this system, landowners subdivided large plantations into farms of thirty to fifty acres and rented them to freedmen under annual leases for a share of the crop, usually one-half.

Although the wage system continued on sugar and rice plantations, by 1870 the plantation tradition had yielded to sharecropping in the cotton South. By 1880 sharecroppers, white and black, farmed 80 percent of the land in cotton-producing states. In fact, white sharecroppers outnumbered black, although a higher proportion of southern blacks, almost 75 percent, were involved in the system. Changes in marketing and finance, meanwhile, made the sharecroppers' lot increasingly precarious.

Toward a Crop-Lien Economy

Before the Civil War planters had depended on factors, or middlemen, who sold them supplies, extended credit, and marketed their crops through urban merchants. Because the high value of slave property had backed these long-distance credit arrangements, this system collapsed with the end of slavery.

Into this gap stepped rural merchants, who advanced supplies to tenants and sharecroppers on credit and sold their crops to wholesalers. Because renters had no property to serve as collateral, merchants secured their loans with a lien, or claim, on each farmer's next crop. Exorbitant interest rates, 50 percent or more, quickly forced many tenants and sharecroppers into a cycle of indebtedness. The sharecropper might well owe part of his crop to the landowner and another part (the rest of his crop, or more) to the merchant. Illiterate tenants who could not keep track of their financial arrangements were at the mercy of sometimes unscrupulous merchants. Once a tenant's real or alleged debts exceeded the value of his crop, he was tied to the land, to cotton, and to sharecropping.

Trapped in perpetual debt, tenant farmers became the chief victims of the new agricultural order. As an easily marketable cash crop, cotton remained the only survival route open to poor farmers, regardless of race. Yet low income from cotton locked them

into sharecropping and crop liens, and the failure to diversify crops exhausted the soil. African-American tenants, for whom neither landownership nor economic independence ever materialized, saw their political rights dwindle as rapidly as their hopes for economic freedom.

New Concerns in the North

The nomination of Ulysses S. Grant for president in 1868 launched a chaotic era in national politics. His eight years in office featured political scandals, a party revolt, a massive depression, and a steady retreat from Reconstruction. By the mid-1870s northern voters cared more about unemployment, labor unrest, and currency problems than the "southern question." Eager to end sectional conflict, Republicans turned their backs on the freedmen.

A war hero, Grant was endorsed by veterans, admired throughout the North, and unscathed by the bitter feuds of Reconstruction politics. To oppose Grant, the Democrats nominated Horatio Seymour, arch-critic of the Lincoln administration and an opponent of Reconstruction and greenbacks. Grant ran on his personal popularity more than on issues. Although he carried all but eight states, the popular vote was close; newly enfranchised freedmen provided Grant's margin in the South.

Grant's presidential leadership proved as weak as his war leadership had been strong, and a string of scandals plagued his administration. For example, near the end of Grant's first term, his vice president, Schuyler Colfax, got caught up in the Crédit Mobilier scandal, an elaborate scheme to skim off the profits of the Union Pacific Railroad. Then in 1875 Grant's personal secretary, Orville Babcock, was found guilty of accepting bribes from the "whiskey ring," distillers who preferred bribery to payment of federal taxes.

Although Grant was not personally involved in the scandals, he did little to restrain such activities, and "Grantism" came to stand for fraud, bribery, and corruption in office. Such evils, however, spread far beyond Washington. The New York City press in 1872 revealed that Democrat boss William M. Tweed led a ring that had looted the city treasury and collected some $200 million in kickbacks and bribes.

As the election of 1872 approached, dissident Republicans feared that "Grantism" would ruin the party. Former Radicals and other Republicans left out of Grant's "Great Barbecue" formed their own party, the Liberal Republicans.

The Liberals' Revolt

The Liberal Republican revolt split the Republican party and undermined Reconstruction. Liberals demanded civil service reform to bring the "best men" into government. In the South they demanded an end to "bayonet rule" and argued that African-Americans, now enfranchised, could fend for themselves.

New York Tribune editor Horace Greeley, inconsistently supporting both a stringent Reconstruction policy and leniency toward the ex-Confederates, received the Liberal Republican nomination, and the Democrats endorsed Greeley as well.

Despite Greeley's arduous campaigning (he literally worked himself to death on the campaign trail and died a few weeks after the election), Grant carried 56 percent of the popular vote and won the electoral vote handily. But his victory had come at a high price: to nullify the Liberals' issues, "regular" Republicans passed an amnesty act allowing all but a few hundred ex-Confederates to resume office. And during Grant's second term Republicans' desire to discard the "southern question" grew as a depression gripped the nation.

The Panic of 1873

The postwar years brought accelerated industrialization, rapid economic expansion, and frantic speculation as investors rushed to take advantage of seemingly unlimited opportunities.

In 1869 Philadelphia banker Jay Cooke took over a new transcontinental railroad line, the Northern Pacific. For four years Northern Pacific securities sold briskly, but in 1873 construction costs outran bond sales. In September Cooke, his bank vaults stuffed with unsalable bonds, defaulted on his obligations. His bank, the largest in the nation, shut down. Then the stock market collapsed and smaller banks and other firms followed; and the Panic of 1873 plunged the nation into a devastating five-year depression. Thousands of businesses went bankrupt. By 1878 unemployment had risen to more than 3 million. The depression of the 1870s demonstrated ruthlessly that conflicts born of industrialization had replaced sectional divisions.

Reconstruction and the Constitution

During the 1870s the Supreme Court also played a role in weakening northern support for Reconstruction. The process began with the *Slaughterhouse* decision of 1873. In this case the Court ruled that the Fourteenth Amendment protected the rights of *national* citizenship, such as the right to interstate travel, but that it did not protect the civil rights that individuals derived from *state* citizenship. The *Slaughterhouse* decision effectively gutted the Fourteenth Amendment, which was intended to secure freedmen's rights against state encroachment.

The Supreme Court retreated even further from Reconstruction in two cases involving the Enforcement Act of 1870. In *U.S. v. Reese* (1876), the Court threw out the indictment of Kentucky officials who had barred African-Americans from voting. Another decision that same year, *U.S. v. Cruikshank*, again weakened the Fourteenth Amendment. In the *Cruikshank* case, the Court ruled that the amendment barred *states*, but not *individuals*, from encroaching on individual rights.

Continuing this retreat from Reconstruction, the Supreme Court in 1883 invalidated both the Civil Rights Act of 1875 and the Ku Klux Klan Act of 1871; later it would uphold segregation laws (see Chapter 21). Taken cumulatively, these decisions dismantled Republican Reconstruction and confirmed rising northern sentiment that Reconstruction's egalitarian goals were unenforceable.

Republicans in Retreat

The Republicans gradually disengaged from Reconstruction, beginning with the election of Grant as president in 1868. Grant, like most Americans, hesitated to approve the use of federal authority in state or local affairs.

In the 1870s Republican idealism waned. Instead, commercial and industrial interests dominated both the Liberal and "regular" wings of the party, and few had any taste left for further sectional strife. When Democratic victories in the House of Representatives in 1874 showed that Reconstruction had become a political liability, the Republicans prepared to abandon it.

Reconstruction Abandoned

An angry white majority had led a Democratic resurgence throughout the South in the 1870s, and by the end of 1872 four ex-Confederate states had already returned the Democrats to power. By 1876 Republican rule survived in only three southern states. Political bargaining in 1877 ended what little remained of Reconstruction.

"Redeeming" the South

After 1872 the Republican collapse in the South accelerated. Congressional amnesty enabled virtually all ex-Confederate officials to regain office, divided Republicans lost their grip on the southern electorate, and attrition diminished Republican ranks. Carpetbaggers returned North or joined the Democrats, and scalawags deserted the Republicans in large numbers. Unable to win new white votes or retain the old ones, the fragile Republican coalition crumbled.

Meanwhile, the Democrats mobilized formerly apathetic white voters. Although still faction-ridden—businessmen who dreamed of an industrialized "New South" had little in common with the old planter elite, the so-called Bourbons—the Democrats shared one goal: kicking the Republicans out. The Democrats' tactics varied. In several Deep South states Democrats resorted to violence. In Vicksburg in 1874 rampaging whites slaughtered about 300 blacks and terrorized thousands of potential voters. Vigilante groups in several southern states disrupted Republican meetings and threatened blacks who had registered to vote. Terrorism did not completely squelch black voting, but it did deprive Republicans of enough African-American votes to win state elections.

Redemption, the word that Democrats used to describe their return to power, introduced sweeping changes. States rewrote constitutions, cut expenses, lowered taxes, eliminated social programs, limited the rights of tenants and sharecroppers, and shaped laws to ensure a stable African-American labor force. Legislatures restored vagrancy laws, strengthened crop-lien statutes, and remade criminal law. New criminal codes directed at African-Americans imposed severe penalties for what formerly were misdemeanors: stealing livestock or wrongly taking part of a crop became grand larceny, punishable by five years at hard labor. Freedmen whose hopes had been raised by Republicans saw their prospects destroyed by the redeemers.

The Election of 1876

By autumn 1876, with redemption almost complete, both parties were moving to discard the animosity left by the war and Reconstruction. The Republicans nominated Rutherford B. Hayes, the governor of Ohio, for president. Popular with all factions and untainted by the Grant scandals, Hayes, a "moderate," favored "home rule" in the South and civil and political rights for all—clearly contradictory goals. The Democrats nominated Governor Samuel J. Tilden of New York, a political reformer known for his assaults on the Tweed Ring that had plundered New York City's treasury.

Tilden won the popular vote by a small margin, but the Republicans challenged pro-Tilden electoral votes from South Carolina, Florida, and Louisiana. Giving those nineteen electoral votes to Hayes would make him the winner. The Democrats, for their part, requiring a single electoral vote to put Tilden in the White House, challenged one electoral vote from Oregon. But Southern Republicans managed to throw out enough Democratic ballots in the contested states to proclaim Hayes the winner.

The nation now faced an unprecedented dilemma. Each party claimed victory, and each accused the other of fraud. In fact, both parties were guilty. In January 1877 Congress created a special electoral commission to resolve the conflict. With eight Republicans and seven Democrats, the commission gave the Republican Hayes the election by an 8–7 vote.

Congress now had to certify the new electoral vote. But the Democrats controlled the House, and some planned to forestall approval of the electoral vote. During informal negotiations, Ohio Republicans and southern Democrats agreed that if Hayes won the election, he would remove federal troops from all southern states. Other negotiations led to the understanding that southerners would receive federal patronage, federal aid to railroads, and federal support for internal improvements. In turn, southerners promised to accept Hayes as president and to treat the freedmen fairly.

Congress thus ratified Hayes's election. Once in office, Hayes fulfilled many of the agreements made by his colleagues. Republican rule toppled in Louisiana, South Carolina, and Florida. But some of the bargains struck in the so-called Compromise of 1877 fell apart, particularly Democratic promises to treat the freedmen fairly and Hayes's pledges to ensure the freed slaves' rights.

CHRONOLOGY

1863 President Abraham Lincoln issues Proclamation of Amnesty and Reconstruction.

1865 Freedmen's Bureau established.
Civil War ends.
Lincoln assassinated; Andrew Johnson becomes president.
Johnson issues Proclamation of Amnesty and Reconstruction.
Ex-Confederate states hold constitutional conventions (May–December).
Thirteenth Amendment added to the Constitution.
Presidential Reconstruction completed.

1866 Congress enacts the Civil Rights Act of 1866 and the Supplementary Freedmen's Bureau Act over Johnson's vetoes.
Ku Klux Klan founded in Tennessee.
Congress proposes the Fourteenth Amendment.
Race riots in southern cities.
Thirty-ninth Congress begins debates over Reconstruction policy.

1867 Reconstruction Act of 1867.
Constitutional conventions meet in the ex-Confederate states.
Howard University founded.

1868 President Johnson is impeached, tried, and acquitted.
Fourteenth Amendment added to the Constitution.
Ulysses S. Grant elected president.

1869 Transcontinental railroad completed.

1870 Fifteenth Amendment added to the Constitution.
Enforcement Act of 1870.

1871 Second Enforcement Act.
Ku Klux Klan Act.

1872 Liberal Republican party formed.
Grant reelected president.

1873 Panic of 1873 begins (September–October), setting off a five-year depression.

1875 Civil Rights Act of 1875.

1876 Disputed presidential election: Rutherford B. Hayes versus Samuel J. Tilden.

1877 Electoral commission decides election in favor of Hayes.
The last Republican-controlled governments overthrown in Florida, Louisiana, and South Carolina.

FOR FURTHER READING

Eric Foner, *Reconstruction: America's Unfinished Revolution, 1863–1877* (1988). A thorough exploration of Reconstruction that draws on recent scholarship and stresses the centrality of the African-American experience.

John Hope Franklin, *Reconstruction After the Civil War* (1961). An overview that dismantles the traditional view of Reconstruction as a disastrous experiment in radical rule.

William Gillette, *Retreat from Reconstruction, 1869–1879* (1979). A survey of the era's national politics, indicting Republican policy makers for vacillation and lack of commitment to racial equality.

Leon Litwack, *Been in the Storm So Long: The Aftermath of Slavery* (1979). A comprehensive study of the African-American response to emancipation in 1865–1866.

Roger L. Ransom and Richard Sutch, *One Kind of Freedom: The Economic Consequences of Emancipation* (1977). Economic assessment of the impact of free black labor on the South and explanation of the rise of sharecropping and the crop-lien system.

Kenneth M. Stampp, *The Era of Reconstruction, 1865–1877* (1965). A classic revisionist interpretation of Reconstruction, focusing on the establishment and fall of Republican governments.

Joel Williamson, *The Negro in South Carolina During Reconstruction, 1861–1877* (1965). A pioneer study of African-American life and institutions after emancipation.

Appendix

Declaration of Independence

IN CONGRESS, JULY 4, 1776

The Unanimous Declaration of the Thirteen United States of America

When, in the course of human events, it becomes necessary for one people to dissolve the political bands which have connected them with another, and to assume, among the powers of the earth, the separate and equal station to which the laws of nature and of nature's God entitle them, a decent respect to the opinions of mankind requires that they should declare the causes which impel them to the separation.

We hold these truths to be self-evident: That all men are created equal; that they are endowed by their Creator with certain unalienable rights; that among these are life, liberty, and the pursuit of happiness; that, to secure these rights, governments are instituted among men, deriving their just powers from the consent of the governed; that whenever any form of government becomes destructive of these ends, it is the right of the people to alter or to abolish it, and to institute new government, laying its foundation on such principles, and organizing its powers in such form, as to them shall seem most likely to effect their safety and happiness. Prudence, indeed, will dictate that governments long established should not be changed for light and transient causes; and accordingly all experience hath shown that mankind are more disposed to suffer, while

evils are sufferable, than to right themselves by abolishing the forms to which they are accustomed. But when a long train of abuses and usurpations, pursuing invariably the same object, evinces a design to reduce them under absolute despotism, it is their right, it is their duty, to throw off such government, and to provide new guards for their future security. Such has been the patient sufferance of these colonies; and such is now the necessity which constrains them to alter their former systems of government. The history of the present King of Great Britain is a history of repeated injuries and usurpations, all having in direct object the establishment of an absolute tyranny over these states. To prove this, let facts be submitted to a candid world.

He has refused his assent to laws, the most wholesome and necessary for the public good.

He has forbidden his governors to pass laws of immediate and pressing importance, unless suspended in their operation till his assent should be obtained; and, when so suspended, he has utterly neglected to attend to them.

He has refused to pass other laws for the accommodation of large districts of people, unless those people would relinquish the right of representation in the legislature, a right inestimable to them, and formidable to tyrants only.

He has called together legislative bodies at places unusual, uncomfortable, and distant from the depository of their public records, for the sole purpose of fatiguing them into compliance with his measures.

He has dissolved representative houses repeatedly, for opposing, with manly firmness, his invasions on the rights of the people.

He has refused for a long time, after such dissolutions, to cause others to be elected; whereby the legislative powers, incapable of annihilation, have returned to the people at large for their exercise; the state remaining, in the mean time, exposed to all the dangers of invasions from without and convulsions within.

He has endeavored to prevent the population of these states; for that purpose obstructing the laws of naturalization of foreigners; refusing to pass others to encourage their migration hither, and raising the conditions of new appropriation of lands.

He has obstructed the administration of justice, by refusing his assent to laws for establishing judiciary powers.

He has made judges dependent on his will alone, for the tenure of their offices, and the amount and payment of their salaries.

He has erected a multitude of new offices, and sent hither swarms of officers to harass our people and eat out their substance.

He has kept among us, in times of peace, standing armies, without the consent of our legislatures.

He has affected to render the military independent of, and superior to, the civil power.

He has combined with others to subject us to a jurisdiction foreign to our constitution, and unacknowledged by our laws, giving his assent to their acts of pretended legislation:

For quartering large bodies of armed troops among us;

For protecting them, by a mock trial, from punishment for any murders which they should commit on the inhabitants of these states;

For cutting off our trade with all parts of the world;

For imposing taxes on us without our consent;

For depriving us, in many cases, of the benefits of trial by jury;

For transporting us beyond seas, to be tried for pretended offenses;

For abolishing the free system of English laws in a neighboring province, establishing therein an arbitrary government, and enlarging its boundaries, so as to render it at once an example and fit instrument for introducing the same absolute rule into these colonies;

For taking away our charters, abolishing our most valuable laws, and altering fundamentally the forms of our governments;

For suspending our own legislatures, and declaring themselves invested with power to legislate for us in all cases whatsoever.

He has abdicated government here, by declaring us out of his protection and waging war against us.

He has plundered our seas, ravaged our coasts, burned our towns, and destroyed the lives of our people.

He is at this time transporting large armies of foreign mercenaries to complete the works of death, desolation, and tyranny already begun with circumstances of cruelty and perfidy scarcely paralleled in the most barbarous ages, and totally unworthy of the head of a civilized nation.

He has constrained our fellow-citizens, taken captive on the high seas, to bear arms against their country, to become the executioners of their friends and brethren, or to fall themselves by their hands.

He has excited domestic insurrection among us, and has endeavored to bring on the inhabitants of our frontiers the merciless Indian savages, whose known rule of warfare is an undistinguished destruction of all ages, sexes, and conditions.

In every stage of these oppressions we have petitioned for redress in the most humble terms; our repeated petitions have been answered only by repeated injury. A prince, whose character is thus marked by every act which may define a tyrant, is unfit to be the ruler of a free people.

Nor have we been wanting in our attentions to our British brethren. We have warned them, from time to time, of attempts by their legislature to extend an unwarrantable jurisdiction over us. We have reminded them of the circumstances of our emigration and settlement here. We have appealed to their native justice and magnanimity; and we have conjured them by the ties of our common kindred, to disavow these usurpations, which would inevitably interrupt our connections and correspondence. They, too, have been deaf to the voice of justice and of consanguinity. We must, therefore, acquiesce in the necessity which denounces our separation, and hold them, as we hold the rest of mankind, enemies in war, in peace friends.

We, therefore, the representatives of the United States of America, in General Congress assembled, appealing to the Supreme Judge of the world for the rectitude of our intentions, do, in the name and by the authority of the good people of these colonies, solemnly publish and declare, that these United Colonies are, and of right ought to be, FREE AND INDEPENDENT STATES; that they are absolved from all allegiance to the British crown, and that all political connection between them and the state of Great Britain is, and ought to be, totally dissolved; and that, as free and independent states, they have full power to levy war, conclude peace, contract alliances, establish commerce, and do all other acts and things which independent states may of right do. And for the support of this declaration, with a firm reliance on the protection of Divine Providence, we mutually pledge to each other our lives, our fortunes, and our sacred honor.

JOHN HANCOCK [*President*]
[*and fifty-five others*]

Constitution of the United States of America

PREAMBLE

We the people of the United States, in order to form a more perfect union, establish justice, insure domestic tranquility, provide for the common defense, promote the general welfare, and secure the blessings of liberty to ourselves and our posterity, do ordain and establish this Constitution for the United States of America.

ARTICLE I

Section 1. All legislative powers herein granted shall be vested in a Congress of the United States, which shall consist of a Senate and a House of Representatives.

Section 2. The House of Representatives shall be composed of members chosen every second year by the people of the several States, and the electors in each State shall have the qualifications requisite for electors of the most numerous branch of the State Legislature.

No person shall be a Representative who shall not have attained to the age of twenty-five years, and been seven years a citizen of the United States, and who shall not, when elected, be an inhabitant of that State in which he shall be chosen.

Representatives and direct taxes shall be apportioned among the several States which may be included within this Union, according to their respective numbers, *which shall be determined by adding to the whole number of free persons, including those bound to service for a term of years and excluding Indians not taxed, three-fifths of all other persons.* The actual enumeration shall be made within three years after the first meeting of the Congress of the United States, and within every subsequent term of ten years, in such manner as they shall by law direct. The number of Representatives shall not exceed one for every thirty thousand, but each State shall have at least one Representative; *and until such enumeration shall be made, the State of New Hampshire shall be entitled to choose three, Massachusetts eight, Rhode Island and Providence Plantations one, Connecticut five, New York six, New Jersey four, Pennsylvania eight, Delaware one, Maryland six, Virginia ten, North Carolina five, South Carolina five, and Georgia three.*

When vacancies happen in the representation from any State, the Executive authority thereof shall issue writs of election to fill such vacancies.

The House of Representatives shall choose their Speaker and other officers; and shall have the sole power of impeachment.

Section 3. The Senate of the United States shall be composed of two Senators from each State, *chosen by the legislature thereof,* for six years; and each Senator shall have one vote.

Immediately after they shall be assembled in consequence of the first election, they shall be divided as equally as may be into three classes. The seats of the Senators of the first class shall be vacated at the expiration of the second year, of the second class at the expiration of the fourth year, and of the third class at the expiration of the sixth year, so that one-third may be chosen every second year; *and if vacancies happen by resignation or otherwise, during the recess of the legislature of any State, the Executive thereof may make*

NOTE: Passages no longer in effect are printed in italic type.

temporary appointments until the next meeting of the legislature, which shall then fill such vacancies.

No person shall be a Senator who shall not have attained to the age of thirty years, and been nine years a citizen of the United States, and who shall not, when elected, be an inhabitant of that State for which he shall be chosen.

The Vice President of the United States shall be President of the Senate, but shall have no vote, unless they be equally divided.

The Senate shall choose their other officers, and also a President *pro tempore,* in the absence of the Vice President, or when he shall exercise the office of the President of the United States.

The Senate shall have the sole power to try all impeachments. When sitting for that purpose, they shall be on oath or affirmation. When the President of the United States is tried, the Chief Justice shall preside: and no person shall be convicted without the concurrence of two-thirds of the members present.

Judgment in cases of impeachment shall not extend further than to removal from the office, and disqualification to hold and enjoy any office of honor, trust or profit under the United States; but the party convicted shall nevertheless be liable and subject to indictment, trial, judgment and punishment, according to law.

Section 4. The times, places and manner of holding elections for Senators and Representatives shall be prescribed in each State by the legislature thereof; but the Congress may at any time by law make or alter such regulations, except as to the places of choosing Senators.

The Congress shall assemble at least once in every year, and such meeting *shall be on the first Monday in December, unless they shall by law appoint a different day.*

Section 5. Each house shall be the judge of the elections, returns and qualifications of its own members, and a majority of each shall constitute a quorum to do business; but a smaller number may

adjourn from day to day, and may be authorized to compel the attendance of absent members, in such manner, and under such penalties, as each house may provide.

Each house may determine the rules of its proceedings, punish its members for disorderly behavior, and with the concurrence of two-thirds, expel a member.

Each house shall keep a journal of its proceedings, and from time to time publish the same, excepting such parts as may in their judgment require secrecy; and the yeas and nays of the members of either house on any question shall, at the desire of one-fifth of those present, be entered on the journal.

Neither house, during the session of Congress, shall, without the consent of the other, adjourn for more than three days, nor to any other place than that in which the two houses shall be sitting.

Section 6. The Senators and Representatives shall receive a compensation for their services, to be ascertained by law and paid out of the treasury of the United States. They shall in all cases except treason, felony and breach of the peace, be privileged from arrest during their attendance at the session of their respective houses, and in going to and returning from the same; and for any speech or debate in either house, they shall not be questioned in any other place.

No Senator or Representative shall, during the time for which he was elected, be appointed to any civil office under the authority of the United States, which shall have been created, or the emoluments whereof shall have been increased, during such time; and no person holding any office under the United States shall be a member of either house during his continuance in office.

Section 7. All bills for raising revenue shall originate in the House of Representatives; but the Senate may propose or concur with amendments as on other bills.

Every bill which shall have passed the House of Representatives and the Senate, shall, before it become a law, be presented to the President of the United States; if he approve he shall sign it, but if not he shall return it with objections to that house in which it originated, who shall enter the objections at large on their journal, and proceed to reconsider it. If after such reconsideration two-thirds of that house shall agree to pass the bill, it shall be sent, together with the objections, to the other house, by which it shall likewise be reconsidered, and, if approved by two-thirds of that house, it shall become a law. But in all such cases the votes of both houses shall be determined by yeas and nays, and the names of the persons voting for and against the bill shall be entered on the journal of each house respectively. If any bill shall not be returned by the President within ten days (Sundays excepted) after it shall have been presented to him, the same shall be a law, in like manner as if he had signed it, unless the Congress by their adjournment prevent its return, in which case it shall not be a law.

Every order, resolution, or vote to which the concurrence of the Senate and House of Representatives may be necessary (except on a question of adjournment) shall be presented to the President of the United States; and before the same shall take effect, shall be approved by him, or being disapproved by him, shall be repassed by two-thirds of the Senate and House of Representatives, according to the rules and limitations prescribed in the case of a bill.

Section 8.   The Congress shall have power

To lay and collect taxes, duties, imposts, and excises, to pay the debts and provide for the common defense and general welfare of the United States; but all duties, imposts and excises shall be uniform throughout the United States;

To borrow money on the credit of the United States;

To regulate commerce with foreign nations, and among the several States, and with the Indian tribes;

To establish an uniform rule of naturalization, and uniform laws on the subject of bankruptcies throughout the United States;

To coin money, regulate the value thereof, and of foreign coin, and fix the standard of weights and measures;

To provide for the punishment of counterfeiting the securities and current coin of the United States;

To establish post offices and post roads;

To promote the progress of science and useful arts by securing for limited times to authors and inventors the exclusive right to their respective writings and discoveries;

To constitute tribunals inferior to the Supreme Court;

To define and punish piracies and felonies committed on the high seas and offenses against the law of nations;

To declare war, grant letters of marque and reprisal, and make rules concerning captures on land and water;

To raise and support armies, but no appropriation of money to that use shall be for a longer term than two years;

To provide and maintain a navy;

To make rules for the government and regulation of the land and naval forces;

To provide for calling forth the militia to execute the laws of the Union, suppress insurrections, and repel invasions;

To provide for organizing, arming, and disciplining the militia, and for governing such part of them as may be employed in the service of the United States, reserving to the States respectively the appointment of the officers, and the authority of training the militia according to the discipline prescribed by Congress;

To exercise exclusive legislation in all cases whatsoever, over such district (not exceeding ten miles square) as may, by cession of particular States, and the acceptance of Congress, become the seat of government of the United States, and to exercise like authority over all places purchased by the consent of the legislature of the State, in which the same shall be, for erection of forts, magazines, arsenals, dock-yards, and other needful buildings;—and

To make all laws which shall be necessary and proper for carrying into execution the foregoing powers, and all other powers vested by this Constitution in the government of the United States, or in any department or officer thereof.

Section 9. *The migration or importation of such persons as any of the States now existing shall think proper to admit shall not be prohibited by the Congress prior to the year 1808; but a tax or duty may be imposed on such importation, not exceeding $10 for each person.*

The privilege of the writ of habeas corpus shall not be suspended, unless when in cases of rebellion or invasion the public safety may require it.

No bill of attainder or ex post facto law shall be passed.

No capitation, or other direct, tax shall be laid, unless in proportion to the census or enumeration herein before directed to be taken.

No tax or duty shall be laid on articles exported from any State.

No preference shall be given by any regulation of commerce or revenue to the ports of one State over those of another; nor shall vessels bound to, or from, one State, be obliged to enter, clear, or pay duties in another.

No money shall be drawn from the treasury, but in consequence of appropriations made by law; and a regular statement and account of the receipts and expenditures of all public money shall be published from time to time.

No title of nobility shall be granted by the United States: and no person holding any office of profit or trust under them, shall, without the consent of the Congress, accept of any present, emolument, office, or title, of any kind whatever, from any king, prince, or foreign state.

Section 10. No State shall enter into any treaty, alliance, or confederation; grant letters of marque and reprisal; coin money; emit bills of credit; make anything but gold and silver coin a tender in payment of debts; pass any bill of attainder, ex post facto law, or law impairing the obligation of contracts, or grant any title of nobility.

No State shall, without the consent of Congress, lay any imposts or duties on imports or exports, except what may be absolutely necessary for executing its inspection laws: and the net produce of all duties and imposts, laid by any State on imports or exports, shall be for the use of the treasury of the United States; and all such laws shall be subject to the revision and control of the Congress.

No State shall, without the consent of Congress, lay any duty of tonnage, keep troops or ships of war in time of peace, enter into any agreement or compact with another State, or with a foreign power, or engage in war, unless actually invaded, or in such imminent danger as will not admit of delay.

ARTICLE II

Section 1. The executive power shall be vested in a President of the United States of America. He shall hold his office during the term of four years, and, together with the Vice President, chosen for the same term, be elected as follows:

Each state shall appoint, in such manner as the legislature thereof may direct, a number of electors, equal to the whole number of Senators and Representatives to which the State may be entitled in the Congress; but no Senator or Representative, or person holding an office of trust or profit under the United States, shall be appointed an elector.

The electors shall meet in their respective States, and vote by ballot for two persons, of whom one at least shall not be an inhabitant of the same State with themselves. And they shall make a list of all the persons voted for, and of the number of votes for each; which list they shall sign and certify, and transmit sealed to the seat of government of the United States, directed to the President of the Senate. The President of the Senate shall, in the presence of the Senate and the House of Representatives, open all the certificates, and the votes shall then be counted. The person having the greatest number of votes shall be the President, if such number be a majority of the whole number of electors appointed; and if there be more than one who have such majority, and have an equal number of votes, then the House of Representatives shall immediately choose by ballot one of them for President; and if no person have a majority, then from the five highest on the list said house shall in like manner choose the President. But in choosing the President the votes shall be taken by States, the representation from each State having one vote; a quorum for this purpose shall consist of a member or members from two-thirds of the States, and a majority of all the States shall be necessary to a choice. In every case, after the choice of the President, the person having the greatest number of votes of the electors shall be the Vice President. But if there should remain two or more who have equal votes, the Senate shall choose from them by ballot the Vice President.

The Congress may determine the time of choosing the electors and the day on which they shall give their votes; which day shall be the same throughout the United States.

No person except a natural-born citizen, *or a citizen of the United States at the time of the adoption of this Constitution,* shall be eligible to the office of President; neither shall any person be eligible to that office who shall not have attained to the age of thirty-five years, and been fourteen years a resident within the United States.

In case of the removal of the President from office or of his death, resignation, or inability to discharge the powers and duties of the said office, the same shall devolve on the Vice President, and the Congress may by law provide for the case of removal, death, resignation, or inability, both of the President and Vice President, declaring what officer shall then act as President, and such officer shall act accordingly, until the disability be removed, or a President shall be elected.

The President shall, at stated times, receive for his services a compensation, which shall neither be increased nor diminished during the period for which he shall have been elected, and he shall not receive within that period any other emolument from the United States, or any of them.

Before he enter on the execution of his office, he shall take the following oath or affirmation:—"I do solemnly swear (or affirm) that I will faithfully execute the office of the President of the United States, and will to the best of my ability preserve, protect and defend the Constitution of the United States."

Section 2. The President shall be commander in chief of the army and navy of the United States, and of the militia of the several States, when called into the actual service of the United States; he may require the opinion, in writing, of the principal officer in each of the executive departments, upon any subject relating to the duties of their respective offices, and he shall have power to grant reprieves and pardons for offenses against the United States, except in cases of impeachment.

He shall have power, by and with the advice and consent of the Senate, to make treaties, provided two-thirds of the Senators present concur; and he shall nominate, and by and with the advice and consent of the Senate, shall appoint ambassadors, other public ministers and consuls, judges of the Supreme Court, and all other officers of the United States, whose appointments are not herein otherwise provided for, and which shall be established by law: but Congress may by law vest the appointment of such inferior officers, as they think proper, in the President alone, in the courts of law, or in the heads of departments.

The President shall have power to fill up all vacancies that may happen during the recess of the Senate, by granting commissions which shall expire at the end of their next session.

Section 3. He shall from time to time give to the Congress information of the state of the Union, and recommend to their consideration such measures as he shall judge necessary and expedient; he may, on extraordinary occasions, convene both houses, or either of them, and in case of disagreement between them, with respect to the time of adjournment, he may adjourn them to such time as he shall think proper; he shall receive ambassadors and other public ministers; he shall take care that the laws be faithfully executed, and shall commission all the officers of the United States.

Section 4. The President, Vice President and all civil officers of the United States shall be removed from office on impeachment for, and on conviction of, treason, bribery, or other high crimes and misdemeanors.

ARTICLE III

Section 1. The judicial power of the United States shall be vested in one Supreme Court, and in such inferior courts as the Congress may from time to time ordain and establish. The judges, both of the Supreme and inferior courts, shall hold their offices during good behavior, and shall, at stated times, receive for their services a compensation which shall not be diminished during their continuance in office.

Section 2. The judicial power shall extend to all cases, in law and equity, arising under this Constitution, the laws of the United States, and treaties made, or which shall be made, under their authority;—to all cases affecting ambassadors, other public ministers and consuls;—to all cases of admiralty and maritime jurisdiction;—to controversies to which the United States shall be a party;—to controversies between two or more States;—*between a State and citizens of another State;*—between citizens of different States;—between citizens of the same State claiming lands under grants of different States, and between a State, or the citizens thereof, and foreign states, citizens or subjects.

In all cases affecting ambassadors, other public ministers and consuls, and those in which a State shall be party, the Supreme Court shall have original jurisdiction. In all the other cases before mentioned, the Supreme Court shall have appellate jurisdiction, both as to law and fact, with such exceptions, and under such regulations, as the Congress shall make.

The trial of all crimes, except in cases of impeachment, shall be by jury; and such trial shall be held in the State where said crimes shall have been committed; but when not committed within any State, the trial shall be at such place or places as the Congress may by law have directed.

Section 3. Treason against the United States shall consist only in levying war against them, or in adhering to their enemies, giving them aid and comfort. No person shall be convicted of treason unless on the testimony of two witnesses to the same overt act, or on confession in open court.

The Congress shall have power to declare the punishment of treason, but no attainder of treason shall work corruption of blood, or forfeiture except during the life of the person attainted.

ARTICLE IV

Section 1. Full faith and credit shall be given in each State to the public acts, records, and judicial proceedings of every other State. And the Congress may by general laws prescribe the manner in which such acts, records, and proceedings shall be proved, and the effect thereof.

Section 2. The citizens of each State shall be entitled to all privileges and immunities of citizens in the several States.

A person charged in any State with treason, felony, or other crime, who shall flee from justice, and be found in another State, shall on demand of the executive authority of the State from which he fled, be delivered up, to be removed to the State having jurisdiction of the crime.

No person held to service or labor in one State, under the laws thereof, escaping into another, shall, in consequence of any law or regulation therein, be discharged from such service or labor, but shall be delivered up on claim of the party to whom such service or labor may be due.

Section 3. New States may be admitted by the Congress into this Union; but no new State shall be formed or erected within the jurisdiction of any other State; nor any State be formed by the junction of two or more States, or parts of States, without the consent of the legislatures of the States concerned as well as of the Congress.

The Congress shall have power to dispose of and make all needful rules and regulations respecting the territory or other property belonging to the United States; and nothing in this Constitution shall be so construed as to prejudice any claims of the United States, or of any particular State.

Section 4. The United States shall guarantee to every State in this Union a republican form of government, and shall protect each of them against invasion; and on application of the legislature, or of the executive (when the legislature cannot be convened), against domestic violence.

ARTICLE V

The Congress, whenever two-thirds of both houses shall deem it necessary, shall propose amendments to this Constitution, or, on the application of the legislatures of two-thirds of the several States, shall call a convention for proposing amendments, which, in either case, shall be valid to all intents and purposes, as part of this Constitution, when ratified by the legislatures of three-fourths of the several States, or by conventions in three-fourths thereof, as the one or the other mode of ratification may be proposed by the Congress; provided *that no amendments which may be made prior to the year one thousand eight hundred and eight shall in any manner affect the first and fourth clauses in the ninth section of the first article;* and that no State, without its consent, shall be deprived of its equal suffrage in the Senate.

ARTICLE VI

All debts contracted and engagements entered into, before the adoption of this Constitution, shall be as valid against the United States under this Constitution, as under the Confederation.

This Constitution, and the laws of the United States which shall be made in pursuance thereof; and all treaties made, or which shall be made, under the authority of the United States, shall be the supreme law of the land; and the judges in every State shall be bound thereby, anything in the Constitution or laws of any State to the contrary notwithstanding.

The Senators and Representatives before mentioned, and the members of the several State legislatures, and all executive and judicial officers, both of the United States and of the several States, shall be bound by oath or affirmation to support this Constitution; but no religious test shall ever be required as a qualification to any office or public trust under the United States.

ARTICLE VII

The ratification of the conventions of nine States shall be sufficient for the establishment of this Constitution between the States so ratifying the same.

Done in Convention by the unanimous consent of the States present, the seventeenth day of September in the year of our Lord one thousand seven hundred and eighty-seven and of the Independence of the United States of America the twelfth. In witness whereof we have hereunto subscribed our names.

[Signed by]
Gº WASHINGTON
Presidt and Deputy from Virginia
[*and thirty-eight others*]

Amendments to the Constitution

ARTICLE I*

Congress shall make no law respecting an establishment of religion, or prohibiting the free exercise thereof; or abridging the freedom of speech, or of the press; or the right of the people peaceably to assemble, and to petition the government for a redress of grievances.

ARTICLE II

A well-regulated militia being necessary to the security of a free State, the right of the people to keep and bear arms shall not be infringed.

ARTICLE III

No soldier shall, in time of peace, be quartered in any house without the consent of the owner, nor in time of war, but in a manner to be prescribed by law.

ARTICLE IV

The right of the people to be secure in their persons, houses, papers, and effects, against unreasonable searches and seizures, shall not be violated, and no warrants shall issue but upon probable cause, supported by oath or affirmation, and particularly describing the place to be searched, and the persons or things to be seized.

ARTICLE V

No person shall be held to answer for a capital, or otherwise infamous crime, unless on a presentment or indictment of a grand jury, except in cases arising in the land or naval forces, or in the militia, when in actual service in time of war or public danger; nor shall any person be subject for the same offense to be twice put in jeopardy of life or limb; nor shall be compelled in any criminal case to be a witness against himself, nor be deprived of life, liberty, or property, without due process of law; nor shall private property be taken for public use without just compensation.

ARTICLE VI

In all criminal prosecutions, the accused shall enjoy the right to a speedy and public trial, by an impartial jury of the State and district wherein the crime shall have been committed, which district shall have been previously ascertained by law, and to be informed of the nature and cause of the accusation; to be confronted with the witnesses against him; to have compulsory process for obtaining witnesses in his favor, and to have the assistance of counsel for his defense.

ARTICLE VII

In suits at common law, where the value in controversy shall exceed twenty dollars, the right of trial by jury shall be preserved, and no fact tried by a jury shall be otherwise reexamined in any court of the United States, than according to the rules of the common law.

ARTICLE VIII

Excessive bail shall not be required, nor excessive fines imposed, nor cruel and unusual punishments inflicted.

ARTICLE IX

The enumeration in the Constitution, of certain rights, shall not be construed to deny or disparage others retained by the people.

---

*The first ten Amendments (Bill of Rights) were adopted in 1791.

ARTICLE X

The powers not delegated to the United States by the Constitution, not prohibited by it to the States, are reserved to the States respectively, or to the people.

ARTICLE XI   [Adopted 1798]

The judicial power of the United States shall not be construed to extend to any suit in law or equity, commenced or prosecuted against one of the United States by citizens of another State, or by citizens or subjects of any foreign state.

ARTICLE XII   [Adopted 1804]

The electors shall meet in their respective States, and vote by ballot for President and Vice President, one of whom, at least, shall not be an inhabitant of the same State with themselves; they shall name in their ballots the person voted for as President, and in distinct ballots the person voted for as Vice President, and they shall make distinct lists of all persons voted for as President, and of all persons voted for as Vice President, and of the number of votes for each, which lists they shall sign and certify, and transmit sealed to the seat of government of the United States, directed to the President of the Senate;—the President of the Senate shall, in the presence of the Senate and House of Representatives, open all the certificates and the votes shall then be counted;— the person having the greatest number of votes for President shall be the President, if such number be a majority of the whole number of electors appointed; and if no person have such majority, then from the persons having the highest numbers not exceeding three on the list of those voted for as President, the House of Representatives shall choose immediately, by ballot, the President. But in choosing the President, the votes shall be taken by States, the representation from each State having one vote; a quorum for this purpose shall consist of a member or members from two-thirds of the States, and a majority of all the States shall be necessary to a choice.

And if the House of Representatives shall not choose a President whenever the right of choice shall devolve upon them, before *the fourth day of March* next following, then the Vice President shall act as President, as in the case of the death or other constitutional disability of the President.

The person having the greatest number of votes as Vice President shall be the Vice President, if such a number be a majority of the whole number of electors appointed; and if no person have a majority, then from the two highest numbers on the list the Senate shall choose the Vice President; a quorum for the purpose shall consist of two-thirds of the whole number of Senators, and a majority of the whole number shall be necessary to a choice. But no person constitutionally ineligible to the office of President shall be eligible to that of Vice President of the United States.

ARTICLE XIII   [Adopted 1865]

Section 1. Neither slavery nor involuntary servitude, except as a punishment for crime whereof the party shall have been duly convicted, shall exist within the United States, or any place subject to their jurisdiction.

Section 2. Congress shall have power to enforce this article by appropriate legislation.

ARTICLE XIV   [Adopted 1868]

Section 1. All persons born or naturalized in the United States, and subject to the jurisdiction thereof, are citizens of the United States and of the State wherein they reside. No State shall make or enforce any law which shall abridge the privileges or immunities of citizens of the United States; nor shall any State deprive any person of life, liberty, or property, without due process of law; nor deny to any person within its jurisdiction the equal protection of the laws.

Section 2. Representatives shall be apportioned among the several States according to their respective numbers, counting the whole number of persons in each State, excluding Indians not taxed. But when the right to vote at any election for the choice of Electors for President and Vice President of the United States, Representatives in Congress, the executive and judicial officers of a State, or the members of the legislature thereof, is denied to any of the male inhabitants of such State, being twenty-one years of age and citizens of the United States, or in any way abridged, except for participation in rebellion, or other crime, the basis of representation therein shall be reduced in the proportion which the number of such male citizens shall bear to the whole number of male citizens twenty-one years of age in such State.

Section 3. No person shall be a Senator or Representative in Congress or Elector of President and Vice President, or hold any office, civil or military, under the United States, or under any State, who, having previously taken an oath, as a member of Congress, or as an officer of the United States, or as a member of any State legislature, or as an executive or judicial officer of any State, to support the Constitution of the United States, shall have engaged in insurrection or rebellion against the same, or given aid and comfort to the enemies thereof. Congress may, by a vote of two-thirds of each house, remove such disability.

Section 4. The validity of the public debt of the United States, authorized by law, including debts incurred for payment of pensions and bounties for services in suppressing insurrection or rebellion, shall not be questioned. But neither the United States nor any State shall assume or pay any debt or obligation incurred in aid of insurrection or rebellion against the United States, or any claim for the loss or emancipation of any slave; but all such debts, obligations, and claims shall be held illegal and void.

Section 5. The Congress shall have the power to enforce, by appropriate legislation, the provisions of this article.

ARTICLE XV [Adopted 1870]

Section 1. The right of citizens of the United States to vote shall not be denied or abridged by the United States or by any State on account of race, color, or previous condition of servitude.

Section 2. The Congress shall have power to enforce this article by appropriate legislation.

ARTICLE XVI [Adopted 1913]

The Congress shall have power to lay and collect taxes on incomes, from whatever source derived, without apportionment among the several States, and without regard to any census or enumeration.

ARTICLE XVII [Adopted 1913]

Section 1. The Senate of the United States shall be composed of two Senators from each State, elected by the people thereof, for six years; and each Senator shall have one vote. The electors in each State shall have the qualifications requisite for electors of [voters for] the most numerous branch of the State legislatures.

Section 2. When vacancies happen in the representation of any State in the Senate, the executive authority of such State shall issue writs of election to fill such vacancies: Provided, that the Legislature of any State may empower the executive thereof to make temporary appointments until the people fill the vacancies by election as the Legislature may direct.

Section 3. This amendment shall not be so construed as to affect the election or term of any Senator chosen before it becomes valid as part of the Constitution.

ARTICLE XVIII [Adopted 1919; repealed 1933]

Section 1. *After one year from the ratification of this article the manufacture, sale, or transportation of intoxicating liquors within, the importation thereof into,* *or the exportation thereof from the United States and all territory subject to the jurisdiction thereof, for beverage purposes, is hereby prohibited.*

Section 2.   *The Congress and the several States shall have concurrent power to enforce this article by appropriate legislation.*

Section 3.   *This article shall be inoperative unless it shall have been ratified as an amendment to the Constitution by the legislatures of the several States, as provided by the Constitution, within seven years from the date of the submission thereof to the States by the Congress.*

ARTICLE XIX   [*Adopted 1920*]

Section 1.   The right of citizens of the United States to vote shall not be denied or abridged by the United States or by any State on account of sex.

Section 2.   The Congress shall have the power to enforce this article by appropriate legislation.

ARTICLE XX   [*Adopted 1933*]

Section 1.   The terms of the President and Vice President shall end at noon on the 20th day of January, and the terms of Senators and Representatives at noon on the 3d day of January, of the years in which such terms would have ended if this article had not been ratified; and the terms of their successors shall then begin.

Section 2.   The Congress shall assemble at least once in every year, and such meeting shall begin at noon on the 3d day of January, unless they shall by law appoint a different day.

Section 3.   If, at the time fixed for the beginning of the term of the President, the President-elect shall have died, the Vice President-elect shall become President. If a President shall not have been chosen before the time fixed for the beginning of his term, or if the President-elect shall have failed

to qualify, then the Vice President-elect shall act as President until a President shall have qualified; and the Congress may by law provide for the case wherein neither a President-elect nor a Vice President-elect shall have qualified, declaring who shall then act as President, or the manner in which one who is to act shall be selected, and such persons shall act accordingly until a President or Vice President shall have qualified.

Section 4.   The Congress may by law provide for the case of the death of any of the persons from whom the House of Representatives may choose a President whenever the right of choice shall have devolved upon them, and for the case of the death of any of the persons from whom the Senate may choose a Vice President whenever the right of choice shall have devolved upon them.

Section 5.   Sections 1 and 2 shall take effect on the 15th day of October following the ratification of this article.

Section 6.   This article shall be inoperative unless it shall have been ratified as an amendment to the Constitution by the Legislatures of three-fourths of the several States within seven years from the date of its submission.

ARTICLE XXI   [*Adopted 1933*]

Section 1.   The eighteenth article of amendment to the Constitution of the United States is hereby repealed.

Section 2.   The transportation or importation into any State, Territory, or Possession of the United States for delivery or use therein of intoxicating liquors, in violation of the laws thereof, is hereby prohibited.

Section 3.   This article shall be inoperative unless it shall have been ratified as an amendment to the Constitution by conventions in the several States, as provided in the Constitution, within seven years from the date of submission thereof to the States by the Congress.

ARTICLE XXII   [*Adopted 1951*]

Section 1.   No person shall be elected to the office of President more than twice, and no person who has held the office of President, or acted as President, for more than two years of a term to which some other person was elected President shall be elected to the office of President more than once. But this article shall not apply to any person holding the office of President when this article was proposed by the Congress, and shall not prevent any person who may be holding the office of President, or acting as President, during the term within which this article becomes operative from holding the office of President or acting as President during the remainder of such term.

Section 2.   This article shall be inoperative unless it shall have been ratified as an amendment to the Constitution by the legislatures of three-fourths of the several States within seven years from the date of its submission to the States by the Congress.

ARTICLE XXIII   [*Adopted 1961*]

Section 1.   The District constituting the seat of Government of the United States shall appoint in such manner as the Congress may direct:

A number of electors of President and Vice President equal to the whole number of Senators and Representatives in Congress to which the District would be entitled if it were a State, but in no event more than the least populous State; they shall be in addition to those appointed by the States, but they shall be considered for the purposes of the election of President and Vice President, to be electors appointed by a State; and they shall meet in the District and perform such duties as provided by the twelfth article of amendment.

Section 2.   The Congress shall have the power to enforce this article by appropriate legislation.

ARTICLE XXIV   [*Adopted 1964*]

Section 1.   The right of citizens of the United States to vote in any primary or other election for President or Vice President, for electors for President or Vice President, or for Senator or Representative in Congress, shall not be denied or abridged by the United States or any State by reason of failure to pay any poll tax or other tax.

Section 2.   The Congress shall have the power to enforce this article by appropriate legislation.

ARTICLE XXV   [*Adopted 1967*]

Section 1.   In case of the removal of the President from office or of his death or resignation, the Vice President shall become President.

Section 2.   Whenever there is a vacancy in the office of the Vice President, the President shall nominate a Vice President who shall take office upon confirmation by a majority vote of both Houses of Congress.

Section 3.   Whenever the President transmits to the President pro tempore of the Senate and the Speaker of the House of Representatives his written declaration that he is unable to discharge the powers and duties of his office, and until he transmits to them a written declaration to the contrary, such powers and duties shall be discharged by the Vice President as Acting President.

Section 4.   Whenever the Vice President and a majority of either the principal officers of the executive departments or of such other body as Congress may by law provide, transmit to the President pro tempore of the Senate and the Speaker of the House of Representatives their written declaration that the President is unable to discharge the powers and duties of his office, the Vice President shall immediately assume the powers and duties of the office as Acting President.

Thereafter, when the President transmits to the President pro tempore of the Senate and the

Speaker of the House of Representatives his written declaration that no inability exists, he shall resume the powers and duties of his office unless the Vice President and a majority of either the principal officers of the executive department[s] or of such other body as Congress may by law provide, transmit within four days to the President pro tempore of the Senate and the Speaker of the House of Representatives their written declaration that the President is unable to discharge the powers and duties of his office. Thereupon Congress shall decide the issue, assembling within forty-eight hours for that purpose if not in session. If the Congress, within twenty-one days after receipt of the latter written declaration, or, if Congress is not in session, within twenty-one days after Congress is required to assemble, determines by two-thirds vote of both Houses that the President is unable to discharge the powers and duties of his office, the Vice President shall continue to discharge the same as Acting President; otherwise, the President shall resume the powers and duties of his office.

ARTICLE XXVI   [*Adopted 1971*]

Section 1.   The right of citizens of the United States, who are eighteen years of age or older, to vote shall not be denied or abridged by the United States or by any State on account of age.

Section 2.   The Congress shall have power to enforce this article by appropriate legislation.

ARTICLE XXVII*   [*Adopted 1992*]

No law, varying the compensation for services of the Senators and Representatives, shall take effect, until an election of Representatives shall have intervened.

---

*Originally proposed in 1789 by James Madison, this amendment failed to win ratification along with the other parts of what became the Bill of Rights. However, the proposed amendment contained no deadline for ratification, and over the years other state legislatures voted to add it to the Constitution; many such ratifications occured during the 1980s and early 1990s as public frustration with Congress's performance mounted. In May 1992 the Archivist of the United States certified that, with the Michigan legislature's ratification, the article had been approved by three-fourths of the states and thus automatically became part of the Constitution. But congressional leaders and constitutional specialists questioned whether an amendment that took 202 years to win ratification was valid, and the issue had not been resolved by the time this book went to press.

Index